Roger Ar

THE FUR TRADE
AND THE NORTHWEST

E. E. RICH

THE
FUR TRADE
AND THE
NORTHWEST
TO 1857

The Canadian Centenary Series

McClelland and Stewart Limited

The Canadian Publishers
McClelland and Stewart Limited
25 Hollinger Road, Toronto 16

THE CANADIAN CENTENARY SERIES

A History of Canada

W. L. Morton, EXECUTIVE EDITOR

D. G. Creighton, ADVISORY EDITOR

VOLUMES STARRED ARE PUBLISHED

CONTENTS

The Fur Trade and the Northwest, to 1857

MAPS AND ILLUSTRATIONS

The Canadian Centenary Series

Half a century has elapsed since *Canada and Its Provinces*, the first large-scale co-operative history of Canada, was published. During that time, new historical materials have been made available in archives and libraries; new research has been carried out, and its results published; new interpretations have been advanced and tested. In these same years Canada itself has greatly grown and changed. These facts, together with the centenary of Confederation, justify the publication of a new co-operative history of Canada.

The form chosen for this enterprise was that of a series of volumes. The series was planned by the editors, but each volume will be designed and executed by a single author. The general theme of the work is the development of those regional communities which have for the past century made up the Canadian nation; and the series will be composed of a number of volumes sufficiently large to permit an adequate treatment of all the phases of the theme in the light of modern knowledge.

The Centenary History, then, was planned as a series to have a certain common character and to follow a common method but to be written by individual authors, specialists in their fields. As a whole it will be a work of specialized knowledge, the great advantage of scholarly co-operation, and at the same time each volume will have the unity and distinctive character of individual authorship. It was agreed that a general narrative treatment was necessary and that each author should deal in a balanced way with economic, political and social history. The result, it is hoped, will be an interpretive, varied, and comprehensive account, at once useful to the student and interesting to the general reader.

The difficulties of organizing and executing such a series are apparent: the overlapping of separate narratives, the risk of omissions, the imposition of divisions which are relevant to some themes but not to others. Not so apparent, but quite as troublesome, are problems of scale, perspective, and scope, problems which perplex the writer of a one-volume history and are magnified in a series. It is by deliberate choice that certain parts of the history are told twice, in different volumes from different points of view, in the belief that the benefits gained outweigh the unavoidable disadvantages.

The editors have attempted in the Series to point out the distinct and independent character of Canadian history by stressing the place of the North in the development of the present Canada. Three volumes are devoted to that theme, one by the late Professor T. J. Oleson, one being written by Professor Morris Zaslow, and this volume by Professor E. E. Rich.

Professor Rich, in carrying the work forward, has illustrated with admirable historical skill the long dominance of regions later part of Canada by the maritime approach from overseas. At the same time he has woven together with insight and impartiality the inland and maritime threads of development in the Canadian Northwest, combining with novel emphasis the three elements in its history: the advance into the Northwest from the St Lawrence, the advance from Hudson Bay, and the incorporation of the approach from the Pacific into that development.

If the last point seems to submerge the history of the Pacific coast, it was necessary to do so, in the opinion of the editors, in order to bring out the common rather than the separate aspects of the whole theme of the development of the Northwest fur trade, the development which established British title to the vast lands that became the imperial legacy of the new Canada of 1867.

W. L. MORTON,
Executive Editor.

D. G. CREIGHTON,
Advisory Editor.

The Fur Trade and the Northwest to 1857

A volume on the Northwest is an essential part of a comprehensive history of Canada; and although many treatments would be interesting, the fur-traders could not possibly be left out. Indeed, they must be given priority, for they mastered the dangerous and exhausting routes to the Northwest, they revealed its wealth, and they secured its retention within the Dominion.

Individual traders claim our admiration, but the main interest must be concentrated on the great companies; and since written history is a product of the documents available to the historian, the magnificent archives of the Hudson's Bay Company must inevitably ensure that the present volume accords considerable weight to the policy and activities of that company. The unrivalled opportunities for consulting the Hudson's Bay archives which the author enjoyed over a period of twenty years lay upon him the duty of thanking the Governor and Committee of the Company with far more than the customary warmth for permission to quote from the archives.

But although the Hudson's Bay Company archives have been repeatedly quoted, and though many of the problems and at times even the phrases in which the problems are discussed must be substantially the same as those used in the author's *History of the Hudson's Bay Company*, this is emphatically not a summary of the history of the Company. This is the history of a territory, and of the part played by the fur-traders in opening and developing that territory. Much that would be essential in a history of the Company has no place here, and the outlook and relevance differ materially, so that the Hudson's Bay Company becomes one factor—not always the most important factor—in the history of the territory.

That the volume should end in 1857 instead of in 1870 is not so unfortunate as might at first sight appear. The fur-traders had played their part by 1857; the years which followed were taken up by disputes between the Dominion and the Company, but little that was new emerged, and the result was a foregone conclusion as soon as sanity could be made to prevail. It is, in any case, a condition of historical writing that the story is never complete, nor completely acceptable. There is always something more to be said; and for arranging a terminal date which leaves this volume with its own unity but yet integrates it with the other volumes in the Centenary Series, as well as for thoughtful scholarship in so many of the problems involved, the author owes sincere thanks to the Editors of the series.

E. E. RICH.

CHAPTER 1

The Northwest:
The Geographical
Background

The North West Territories and the Yukon Territory between them contain almost half of the total area of the present Canada; at the date of Confederation the proportion of "Rupert's Land and the North-Western
Territory" to the whole area was even greater. This was partly due to the
fact that British Columbia, Prince Edward Island, and Newfoundland had
not yet been admitted to the Dominion, to swell the total area; but more
to the fact that Rupert's Land and the North-Western Territory then included vast districts which have since been separated off—Manitoba,
Saskatchewan and Alberta, the District of Ungava, and the northern part
of the Province of Ontario.

This decrease in the area of the North West Territories shows the advance
of human settlement into the empty spaces of the North American continent. The changes indicate a population which needs the machinery of
local and provincial government and which, also, can operate that
machinery. Nevertheless, great areas of the present Canada are still so
thinly populated as to play almost no part in the life of the country, and
the North West Territories and Yukon, as they now stand, support only
40,000 people in all their enormous extent.[1]

Development since Confederation has shown that the territories of
Rupert's Land and the Northwest then included some lands which were
capable of settlement, and far more which were not. This distinction was
not at all clear to the Fathers of Confederation. Their vision was of a land
which would prove capable of development throughout, and they included
the North West Territories within their already complicated federal scheme
because they hoped that all was valuable. With limited and fragmentary
knowledge, they assumed that almost endless good land lay in these territories and that settlement would become possible as soon as proprietary
rights had been abolished, transportation had made access possible, and
sound government had been established. Seeing the way in which immi-

grants were flocking into the midwestern lands of the United States, and knowing that a "Fertile Belt" ran westwards from Lake Winnipeg, they were convinced that the reason why the "Fertile Belt" stood empty was that alleged proprietary rights prevented settlement. Accordingly, their first preoccupations were the legal and constitutional problems of abolishing or absorbing those proprietary rights. But although the Fathers of Confederation knew that the "Fertile Belt" ran westwards from Lake Winnipeg, they did not know its extent or its limitations; and even its fertility was denied by the Hudson's Bay Company's officials, who had almost a monopoly of first-hand knowledge.

Not only had proprietary rights to be abolished before the "Fertile Belt" could be settled; it was also necessary to provide a means of access—a railway. A railway across the prairies, running from coast to coast with strategic, mercantile, and imperial possibilities, was an attractive dream. The notion emerged in the moderate and balanced evidence given to the Parliamentary Commission of 1857 by Chief Justice Draper, as he gave his "very visionary" idea of such a railway. As it became clear that Rupert's Land and the North-Western Territory contained endless miles of deep rich soil, it was accepted that a railway was a necessity if the prairies were to be opened for settlement. When the debate on Confederation began there was only one stable agricultural community in the whole vast area —Red River Colony at the junction of the Red and the Assiniboine rivers— and the Red River colonists had been brought in along the forbidding route from Hudson Bay, most of them spending a winter under canvas by the shores of the Bay before they could start on the overland journey. The colony had made it abundantly clear that, despite the double talk before the Parliamentary Commission of 1857, there was an abundance of fertile soil; it had also made it clear that any settler faced difficulties not all of which were attributable to the Hudson's Bay Company.

In the "Fertile Belt," and still more in the frozen north, there were serious—perhaps insurmountable—obstacles to be overcome. Even as the railway reached the prairies, taking immigrants inland and bringing crops to the seaboard and to the markets of the world, it remained open to question whether the "very visionary" railway would prove the answer; for as the Red River Colony developed its own transport system it led south to St Paul and St Louis, not to the St Lawrence and Canada. Over the greater spaces of the Northwest there hung a heavier question-mark. They were frozen; and they were inaccessible in a way quite distinct from the difficulties which cut off the "Fertile Belt" from the St Lawrence, quite distinct if only because the obstacles to access to the Northwest were superimposed on the obstacles to access to the "Fertile Belt."

The "Fertile Belt" itself was cut off from the St Lawrence basin, and the

Atlantic and the markets of Europe, by the Great Shield of Canada. This great barrier impedes access westwards and northwards from the St Lawrence basin and marks off the eastern provinces of Canada from the rest of North America. It interrupted movement both because of its extent and because of its nature. Composed of Precambrian rock which had been scoured of its top-soil by the ice-movements of the Glacial Period, it presents a surface of hard rock overlaid with shallow soil lying in small pockets.[2] Agriculture is possible only in small basins or valleys. The great ice-field which had spread outwards from west of Hudson Bay and from the heart of the Labrador Peninsula had smoothed down the topography, polished and levelled the rock surfaces, scattered debris irregularly, and disorganized the drainage system. Therefore the Shield contains many small hills but no great eminences, it boasts a profusion of lakes and streams, and its rock-formations have proved in modern times to be the source of a great variety of mineral wealth.[3] Intractable and difficult in itself, the Great Shield interposed its barrier between arrival from Europe by the St Lawrence and any break-out to the west; and it spread from the St Lawrence to Ungava and almost to the shores of Hudson Bay. There the clay belt of what is now Northern Ontario intervenes. The Shield continues on westwards from Lake Superior to Lake Winnipeg and so north-west; southwards it extends across the Canadian frontier into Michigan and Minnesota.

The Great Shield presents a formidable barrier to penetration and a strong deterrent to settlement. But it is not impenetrable. In North America, however, as in most new territories, the early means of access to the hinterland were the waterways. The way in which the Shield dominated the watersheds and drainage systems therefore assumed a particular importance. Cut off by the Shield, the Atlantic Basin and the St Lawrence Basin are, in geographic terms, self-contained and comparatively small parts of Canada. Whereas the Hudson Bay drainage system covers 1,379,160 square miles and the Arctic Basin drains 947,188 square miles, the drainage areas of the Atlantic Provinces and the St Lawrence between them cover only 420,000 square miles. Far the greater part of Canada drains to the north, not to the south; and between the rivers which run one way or the other lies a series of watersheds, varying in length and in difficulty but all serving to make access by water arduous and costly.[4] The Shield and its watershed made portages necessary. They confined traffic to vessels and cargo which could head up the rivers of Canada to the portages and which could then cross by carrying-place to the drainage-basins of the north; and they confined this traffic to men who would face such methods of travel. These would be adventurers and traders, seldom settlers.

Geography and history cannot properly, or for long, be kept in separate compartments. The overwhelming feature of the Shield, though not as yet

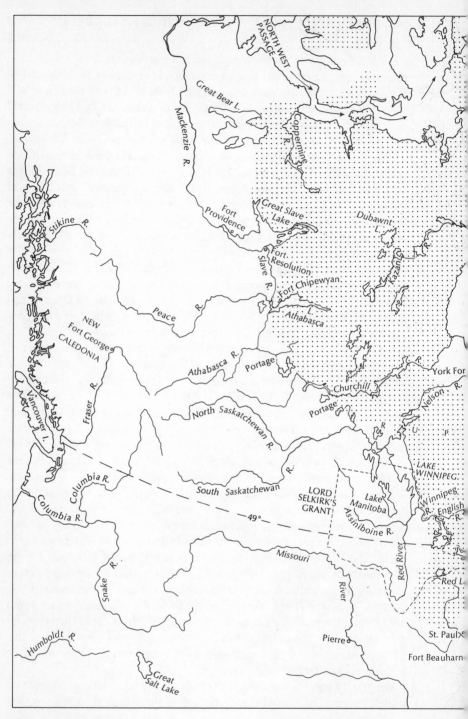

The Canadian Shield

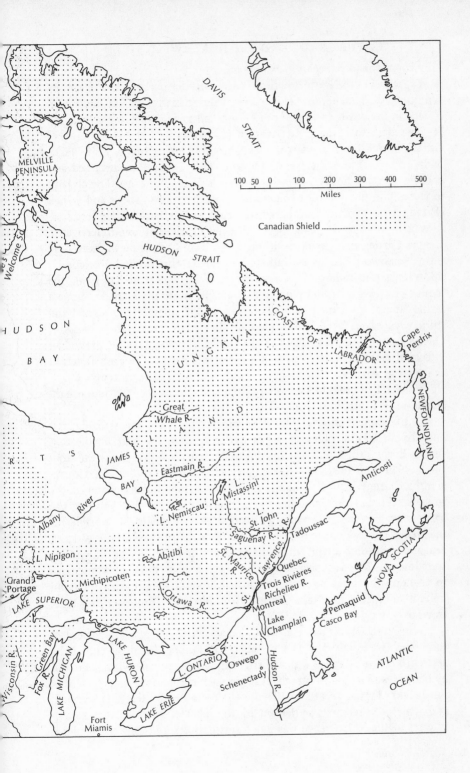

DAVIS STRAIT

MELVILLE PENINSULA

West Welcome Sd.

HUDSON STRAIT

HUDSON BAY

COAST OF LABRADOR

Cape Perdrix

100 50 0   100   200   300   400   500
              Miles

Canadian Shield .... :::::::::

U · N · G · A · V · A

NEWFOUNDLAND

Great Whale R.

L · A · N · D

R T 'S

JAMES BAY

Eastmain R.

L. Mistassini

Anticosti

Albany River

L. Nemiscau

St. John

Saguenay R.   Tadoussac

L. Nipigon

L. Abitibi

St. Maurice R.

St. Lawrence

NOVA SCOTIA

Grand Portage

Michipicoten

Ottawa R.

Quebec

Trois Rivières
Richelieu R.

LAKE SUPERIOR

Montreal

Pemaquid

Casco Bay

Wisconsin R.

Green Bay

Fox R.

LAKE MICHIGAN

LAKE HURON

Lake Champlain

ATLANTIC

OCEAN

L. ONTARIO

Oswego

Hudson R.

Schenectady

LAKE ERIE

Fort Miamis

fully comprehended, began to assume importance right from the first European approaches to North America. To the early Europeans Canada was, by definition, the land approached by way of the St Lawrence. The first North American Indians to be brought to Europe had so described it. For them the St Lawrence was "the great river of Hochelaga and the route towards Canada";[5] and Canada was the region around Quebec (not yet, of course, built as a city) and the Isle of Orleans. This Canada, so described and defined, was specifically a French preserve, la Nouvelle France, French both in fact and in the purpose to maintain it so. French institutions and French characteristics expanded inland wherever the St Lawrence offered access.

When in 1534 the middle-aged and experienced Malouin navigator, Jacques Cartier, first explored the "great river" of Canada he was searching for a Northwest Passage to Cathay. He realized that he had not found a salt-water strait leading to the Pacific, but he knew that he had found the mouth of a vast river, draining down from the west, and he had come to a fertile land at an attractive time of year, in late summer. His second and third voyages, in 1535 and 1541, took him up the river, to the sites of Quebec and of Montreal. There, as he climbed Mount Royal at the Indian village of Hochelaga, he came to grips with the Shield. The great rapids in the river at his feet—the Lachine Rapids—barred further progress in the ships which had brought him so far. There was "no passage to the Southern Ocean"; at least not in seagoing ships.

But the rapids, and the Shield of which they were the sign, did not entirely cut off the valley of the St Lawrence from the heart of the continent. Beyond the rapids, the Indians told Cartier, the great river ran from the west in a broad stream, smooth and with easy navigation, for a three-months' journey. And although to the north the mountains threatened, the Indians said that there another river, the Ottawa, offered a way past the barriers to the west. Cartier was assured that it would be possible for the French to break out to the west, to continue their search for the Western Sea, and to open up a land which they had seen to be fertile and which they were told was rich in copper and perhaps even in gold. But they would have to abandon the seagoing craft which had brought them over a thousand miles inland; they must take to the Indians' birch-bark canoes or they must travel overland.

Having reached this point, at which a determined reappraisal was needed, the French were halted by lack of support in Europe. Until the end of the sixteenth century France was so distracted by her struggle with Spain and by her civil and religious wars that Cartier's achievement was not challenged until Henry IV had secured the Treaty of Vervins, had defeated the League, and achieved a religious settlement by the Edict of Nantes. Some sort of interest in the St Lawrence was indeed maintained, and Cartier's nephew,

Jacques Noël, made his way up the river in 1587 and gazed again on the prospects which had fascinated Cartier.

But Noël also was stopped at the rapids; and not only was Cartier's achievement not surpassed for the next half-century, but the French hold on North America declined. The small garrison which Cartier had left where the river narrows at Quebec was withdrawn in 1543, and such interest as remained was focussed on weak efforts to establish a colony on the Atlantic coast, in Acadia. Contact with the valley of the St Lawrence was nevertheless maintained through this period of recession because by the end of the sixteenth century a steady trade in furs had developed, deriving for the most part from furs traded from Indians at Tadoussac, on the north shore of the river, where the Saguenay flows down from Lac St Jean and the north.

During this period the crossing of the Atlantic had become a commonplace achievement for the Breton, Norman, and Basque fishermen who every year went to catch cod on the Grand Banks of Newfoundland. As many as three hundred ships a year habitually made the voyage, and as the fishermen landed to tend their ships, dry their fish, and mend their nets, they met Indians and traded furs for small European articles, especially for clothing and for ironware. With the passage of years there developed a steady trade which caused both a new European pattern of commerce and a revolution in the social economy of the North American Indians. It also drew the French, and then the English, into the northwest lands of Canada.

The furs which went up from the Breton and Norman fishing ports to Paris stimulated an active and lucrative trade there. They were of prime quality, taken in hard arctic conditions; and although they included almost all the common skins, they contained a preponderance of beaver. This revolutionized the fur trade of Europe, for it brought the felting industry to the forefront on an international scale. While a furrier used skins "in the pelt" for clothing or for adornment, the felter used the hair only, discarding the skin. He felted the hair into a compost with fixatives, to form a material which had great strength, durability, and flexibility; and since the winter coat of a beaver carried a thick under-fur of beaver wool, or *duvet*, every hair of which was barbed at the root, it was admirable raw material for the felter. Moreover, beaver skins carried not only the coat of beaver wool but a topcoat of fine "guard-hairs" as well. If the beaver wool could be removed without spoiling the skin, the merchant had a handsome pelt for use by the furrier as well as a load of beaver wool for the felter. The European trade system which developed as supplies of beaver began to arrive regularly in Paris from the Norman and Breton ports took the beaver skins to Russia, where they were put through a process known as "combing." The Russian process was a closely guarded secret; but the Dutch quickly monopolized the trade of taking the beaver to Archangel, or to Narva, and of bringing back the beaver pelts and the beaver wool for distribution to the felters and the furriers of western Europe. Amsterdam became the centre of this trade, but the French remained the chief source of supply as felt was developed for a variety of uses (even as the main material for much of the armour of the period) and the great beaver hat swept the world of fashion.[6]

Tadoussac, with the Saguenay draining down through the Shield and bringing Algonquins and Montagnais to trade, had become the site of an annual rendezvous, from which much of the fur was derived, as early as 1550. The trade grew steadily; it was reckoned to be worth 20,000 crowns a year in the 1580's, and while the merchants of Normandy and of Britanny staked their claims to participate or to monopolize and a succession of nobles and courtiers secured grants for trade and mineral development (and for colonization), furs predominated over all other French interests.

This was to be expected. For by 1600 it was clear that, whatever the prospects might be of a French colony being established at Sable Island or elsewhere, they were negligible in the St Lawrence valley; still less further afield, past the barriers which shut in the valley. But the fur trade was so attractive that there were those who would promise to develop a colony in return for a grant of monopoly. Such a group planted a small garrison at Tadoussac itself in 1600, but the post was withdrawn in 1601. When the remains of the same syndicate sent out two ships under the experienced Breton trader, François de Pontgravé, in 1603, they went again direct to Tadoussac. Their object was furs; their horizon was bounded by the valley of the great river. But they had aboard as observer Samuel de Champlain; and he was destined to pioneer the French break-out past the barrier of the Shield into the wider territories of the north and west.

After a boyhood spent at sea (perhaps even in voyages to the Grand Banks), a youth of fighting in the Wars of Religion, and then a voyage under Spanish command to the Caribbean, Champlain had formed his own views about the overseas world, the importance of her colonial empire to Spain, and the possibility of France winning wealth and power from a comparable empire. His role in 1603 was to see the country of Canada and to assess its capacity; and he revealed much.[7]

At Tadoussac Champlain and Pontgravé found a band of Algonquins, come to trade and anxious to secure the alliance of the French against their enemies. Since Cartier's time the traffic in furs had spread the use of European implements far beyond the lands of the Indian tribes who made contact with the French. This had seriously affected the patterns of Indian settlement. The Algonquins who dominated the trade route which came from the west by way of the Ottawa River, and the Montagnais who controlled the route down from the north by way of the Saguenay, had driven out the Iroquois who had been masters of the St Lawrence when Cartier met them. The Iroquois had moved south of the St Lawrence, and the Hurons who had been at Hochelaga had moved westwards to Georgian Bay. The Algonquins and the Montagnais had created an effective monopoly of the trade with the French, and they were now anxious to confirm and exploit their advantage. While they offered their country to the French for settlement (a phrase which probably meant little to them) and sought a French alliance in their war against the Iroquois, they nevertheless showed an obstinate determination to obstruct French penetration into the northern and western lands where the furs were taken and·to prevent them from making contact with the fur-hunting tribes of those lands.

So although Champlain got a reasonably accurate description of Saguenay River, Lac St Jean, and the waterways of the north, heavy emphasis was placed on the rapids and other difficulties, and when he tried to make his way up the river he got little help from his Indian friends and was stopped by the rapids when he had gone only about a dozen leagues. But the need to break out to the north was still in his mind as Champlain sailed on up the St Lawrence, and when he came to Trois Rivières he noted that the St Maurice River would provide a route by which the French could reach Lac St Jean and tap the trade which was taken down to Tadoussac. The route would be broken by portages (for it must get out past the Shield); and Champlain himself failed to make any distance up the St Maurice.

Continuing on up the St Lawrence, Champlain, like Cartier before him, was halted at Lachine Rapids. He had with him a skiff specially brought to mount the rapids; but it was quite impossible to do so. Once more he was hemmed in by the valley of the St Lawrence, and once more he was told by the Indians of what lay beyond. He was given some notion of Lake Ontario, of the great falls at Niagara, of Lake Erie, of the straits at Detroit, and of a further lake whose water was salt, whose western shore the Indians had never seen, and where the current ceased to flow eastwards. This, Champlain concluded, must be the South Sea. It was in fact Lake Huron.

At the rapids also Champlain found that the Algonquins had created for themselves a monopoly of the trade between the French and the northern and western Indians. In particular, as the Hurons had withdrawn to Georgian Bay, the Algonquins had assumed control of the way westwards which avoided the Lachine Rapids and the Iroquois lands by a more northern route on the Ottawa River.

By the time that he turned again for France, Champlain had penetrated no further into the Northwest than Cartier had done. He had been stopped by the same barriers at the same places. But he had got more purposeful notions of the possibility of breaking out through the cataracts and the rough inhospitable country, and his ideas were the more attractive by reason of the great error which they contained—the conclusion that the South Sea could be reached by a moderate drive to the west. Less attractive but more realistic was his conclusion that a salt water to the north, of which he heard rumours, must be some branch or gulf of the north Atlantic and could be reached by ship; it was Hudson Bay of which he had heard.

The report which Champlain made on his return to France met a ready response, and in 1604 Henri IV granted to the powerful Huguenot, the Sieur de Monts, the whole of New France—an area defined as running from the 40th to the 46th parallel of latitude; by implication any more southern claim was abandoned by the French. De Monts was to Christianize the Indians and was to establish a French colony. More to the point was his ten-years' monopoly of the fur trade, and Champlain and Pontgravé, who worked with him, devoted most of their care to the trade. Feeble ventures in colonization were made at St Croix on the Maine coast and then at Acadia, while Champlain himself cruised down the Atlantic coast seeking an opening which would lead him westwards. Not until the colony in Acadia had been abandoned and de Monts could only secure a renewal of his monopoly (for a single year) on condition that a new colony should be established, in the St Lawrence valley, did the river receive attention as anything else but an artery of the fur trade. Even then it is probable that fur-trade motives predominated; for the outcome was a decision to set up a Habitation at Quebec.

At Tadoussac in 1608 Champlain and Pontgravé, though armed with de Monts' monopoly, had been defied by a party of Basque traders; and they had failed (once more) to get away from the conditions of trade at Tadoussac by finding a way into the north by the Saguenay River. At Quebec, where the St Lawrence narrows, the monopoly could more easily be enforced than at Tadoussac, and there in 1608 they built a small post. Of the twenty-eight men who spent the winter there with Champlain twenty died of scurvy or dysentery, and the hardships of a Canadian winter were appreciated in their full severity. Nevertheless, in the summer of 1609, instead of drawing out, Champlain went on up-stream, and, about seventy miles above Quebec, he met a party of Hurons coming down from Georgian Bay to seek a French alliance. In return, said Champlain, the Hurons agreed "to help us in our discoveries in the country of the Iroquois, with whom they are in mortal conflict."

The Hurons offered the chance for the French to move both south into the Iroquois lands and west into Huronia, and Champlain accepted their alliance. He travelled with them from the St Lawrence by the Richelieu River to Lake Champlain and then to a battle with the Iroquois near the site of Fort Ticonderoga at the back of the Adirondacks. His presence, and the power of his arquebus, ensured a Huron victory. This entailed the lasting hostility of the Iroquois; but they (or at least the Mohawks of that confederacy, who were particularly concerned with the valley of the St Lawrence) had probably been opposed to the French since Cartier's time and had certainly resented the power which French trade and friendship gave to their enemies. Whether it was existent before or not, from the time that Champlain went on the warpath with the Hurons the French could be assured of Iroquois hostility.

Champlain had, however, also won the friendship and admiration of the Hurons. But he was not able to exploit these advantages until 1613. In the meantime he tried, again in vain, to work north on the Saguenay River, and in 1610 he again went on the warpath with the Hurons. On this occasion he got them to take a young Frenchman, Etienne Brulé, back to live with them and to learn their language. In 1611 Brulé brought down a powerful group of Hurons and Algonquins to trade, and Champlain got them to agree to come again in the following year to a rendezvous at Lachine (away from the competition at Tadoussac) while he persuaded the Algonquins to take back with them another young man, Nicolas de Vignau, to winter with them up the Ottawa River at Lac des Allumettes. Champlain was acquiring knowledge of the routes which would lead out of the valley. He was also acquiring expertise in the techniques of travel, and in 1611 he ran Lachine Rapids in a canoe. Champlain could not swim, and one of his men, who also made the attempt, was drowned.

As the momentum for a break-out gathered, the fur trade played its part. To get away from Tadoussac, to bring the Hurons and the Algonquins to trade at Lachine, was in itself a thrust towards the interior; and in 1611 Champlain began to prepare a site for a post at Montreal, promising the Indians that he would make a settlement there. His plans were helped when, during the winter of 1612, the monopoly of the fur trade was granted to the Comte de Soissons and then, on his death, to the Prince de Condé, who became Viceroy of New France. Champlain was made lieutenant to the Viceroy, and while the fur trade was reorganized under the *Compagnie de Rouen* (sometimes called the *Compagnie de Champlain*) under Condé's licence, Champlain was empowered to make treaties with Indian chiefs, to take part in wars, to organize exploration in the valley of the St Lawrence, and to discover a route to China and the East Indies.

At this juncture Vignau came in from his winter with the Algonquins to report that he had travelled with the Indians, a seventeen days' journey to a northern sea where, he said, an English ship had been wrecked. He proved to have heard an Indian rumour of the last voyage of Henry Hudson, into James Bay, in 1610-11, and his report was substantially accurate except on the one point which he would certainly have got right if he had made the journey himself—the length of the journey from Lachine to the Northern Sea. Champlain, however, found the report acceptable. It fitted in with his conviction that a northern sea lay beyond the land masses, that it should be possible to sail there direct from Europe, and that once the immediate obstacles of the rapids enclosing the St Lawrence valley had been overcome the same territories could be reached by overland travel. In 1613 he set off from Lachine in May, with two canoes and four other Frenchmen (including Vignau), intent on making his way to the Northern Sea. They had only one Indian guide, and they had to learn the techniques of canoe-travel as they went up past the portages on the Ottawa. Champlain himself was almost drowned, but eventually, accompanied by some Algonquins whom they had met, they went past the site of the present city of Ottawa, past the tumultuous junction of the Ottawa River and the Gatineau coming down from the north and the great Rideau Falls, to Lac des Chats and Lac des Allumettes. On one portage, which lasted three days, Champlain lost the astrolabe which he had carried so far; it was turned up by a ploughteam in 1867!

At Lac des Allumettes Champlain came to the main encampment of the Algonquins, a remote and unattractive site but one which enabled that tribe to control the fur trade of the Northwest as it went to meet the French by way of the Ottawa River. Here Vignau, who had come under suspicion as the difficulties of the route were revealed, was unmasked. The Algonquins convinced Champlain that the young man had spent the whole of the previous winter with them. He had certainly not gone on a journey to the Northern Sea; and even if such a journey should prove possible it would be immensely difficult and dangerous. This Champlain could well believe. His plans to go further west, to meet the Nipissings and to "view the Northern Sea," must be abandoned.

Frustrating as this outcome was, Champlain had explored the Ottawa River, a route which could lead to Lake Superior and the Northwest. It avoided both the geographical and the tribal difficulties which made the St Lawrence itself impossible, and for two centuries the Ottawa was to serve the French as their best approach to the Northwest. It offered a way past the barrier of the Shield at the same time as it evaded the Iroquois cordons which made the southern route dangerous.

The Ottawa was quickly exploited. The publication of Champlain's *Voyages* brought favourable publicity in France, Condé secured a renewal of his monopoly of the fur trade, and a powerful company of merchants (sometimes known as the *Compagnie de Canada*) was formed to manage the trade. Colonization was still neglected. But when Champlain came back from France in 1615 he brought with him four members of the Franciscan Minorites order, the Recollects. He had tried before to get a Jesuit mission for the St Lawrence, but the Jesuits had turned their attention to Acadia instead. Now the Recollects brought such enthusiasm that Champlain could hardly keep up with them. Before Champlain had even arrived at Lachine, Father le Caron had pushed west, had met the Hurons as they came to trade, decided to establish a mission in Huronia, and set off back to Quebec to assemble equipment. Champlain had long wanted to visit Huronia, and he decided to accompany the priest; but le Caron and twelve Frenchmen had already left Lachine in company with the Hurons before Champlain could set off. He knew the way as far as Lac des Allumettes; after that he was in new country, following the Ottawa up into the granite of the Shield, through a barren wilderness to Mattawa. Here he left the Ottawa and followed the Mattawa River to Trout Lake, down over the height of land, into the basin of Lake Huron. He had broken through to the west.

Champlain's great achievement was, of course, new only in that Europeans had not previously found a way to the west. Indians habitually crossed the heights of land and linked the water-systems of the continent. And when Champlain arrived among the Nipissing Indians he found them a people who knew the ways north to meet the Crees of the Northern Sea, west to Sault Ste Marie and Lake Superior, and south to Georgian Bay and on to Lake Michigan. From all these directions they traded furs which they passed onwards to the French rendezvous at Lachine, and they told much to Champlain and took him southwest by the French River, once more through the Shield, to Lake Huron, the Freshwater Sea. The ramifications of the Indian trade which brought the furs of the north and west down to Lachine were clear; equally clear was the ease with which bands of Iroquois could interrupt that trade and divert the furs to the south, to the Richelieu River, the Hudson River, Fort Nassau, New Amsterdam, and Dutch and English merchants.

The Iroquois therefore must be driven back. But Champlain found it hard work to get together a war party of Hurons, to persuade them to take him to Lake Ontario and to the south shore of that lake and then on into Iroquois territory. The precise site of his encounter with the Iroquois is uncertain; it was as he moved towards Lake Oneida. There he suffered a reverse and lost countenance, for his arquebuses were ineffective against a strongly palisaded fort, and he was himself wounded. The Hurons immediately showed the psychological result of the battle when they refused to conduct Champlain back to Lachine by way of Lake Ontario—a journey on which he set much store. The Iroquois too gained immensely in prestige. Their fear of the French was gone; they spread through the valley of the St Lawrence and dominated its fur trade for the next thirty years.

Champlain was forced to spend the winter in Huronia, recovering from

his wound, travelling a little to the west in the spring of 1616 before returning to Lachine by way of the Ottawa. By then he realized (as he had long
suspected) that the widespread Indian trade system lay in the hands of the
middlemen tribes who interposed between the hunting Indians and the
French. The Algonquins were quite capable of preventing the Hurons from
going down to trade, and in 1616 Champlain had to intervene to secure a
passage for the Huron furs. He was obstructed in a plan to go north with a
band of Nipissings, to get furs from the Crees of Hudson Bay; but when the
Nipissings met the Hurons he noted that they handed over quantities of
furs for the Hurons to take down to trade and that many of these furs had
not even been taken by the Nipissings, but by other more distant tribes.

On his return to France Champlain emphasized the danger to the fur
trade from the Iroquois, and he wrote feelingly of the country of Canada and
the need to establish settlements. He maintained the French tradition of
seeking a passage to the west "by way of the St Lawrence," asserting that
the great river came from a lake about a thousand miles long and that
another river also flowed from that lake to run into the South Sea. This
was due to misinterpretation of rumours of the Mississippi, rising just west
of Lake Superior; but that river eventually took the French south to the
Gulf of Mexico, not to the Pacific. Champlain held hopes that it would
enable the French to carry on a profitable trade with China; and here again
the danger was that the English and the Dutch would take over the trade,
as they would take over the fur trade if the Iroquois were not held in check.
To ensure French expansion across the continent, their base in the St Lawrence valley must be made secure. There must be a French colony of settlement, and Quebec must be made into a powerful fortress, strongly
garrisoned.

There was little support in France for such a policy. Henri IV had been
murdered, Condé was in prison, and although the first family of settlers
arrived at Quebec in 1617 (the family of the apothecary Louis Hébert),
Quebec was in despair. But the fur trade meant much. The Compagnie de
Rouen continued to trade under an arrangement with Condé and then,
when he had sold his grant to the Duc de Montmorenci, under a similar
arrangement with the duke. The profits brought interlopers to Canada and
ensured that interest was maintained even in the period following on Henri's
assassination.

But the fur trade, dependent on bringing Indians down to trade at
Lachine, at Tadoussac, or at Trois Rivières, was at odds with plans for settlement, with the missionaries' desire to bring the Indians to a sedentary way
of life, and with Champlain's desire to explore to the north and west. His
wish to Christianize the Indians and to penetrate into the hinterland inevitably brought him into opposition with the merchants; and the clash of

interests was not lessened when the merchants of Rouen and St Malo were deprived of their monopoly and it was given to a new syndicate, the *Compagnie de Montmorenci*, led by two powerful merchants, Ezekiel de Caen and his nephew Guillaume. Guillaume de Caen, the more active partner, was a Huguenot, and the clash between the interests of the merchants and those of the missionaries was emphasized when in 1625 the Jesuits embarked on their mission to Canada.

The establishment of the *Compagnie de Montmorenci* had brought Champlain out, in 1620, as Governor of New France. He was confirmed in office as Richelieu took control in France and Montmorenci sold his position as Viceroy of New France. Champlain was given power to make war and alliances and the duty of discovering a way to the west and to China. He was much taken up with the problems of the little settlement at Quebec, but he was also deeply concerned with the western lands. In 1624 he arranged a peace with the Iroquois and even got them to attend the rendezvous at Lachine and to make an alliance with the Hurons, the Algonquins, and the Montagnais. One of his "young men," Etienne Brulé, at this time (probably in 1623) would seem to have made an important move towards the discovery of the west by travelling from Huronia to Sault Ste Marie and on to Lake Superior.

Champlain supported the Jesuit mission despite the opposition of the Huguenot Guillaume de Caen, and there were vigorous and expansive elements in the small society of which he was governor. But disputes within that society were such that in 1626 an appeal had to be made to the Council in France (where the de Caens had their concession vindicated), and the French were hemmed in not only by the difficulties in travelling but by the animosities of the Indians as Montagnais and Algonquins carried on their hostilities against the Iroquois and as the Hurons strove to maintain their control of the trade coming down from the far west by way of Huronia.

Champlain barely managed to keep his tiny Habitation at Quebec in existence until, in 1628, an English expedition captured Tadoussac and, after leaving him to languish out a winter with no supplies, compelled him to surrender Quebec in July 1629. The blow fell just as it had begun to seem that New France would get from Richelieu the organized support which it had so far lacked. Within the framework of Richelieu's *Compagnie de la Nouvelle France* a group of merchants known as the *Cent Associés* was to control the fur trade, was to take out at least two hundred settlers a year for fifteen years, and was to open up the land, converting the Indians to Christianity and making them into French citizens.[8] The English, at open war with France, captured the first expedition sent out under these auspices and then brought Champlain and the furs stored at Quebec to London. Quebec had, however, been surrendered after peace had been con-

cluded between the two countries, and endless disputes arose as to the ownership of the furs—disputes which revealed that there was in England a group
of merchants and courtiers which had secured recognition as the Canada
Company in 1627 and which was interested in the establishment of an
English colony in Canada, and in the fur trade of the north.

Though forcibly led by David, Lewis, and Thomas Kirke and patronized
by the Earl of Stirling, the English Canada Company was better designed
for plundering expeditions than for the administration of a settlement, and,
by the time that the *Compagnie de la Nouvelle France* resumed control in
1633, Champlain found that three years of English neglect had almost
completely ruined the little colony. With Guillaume de Caen anxious to
make the most of the renewal of his privileges, the French were still preoccupied with the fur trade; and hostilities with the Iroquois had again
broken out. French prestige had suffered greatly, and the situation seemed
completely at odds with the position adopted by Champlain when he
published his *Voyages* in 1632.

Champlain had then summarized his experiences and had maintained
France's right to the whole interior of North America, emphasizing the
need to oppose Dutch and English claims. Knowledgeable and sympathetic,
Champlain took up his role as a paternal governor, drawing the Indians
down to trade again, building up Quebec, Trois Rivières, and Tadoussac as
prosperous little settlements. But his dreams of expansion out from the
valley of the St Lawrence remained with him, and under his auspices the
Jesuits embarked on their missions, and Champlain sent out his "young
men," sometimes in company with the Jesuits, to live with the Indians, to
learn their ideas of the routes to the north and the west, and, when possible,
to travel and explore.

Much effort went into the discovery of a way to Lake Huron and Lake
Superior which would be more direct than the Ottawa River route. The
Recollects had made their way to Lake Erie in 1626, but they had been
forced to withdraw, and French knowledge of the Great Lakes was still
sketchy, as was demonstrated by the map which Champlain included in
the 1632 edition of his *Voyages*. Green Bay was there shown as an inlet
from the north shore of Lake Huron, and Lake Michigan was shown as a
part of Lake Superior. But, probably in 1638, as the French regained control,
one of Champlain's interpreters, Jean Nicolet, who had spent ten years with
the Algonquins, made his way through Lake Huron to Sault Ste Marie and
then, instead of following on into Lake Superior, turned to the Straits of
Michilimackinac and so into Lake Michigan. Here he kept north and west,
into Green Bay and up the Fox River almost to the headwaters of the Wisconsin River. The Wisconsin is a tributary of the Mississippi, and Nicolet

brought back reports of a mighty river and of the South Sea into which it flowed.

Champlain was dead by the time Nicolet brought this report; he died in 1635. But the French continued to probe the ways to the west; and missionary zeal, Iroquois hostility, the fur trade, and the search for the Passage were all present as motives. Knowledge of the Great Lakes and of their rivers was much increased when the Jesuit Father, Isaac Jogues, returning to Sault Ste Marie, was captured by the Iroquois and forced to travel with them until he escaped to the Dutch.

Though he had been mercilessly tortured, Jogues determined to embark on the mission to the Iroquois which quickly earned for itself the name of the "Mission of the Martyrs." For the Iroquois were unspeakably cruel to the missionaries, and they were not to be moved to allow the fur trade which was now concentrated on Lachine to continue. The great Iroquois War was breaking out as Jogues was making his way back to Canada to start his mission, in 1643. Apart from plunder and bloodthirstiness, the Iroquois were determined to cut off the French from supplies of furs from the west and to divert those furs south to the Dutch and English markets on the Atlantic shore. The French wanted to make the way westwards by the upper St Lawrence and Lake Ontario safe for themselves and their Indian allies, and they must maintain the annual rendezvous at Lachine in order to survive.

The religious orders were in the forefront of the struggle. In 1642 the soil of Montreal itself was granted to the religious order of *La Compagnie du Saint Sacrement*, and the city was founded as a military and religious outpost again Iroquois hostility. The need was pressing, and the French settlement barely survived. The Iroquois War continued for almost thirty years, with varying fortunes but with no clear respite. At times Iroquois bands prowled to within fifty yards of the growing fortifications of Montreal, and they ravaged to the north of the St Lawrence as well as to the south.

Little help could be expected from France, for France was in the grip of the Fronde and could offer nothing even when it became clear that the Iroquois War would eventually lead to war with the English and Dutch from whom they drew their arms and support. The costs of the war had to be met from within Canada, and there was only the fur trade from which revenue could be got. As the colony had taken roots, a group of settlers, the *Compagnie des Habitans*, had subcontracted the monopoly of the fur trade from 1632 to 1637 and had prospered so that they then renewed the arrangement for four years, to expire in 1641. By that time the Iroquois menace was serious, and the costs of defence were in excess of revenue, so that the *Compagnie de la Nouvelle France* was only too willing to hand over the fur trade to the *Habitans* once more, in return for responsibility for the costs of administering the colony and for a payment of a thousand beaver skins a year; the *Habitans* were also to bring out at least twenty settlers a year from Europe.

The *Habitans* were thus made responsible for the costs of their own administration and defence; and this was tied to the fur trade, from which they were to derive the revenue. The *Habitans* who undertook this responsibility were a comparatively small group of established settlers, anxious for a consolidated defensive system and for a fur trade under controls which would allow them to enforce their monopoly and to get maximum profits from it. It would seem that the tendency for New France to expand, to break out through the Shield and past the Iroquois cordon, was ended. But the generality of the settlers was not content to be excluded from the fur trade. While the Iroquois hovered round the small settlements, interrupted supplies of furs, and threatened all, there was a premium on the kind of adventurous character who would evade their patrols and go to seek the furs himself. Control was met by smuggling, connivance, and illicit trade; and although the need for control in the interests of revenue was accepted, the arrangement with the *Compagnie des Habitans* was under constant criticism and was modified in 1647, in 1652, in 1653, and again in 1656.

The men who challenged the control of the *Compagnie des Habitans* came, on the whole, from the new colonists who began to build up the population of New France during these years. Sturdy peasants of Breton or Percheron stock, they put down their roots into the soil of Canada. They established a real colony; and when defence and administration had to be paid for, they kept the fur trade going by evading the laws, evading the Iroquois and going to get the furs "in the habitations of the Indians." The *coureur de bois* who emerged under this system had much in common with the "young men" whom Champlain had sent out to live with the tribes; he was tough, resilient, a hardy traveller who could keep up with Indians on the route. His life depended on his being accepted by the Indians. But he differed from Champlain's "interpreters" on important points. He was often a family man with close ties to the interests of the small settlers, travelling with Indians during the winter when farming was out of the question. He was, moreover, interested in trade rather than in discovery; he was not in touch with savants or administrators, nor trained or checked in reporting what he discovered. Since he was, as often as not, acting in defiance of regulations, he was likely to keep to himself anything which might emerge from his journey; and if he made a report it was liable to be regarded with some suspicion.

Nevertheless the *coureurs de bois* had magnificent qualities. It was they who, in the unpropitious times which followed on Champlain's death, perpetuated his conviction that French interest in Canada must not stop at

Lachine Rapids. Their individual exploits are not easy to ascertain, but it is clear that up to the time when, in 1663, the *Compagnie de la Nouvelle France*, and with it the *Compagnie des Habitans*, disappeared and a new regime was instituted, the *coureurs* were making a succession of adventurous voyages into the territories of the middle west and were building up a reliable notion of the geography of the region of the lakes and of the territory to the north and west. The *coureurs*, too, developed their own theories about the routes for further expansion; and by 1660 a pair of them, related by marriage—Médard Chouart, Sieur des Groseilliers and Pierre Esprit Radisson—had formed their own view of the commonly accepted notion that there was a passage "from the west sea to the south sea, and a great trade of beaver in that passage." The peculiarity of their view lay in their conviction that the passage lay to the north, by way of Hudson Bay; not by way of the St Lawrence or, alternatively, by way of the Ottawa River and Lake Superior.[9]

This conviction was the result of actual travel and of conversations with Indians, not of speculation and theory. Groseilliers, a typical immigrant of the period, had been brought to Canada from Charly-sur-Marne as a child. He had served with the Jesuit missions in Huronia from 1646 onwards and had seen the way in which the Iroquois had driven the Hurons and their French allies away from Lake Huron and Lake Michigan. Though married, and owning a farm at Trois Rivières, he continued to travel to the west, and from 1654 to 1656 he was sent on an official mission to get the western Indians to bring their furs down to trade despite the Iroquois. It was an important mission, on which the survival of the colony depended. For the French were still hemmed in by the Shield and the Iroquois, confined to the St Lawrence valley and dependent on the Indians bringing their furs to the lower river; and whereas it was estimated that before 1648 about a hundred canoes came each year to trade furs to the value of between two and three thousand livres, in 1652 not a single canoe came.

On his mission Groseilliers probably got as far as Green Bay and there spent the winter. He met the Illinois and the Sioux of the west and the south, and he also met the Crees (the Cristinos) of the far north. The Cree lands reached "as far as the North Sea," and they gave Groseilliers accounts of the "Bay of the North" where seagoing ships, arriving direct from Europe, might meet with the Indians who had themselves trapped the prime arctic furs which were the basis of trade. Groseilliers returned to Canada in 1656 with a considerable private fortune in furs, with a convoy of about thirty Indian canoes whose furs helped to keep the Canadian economy going, and with a determination to open up this new access to the northern territories and the northern furs.

Radisson, in the meantime, had been developing his own views and abilities. He also had been brought to Canada as a boy—from the Papal enclave of Avignon, not from France proper. In 1651 he was captured by an Iroquois band during a raid on Trois Rivières, and for some years he lived with the Mohawk tribe. He was severely tortured and condemned to death for an attempt to escape, but his adoptive family saved his life, and for a further period he travelled with them, learned their skills, and mastered their way of life. He escaped (as Jogues had done) to the Dutch and so was taken to France and thence back to Canada. Though never a particularly religious man, he showed the way in which the religious and the secular elements in Canadian society were combining in efforts to expand the frontier when, in 1657 and 1658, he took part in the Jesuit mission to the Iroquois. He survived unharmed and in 1659 joined Groseilliers in an epoch-making journey in search of furs and of geographical information.

Their prime object was to make contact once more with the Crees and to investigate the possibilities of getting furs through the Bay of the North about which the Crees had spoken to Groseilliers in 1655-56. To maintain control for revenue purposes and to prevent untoward incidents, the Canadian authorities had forbidden trading with the Indians "in their habitations." But Radisson and Groseilliers managed to slip away in company with a band of Indians returning from trade. They went through Lake Superior and spent the winter, 1659-60, with the Sioux in the forests of Wisconsin and then, in spring, returned to Lake Superior and there met the Crees.

Radisson later stated that he and Groseilliers then went north with the Crees, down a river to Hudson Bay. It is unlikely that such a journey could have been managed in the time available, for they were back in Montreal in the late summer of 1660; and in due course, when contact had been established with the Indians of the Bay of the North, they alleged that they had never before seen a white man. But though such a journey is unlikely, Radisson and Groseilliers certainly convinced themselves that it would be possible and would be immensely profitable. For they ascertained that the Bay of the North was the great emporium of the fur trade. Moreover, they concluded that although an overland journey would be possible (even to the extent of saying they had made it) it would be so dangerous and take so much time that access from the sea would be infinitely preferable. Instead of breaking out through the barrier of the Shield to the north and the west, they argued that they must sail round it and approach from the north— though they did not speak in terms of the Shield and its barrier to penetration.

The knowledge on which Radisson and Groseilliers based their views was reliable, but it was second-hand, the fruit of discussions, not of experience. The Crees habitually made the journey between the Bay of the North and

Lake Superior, and the Jesuit Father Dreuillets wrote up an account of such a journey made by an Indian in 1658-60 and sent it to the Governor. The journey was clearly possible, and the Bay itself was getting to be reasonably well known too. From the early voyages of John Cabot, of the brothers Corte-Real, and then of Sebastian Cabot, it was known by 1509 that Hudson Strait led westwards into a great bay which dropped down into the heart of the land from the north; and during the Elizabethan period the endless search for the "Straits of Anian," leading to a Northwest Passage, established the outlines of the coasts of Greenland, of Labrador, and of Baffinland. Dutch and Danes took their part, but the English led, and they gained a knowledge of northern waters and a competence in arctic navigation which stood them in good stead.

The quest was continued in the seventeenth century, with George Weymouth sailing through Hudson Strait in 1602 and the East India Company and the Muscovy Company both anxious to discover a passage to the Indies. Henry Hudson himself added as much to the myth as to the knowledge of the problem. For (after his voyages of 1607 and 1608 had taken him further north than had previously been achieved and his 1609 voyage had given possession of the Hudson River and its fur trade to the Dutch whose employee he then was) his last tragic voyage of 1610-11 took him through the Strait and down into the "Bottom of the Bay." He was in the deep indentation of James Bay, land-locked and with the west coast of Hudson Bay stretching north to Melville Peninsula to thwart him if he tried for a passage. But he and the mutineers, who put him ashore to die and then sailed on back to Ireland, believed that he had broken into the Western Sea. It remained only to sail on to the western shore of the vast body of water into which Hudson had entered; and English merchants and courtiers, bound together as "discoverers of the North-West Passage," took the mutineers into their employment and sent out a series of voyages with that object in view.

In 1612 Thomas Button probed the western shore of the Bay as far north as Roe's Welcome, and he wintered at the mouth of the Nelson River (which he named). But though he took possession of the western shore and of the river mouth in the name of the King of England, he was disappointed in that he was in search of a passage; and he did nothing to stimulate an English fur trade—indeed, he saw no Indians. The Passage dominated the period, through voyages by Bylot and Baffin in 1616, by Hawkridge in 1617, and by the Dane Jens Munck in 1619-20. The western shore of the Bay held them all, and English pre-eminence may be judged from the fact that Munck was obliged to take English pilots on the disastrous expedition which ended in starvation and scurvy in the mouth of the Churchill River. Hopes of a break-through on the west coast of the Bay remained uppermost, and when the Merchant Venturers of Bristol sent out Thomas James and Luke Fox in 1631, it was to the Churchill River that they also went, to "the very place where the Passage should be." Between them they explored the south coast of the Bay from the Nelson River east to Cape Henrietta Maria while James went to the Bottom of the Bay and wintered on Charlton Island before returning home.

James and Fox added to the already considerable knowledge of Hudson Bay which was available as Radisson and Groseilliers began to think seriously and constructively about the Bay of the North. The knowledge was, however, almost entirely in the possession of Englishmen; and their interests were in silks and a passage to the East, not in furs and possession of the frozen lands in which (if they were unfortunate) they were forced to winter. But it was becoming clear to the English that the Northern Sea might yield its own kind of profits. Huguenot refugees stimulated an industry of felting, among others, and a Feltmakers' Company was started in London in 1629 while the furs which were bought to London when the Canada Company captured Quebec in that year brought notions of a profitable fur trade to simmer in the minds of English merchants.

Accordingly, by the time that Radisson and Groseilliers got back from their great journey to the west in the summer of 1660, convinced that the best approach to the furs of the north must be by sea into the Bottom of the Bay, it was always possible that they might have to turn to England for support in such a venture. They would prefer French-Canadian support. But they had broken most of the Canadian regulations in setting forth, and on their return they were fined, punished, and forced to pay duty on the furs which they brought back. Convinced that the Canadian authorities would never support their plan, they took it to France and, failing support there, back to Canada again. Regulations meant little to such men, provided they could get backing, and they managed to launch an illicit expedition to test their views. This failing, they turned to the New Englanders of Boston and managed to get a ship for their purposes in 1663. But they had made a late start, the captain was unwilling to chance wintering in the Bay, and they returned "re infecta" to Boston. There, as they tried to organize a second voyage, they were thrown into the company of the boundary commissioners whom England had sent out to delimit the frontiers after the capture of the Dutch colonies of New Amsterdam and Manhattan. "Frivolous placemen" though these Stuart courtiers may have been, they were alive to the possibilities of the Canadians' plans.

Somehow, probably by the intervention of Colonel George Cartwright (who was alleged to be a Papist and who was certainly a friend of James, Duke of York), the two coureurs were got to London. It was an eventful journey, in which they were captured at sea by a Dutchman, were landed in Spain, and made their way to London only to find, in 1665, that the Court had been driven down to Oxford by the plague. They were, however, such men as the Court of the restored Stuarts delighted to make much of. The savants of the newly founded Royal Society discussed the climate and geography of the Arctic with them, the bankers talked of the profits of the fur trade, and the King himself thoroughly enjoyed their talk and their company and gave Radisson a medallion-portrait of himself.

Statesmen, too, working out a thesis for an imperial economy in which northern lands would counterbalance tropical territories and in which control of trade routes would be all-important, found the flow of information about the possibilities of living, trading, and travelling in the Sea of the North fascinating. Prince Rupert the King's cousin, Rupert's secretary James Hayes, and the great statesman Sir George Carteret, treated Radisson and Groseilliers as the serious proponents of an important doctrine; they were kept at Oxford until the Court moved back to London in 1666, and then supported and encouraged while the frustrating business of fitting out a voyage to test their idea was put in hand.

Though there were delays and ineptitude in plenty, there seems to have been little doubt that such a voyage would indeed be launched. Radisson and Groseilliers were promised that a royal ship would be lent them for the voyage, and they were made the personal protégés of Sir Peter Colleton, who was one of the most powerful and purposeful of the group of courtiers concerned with such matters. Their notion fitted the English approach. Whereas the French were committed to the lower St Lawrence as their starting-point and sought an answer to the confinement of the Shield by breaking out overland by trail and portage over the height of land, the English had accumulated a knowledge of the direct approach from the Atlantic to the Bottom of the Bay and had evolved a theory of a passage to the Far East which ensured support for the two *coureurs*.

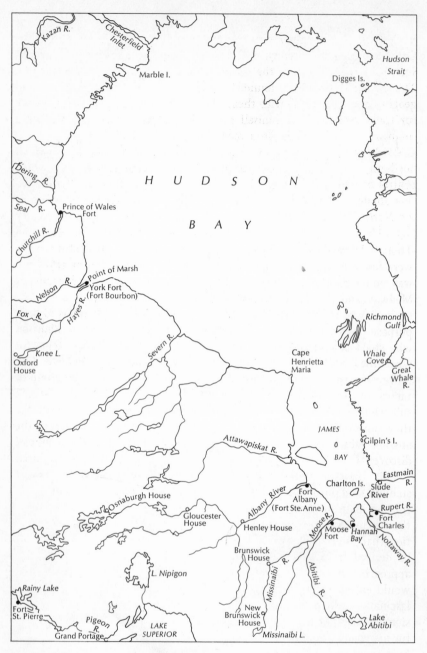

Hudson's Bay

CHAPTER 2

The
Hudson's Bay Company
at the Bottom of the Bay

Though Groseilliers and Radisson were supported and encouraged, there were few resources which could be put at their disposal. The Dutch War was going badly, the English fleet was sacked at its moorings in the Medway, and Van Tromp controlled the Channel. Preparations for a voyage to the Bay in 1667 had to be abandoned; the ship which was bought for the purpose proved completely unsatisfactory. The well-connected supporters who stood behind Groseilliers and Radisson had many defects, especially when they were involved in the troubles of a nation at war. They were, however, adepts at manipulation. Diverse as were their interests—scientific, mercantile, or imperial—they were brought together by the need for joint subscription to maintain the two Frenchmen; and from a loose syndicate they gained coherence when, in 1667, the King granted them a royal commission which promised "the sole trade of what countryes they shall discover."[1]

This grant in itself brought support from financiers who gave credit, stability, and purpose. Small investments by interested, wealthy, and powerful men indicate that there was a general awareness of the possibilities of the scheme proposed by the two Canadians, rather than any clear conviction that the scheme was feasible in itself or that any great wealth could be derived from its exploitation. A notable difference from the French approach was that the project did not get support from merchants who would expect to organize and profit from the fur trade; this despite the fascination which the furs held for Groseilliers and Radisson, the professional advisers of the group which was forming. The nearest approach to a fur merchant who interested himself was John Kirke; the whole family had been concerned in the capture of Quebec in 1629 and in the sale of the furs accumulated there, and John Kirke was a merchant of London and agent for several European merchants. He was the only one among the sponsors of the venture who had any traceable connection with furs, and even that connection was remote and conjectural. The cargo of trade goods which was got together in London was based on the assumption that the Crees of the Northern Sea would have become used to that sort of European goods which had hitherto been exchanged for their furs by the Algonquins and the Montagnais and which would have been brought up from Canada by these tribes. French brandy and tobacco were therefore purchased and assembled in the London warehouses by Kirke, helped in this by the two experienced Canadians.

As the English preparations were going forward, attempts were made to entice Groseilliers and Radisson away from England, and the French court began to interest itself, at last, in a voyage to the Bottom of the Bay. But the two Canadians stood firm, and in June 1668 their expedition was at last launched. It consisted of the *Eaglet* ketch, lent by Charles II and under the command of Captain William Stannard, and of the *Nonsuch* ketch, bought from Sir William Warren, a great London timber merchant, and commanded by Zachariah Gillam, a tough Boston seaman who had already had some experience of sailing north from the New England ports. Groseilliers sailed aboard the *Nonsuch*, Radisson aboard the *Eaglet*. Neither of the ships was built for the sort of work which was in hand, and their defects soon became obvious. The *Eaglet*, of fifty-four tons burthen, forty feet long and sixteen feet in the beam, soon revealed that she was "unable to endure the Violent Stormes" of the Atlantic and put back to Plymouth. The *Nonsuch* was even smaller, of only forty-three tons, thirty-six feet long and fifteen feet in the beam. But with Groseilliers aboard she ploughed on, passed through Hudson Strait, and was down in the Bottom of the Bay in the late summer.

At the Bottom of the Bay the *Nonsuch* was met by friendly Indians and was guided by them into the mouth of the Rupert River. This was completely frozen by early in December, and for the next six months the ship was "environed with ice." The ketch had been hauled on shore, and the crew built a house, dug a hole to preserve their beer from frost, brewed small beer from malt, and lived reasonably well through the winter. Game and fish were abundant, especially partridges and pike. Though the Indians were friendly, they were apt to pilfer unwanted trifles. They followed a nomadic way of life, and in the spring a band of about three hundred came to the ship to trade. As winter ended Gillam was able to report that he had not lost a single man by illness or hardship, only "some trouble with scurvy in their mouths."

In a memorandum submitted to the Council in 1683, in which this winter was described, it was claimed that a friendly trade was established and that Gillam "discovered a River in the bottome of the said Bay, upon the East Maine, where he mett with the native Indians, and having made a League of Friendship with the Captain of the said River, and formally purchased both the River itself and the Lands thereabouts, he gave it the name of Rupert River." [2] In view of the different notions of personal property and of landed property, the bargain cannot have meant much to the Indians, whatever it meant to the white men. Nevertheless, such a bargain placed the English in a strong position as against other European claimants, and it had the merit of paying at least some attention to Indian claims.

It was probably Groseilliers, with his knowledge of Indian ways (and perhaps even of the Cree language), who conducted these negotiations, although the ship's captain was officially in command of the voyage. Aboard ship Groseilliers and Radisson had no powers; they were only advisers. The captains must remain in command; the Canadians were no more than supercargoes. They were, of course, to be treated with respect, and their knowledge was all-important. But they could not dominate the voyage even though the ships' captains were instructed "to use the said Mr Gooseberry and Mr Radisson with all manner of civility and courtesy" and were told that they were "the persons upon whose Credit wee have undertaken this expedition." Even the trade goods were under the control of the ships' captains, who were to hand them over to the Canadians in lots of fifty pounds' value. Probably the purchase of their lands from the Indians would easily fall into the category of a fifty-pound deal by Groseilliers.

The Instructions [3] for the two ships make it clear that, despite the range of interests which this voyage served, trade dominated by the time the ships sailed. The Canadians had led their English supporters to believe that they might well find a practicable route to the South Sea—"haveing told us that it is but 7 daies padling or sailing from the River where they intend to trade until the Stinking Lake and not above 7 daies more to the streight which leads into that sea they call the South Sea and from thence but forty or fifty leagues to the sea itself, in all which streight it Ebbs and flowes by meanes whereof the passage up and downe will be quicke." The Canadians carried into the English context the French notion that there existed, somewhere, an easy water-route from the Bay of the North to the Stinking Lake (the Lac des Puants, which ultimately proved to be Green Bay, Lake Michigan), [4] and on from Lake Michigan, still by water, to the South Sea. This, misunderstood, was a version of the route from the Middle West to the Gulf of Florida by way of the Mississippi. The possibility was there and was included in the Instructions with which the ships set sail. But exploration in search of a passage was not a prime object of this particular expedition. If the preliminary reports seemed to justify it, a ship specially prepared to seek for a passage would be sent out to the Bay in the following year.

In the meantime the Northwest Passage was comparatively unimportant and took no priority over additional objectives such as the development of copper and other minerals and the setting up of an English colony. All these possibilities were of less importance than the furs which would be traded from the Crees; since the whole voyage was based on the information given by Groseilliers and Radisson and since furs were their obsession, this should cause no surprise. Both the *Eaglet* and the *Nonsuch* were meant to winter in the Bay; but in the spring of 1669 the two captains were to change ships; Stannard and Groseilliers were to come home in the *Nonsuch*, bringing the furs which had by then been traded, while Radisson and Gillam were to stay on with the *Eaglet* for a second winter in the Bay. The failure of the *Eaglet* meant that these Instructions went by the board, but this first voyage revealed that furs from the Bay would command a market and could make generous profits. The furs which the *Nonsuch* brought home sold handsomely and with little delay.

While the *Nonsuch* and her cargo brought the fur trade of the Northwest to London, the syndicate which had sent her out had already organized into a more closely knit body during her absence. Perhaps the ebullient Radisson had something to do with this, for soon after the *Eaglet* had returned to England the sponsors had announced that they would send out another expedition as soon as the weather improved; and they begged the use of the *Hadarine* pink from the navy for the purpose. Disappointed in this, they nevertheless bound themselves into a legal corporation of which the unit was the holding of a three-hundred-pounds share. A remarkable and important body of men joined on these terms, though not all of them at once paid the comparatively small sum involved in the purchase of a share: Prince Rupert, the Duke of Albemarle, the Earl of Craven, the Earl of Arlington, Anthony Ashley Cooper (later Earl of Shaftesbury), Sir John Robinson the Lieutenant of the Tower, and a small group of bankers and merchants. Most, if not all, of these men had already paid in something towards the costs of the 1668 voyage, and in June 1669 those subscribers who were primarily interested in the trading possibilities, a group of six City men, secured a monopoly of the trade of the "northern parts of America."[5] The men who secured this grant were acting on behalf of the wider group who had already paid in the money needed for the voyage and who held together and organized their further joint action within the convention of a three-hundred-pounds share or unit. They were securing precision for the vague royal support which had been already obtained and which had given rise to rumours that the supporters of the voyage had won a royal grant of trade and of ownership of the land.

Whatever the story behind the grant of exclusive trade, secured in June 1669, it is evident that a powerful group among the subscribers to the *Nonsuch* voyage wanted, above all things, to secure the trade in furs to themselves. When the *Nonsuch* returned, their preoccupation was justified;

even the seamen who had "carried out no trade" had made considerable sums by exchanging their spare clothing, knives, and needles for furs with the Indians. The grant of exclusive trade was renewed two days after the *Nonsuch* had cleared her furs through the customs, on October 21, 1669.[6] Again the outstanding fact was that there had emerged a group of English businessmen anxious to secure a monopoly of the trade from the Bay. But they were acting on behalf of a wider group, and the grant itself contained many clauses which had little direct concern with trade. This time the propriety of the seas, straits, and lands within the entrance to Hudson Strait was granted, together with all mineral rights within the territory; and the grant of land was made in due form according to English law, in free socage, direct from the Crown, on the same terms as the Manor of East Greenwich was held. The service to be rendered in payment was to be two elk skins and two black beaver skins a year, whenever the King of England or his heirs or successors should set foot on the territories. Much of this was the common form of grant for English colonizing, and it had the great merit that such a grant would bring an English colony into a known and firm relationship with English law and English society. The *Nonsuch*, however, had just returned from her winter in the Bay and had brought no reports of mineral deposits or of the serious possibility of establishing an English colony. She had brought furs and reports of a boundless wealth in furs, and the grant of October 1669 must be taken as little more than the full specification of the earlier grant of June, with the legal formalities filled in but with the emphasis still focussed on the clause giving the sole commerce to the grantees.

This was still not the full and final charter of the Hudson's Bay Company. Although other possibilities were mentioned, trade was the dominant consideration, and the men named in this grant of October 1669 were those who were chiefly concerned with trade. The land owners, scientists, economists, and statesmen who had subscribed varying sums of money for the maintenance of Groseilliers and Radisson and for the *Nonsuch* voyage were content to see the whole business brought into the common form of the period. They were content, too, to push the project a further step forward. It was Prince Rupert's secretary, James Hayes, an unlovable character not to be suspected of devotion to anything which did not hold promise of rewards, who kept the various elements together and piloted through court and chancery the ultimate Charter, in which all their interests were combined. Rupert was already committed, though he had paid in his money with considerable caution; and in April 1670 he placed before the Council a full draft charter. The Prince's "docket on Hudson's Bay" went to the Privy Council of April 13, received the Privy Seal on the 18th, and emerged on May 2, 1670, under the Great Seal of England as the Charter of the

Governor and Company of Adventurers of England trading into Hudson's Bay.[7]

Its Charter granted to the Hudson's Bay Company all "those Seas Streightes Bayes Lakes Creekes and Soundes in whatsoever Latitude they shall bee that lye within the entrance of the Streightes commonly called Hudson's Streightes together with all the Landes and Territoryes upon the Countryes Coastes and confynes of the Seas Bayes Lakes Rivers Creekes and Soundes aforesaid that are not actually possessed by or granted to any of our Subjectes or possessed by the Subjectes of any other Christian Prince or State." The Governor and Adventurers of the Company were made "true and absolute Lordes and Proprietors" of this enormous and ill-defined territory, which they were to hold, once more, according to the terms of the Manor of East Greenwich, on payment of two elks and two black beaver a year whenever the King or his heirs or successors should enter the territory. In effect this granted to the English company the drainage-basin of Hudson Bay; and at that date it was not known what this might imply.

The Charter apparently made an exception in favour of the prior rights of any Christian prince. But this was no more than a form of words, uncertain in its meaning and European in its origin. It had little relevance to possession of the Northwest, and the whole English undertaking was based on the assumption that France refused to concern herself with these lands and with the maritime approach to them. The result of the Charter was therefore that the English company, with proprietary rights derived from the English Crown according to the accepted forms of English law, was brought on to the back of the French territories and athwart the efforts of the Canadians to break out from the basin of the St Lawrence. As knowledge broadened out it became clear that the Charter granted land right through to the watershed of the Rockies and up to the height of land north of Lake Winnipeg. As yet it could not be known what lands would be comprised in the area delineated, but the territory so granted was called Rupert's Land, and elaborate regulations were set out to make it possible for a colony to be established there, with governors, councils, and courts of law.

Unrealistic as many features of the Hudson's Bay Company's Charter may appear in the light of later knowledge of the climate and territory, they were meant to take account of all contingencies. Such terms were necessary if what had come to be accepted as the first simple object of the English in Hudson Bay was to be achieved—the establishment of a trade in furs. For if the French should claim and vindicate a right to the territory itself, any English fur trade would be destroyed. Accordingly, in order that a fur trade might be maintained, the territory itself had to be claimed under a national flag and then granted away with legal formalism to a company and a colony; and since the English fully supported the dictum that "prescription without possession availeth nothing," it had to be made clear that real occupation of the lands was in view.

Rivalry for ownership of the lands within the Hudson Bay drainage-basin came later. It was trade and access to the "northern Indians" of the Bay which were the immediate issues and which brought a well-connected and strongly-organized English chartered company into rivalry with the French of Canada. Profiting by the mishandling of Groseilliers and Radisson, the English had gained control of the sea route to the Northwest, or at least of the approach to that territory, and they had by the Charter placed that control in the hands of a small group of men whose motives were so mixed and whose personal investments were so small in relation to their wealth that they could persist in their claims even when the fur trade, which had become their prime motive, could not be made to pay.

As the pioneer voyage under the Charter took shape, matters other than the fur trade received due attention. Part of the outward cargo consisted of bricks and mortar for the construction of a post, and of "great Gunns" for defence. This would indicate some sort of settlement which would be far removed from anything which a *coureur de bois* would have thought necessary, or even helpful, for trading with Indians. At least it would indicate a "factory" constructed as a focus for the local trade, an emporium to which the Indians would be drawn, and a depot to which the ships would sail; probably more. The Charter had envisaged the foundation of a colony in Rupert's Land and had even made it possible for the governor and the controlling power to be transferred from London to the colony. In the event, such a colony did not begin to take shape until the nineteenth century; but as yet the geographical circumstances were little appreciated, and actual "possession" of the land might well be required to counter French claims. Thus the notion of a "plantation" could not be put on one side; Gillam's treaty with the Indians must be reinforced by possession, and a settlement of some sort must be made.

Affairs in Rupert's Land were to be under the control of a governor; and the governor appointed to go out on the first chartered voyage and to remain in Rupert's Land had no previous knowledge of the fur trade and had given no signs that he would seriously concern himself with so worldly a business. Charles Bayly, first Governor of Rupert's Land, is in many ways an enigma. The one aspect of his appointment which is certain is that he was a royal nominee thrust upon a company which knew little of him and which had every reason for misgiving. Bayly was in fact in prison in the Tower at the time of his appointment. His offence was that as a Quaker (he was described as "an old Quaker with a long beard") he had reproved the King for "rioting and excess, chambering and wantonness" and had denounced in turn the established church, Roman Catholicism, and the loose morals of the Restoration court. He was released from the Tower on the express condition that he should betake himself to "the Navigation in Hudson's Bay." Although he had behind him some experience as a resident in Maryland and although the Governor of the Tower in whose particular care he was put was Sir John Robinson (an early member of the Hudson's Bay Company, later to become Treasurer and Deputy Governor), these connections are not enough to explain why the Company should accept such a governor, nor do they make it clear why the arrangement for his release should stipulate that he must receive "such conditions and Allowances as may be agreeable to reason and the nature of his Employment."

The Company was, however, considering a governor who was primarily a resident magistrate, not a fur-trader. That the Crown should express an interest and that Charles II should stir himself on behalf of Bayly calls for comment. But it has long been known that Bayly had enjoyed at least one audience with the King, and it has recently been shown that Bayly, being of French extraction, had been taken up by Charles's mother, the French-born Henrietta Maria, as a playmate for the young prince who was later to become Charles II.[8] Hence the familiarity and the affection between the King and the Quaker, and the revelation of royal interest in the appointment of the first Governor of Rupert's Land. Other signs of royal interest were there, too—the nomination of Rupert himself as the first Governor of the Company, to be followed by James, Duke of York (later to become King James II), as the second Governor.

But trade was not neglected. Fresh money had been invested in the purchase of a cargo of trade goods and in the long-term commitment of a ship —the Prince Rupert, specially built for such voyages. When an expedition set forth in June 1670 it consisted of the Prince Rupert and the Wivenhoe (again borrowed from the Royal Navy, and again signifying royal interest), and it took with it Bayly as Governor, Groseilliers and Radisson as traders, Zachariah Gillam, who knew the navigation, and Thomas Gorst who had been on the voyage of the Nonsuch. Gorst represented the interests of the investors and wrote up an account of the voyage for them,[9] from which it is possible to form a narrative of this first chartered expedition. There can be no mistaking the fact that the knowledge and experience of Radisson and Groseilliers gave them great power, and that preoccupation with the fur trade overrode all other interests.

At Digges Island the Rupert and the Wivenhoe separated, the Rupert taking Gillam and Groseilliers to Charles Fort in the Rupert River, where they had been in the previous year. The Wivenhoe took Radisson and Governor Bayly further west, with the intention of setting up the main English post in the Nelson River or in the Hayes River. Early voyages had built up a fair knowledge of the western shore of the Bay, derived from seagoing expeditions. But nothing was known of the territory opened up by the rivers, or indeed of the navigability of the rivers except what could be got from Canadian *coureurs*—of whom Groseilliers and Radisson were outstanding examples. The *coureurs* however, despite their assertions, had not yet travelled down the rivers to the Northern Sea. They were dependent on Indian rumour for details, although it was accepted that, in some way or other, the rivers which ran north to the Bay drained the territory at the back of the Shield which hemmed in Canada and the St Lawrence basin.

The available knowledge therefore allowed Radisson and Bayly to sail the *Wivenhoe* direct to the Nelson River, but gave them little idea of what they would find when they got there. They almost wrecked their ship getting her into the river mouth and, after Bayly had gone ashore and taken possession in the name of the King, the *Wivenhoe* was carried out to sea in a violent storm, winter set in, the ship's captain went sick and died, and Bayly decided to sail over to join the *Rupert* in the Rupert River. The western shore of the Bay was in effect abandoned, and effort was concentrated on the Bottom of the Bay. Even so, the experience of the winter was such that the men would not stay, and in the spring both ships and all the men sailed for England, abandoning the small fort which they had built. Disappointing as this result must have been, the profits on the beaver which had been traded were satisfying, and an active market in furs began to develop in London, with the Hudson's Bay Company's sales by auction at its centre.

Meanwhile in France the threat that the Iroquois might overthrow the colony in Canada had been taken so seriously that in 1665, when the danger to the eastern frontier of Christian Europe from the Turks was for the moment held in check, and when France's quarrel with the Papacy was also in suspense, the Carignan-Salières regiment was sent to Canada, and the Chevalier de Tracy took command as Lieutenant-General of the French forces. A winter campaign against the Iroquois was, however, ineffective, and an invasion of their lands, led by Tracy himself in the summer of 1666, achieved little.[10] The episode nevertheless prevented Governor Richard Nichols of New York from taking sides with the Iroquois against the French colony. Nichols had contemplated such action in view of the fact that England and France were officially at war from early in 1666 onwards; but he had been unable to persuade the other New England colonies to attack the French, and when Tracy's campaign had failed to give complete victory either to the French or to the Iroquois, he agreed with Tracy that English and French were to live in North America "en bonne intelligence et réciproque courtoisie." If so much could be achieved when the two kingdoms were at war, when their mutual hostility to the Dutch had brought them to peace (at Breda in 1667) and then to an alliance in which their combined fleets fought under the Duke of York, the vague threat to French ambitions which the Hudson's Bay Company seemed to pose was unlikely to come between even such uneasy allies.

The French under Colbert were nevertheless acutely aware of the English interest in the Northern Sea, and of the potential danger to their own designs. Acceptance of amicable relations in North America did not prevent Colbert from taking into French service the Dutchman Van Heemskerk, who had sailed with Radisson on his abortive voyage of 1669 and who knew about English plans. Colbert gave to Heemskerk "all the lands which have been and shall be discovered by him in all North America entered from above Canada towards the North Pole."[11] The grant was to extend to the South Sea if Heemskerk could reach so far, and he himself was romancing about a land which he called the "Floride du nord," where he would find safe anchorages and good rivers to lead him to the interior.[12]

In August 1670 Heemskerk was sent out from Dieppe. But he was an important month behind Bayly and his men, he failed to get into the Bay, and his voyage was a complete failure. Heemskerk nevertheless reveals the interest which Colbert was taking in the Northern Sea; and the English protest evoked a reply based on the doctrine of effective occupation,[13] which made the abandonment of the Bottom of the Bay by Bayly in 1671 all the more potentially dangerous for any English claims.

In the Northwest neither French nor English in 1671 had achieved anything which could be described as effective occupation. But in view of the need for an alliance against the Dutch it was important for both countries that the North American situation should be allowed to take whatever shape circumstances dictated, without precipitating a major confrontation. The personalities of the agents of the two countries would inevitably count for much; and the French of Canada were well led by the great Intendant, Jean Talon, who had arrived in Canada in 1665, served for three decisive years in which the economy of the colony was revitalized on Colbertist lines, and returned for a second period of office in 1670.[14] As the problem of Hudson Bay began to develop, and information of the English achievement began to be available, Talon was convinced that Canada had survived its period of defence and inactivity. Part of his economic policy hinged on developing a Canadian economy which should be a counterpart to that of the French West Indies (an idea implicit in the formation of the Compagnie de l'Occident). But although he was insistent in his efforts to diversify the economy of Canada he realized that as yet it was the fur trade which must pay for all, and that the Canadian fur trade was open to a two-pronged threat. From the south the New England colonies with their Iroquois allies were long-acknowledged rivals; to the north a new threat might be seen in Hudson Bay.

Reports from New England spoke freely of Talon's desire to engross the whole beaver trade and of the way in which French fur posts had been advanced towards Albany.[15] In the north he was equally concerned to establish French control of the trade. The possibility of reaching the Northern Sea by overland travel from Canada was shown by the rapidity with which Indian rumour brought news of the English to Talon. Apparently he was informed of Bayly's arrival within little more than a month of the Indians' first sight of the English ships; and Talon decided to counter the English, and any pretensions which they might make in the future, by an overland expedition. His vision was of a New France which had broken through the confines of the Shield, of a land whose boundaries could scarcely be envisaged (as he wrote to Colbert), so distant were they from the confines of the Canada which was known; in 1670 he asked for royal medals, to be distributed to explorers searching for new forests and mines and industries. In passing on to Paris his report of the two English ships at the Bottom of the Bay, Talon announced his decision to send north some men of resolution who would persuade the Crees to bring their furs to the St Lawrence. They would also make notes about the country and above all would find out whether it might be possible to build houses in which Europeans might winter.[16]

The French had long had some sort of information of the routes by which the Northern Sea might be reached from Canada. In particular, in the *Jesuit Relation* of 1657-58 Father Drueillettes had set out five ways of making the journey. It was certain that access to the Bay from the St Lawrence was possible for skilled travellers, and in the early summer of 1671 Talon sent off the Jesuit Father Albanel. The Jesuit had been in Canada since 1649 and had a perfect knowledge of the Montagnais and their language, as well as the habits of Indian travel. He was accompanied on this journey by the Sieur de Saint Simon, a recently-ennobled young man of twenty-three, and by another Frenchman named Sebastian Provencher of Pennara. They were to make notes of the geography of the Bay and to report whether ships might be wintered there, to act as supply ships for further exploration in search of the Northwest Passage. They were to encourage a trade in furs; and above all they were to deny any English pretensions. Asserting that the lands by the shores of the Bay had originally been discovered by Frenchmen, they were to claim possession and were to set up the arms of the King of France as tokens of French sovereignty.

Travelling with a party of eight Indians, Albanel reached Lac St Jean in early September and there learned that the English ships had passed the winter 1670-71 by the Bay. He settled down for the winter, set out again in June 1672, and reached the mouth of the Rupert River by way of Lake Mistassini and Lake Nemiscau at the end of that month. The English post at the Rupert River was deserted, since Bayly had taken all his men back to England. So the Frenchmen wandered by the shore of the Bay, met bands of Indians, made presents to them, and even converted some of them to Christianity. They formally set up the French arms and declared French sovereignty; and this met no opposition from the Indians despite the "sale" of these lands to Gillam and the earlier presence of the English. The Indians were not thinking in terms of European doctrines of land ownership. Their problem was to obtain European allies against their enemies and to prevent Europeans from intervening between them and the market for furs on the St Lawrence. They tried to persuade the French not to undertake a voyage which would expose the background of the trade which arrived in Indian hands at the markets in Canada (as they had tried to dissuade Champlain), but Albanel and his companions broke through this secrecy. They confirmed that English ships had wintered by the Bay and that French ships might well do the same, they showed that Canadians could make an overland journey to the Bay, and they made a forthright claim both to the territory itself and to the loyalty of the northern Indians.[17]

Albanel finished his mission and started back for Canada just before a new English expedition, which must have challenged his actions despite the "réciproque courtoisie" between the two nations, arrived at the Bottom of the Bay. The expedition consisted of three ships—the *Rupert* once more, the barque *Employ*, and a small fishing vessel (a dogger), the *Messenger*—and was again under command of Bayly. The size of the English expedition has significance since Bayly had reported that if trade alone were under consideration one ship a year would be adequate. But for a settlement, said Bayly, the *Rupert* would need at least one consort, at least thirty men must be sent out, and "Mousebae" would be the best site. This should not be taken as indicating that in 1672 the decision to send out three ships signified a determination to found a colony of settlers. The distinctions were derived from overseas trade to the East and to Africa, where a continuous trade necessitated a "fort" or a "factory," where a "factor" could maintain relations and prepare cargoes ready for the arrival of shipping. The weakness of such a method of trade was the "interloper" who took advantage of its security without sharing the costs, and its alternative was the "fugitive" trade which maintained itself without any shore establishments. When the Hudson's Bay Committee decided to send out Bayly in 1672 with resources to make a "settlement," it was a "factory" which was intended, not a colony.

The decision meant that a permanent English post was to be set up; and this would mean that the northern Indians would know that there would always be English goods to be got at the Bay and that their furs would always find a market there. A "fugitive" trade would not have such effects, and the Hudson's Bay men were staking a permanent interest in the Bay when they sent out a further supply of bricks and mortar and ordered one of their ships to winter in the Bay. As against French claims the decision had its significance; but it was a decision made in relation to trade rather than in relation to sovereignty. It went along with a firm decision that all trade must be conducted by the Company alone and that the private trade of servants and sailors (and even of governors) which had marked the previous voyages must cease. Henceforth only the Company's men, trading on behalf of the Company and with the Company's goods, were to trade with Indians throughout the vast territory which the Charter had conferred.

Bayly, with his three ships, went straight to the Rupert River, and there settled down to a prosperous but unenterprising trade, so that in the early summer of 1673 he was able to send home a good cargo of furs in two of his ships. Radisson went back to England with the furs, but Groseilliers stayed out and was sent to explore the western parts of the Bay and to settle "Port Nelson." At the Nelson River he found remains of Thomas Button, but no Indians were there during his stay and he returned to Bayly disappointed. Bayly also was in trouble, beset by rumours that the French were encouraging the Indians to attack his post and faced by French rivalry for furs. Even at the considerable distances which separated French *coureurs* from the mouth of the Rupert River their influence was felt, and Bayly was obliged to give better prices for furs than he had intended. The element of competition, exploited by the Indians, offset the rigidity which would otherwise have settled on the English trade. For within its monopoly the Hudson's Bay Company felt able to insist on a "standard of trade," which had been set out by Radisson, and to allow individual traders no margin for haggling. In fact, from these early days, the need to counter the flexibility of the French traders led to systematic evasion of the "standard of trade" set out by the company, and the English employees adopted their own standards. These were indeed rigid by comparison with the bargaining methods of the *coureurs*, but they gave local variants in price according to circumstances.

Behind the problems raised by the ability of the Indians to exploit competition between the two European systems lay the fact that the two great powers, despite their *entente*, despite the fact that they were actually in alliance against the Dutch from the Treaty of Dover in 1670 and were comrades in arms from 1672 onwards, were committed to hostility in the Bay. The journey of Albanel and Saint Simon had been followed up by traders from Quebec, and a French post had been established only a week's travel up-river from the English factory. The Rupert River was so much interrupted as an avenue of trade that the English sent a party to Moose, and Bayly himself took a party to experiment with trade at the Albany River. Both ventures were comparative failures. What was emerging was that the Indians of the Bay (the Crees in particular) had already come to depend on regular English trade and to expect the arrival of ships with goods, but that nevertheless the pattern of trade was not so regular or so immune from French intervention that the English could neglect their opportunities. They were forced to probe the shores of the Bay, not so much in search of any passage to the Far East, rather in the hope of finding some attractive harbour at the mouth of a river which would bring down to their post tribes of Indians who would not be subject to the competition of the French *coureurs*. They were getting to know the shoreline of the Bay, the Eastmain, the Bottom of the Bay, the Rupert, Albany, Hayes, and Nelson rivers, and in 1674 Bayly made his way to Cape Henrietta Maria and to the New Severn River.

He returned to Fort Rupert to find once more that the "French of Canada" were on his doorstep. It was Albanel again. His journey to the Bay in 1674 was made with the explicit object of enticing Radisson and Groseilliers back to the French allegiance. The move can be traced directly to Louis de Buade, Comte de Frontenac, who had been made Governor of Canada in 1672. Frontenac was greatly concerned with the fur trade—more, perhaps, than was consonant with his duties as governor—and in a letter to Colbert of 1673 he had explained at length the harm which Groseilliers was inflicting on the trade of Canada.[18] Albanel was therefore sent north again, carrying a personal message to Groseilliers in the hope of luring him back to the French allegiance. The convention of mutual respect which de Tracy had established still prevailed, and so Albanel carried a letter of introduction to Bayly as well as his letter to Groseilliers;[19] and on his arrival he was in need of the succour which the kindly Quaker gave him.

Bayly in the meantime had been relieved of his command by a trained fur-trader, with experience in Russia. But the ships bringing out this replacement had not yet arrived when Albanel got to the Bay, and so Bayly was still in command of the English post. As he observed the Jesuit's connivance with Groseilliers and then with Radisson, he decided to place Albanel in custody and to send him to London, with the two Canadians, for the Committee to deal with. The ships of 1674 were so late in arriving, however, that neither Bayly nor the Jesuit nor the Canadians could get out of the Bay that year. During the winter the professional fur-trader who was to replace Bayly wearied of conditions, and in September 1675 it was he who sailed for England with the Jesuit and the Canadians, leaving Bayly once more in command.[20]

In 1675 Bayly had only four men left with him. But by the time the French next visited the Bay, in 1679, he was able to boast that he had three forts, at Moose, at Rupert (or Fort Charles), and at Albany, each driving a prosperous trade. He added that another post was being set up at New Severn and another was planned at the mouths of the rivers which "ran up" to Lake Superior. By this Bayly would mean the mouth of the Nelson or the Hayes river, and he would be showing that the English knew that the furs which came to the Bay came in part from the area "on the back" of the French possessions. With over sixty men under his command the Quaker was confident; he was also able to boast that the *Rupert* had spent the winter in the Bay as a guard-ship, with her strong armament of twelve guns, that he had another ship of fifteen tons, built for trade along the coast, and that although he had just lost a barque of forty tons he was in no serious difficulty for that reason. He was able to get all the beaver which he could handle, and within six years or so he was confident that the English would be complete masters of all the trade of the Assiniboines.[21] Notions of geography and of tribal distribution were of course vague and inaccurate, but by this Bayly would mean that the Hudson's Bay trade system would spread from the area of the Crees (reaching from the east side of Lake Winnipeg northwards) to the area from the west of Lake Winnipeg and the lower Saskatchewan northwards to the Bay. This was the land of the Wood Assiniboines, distinguished from the Assiniboines of the Plains to the west and south of Lake Winnipeg. The confident statement was, once more, an indication that in Bayly's time it was already appreciated that the trade brought to the Bay came from Indians who would otherwise take their furs to the French or to whom the French would penetrate in search of trade.

The chance which gave Bayly this opportunity to enlarge on his successes and on his plans was due to the arrival at his post of the brothers Louis and Zacharie Jolliet. Accepting the fur trade as the basis of the Canadian economy, and accepting the need for close regulation of that trade, Frontenac, as Governor of New France, was faced with a dilemma. He was a determined expansionist, deeply involved in plans for breaking out from the valley of the St Lawrence; but he was on the whole more concerned for expansion to the south than to the north. His ambitions inevitably brought him face to face with the Iroquois, determined to confine the French within their river valley and there to cut them off from access to other Indian tribes. In all his plans Frontenac was so aware of the financial possibilities of the fur trade that his motives were called in question, and since he used fur-traders in his schemes he was in no position to enforce the limitations on their free activity which were a part of French policy and which, from some points of view, he supported. In his efforts to extend

French influence down the valley of the Richelieu River towards Lake Champlain and the south he had met the Iroquois at Lake Ontario in 1673 and had promised French protection to them;[22] there he built Fort Frontenac (in a situation which was at least as appropriate for managing the fur trade as it was for any defence against the Iroquois), and in due course he handed over that post to the Chevalier de la Salle, a notable trader as well as an explorer.[23]

But Frontenac had been informed by the Jesuit Father Nouvel that by 1673 the English traders in the Bay had already diverted many of the Crees from bringing their furs south to the French.[24] The question of restraining or of encouraging the *coureurs* in their opposition to this trade was the more difficult since the Canadian economy needed more closely controlled supplies of furs, not a sheer increase in quantity. Each year the *coureurs* were forbidden to absent themselves from the settlements without licences; but Frontenac was at odds with his intendant Duchesnau, and each accused the other of connivance which made such vetoes useless. The outcome was that the *coureurs* maintained their own form of rivalry to the English posts with small hindrance, that Frontenac, little as he admired the Jesuits and much as he focussed his attention on the southern trade, had sent Albanel north on his second voyage, and that he followed this up with the brothers Jolliet in 1679.

Louis and Zacharie Jolliet had been used by Frontenac for exploration to the south, and Louis had completed a voyage from Lake Ontario to the Gulf of Mexico[25] which had gone far towards clearing up the problem of the "South Sea." His mission to Hudson Bay was purely one of reconaissance, to report on the position and strength of the English there. Little was required in the way of exploration, for the *coureurs* had already approached to within one day's journey of Fort Charles. Jolliet left Quebec in May 1679 and arrived at the Bay via the Saguenay River, Lake Mistassini, and the Rupert River, early in June. It was a speedy journey, and it showed the easy interrelationship between the trade area of the Bottom of the Bay and that of the lower St Lawrence. He took a priest as far as Lake Nemiscau, but his purpose was strictly secular. Zacharie Jolliet had also dropped off somewhere *en route*, perhaps also at Nemiscau, and Louis arrived at Fort Charles in need of help—which Bayly gladly gave him. So little was Bayly impressed that he thought it reasonable to offer Jolliet employment with the English. Jolliet in his turn reported that the English "forts" were not defensible, that they were built to resist the cold, not an attack from the land, and that, "Whenever it shall please His Majesty to wish to expel the English from this Bay in order to be Master of all the country and the Beaver trade, it will be Easy to provide the means and put them into Execution."[26]

The Jolliet expedition of 1679 illustrates the national rivalry which was rising in the fur trade behind the veneer of reciprocal understanding or even of alliance against the Dutch. It illustrates too the contrast between the English governor boasting of his ships and his command of the coasts, and the Frenchman shrewdly reckoning up the possibility of an overland approach and accepting the underlying hostility of the two nations as something to be brought out into the open "Whenever it shall please His Majesty to wish." In the meantime the peculiar climate of English politics during the period of the Exclusion Bill crisis made it possible for Albanel to be made much of in London, for him to be allowed to return to France, and for him to lure Groseilliers and Radisson to follow him, to add their knowledge and ideas to the information there available.

The English company was split and weakened by the Exclusion Bill crisis, while the end of the Dutch War and the marriage between William of Orange and Mary Stuart cast a blight on the "good understanding" between the two nations. The French were seriously weighing the value of the "good understanding" in the Bay, and Radisson in Paris was setting out his notion that the proper approach to Hudson Bay, and to further search for a Northwest Passage, should be sea-borne.[27] He was sufficiently aware of the other ambitions which were current to couple his proposal to oust the English from the Bay with a proposal to seek a passage and with a plan to reach the Western Sea by way of the "Freshwater Lake," to link up exploration southwards down the Mississippi with this westwards thrust, and to block off the fur-trading Indians from the New England colonies and New York by a couple of forts on Lake Erie. He was, in fact, co-ordinating Frontenac's desire to press southwards with his own commitment to Hudson Bay.

The difficulties which fell on the Hudson's Bay Company proved helpful in the end; for they brought a rift in the courtiers who had supported the Company and left control in the hands of a group of financiers, concerned with little else but trade. Bayly was replaced as governor by John Nixon, a shrewd observer; and the English approach was emphasized by the sending out of three ships for use in the Bay. But the ships were not only a means of exploration and trade; they carried great guns such as could not be dragged overland from Canada, and they were reckoned to be the best form of defence which could be provided. The need to anticipate French ambitions was further emphasized when, in his Instructions, Nixon was told that he must set up posts at Port Nelson and New Severn, and that this must be "suddenly put in execution." Emphasis on maritime defence against a land attack came out further in the order that Hayes Island, off Moose, was to be made the site of Nixon's chief post, for it was defensible by ships from any attack from the mainland. In the same vein, Charlton Island was to be the rendezvous for ships from England, and a great warehouse was to be built there.

Throughout the Instructions which were given to Nixon there was an awareness of the underlying conflict with the French. He was to make treaties with the Indians (after the manner of Gillam) so that "it might be understood by them that you have purchased both the lands and rivers of them, and that they had transferred the absolute propriety to you, or at least the only freedom of trade"; and the Union flag, whose use the Company claimed by its Charter, was to be employed to seal the bargain and to impress the Indians. In similar vein, and copying the French technique, wooden plaques were to be nailed to trees.[28] Nixon was critically aware of the inability of the London business men to estimate the realities of life at the Bottom of the Bay; nevertheless they felt responsibility, they were accumulating knowledge, and their interest was engaged. They sent detailed instructions about the use of country food, both because of cost and because a steady diet of ship's provisions and "hard tack" through the winter had revealed the danger of scurvy; they sent out seeds to plant, and hens and pigs and goats, and they gave advice as to the building of substantial warehouses and the conduct of the business at trade time "after a method."

Unrealistic as Nixon's instructions may have been in some respects, they showed a lively interest and a firm purpose; and this was remarkable because of the difficulties through which the Hudson's Bay Company was going and because their homewards-bound ship miscarried and they were without news of the actual situation in the Bay. In France, by contrast, there was little support for Radisson's proposal to rival the English by a sea-borne expedition to the Bay. It met with approval from a few, particularly from a well-known merchant connected with the *ferme* of the revenues of the colony and of considerable repute in France—Charles Aubert de la Chesnaye, who was later to secure acceptance of his views. In 1679-80, however, La Chesnaye failed to win support for a maritime and outspokenly anti-English policy. He had already sent a shallop to trade in the Bay, in 1676, and had been fined for so doing since he thereby infringed the privileges of Tadoussac; and in 1679-80 he sent another ship, under pretence of a fishing expedition, to Anticosti, under command of Zacharie Jolliet, to trade furs in the Bay.[29] The episode ended with the furs being traded to the English, and La Chesnaye was in any case opposed by Frontenac. For although the Governor was anxious to know the situation in the Bay and was keenly interested in the fur trade, he was embroiled in bitter controversy over every aspect of the trade and was impressed with the need to thrust out to the south and to the west rather than to the north. Behind everything lay the two major problems—whether any expansion of the settled area of Canada, to south, west, or north, was compatible with the determination to achieve a closely integrated colonial society, as Frontenac himself desired and as Colbert ordered; and whether any expansion of the fur trade could possibly result in anything but a collapse of fur prices in Europe and a consequent collapse of the Canadian economy.

The Canadian argument was to some extent academic, since Frontenac was not to be deterred from his policy of expansion to the south and west. In 1678 he had licensed Daniel Greysolon Dulhut to lead a party to the "extremity of Lake Superior." Ostensibly a move in the search for the Western Sea, this expedition also gave control of trade at the western end of Lake Superior to the French; and in due course Dulhut was diverted from Lake Superior southwards towards the Mississippi. Moreover, the Canadian fur trade was in a crisis over the use of brandy. Despite the restrictions on trading spirits for furs, which had been put through after the "Brandy Parliament" of 1678, Canadians were not seriously alarmed at the practice, and Frontenac and his officials never adequately enforced the official policy. Perhaps they were genuinely unable to do so; at any rate it was common knowledge that, notwithstanding the laws requiring licences before any *habitant* could go off to trade, the meagre population of Canada was supporting some five or six hundred *coureurs*, "living in the woods." The connivance needed to bring these facts into relation with royal edicts was considerable. The formulation of an effective policy was not made easier because the Governor and the Intendant each accused the other of fostering evasion of the edicts.

But Frontenac and Duchesnau were agreed in feeling that the position of the English in the Bay should be challenged whenever it seemed appropriate, and Colbert himself was increasingly prepared to oust the English. He had his agents in England, who kept him informed of the claims and activities of the Hudson's Bay Company, and he was in support of the moves which led to the enticement back to France of Radisson. Several copies of the Charter of the Company were circulating in Paris at a time when nobody in London, outside the Committee of the Company, was able to discover exactly what the terms of that magnificent grant of privilege and monopoly were.

The upshot was that in 1681 La Chesnaye brought back a profitable shipload of furs to France and that he managed to secure a charter for a French *Compagnie de la Baie D'Hudson*.[30] The English were warned, for Radisson came over to London in 1681 in order to take his wife to France, and the warning was passed on to the Bay. Up to this point Nixon had been urged to develop the western areas of the Bay, to open the route to the Crees, the Algonquins, and the Hurons of the vicinity of Lake Winnipeg and the route on to Lake Superior. This accorded with Nixon's own suggestion that the English should establish posts in the "rivers that goe doun into

Kennedy [Canada]"—but with a difference. Nixon insisted that the Indians must first be enticed down to trade at the Bay, including even the "Poyets" of far Athabasca; then the English must send men inland to trade and would become involved in the task of maintaining peace between the inland tribes. The London Committee was reluctant to send its own men inland to trade. But in urging the immediate settlement of Port Nelson it accepted the need to draw trade from the "rivers that goe doun into Kennedy." The English wanted the trade of the Lake Winnipeg and Saskatchewan areas as well as the trade of the Rupert River and Lake Nemiscau; but they were not ready to send their own men inland to seek that trade.

La Chesnaye found on his return to Canada that Frontenac was still averse from a direct maritime challenge to the English, or indeed from an expansion of the fur trade to the north. The utmost for which La Chesnaye could get permission from Frontenac was to fit out a fishing voyage to work off the coast of Anticosti. Such permits had proved the cover for trade to the Bay on previous occasions, and perhaps Frontenac was knowingly sending off a fur-trading voyage on such terms that when the English protest arrived he could maintain his ignorance and continue on that basis of friendly relations on which he set so much store. The Iroquois war had broken out with renewed fierceness from 1680 onwards, and he would naturally not want to provoke his English neighbours at this crisis. But in 1682 both Frontenac and Duchesnau were recalled to France (for the Iroquois war was going badly, and there were many memorials about the involvement of both of them in the fur trade), and Frontenac was replaced by Joseph Lefebvre de la Barre, who was to prove much less effective, but much less restrained, in his dealings both with the Iroquois and with the English. At the same time the restraining influence of Colbert was removed as his son the Marquis de Seignelay took charge of Canadian affairs from 1681 onwards and of the Ministry of the Marine on his father's death in 1683. La Barre was specially instructed by Seignelay before his departure for Canada, and Louis XIV himself sent for him to give his views. It was impressed on him that changes in policy must be made; and under his governorship the long-threatened French incursion into the Bay at last took shape.

CHAPTER 3

The French in the Bay

Much of the reluctance to stage a forthright challenge to the English in the Bay stemmed from the precarious instability of the Canadian economy. When the Canadian fur trade had come under the French Crown in 1663, the *Compagnie des Indes Occidentales* had been established to control the trade of both Canada and the French West Indian islands. The *Compagnie* failed to meet the wishes of the *habitants*, it failed to satisfy the revenue requirements of the Crown, and it failed to make money for its members. Its charter was revoked in 1674, when the powerful financier Jean Oudiette bought its rights, including the monopoly of the fur trade of Tadoussac, the *ferme* of all dues on the fur trade, and all other revenues in Canada; at the same time he was made responsible for the costs of administration of the colony. He also took over the sugar dues from the West India islands, which made his bargain for Canada seem less unattractive.[1]

Oudiette soon discovered that Canada was producing more beaver than the French market could absorb and that it was producing the wrong kinds of beaver. The French market needed about forty thousand coat beaver a year and not more than twenty thousand parchment skins. But Canada was sending home about ninety-two thousand skins a year (in 1677), of which only about four thousand were coat beaver; the remainder were parchment, and not always even good parchment.[2]

The distinction between coat beaver and parchment was fundamental to the fur trade, underlying the fine distinctions which the traders drew. For his trade the felter wanted the under-fur, the beaver wool or *duvet*, and as the French trade grew up it had got this beaver wool by sending its skins to Russia for combing. The process involved Holland and Russia, but it left a fine pelt composed of the glossy guard-hairs as well as the sacks of beaver wool, and it accorded well with the Canadian background of the French trade. For the Indians who traded to the St Lawrence mostly brought down skins which carried both kinds of fur. They had been sun-dried as they were taken from the beaver, and were naturally known as parchment. But as the northern trade developed two new factors emerged. The northern skins carried a heavier load of beaver wool, especially if they had been taken in winter; and the northern Indians often wore the skins before they brought them into trade, and thereby they greased the skin into the condition of a supple leather while they rubbed off the guard hairs. Coat beaver therefore had many advantages; it carried nothing but beaver wool, and since it normally came from the north it usually carried a thick coat of it. No elaborate process was needed to get the beaver wool from the skin. It could easily be shaved off, leaving a useful leather. There was no need to call in the Russians or the Dutch if coat beaver could be got.

A proportion of parchment skins was still needed to keep the old trades going and to provide the fine beaver fur which was left after combing had been finished. But Oudiette's problem of a surplus of "shoddy parchment" was in effect a problem of too many beaver from the south and too few from the north. His quandary was underlined when Governor Nixon began to get some order into the English trade. The cargo which he sent home in 1680 sold for more than the total capital invested in the Hudson's Bay Company, and much of it soon found its way to the European market, in direct rivalry to the furs of Canada. This was the first sign that the coat beaver of the Bay might affect the European market, and the prosperity which followed enabled the Hudson's Bay Company to pay its first dividend in 1684—after fourteen years of continuous trade without a dividend. The long period without reward indicates that the Company was maintained by wealthy men who were involved only for small stakes, not by professional fur-traders struggling for survival. But as the trade got under way and the coat beaver of the Bay began to secure a market in Europe, the merchants of Quebec and Montreal were forced to try endless expedients to stimulate the flow of coat beaver and to discourage the trading of parchment.

Controlled prices, varying according to detailed schedules but making a basic distinction in favour of prime coat beaver, were tried. But in the last resort the French either had to buy the furs which the Indians had brought to trade or drive them away dangerously disappointed—probably to go to the English next year. So the Indian trade continued without regard for ultimate consumption, the more easily because the *fermier* was there as a buffer between the *habitants* and the realities of their economic situation, compelled to buy all beaver at controlled prices and steadily accumulating a surplus of unsaleable low-grade parchment skins in his warehouse.

Though the process sounds a simple one, it was said that the Hurons and the Algonquins who were the main supporters of the French trade did not know how to *"engraisser"* their beaver, turning it into *"castor gras"* or coat.[3] So prime coat beaver from the north would be acceptable to the

Canadians. There seemed to be little chance of creating a glut of coat skins to match the glut of parchment. Oudiette himself favoured schemes for securing the northern skins, while those who, like La Chesnaye, could see their way to sharing in the trade to Hudson Bay, could make their plans without fear of oversetting the balance of Canadian trade, although they would have to find their way round a formidable barrier of regulations.

The open question was whether the best approach to the Crees and other northern Indians would be by sea or by overland route; and while Frontenac was opposed to La Chesnaye (and a maritime approach), Duchesnau favoured the creation of French posts on the rivers which ran down to the Bay.[4] This would draw the trade to Canada's market and put it under tribute to Canadian revenue. It would stifle the English trade without a direct confrontation, and it brought French traders to within a day's journey of the English posts. But such a policy could only succeed within limits. Jolliet had reported of the English posts that "there is no doubt that if they are left in the Bay they will render themselves masters of the trade of all Canada inside six years."[5] If the French wanted prime coat beaver (as they did) they would have to challenge the English in the north. In 1682 all the signs were that they were prepared to do so.

Warned by Radisson, the English prepared to meet the threat. Nixon was to send men up into the country. But, unlike the French, the English were not to trade inland. They were merely to "use all fair persuasion" to get the Indians down to trade at the Bayside posts. In addition, in 1682, two ships were sent out under the independent command of John Bridgar, with the specific task of settling the Nelson River. He was not only instructed to settle the "rivers that goe doun into Kennedy"; he was also told to "use your diligence to Penetrate into the Countrey to make what discoveries you can," and "to make such Contacts with the Natives of the River in and above Port Nelson as may in future times ascertain to us a right and property therein and the Sole Liberty of trade and Commerce there."[6]

The French were not the only rivals whom the Hudson's Bay Committee had to counter in 1682–83. As their ships assembled in the Thames they found that their ships' captains were ready to defy the Company's discipline, especially in its veto on all private trade. The oldest and most experienced of the captains, Zachariah Gillam, was toying with the idea of sending out an interloping expedition from New England; and in fact his son Benjamin Gillam did set out from Boston for the Bay.[7] The captains were, with some difficulty, brought to order. But the coat beaver from the Bay were bound to provoke challenge from within England as well as from the French, and soon after their ships had sailed an interloper, the *Expectation*, with four of the Company's former servants aboard, sailed from Dartmouth. Yet another ship was hastily hired and sent to intercept the *Expectation*. But the interloper was daunted by the difficulties of navigation and put in to shelter in an Irish port. She was wrecked in the next year when she made the venture. In the meantime the hired ship which had been sent in pursuit was lost at sea with all hands, her fate unknown.

The episode emphasizes the English Company's advantage in the maritime approach to the Bay, and, further, that they alone could exploit such an advantage. Despite the obvious defects in their ships' captains,[8] the Company maintained an astonishingly successful tradition of navigation into the Bay, in marked contrast with its rivals. Part of the reason for the ability shown by the English captains must be ascribed to experience, for year by year the route became better known, and the ships were used for cruising along the shores of the Bay during the summer months. But much must be ascribed to simple rule of thumb; the English had a time-table to which they adhered. When the time-table was departed from—as when the hired ship was sent in pursuit of the interloper at a late date—disaster was to be expected. The Committee always got its ships off from the mouth of the Thames by May 25 at the latest, to make the Atlantic crossing in a northern latitude in the best summer conditions and to arrive off Hudson Strait after the ice had broken. If they did not time their arrival aright they were condemned to cruise to and fro, in grave danger, until the straits were clear; but the English ships seldom made a mistake and were able to sail down to the Bottom of the Bay, impress the Indians who had come from inland to trade, perhaps undertake a coastal voyage for the Governor, unload their cargo, load with furs and with ballast (for furs were light but comparatively bulky), and be out in the open sea on their way back to England by the time winter had closed the straits again. The story of English trade to the Bay had its quota of shipwrecks, but by comparison with rivals of any nationality the Hudson's Bay Company had an undoubted advantage in its ability to get ships into and out from the Bay with reasonable certainty. The French were not good mariners, they feared the ice, and their ships were slight and unable to stand up to northern navigation, while the English were robust, hardy, and adventurous, they knew all the seas of the world, and they had large and sturdy ships. That was Radisson's verdict. He was back in English service by the time he made this comparison.[9] But the first formal French challenge for possession of the maritime route to the Bay seemed fully to confirm his point.

On top of the challenges from interlopers, in January 1683 the Hudson's Bay Company received for comment a memorandum which had originated with La Barre, in which he had put to the French government his contention that the English were making settlements in territory which belonged to France. He was, he said, ready to leave them their "commerce de la Mer," but if they set up their obnoxious little posts inland he would feel obliged to drive them out and (echoing Jolliet's words) he said he could easily achieve this since they were very weak.[10] At that time the English had no posts inland at all. La Barre's memorandum must be taken as evidence of his view that he must carry the war into Iroquois territory and that he must convince the English that any help given to the Iroquois would result in their own expulsion from the Northwest. It is evidence, also, of his recent arrival in Canada and of the influence which Oudiette and La Chesnaye exercised over him. The Hudson's Bay Committee, instead of stating simply that they had no "obnoxious little posts inland," set out to show that Englishmen had frequented the Bay for over a hundred years, whereas no Frenchmen had ever been known to sail or to trade in the Bay. They then advanced the Company's case on the strength of Gillam's treaty with the Indians, the royal charter, the building of Fort Charles and the subsequent development of trade, Bayly's confirmation of the treaty with the Indians, and the fact that Frontenac "did conciliate a good Intelligence and amity without complaineing of any Injury done by the Company in building Forts and makeing Settlements."[11]

The Company received support from the English government, although James, Duke of York (who was the Company's new governor in succession to Rupert), proved of little use in the crisis. The English government produced a full-scale rebuttal of French claims, categorically stating, for the first time, the English claim to the Northwest. The rebuttal took up the arguments which the Company had furnished and added that the Company had the right not only to erect posts by the shores of the Bay but also to extend on the mainland.[12]

While this diplomatic episode was taking place, Radisson and Groseilliers had sailed from Quebec in two small and ill-found ships. La Chesnaye was aboard with them; the expedition was organized by him, and it was sailing under the permit to fish off Anticosti which he had obtained. But Radisson took control of the expedition and conducted it into the mouth of the Hayes River on August 19 or 20, 1682. A low point of land, the Point of Marsh, separates the mouth of the Hayes River from the mouth of the Nelson, so that it was some days before Radisson became aware that while he was settling in for the winter in the Hayes River, another interloping expedition was similarly occupied in the Nelson River. This was the Boston, New England, expedition under Benjamin Gillam, son of the Hudson's Bay captain. There is no way of checking accounts of the affair to within a day or so, but it appears reasonably certain that young Gillam arrived at least one day ahead of the Frenchmen, perhaps more. Admirable as the Hudson's Bay Company's timing of its voyages might be from the point of view of the weather, on this particular occasion the Company's ships were the last to arrive.

John Bridgar lost his special convoy, and with the veteran Zachariah Gillam to command and pilot her, the *Rupert* arrived alone. The captain of the *Albemarle* had died at sea, and she made for the Bottom of the Bay and spent the winter there. Radisson being already in the Nelson River, he maintained that he had taken possession for the French, and he kept the English out from an anchorage, so that the *Rupert* was eventually carried out to sea and lost in the gathering ice. Old Gillam perished with his ship, and the equipment which he had brought out for the settlement of the Nelson River was lost with him. Bridgar and some of his men were already ashore, but they had no equipment, and they finished the winter as prisoners of the French—as did young Gillam and his bachelor New Englanders.

Radisson took complete control of the situation, and when the French ships proved their weakness and were cut through by the ice swirling in the river at springtime, he knocked the remnants together into one barely serviceable craft on which he sent the Hudson's Bay men (except Bridgar) to the Bottom of the Bay, while he took the Boston ship, *Bachelors' Delight*, and, with Bridgar and the New Englanders as his prisoners, set sail for Quebec with a fine cargo of furs. Badly organized as his outfit had obviously been, he had enough goods left (some of them taken from his rivals) to leave behind him a French post under command of Groseilliers' son, Jean Baptiste Chouart, on an island in the Hayes River. The post contained only seven men, but it turned Radisson's voyage from a mere interloping expedition into something of more durability and purpose. The little French post in the Gargousse (as the French called the river) stood for a French intention to maintain a permanent trade and for a denial of any English claim to sovereignty.[13]

But the French were once more unwilling to face a definite confrontation with England over the Northwest, while the English were prepared to push their claims to their logical conclusion. They ended by a forthright declaration that Hudson Bay was not a "Dependence of Canada" but that "The Country of Canada and that of Hudson's Bay are two different Provinces and have no relation but that of Neighbourhood."[14] Against this, the French entered on a detailed examination of the past history of the Bay, from Verezzano's discoveries in 1527 onwards. They paid particular attention to a voyage which Jean Bourdon was alleged to have made in 1656, from Tadoussac north by sea and through a passage in 68° into a great bay, of which he took possession in the name of the *Compagnie de Canada*. There followed an embassy to Quebec from the Indians of the Baie du Nord, in 1661, and in 1663 the Jesuit Father Couture went overland to the Bay, taking with him the Sieur de la Chesnaye.[15] They took possession of the land, erected a cross, and set up the royal arms of France at the foot of a great tree. These assertions are hard to reconcile with the novelty of the information which Radisson and Groseilliers gathered when they wintered with the Sioux of Wisconsin in 1659-60. There are, moreover, anomalies in the French statements : Couture himself and a companion of his on this journey later stated that he did not get to the Bay; and it would be hard to find a "great tree" to which to nail the royal arms.[16]

But there was some substance in the French allegations. There were certainly rumours circulating in Quebec about the Bay while Radisson and Groseilliers were trying to get support for a sea voyage, and it may be that the lack of support which they met was due to the comparative failure of Bourdon's voyage in 1656 and the conclusion that the best approach to the Bay would be overland from Canada by way of Nemiscau. The English could not deny the story; they fell back on a declaration that, "Whatever Chance Voyage may have been made or missionaries sent for the sake of Religion with soldiers to protect the Missionaries, the same could not bring any prejudice to the Right of His Majesties Subjects."[17]

While the English government was outspoken, the French government wavered. Anxious not to embarrass James, Duke of York, Governor of the Company and heir to the throne, round whom the Exclusion Bill controversy had raged, they were affected by the powerful group which favoured Canadian expansion to the south and the Mississippi rather than to the north, and they were greatly influenced by the failure of La Barre in his Iroquois war and by a movement for the recall of Frontenac to power, with the consequent emphasis on maintaining good relations with the English in the north. The very success which Radisson and La Chesnaye had achieved brought difficulties, for it was a problem what to do with the *Bachelors' Delight*. She could not be judged a prize of war since she had been taken in time of peace, and in the end she was released. Equally the furs raised the question whether they should be subjected to the tax of the *Quart* in Canada, or whether the trade to Hudson Bay might be run direct from France without deviation to any Canadian *entrepôt*. On these points La Barre, anxious to favour La Chesnaye, fell out with Seignelay, who insisted on maintaining the controls of Oudiette and the overriding importance of the Canadian revenue system.[18]

The result was that while the English tightened their position by orders to seize all interlopers of whatever nationality, by exacting an oath of loyalty from their servants, and by declaring that the French of Canada were "a standing enemy from whome you are never to expect any Friendship or Faire Dealing,"[19] the French government ordered Radisson to make his peace with the English. Seignelay, now Minister of Marine, and François de Callières suggested to the English ambassador, Lord Preston, that Radisson should go to the Bay under English auspices, disband his post, and leave "the rivers that goe doun into Kennedy" in English hands. The French were anxious to reduce the episode to the status of "an affair merely of merchants" on which they could yield with grace, but they were unwilling to yield on the deeper issues of legal possession and access.[20] On this they temporized and yielded nothing as of right. So it was the end of April 1684 before Lord Preston reported that the French had agreed to restore Port Nelson and all which they had violently taken.[21] Though this might be accepted as conceding the abandonment of any French claim to the territory, so much was not said; and the restoration of property was, in fact, never carried out.

As the diplomats wrangled, La Barre got no clear orders in 1683 or again in 1684, and he followed his own inclination—to favour La Chesnaye (whom Intendant de Meules described at this time as the greatest merchant in Quebec and the only man whose advice the Governor would listen to) and to treat the French establishment in the Nelson River as a substantial achievement.[22] In 1683 he allowed La Chesnaye to send out two ships to reinforce the little establishment in the Gargousse River. But the difficulties of penetrating to the Bay by sea were again demonstrated when the ships returned to Quebec with garbled accounts of new discoveries but certainly without getting into the Bay.[23] Not only did Chouart get no reinforcements in 1683; he found a rival at hand. The *Albemarle* had been intended to accompany Bridgar in 1682 but had put in to the Bottom of the Bay and had wintered there. In the summer of 1683 she was sent over to the Nelson River and established an English post alongside the French, and much superior in the eyes of the Indians.[24] In 1684 La Barre acted with more confidence. The Iroquois War was still on hand and a vigorous campaign would have won much support. During the discussion on this problem La Chesnaye's house was a notorious rendezvous of the *coureurs*, and he promised to get down from Michilimackinac at least two hundred active *coureurs* for a campaign against the Iroquois.[25] Though he later had to explain his failure, for the moment his stock stood high; he laid down two ships for northern navigation, and the *habitants* felt that the troubles in the fur trade might better be solved by sending some forty unmarried men on a voyage to the Bay than by taking householders away from their wives and farms for a difficult and dangerous campaign against the Iroquois.

La Barre, given no explicit orders from France, sought at least the friendly inactivity of the New England colonies, overcame his own misgivings, and led his forces against the Iroquois in July 1684; but he had to conclude an ignominious peace. Meanwhile, in June 1684, he had set up the *Compagnie de la Baie d'Hudson*. Sponsored by some half dozen merchants of the colony, this company was dominated by La Chesnaye, and it gave some sort of formal status to the group which had sent Radisson to the Bay and which had tried to reinforce young Chouart; its exact relations to the *Compagnie* which La Chesnaye had managed to establish in France have never been clear, but they must have been close. The *Compagnie de la Baie* was formed explicitly to get furs from Hudson Bay, from "la Rivière Bourbon dit Nelson." But it was not to be exclusively maritime in its approach. Zacharie Jolliet was sent off to take possession of Nemiscau and to interrupt the trade which passed that way for the English posts. He was to regard as an enemy of France any Indian who tried to trade with the English.[26] Having enjoyed English hospitality on his previous journey to the Bay, Jolliet wrote to the English post-masters to warn them that an attack from Canada was imminent, while the Intendant de Meules tried to organize an expedition of twenty canoes to go north, set up posts which would starve the English of trade, and oblige them to withdraw.[27]

While this overland approach to the Bay was in hand, with a permit for three posts to run for thirty years and an arrangement for revenue payments to be made at Quebec, the *Compagnie de la Baie* was at last allowed to send its two ships off to the Bay. The expedition was under command of the Sieur de la Martinière and aboard as chaplain was the Jesuit Père Silvy, who left an account of the voyage.[28] When they arrived in the Hayes River, late in September 1684, they found that the French post which they had come to reinforce no longer existed. The negotiations in Paris had ended in Radisson's being slipped over to London on the understanding that the Hudson's Bay Company would send him out to dismantle the post in the Gargousse River. He wasted no time on the voyage but was back in the Thames by early October, his mission accomplished, the French post abandoned, Chouart and the other Frenchmen seduced into English service and brought home with him, and an English post established in the Nelson River.[29] So La Martinière found the English busy building a post with bastions, a moat, and secure armaments; a half-hearted night attack failed, and La Martinière, with the most impressive force which the French had yet sent into the Bay, was forced to spend his winter without effect and to withdraw in the early summer of 1685, leaving the "rivers that goe doun into Kennedy" in English hands.[30]

Having failed both against the Iroquois and the English, La Barre was recalled in disgrace in June 1685 and replaced by the Marquis de Denonville. The troops and *engagés* whom he brought with him suffered from scurvy and typhus on the voyage, but Denonville had strength enough to put in hand a campaign which at least held the Iroquois at bay. He shared with La Barre the conviction that three things must be achieved: the Iroquois must be subdued; the New England colonies must be subordinated, or at least New York must be secured; and the English must be driven out from Hudson Bay. Relations between England and France were still complex and delicate, with France anxious to set the English against the Dutch and to secure the Stuart dynasty on the English throne.[31] A partition of the colonial world seemed not impossible and was seriously discussed, and Denonville was given no explicit orders to guide his conduct towards the English in the Bay. His own view, however, lay close to that of La Chesnaye; the choice lay between ousting the English from the Bay or accepting the ruin of the Canadian economy—"il faut abandonner ce Commerce aux Anglais ou les chasser de la Baie d'Hudson."[32]

Denonville would probably have moved against the English in the Bay in any case. His hand was forced because La Martinière, as he returned to Quebec, met the Hudson's Bay Company's ships and brought one of them, the *Perpetuana Merchant*, a prisoner to Quebec.[33] No state of war existed, but Denonville decreed that the ship was to be "condemned and made prise of." The only inference was that the English ship had been trespassing in French waters. The affair kept hostility on the boil; once more, the English were amply warned that an attack on their posts might be expected. A French spy had been captured at Albany; from Quebec came news that an overland expedition to capture the posts at the Bottom of the Bay was being organized; and private information from La Rochelle brought the same warning. The English having accepted the notion that Radisson's adventure into the Bay in 1682 was "merely an affair of merchants," the way seemed open to indulge in hostilities in the Bay without interrupting the delicate relations between the two states.[34]

Denonville was above all affected by his realization that in English hands the fur trade of the north was a threat to the Canadian economy.[35] While the English declared that Hudson Bay was not a "Dependence of Canada," the French were increasingly convinced that economically the two areas could not be separated. Whatever the geographical barriers of the Shield— and the Shield had been penetrated many times by 1685—Denonville was convinced that Hudson Bay must be integrated into the trade pattern of Canada. As his troops recovered from their scurvy, typhus, and seasickness, he selected the young Chevalier de Troyes and in February 1686 sent him with about thirty French troops and some sixty Canadian *voyageurs* overland to the Bay. The Canadians were under the command of their natural leaders, Pierre Lemoyne d'Iberville, Jacques de Sainte Hélène, and Paul de Maricourt (three of the eleven sons of Charles Lemoyne, Seigneur de Longueuil et de Châteauguay). Other members of the Lemoyne family were also in the party; and once again the Jesuit priest Silvy went north and once again left an account.[36]

Though characterized throughout by the panache of its Canadian leaders, this expedition was organized by Denonville, it employed regular French troops, and the French government was aware of it.[37] It was different from the quasi-private expeditions which had so far been put in hand, and it was backed alike by the government, by La Chesnaye, and by Oudiette, who had made an arrangement with the Compagnie du Nord and taken a substantial financial stake in the Compagnie.[38] It departed from the previous governmental policy which Jolliet's post at Nemiscau continued and which was still maintained in a map of 1685 which showed French posts at Duluth, north of Lake Superior, on the upper Moose River, at Lake Nemiscau, and at Fort Bourbon, Nelson River, all designated as posts "pour empescher les sauvages de descendre à la Baye de Hudson."[39]

De Troyes left Montreal at the end of March 1686 with thirty-five canoes, travelled by Lake Timiskaming and Lake Abitibi, and was at the Forks of the Moose River on June 19. Though strongly built, with solid bastions and ten cannon for defence, Moose Fort was captured in half an hour. Equal surprise was achieved at Fort Charles, Rupert River, where de Troyes made Bridgar a prisoner and also took the Company's ship, the Craven. He then sailed the Craven back to Moose, armed her with the guns from that post and took her over to attack Albany. Here it is difficult to imagine that surprise was achieved, for de Troyes took three days to site his guns for an attack. But the English were unprepared for resistance and Governor Henry Sergeant (who had with him his wife, his chaplain, and a nurse for his children) soon surrendered. De Troyes and his men had easily taken all the English posts except the new one in the Nelson River. He made no attempt in that direction but, leaving the brothers Lemoyne d'Iberville and Ste Hélène in command of the posts at the Bottom of the Bay, sent the English prisoners over to Nelson River and set out himself for Canada.[40]

Denonville warmly welcomed the young officer on his return to Quebec. He had indeed done remarkably well. But in his official account of the exploit the Governor was careful not to say that he had instructed de Troyes to take the English posts. He had merely told him to take over the fort in which the renegade Radisson was to be found.[41] Radisson was in fact in England; in so far as this instruction had any meaning, it would have entailed the capture of the post in the Nelson River. This was the one post which de Troyes did not reach. The detailed explanation had more relevance to the diplomatic situation in Europe than to the Governor's intentions or to realities in the Bay. He had intended to incapacitate the English posts, and he had almost completely managed to do so.

While Denonville was achieving this triumph in the north, the affair of the Perpetuana Merchant and the claim that she had been trespassing in French waters was absorbed in complex diplomatic exchanges. The hardening of the French attitude was matched by the English, for Governor Sergeant's family party at Albany was the outcome of serious discussion and of a decision that the English would shortly establish a colony of settlement in the Bay.[42] The Hudson's Bay Company secured the sympathy of the English ambassador at Paris, Sir William Trumbull, who, however, was not able to achieve any clear acknowledgement of the English claims. His position was weakened because it was open knowledge that James II, despite his previous connection with the Company, rated possession of the Bay as far less important than a French alliance in Europe.

The French diplomats were therefore able to delay settlement until news had come through to them that de Troyes had been successful; but the English had no knowledge that the Bottom of the Bay was in French hands. Agreement was reached on November 8/19, 1686, on the basis that each country should retain the posts and territories which were in its posses- sion at that time, pending a full enquiry into the legal rights involved.[43] This was a substantial victory for the French, since the Treaty of Neu- trality, as it was called, left Iberville and Ste Hélène in possession of the captured posts and since both nations agreed not to support "wild Indians" with whom the other nation might be at war. The effect of this was that the English abandoned the Iroquois. When Denonville moved against them, he got little help from France, but he alienated the Iroquois from the English by revealing that Governor Dongan of New York held that they were English subjects and could make no treaties without his permission. Dongan's successor, Andros, went further in the same direction and told the Iroquois that they must cease to attack the French since England had made a peace.[44] This was, of course, to presume that the Iroquois and their lands were subject to British sovereignty. But Denonville made an Iroquois treaty which enabled him to reinforce the French posts in the west and to stabilize the farming side of the Canadian economy. He was still convinced that Canada could not survive unless New York could be taken and unless the French hold on the Bay could be confirmed and enlarged. Here, with even James II telling the Hudson's Bay men, as news of de Troyes's exploit came through, that "My honour and your money are concerned, I assure you that I will take a particular care in it and see you righted,"[45] the Hudson's Bay Company formulated its "Case of the Adventurers of Eng- land tradeing into Hudson's Bay in refference to the French." They claimed both the Bottom of the Bay and the Nelson River on grounds of first dis- covery and subsequent settlement, while the French claimed because of their expansion outwards from the valley of the St Lawrence and because they had "Solidly established their Commerce."[46]

While discussions continued, the *Compagnie du Nord* prepared reinforce- ments for Iberville and the English maintained their post in the Nelson River. This proved to be a centre for a trade in fine furs, it gave access to unspoiled Indians, and it opened a backdoor to the lands of Lake Winnipeg and Lake Superior. So "the expedients proposed by the French Commis- sioners" advocated that the three posts at the Bottom of the Bay should be exchanged for Port Nelson. Since the English claimed that all of these posts were theirs by right, the "expedients" were never given serious consideration. Behind the French move lay a realization of the superior advantages of the Nelson River and of the difficulty of expelling the English from their post. If they could get the English to evacuate the Nelson River they could then cut off the Indians from the Bottom of the Bay without committing any warlike actions. Yet, in admitting the English right to the Bottom of the Bay, the French diplomats were giving away ground, and the Hudson's Bay men felt confident that "No Forreigner shall upon any pretence molest us in our rightfull possessions any more."[47] They continued their shipments, added a post in the New Severn River to their establishments, and even set up a small post in the Churchill River. The post in Churchill drove only a meagre trade in whale oil and was destroyed by fire in 1689. But it showed the direction in which the English were looking even when Iberville and his brother ruled at the Bottom of the Bay. They meant to extend westwards and also to control the "rivers that goe doun into Kennedy."

Despite the success which had been won by de Troyes and his party, and the French ability to maintain their gains at the Treaty of Neutrality, this was a time of high confidence for the English. They mopped up another interloping expedition, sent out four ships in 1688, of which two were designated for the resettlement of the Bottom of the Bay, maintained a series of unexampled dividends and, in 1690, trebled their stock and paid a 25 per cent dividend on the increased amount.[48] With all this mercantile success they also managed to secure the acceptance of their case as a matter of state, no more "merely an affair of merchants." Their governor of "York Fort in Hayes River of Port Nelson River" was secured a commission from the Crown as well as from the Company. Thereby he was empowered to make treaties with Indians and to seize any French ships which invaded his domain.[49]

The task of restoring the posts at the Bottom of the Bay was entrusted to two soldiers, Captain John Marsh and Captain Andrew Hamilton. Officially, in view of the Treaty of Neutrality, they were armed only for defence and instructed to build at Albany "without annoying the French or Disturbeing them," and they began to build on an island near the old post which Iberville had occupied and which the French called Ste Anne. The French had come near to starvation during the winter 1686-87, but in the summer of 1687 they received overland supplies from Canada, managed to capture a small English sloop, and sent their furs and prisoners to Quebec; in 1687-88 Iberville went himself to Quebec and then on to France to plead that the French must send ships to the Bay on a regular schedule. The overland route by which he had himself come to the Bay had been tried and would not do for regular communications. "I'll n'est pas possible de pouvoir soutenir l'entreprise de cette baie autrement que par mer," said Iberville's supporters, accepting the English contention that Hudson's Bay was not a "Dependence of Canada."[50]

Iberville was a great character, who matched daring deeds with forceful convictions and conclusive expression. He secured a loan of the best ship in the French navy, the *Soleil d'Afrique*, and in late summer 1688 he also took two ships provided by the *Compagnie du Nord* and left Quebec for the Bay. In the Albany River he found the English under Captain Marsh beginning to build their new post; they desired only to be allowed to live in peace, and in some sort Iberville let them be.[51] But Marsh died of scurvy during the winter, other members of the party were captured, some defected, and when there were only eight men left they surrendered to Iberville on condition that a passage to England was guaranteed to them. Iberville then captured almost all of the English shipping, the two ships which had been sent to the Bottom of the Bay, a sloop, and a further ship which had come over from York Fort. His return to Quebec at the end of the year was a triumph.

The Hudson's Bay Company in London had no definite news of these events until late in 1689, although the failure of their ships to return meant that something had gone wrong with their 1688 venture. They had got back one ship from York Fort with a good cargo and were feeling prosperous and hopeful. For as the Protestant Revolution came to its head the Company could reckon that if James II kept his throne the French would accept a reasonable settlement; and if James should lose his throne to William of Orange (to whom John Churchill, later Duke of Marlborough, Governor of the Company, had just pledged his support) then William's hostility to France would mean that the Company could count on government support.

In 1689 therefore the Hudson's Bay Company was ready to press its claims and develop its policy. The post which it thought had been set up at Albany was to be reinforced, and further advance into the Northwest was projected as a separate ship, the *Northwest Fox*, was sent direct to the Nelson River, to go from there to set up a new post to the north of the Churchill River. The project came to nothing, for following on the Revolution of 1688, war with France (King William's War, or the War of the League of Augsburg) broke out and the *Northwest Fox* and the *Hudson's Bay*, departing from usual practice and sailing down the Channel instead of round the Orkneys, were attacked by French privateers off the Scillies. The *Hudson's Bay* beat off the attack and put back to Plymouth; the *Northwest Fox* was taken prisoner and sailed to Brest. She had been meant to establish the English on the Dering River (formerly called the "Great River" or "Deer River") where they would make contact with the Dogrib

Indians.[52] Travelling back with the Dogribs as they returned from their trade, the English would make contact with the "Poets"—the Assinipoets of Athabasca. The English were in a mood for expansion into the Northwest; they told their governor at York Fort to send men inland on discoveries and even permitted him to vary his Standard of Trade so as to make his posts attractive to Indians.

The Standard of Trade which had been set out by Radisson still ruled in the English posts, and its rigidity marked a notable contrast with the French. The finer techniques of bargaining had not been mastered by the English traders, and the Indians tended to swarm over the posts, to pilfer, and to defraud their creditors. So the whole trade was regimented to a point at which it became true that the Indians were only traded with "through a hole in the wall" and a rigid Standard of Trade reduced the trader to the role of an accountant.[53] As the Standard fossilized, it centred upon the prime beaver skin in good condition. All other skins were reduced to terms of the beaver, which was the unit of accountancy; and so the term "made beaver" assumed a meaning as all other skins were "made" into beaver, for which specified amounts of tobacco, cloth, gunpowder, beads, needles, or other goods were traded. It took nine beaver, or other skins to an equivalent value, to get a three-and-a-half-foot gun in 1684,[54] and the system was often decried as extortionate. But criticism of the Standard often came from interested parties who took no account of the costs of maintaining posts and ships or who took only the good years into consideration.

The Standard was, in any case, not so rigid as might appear. From Bayly onwards the governors had taken liberties with it, and the way in which the Committee themselves ordered in 1689 that the Standard at the new post in the Dering River should be double that in use at York Fort shows that flexibility could be used.[55] Moreover, as the realities of competitive trade were accepted, the traders adopted a "Double Standard" of trade, in which the official Standard was maintained for the purpose of account-keeping but a more flexible standard, higher in some goods or for some skins, lower for others, was used in actual trade with Indians. The Double Standard had to balance out with the official Standard; but it was always suspected as a device whereby the trader oppressed the Indians and accumulated an "Overplus" reserve of purchasing power. These developments were not yet accepted in 1689, and it says much for the Company's determination to move into lands west and south of the Bay that at that time it should have accepted variations in the Standard.

The determination to give "better pennyworths" in order to attract Indians to the English posts was in due course exploited. The Indians played off French and English against each other, and, in particular as beaver became overstocked and martens became "our best furs and turns best to accounte," they played off the flexibility of the French system against the rigidity of the English by trading martens and finer furs to the French inland and bringing beaver and coarser furs down to the Bay, to get standard prices for them. It took some years for the hazards of such a system to be realized by the Hudson's Bay Company. In the meantime the Company was determined to develop westwards, was realistic in accepting a variation in the Standard of Trade, but was out of touch with the situation in the Bay. The Committee were confident that their superior goods would easily enable them to suppress the "straggling French" who traded on the back of their posts, and that the French under Iberville were "in a Despaireing perishing condition."[56] In 1689 they knew nothing of Iberville's success, of his command of the Bottom of the Bay, of his confident contempt for anything they could do.

As the old convention of a "good intelligence" between England and France in North America gave way to overt hostility during the period of the Protestant Revolution and King William's War, Iberville managed to secure government backing and the loan of naval vessels. The Hudson's Bay Company hoped to make its cause a national one in a similar way. The nominal value of its stock was trebled in 1690, to make it "as diffusive amongst their Majesties Subjects as possible, and more a Nationall Interest"; and since the Charter derived only from the royal prerogative and was open to attack as the prerogative itself came under fire, the Company tried to get its privileges confirmed and its claims supported, on a national basis, by Act of Parliament. The Company's governors secured commissions by royal warrant, with powers to maintain English sovereignty in the Bay. But the purposefulness with which the Company tried to expand westwards and to re-establish its hold on the Bottom of the Bay had little relevance to state policy; it was a matter of the fur trade, and the English government held aloof.

Yet the "Case" of the Company met considerable support in Parliament, though it was opposed by the London feltmakers who alleged that the Company was starving them of beaver and maintaining its prices by exporting beaver to the Continent. The merchant communities of New York and New England also opposed the Company's claims as being "very destructive to the Trade of England and the said Colonies," and the opposition produced an "Impartial account of the present State of Hudson's Bay" in which, as against the "boundless charter" with its power to make peace and war, to possess land, exercise jurisdiction, and monopolize trade, the "diminutive trade" of the Company was pilloried and its "forts" were described as no better than pig-sties. Nevertheless, the Company secured a Parliamentary confirmation of its privileges. The grant had two great defects. It was to run for seven years only, and the Company's fur sales were to be controlled in the interests of the felters and furriers. These were serious defects in the Parliamentary grant, but in 1690 the Company was glad to accept them. For it was able to tell its governors that the grant allowed "our Lands and territories to be a Colonie belonging to the Crowne of England."[57]

This was a considerable achievement. But it tied the Company's claims to William's success and to William's interest in that aspect of his problems. The Company was not merely being patriotic when it hoped that "When your Majesties Just Armes shall have given repose to all Christendome, Wee also shall Enjoy our share of those great Benefitts."

In the event, William proved to be so preoccupied with the European situation that the Northwest was treated as a subordinate issue. The saving factor was that the French government was even more engrossed with European affairs. Denonville's claims that no permanent settlement could be reached for Canada until New York and Albany were in French hands therefore met little support, and Denonville found his own position steadily undermined as a movement to restore Frontenac to the governorship gathered way. Frontenac arrived in Canada in the fall of 1689, to find that the Iroquois had taken the chance of open war between England and France to massacre the French settlers and their families at Lachine and that Denonville could only abandon Fort Frontenac and concentrate for the defence of Montreal. Failing to talk the Iroquois into a peace, Frontenac reluctantly decided on a powerful war against their New England allies and, in so doing, accepted much of the policy which Denonville had advocated. In the spring of 1690 a series of lightning attacks on New Hampshire and New York was set off. Schenectady was sacked, the post at Pemaquid was overrun and the Canadians, led by Iberville and his brothers and by the Sieur Hertel, showed a great capacity for this ruthless raiding warfare, travelling fast in company with their Indian allies, spreading devastation, and retiring before the New Englanders could gather for a counterstroke. In the same vein the French destroyed Fort Loyal, Casco Bay; and though the New Englanders replied with a force of eight ships which captured Port Royal, an overland attack on Montreal came to nothing. In October 1690, when Sir William Phips brought his fleet to Quebec, Frontenac was able to defy him until reinforcements came from Montreal and the British withdrew discomfited. A formal attempt to capture Canada, led by an admiral sent from England, had failed.[58] A victory in America which could influence the situation in Europe was never again seriously contemplated during King William's War—and the Hudson's Bay Company and its claims in the Northwest steadily declined in national importance.

For the Canadians the situation was not much more promising. The beaver market in Paris was in a worse state than that of London. With the Bottom of the Bay in French hands, the *Compagnie du Nord* was even able to achieve a glut of coat beaver, a thing not previously to be thought of. In the face of this Iberville argued that possession of the Nelson River would put the French in complete control and enable them to manage the trade entirely in their own interests. Frenchmen, moreover, would be able to winter in the Nelson River and start out in the spring to search for the Straits of Anian and the Northwest Passage.[59] The last suggestion fitted in well with contemporary opinion; Denonville was anxious to improve French geographical knowledge in northern waters, and so was Frontenac, who in 1688 was urging that the doyen of French geographers, Jean Baptiste Franquelin, should be sent north on a surveying expedition.[60] The suggestion that a French post in the Nelson River might be useful in discovering a passage actually came from the Sieur de Riverin, a prominent Canadian who had been secretary to Duchesnau, but who had long been closely connected with the fur trade. He was in charge of the *ferme* and was concerned to make the most of the chance to foster the maritime side of the Canadian economy. Riverin's views do not emerge with great clarity, for while he organized a substantial fishing industry in the Gulf of the St Lawrence he was at the same time concerned to make the most of the bargain between Oudiette as *fermier* of the revenues of Canada and the *Compagnie du Nord* and also to establish a forceful policy for the trade to the south and west.[61] He seems to have been moved, like many Canadians, by three deep convictions—that it was impossible to get too many prime furs; that a glut could be brought about only because the presence of the English made the fur trade competitive, so that the Indians got control and must be offered a price for any furs they brought to market; and that anything which led to a maritime outlook should be supported. At all events, the substantial influence of Riverin lay behind Iberville when he returned to Canada in 1690, with three ships under command to capture the outstanding English post, York Fort, Nelson River.[62]

Iberville arrived at the English post late in August 1690, only to find that the Hudson's Bay Company, encouraged by the passage of its Bill through Parliament, had also sent three ships to the Nelson River. They had already arrived, and the *Hudson's Bay* drove Iberville out of the river. He destroyed the small outpost at the Severn River and with this much success to show made his way back to Quebec, to take his share in the raids into the English colonies which were marking the resumption of control by Frontenac. That policy caused delays in 1691, although a royal ship was again lent in that year for the extirpation of the English post. Again a ship was lent in 1692, but was too late in arriving; and again in 1693 Iberville was lent a fast and powerful frigate. She also arrived late in Quebec and was diverted to other operations.[63]

Frontenac had no love for Iberville; he was anxious to avoid commitments in the north and to increase the raids into New England. The utmost which he permitted was that a supply ship should be sent in 1693 to reinforce the French post at Albany.[64] The ship arrived to find the French post in English hands. The Hudson's Bay Company had profited by the French delays, sending four ships in 1692 to recapture the Bottom of the Bay. They were able to cruise freely in the Bay, to reinforce York Fort, to send the furs from that post back to England, and then to settle down at Gilpin's Island for the winter, ready to attack in the spring. But when spring came there was little left to attack. Without reinforcements or supplies, the French had taken to the woods in efforts to make their way overland back to Canada. Only eight men had been left in the post, and of these two were murdered when the armourer ran amuck. The remaining five fled on the appearance of the English. The Hudson's Bay men took Fort Ste Anne without opposition. So, although Iberville had secured steady support in France, by 1693 the position established by de Troyes had been reversed. The English were in control of the whole of the Bay.[65]

This was enough to divert Frontenac to other problems. Iberville, however, remained determined to drive the English out, especially from York Fort. In Paris he secured the loan of two good ships, he was granted the trade of Nelson River up to 1697 if the booty secured should prove to be of less value than twice the cost of the expedition, and he recruited his crews and a military force on a profit-sharing basis.[66] Once more, in 1694 he could not get his expedition to sea on schedule, and at Quebec he decided to winter in the Rupert River and to attack York Fort in the spring of 1695. He was in some difficulties with Oudiette and with the *Compagnie du Nord* over payment of dues, but he had recruited over a hundred Canadians and, with these to feed, he again changed plans and arrived off York Fort in late September 1694. The English post was well sited, well provisioned, and well manned. But when Iberville had got his guns ashore and started an intermittent bombardment, the English dared not go into the woods to get firewood, and they soon surrendered.[67]

Thus in 1694 the position was again reversed. The English held the Bottom of the Bay but had lost York Fort (Fort Bourbon) to the French. In 1695 Iberville left seventy men under the Sieur de la Forest there and sailed with his furs for Quebec. But en route he changed course and went straight for La Rochelle. His prisoners found their way to England and gave the Hudson's Bay Company their first authentic account of the reverses which Iberville had inflicted. They had their trade from the Bottom of the Bay to comfort them, but this proved too much for the English market to absorb. Finance was therefore difficult. But the incentives were attractive, and English politics were at that time open to complaints from the great companies on whom overseas trade in large part depended and who were suffering heavily from the commerce-raiding of the *guerre de course*. The East India Company, the Africa Company, the Turkey Company, the Barbados Company, and the Company of the Isles of Antilles, all sought naval protection, and the Hudson's Bay Company, as part of the general move to protect the overseas trade of the empire, was able to get the loan of two naval vessels, the *Bonaventure* and the *Seaford*, for the recapture of York Fort. Two company ships were also sent early in June 1696, and a separate ship was sent to restock the now flourishing post at Albany. The English expedition arrived at York only two hours ahead of two French ships, under command of Iberville's brother, de Serigny. He promptly put about and made his way back to France, and the French garrison, after three days' seige, surrendered on terms.[68]

These terms were granted by the captain of the naval vessel, the *Bonaventure*; and whereas the Company had maintained that the lands of the Bay were a national concern, not merely an affair of merchants, it now denied the right of the naval captain to grant terms, insisting that this should have been the prerogative of the Company's representative. The dispute took on colour because the French furs were impounded, and the Company's whole status became involved in the argument over the captured furs. But though the Company's governor, Marlborough, was out of favour, its Parliamentary grant of privileges was due to come up for renewal, and its export market to Europe was disturbed and unreliable in war conditions, the Secretary of the Council of Trade before whom the case for possession of the furs was about to be tried was the Sir William Trumbull who had already done the Company service when he was ambassador at Versailles. Without payment, Trumbull accepted the necessary amount of the Company's stock and in November 1696 was elected Governor of the Company ! This election was perhaps within the prevailing conventions of political behaviour, but it promised more than mere support in the case for possession of the furs taken at York Fort. The war was drawing to its close, and as Secretary of State for the Northern Department, Trumbull was responsible for the negotiations which would define the terms of peace.[69] The Company was securing its seat at the conference table, where ownership of the Bay would be settled.

But William III was to a large extent his own Foreign Minister and, since this was understood to be William's wish, the draft of the terms suggested in July 1696 merely said that "captured colonies in America and the West Indies are to revert to their rightful owners."[70] This seems to have been taken as meaning that the situation should be restored as it had stood in 1688, which for the English meant reversion to the Treaty of Neutrality of 1686, with acceptance of a *status quo* by which the French retained the posts which de Troyes had then just captured at the Bottom of the Bay, and with a commission of enquiry to settle the legal points involved. The Hudson's Bay men easily came to the conclusion that such a treaty would settle nothing—at least, nothing in their favour; their best chance would be to place themselves in a strong position in the hope that, like the previous Treaty of Neutrality, the coming treaty would stabilize the *status quo*. The French adopted a similar attitude. Alongside the "chicaning" of the diplomats, the rival national companies were thus both fitting out expeditions to the Bay in 1696, and both governments were ready to lend officers, men, and ships to help stake a national claim to what was accepted as the gateway to the Northwest.

Exploration was not the only consideration for either side. Whatever the range of argument might be, the fur trade was the motivating force. During the treaty negotiations the French attitude was stiffened by a strong memorandum from Frontenac.[71] His vision was still of the western trade, his focus rested on Michilimackinác. The Straits of Mackinac, between Lake Huron and Lake Michigan, were the centre of the disputes between the Iroquois and the Ottawas and the Hurons; and French prestige at this vital rendezvous had suffered when, in 1686, English traders from Albany (Hudson River) had penetrated there and had offered a range and quality of goods which spoiled the market for the French. During Denonville's and Frontenac's periods of government the French had met increasing difficulty in maintaining the loyalty of their Indian allies, who shrewdly estimated the values and variety of goods to the disadvantage of the French as the war disrupted shipments from Europe. By 1696 Frontenac was convinced that if Indians once enjoyed trade with the English they would never more be content with the French, and as the Iroquois continued to ravage his settlements, all arguments led to a determination to carry the war to the enemy. During the summer of 1696, therefore, a powerful force of over two thousand men set out from Montreal to subdue the Iroquois. Frontenac was over seventy years old, and he had to be carried. The Iroquois retreated into the woods and were never brought to battle. But their villages were destroyed, their confidence was undermined, and their power broken. The Ottawas and the Hurons were saved for the French alliance; they controlled the Straits of Mackinac.

Frontenac's campaign of 1696 brought security to the *habitants* in Canada, while it secured access to the Indians of the west and south and to the routes which led outwards from Michilimackinac. It might be taken as a vindication of Frontenac's policy of maintaining the fur trade as the basis of the Canadian economy, of buttressing that trade against Iroquois attacks, and of focussing it on Michilimackinac and the territories to be reached through that outpost. But no simplification could make the fur trade into a straightforward business. While Canada could not pay her way except by means of the fur trade, every move to protect that trade added to the difficulties. For by 1696 the *fermiers* had on their hands a putrefying mass of unsaleable skins. The western posts and the ventures into Hudson Bay had both contributed to the French surplus; and of the two it appeared in 1696 that the western posts could more easily be controlled. But the furs from the Bay were universally accepted as better in quality than those of the south, they would always command such a market as there was, and without a proportion of coat beaver from the north the Canadian furs would not sell.

Therefore, as a background to the diplomatic negotiations, and despite Frontenac, in 1696 the French minister Pontchartrain ordered that all the western posts except St Louis must be abandoned.[72] Even at St Louis no furs would be traded. It would be maintained simply as a military outpost. All sections of Canadian society broke out in protest against this order, and it was quickly modified so that four posts were left in being—Michilimackinac, St Joseph des Miamis, St Louis des Illinois, and Fort Frontenac. Trading of furs was forbidden at these posts, but there was no means of enforcing the ban; the western and southern trade continued with the added danger that since it was now illicit it tended all the more to run into abuses, and the posts of the west continued to add their quota to the glut from which the fur trade and the economy of Canada were suffering.

As the peace negotiations ran on, this was not yet clear. It seemed that the Iroquois had been dominated, the posts of the west were under control, and the western trade reduced to manageable size. The Canadian fur trade seemed to depend on a proportion of prime coat beaver from the Bay. The French diplomats therefore stood out for their claims in the Bay, and by August 1697 the "Hudson's Bay business" seemed to be the only obstacle to a peace between the two exhausted nations.[73] Well aware that their interests were regarded as of only secondary importance as against the need for a sound peace in Europe, the Hudson's Bay committee sent their own men to the peace conference. They arrived to find that "all places should be put into the same state as before the Breaking out of this Warr." Captured possessions were to be restored by both sides, and commissioners were to settle boundaries between Rupert's Land and Canada. But "the Possession of those Places which were taken by the French during the Peace which preceded this present War, and were retaken by the English during this War shall be left to the French."[74] This would have restored to the French the posts at the Bottom of the Bay which de Troyes had taken during a time of peace and which the English had retaken during the war. This was hard to stomach; but it was accepted that the surrender of York Fort (Fort Bourbon) to the 1696 expedition was valid if the terms of surrender (about which there was considerable discussion arising out of the ownership of the furs then captured) should be observed.

For the Hudson's Bay Company it was a most disappointing peace which was concluded at Ryswick—based neither on historical rights nor on actual possession at the moment. The French had scored a great victory at the conference table, the whole business was based on "an Egregious misinformation," and the Company were "the only sufferers by the peace."[75] They had indeed seen ownership of the Bay, which had been made something of a national interest, subordinated to the situation in Europe. The need for a peace was such that conditions in the Bay could not be allowed to hold up a settlement.

But although the diplomats at Ryswick thought that they had confirmed France in possession of the Bottom of the Bay, and the English in possession of York Fort, exactly the opposite was achieved. At Albany the English remained in firm possession; and the French had taken York Fort while the peace negotiations were in progress. Iberville had been cruising off the coast of Acadia when news came through that the English 1696 expedition had captured his post in the Bourbon River. The French government decided to retake the post, and to use Iberville and five ships for the purpose. In late July 1697, as he made his way through Hudson Strait, he lost one of his ships on ice, and he then lost company with his other ships in a fog. As the fog lifted, one of Iberville's ships, the *Profonde*, found herself sailing in company with an English man-of-war, the *Hampshire*, which the Royal Navy had lent to convoy the Company's ships in that year. The *Profonde* was heavily punished and made off into the ice, apparently sinking. Iberville himself, in the *Pélican*, got clear of the ice and made straight for the Hayes River, arriving ahead of the English, but without any of his consorts. When the English arrived, therefore, the *Pélican* with 44 guns and a sick crew was faced by the *Hampshire* of 52 guns, the *Hudson's Bay* of 32 guns and the *Dering* of 30. The last two were the Company's own ships. The confined anchorage of the Hayes River gave Iberville some advantage, and he fought his ship with consummate skill and daring. The action lasted over two hours, and ended in one of the most dramatic moments in the annals of naval history. The *Pélican* and the *Hampshire* were passing each other on parallel courses, on opposite tacks, and each captain pledged the other in a glass of wine as the ships crossed. Then the *Pélican* fired her broadside at the *Hampshire* and, according to Iberville "sank her immediately, the vessel not passing onward three lengths." There can be no doubt at all that the *Hampshire* was sunk, nor that her captain was killed. But it is unlikely that the *Pélican*'s broadside was heavy enough to sink her, even more unlikely that she could have done it in so sudden and dramatic a manner. The reasonable probability is that the *Hampshire* struck a shoal in the river and ripped her bottom out; that, at least, is what one eyewitness reported as having happened. Whatever the cause of the disaster, the French fought their ship valiantly and skilfully, and the loss of the *Hampshire* demoralized the other English ships. The *Dering* made off out of the river while the *Hudson's Bay* surrendered, leaving Iberville in possession, to await the arrival of his other ships and to reduce the English post at his leisure.[76]

This took him only about a week, and although his triumph was marred when the captured *Hudson's Bay* foundered at her anchorage, Iberville was able to take about £20,000 worth of furs which had been got ready for shipment to London, to leave his brother de Serigny in command of a French post, and to get out of the Bay before ice closed the Strait.

The official terms of the Treaty of Ryswick were signed on September 20, 1697, and Iberville received the surrender of York Fort on September 13. The action therefore took place just within the period of warfare, and the outcome was that, when the terms of the treaty became effective, the Nelson and Hayes rivers were in French possession. The situation which the treaty-makers had assumed had been completely upset.

It was not to be expected that such a change could be absorbed as the terms of the Treaty came into their final form. The Treaty was accepted as it stood. At least it brought a badly-needed period of peace. But for the next sixteen years, until another European war brought another confrontation between England and France and another and more definitive peace, the post in the Nelson River remained in French hands; and the English retained the posts at the Bottom of the Bay although they were explicitly realloted to the French by the terms of the Treaty.

The Beaver, Prime Animal of the Fur Trade, by Mary Baker
in Paul Chrisler Phillips's Fur Trade, Volume I.

A North-west View of Prince of Wales's Fort in Hudson's
Bay, North America, by Samuel Hearne, 1777.

The Wintering Creek in Hayes River, from Henry Ellis's A Voyage to Hudson's Bay, London, 1748.

The Bombardment of York Factory (Fort Nelson) by d'Iberville, 1697, from Bacqueville de la Potherie, Histoire de l'Amerique Septentrionale, Paris, 1753, Volume I.

A Débarquemt des Munitions de guerre et de Bouche. B ciimp de Bourbon. C Mortié caché dans le Bois D Esquimaulees E Fort de Nelson.

York Factory, 1853.

Pierre Lemoine d'Iberville, from a painting by Oliver Flornoy.

Lord Selkirk, from the painting ascribed to Raeburn in Arthur
G. Doughty and Adam Shortt, Canada and Its Provinces, Volume
XIX, Prairie Provinces, Toronto, 1914.

William McGillivray, from an oil painting by Sir
Martin Archer Shee.

CHAPTER 4

The Saskatchewan
and the Prairies

As yet, by the end of King William's War, no one had any clear notion of the lands at the back of the Nelson and Hayes rivers, still less of the lands at the back of the Churchill River. The overland connection between Moose and Albany and the settlements on the St Lawrence was well known to the French and reasonably understood by the English. La Barre had written about the "obnoxious little posts" which the English established inland, but in fact they had no posts out of touch with tidal waters; their policy was to draw the Indians down to trade at the shore.[1] Yet the English maintained their right to send men inland and to establish posts inland if they so wished, and from time to time the governors were instructed to send men up-country.[2] Such instructions were unrealistic in view of the numbers of men available and in view of their lack of skill and experience. It may well be that the real purpose of the instructions was simply to accumulate quotable evidence, for use when the need should arise.

Not only were the Hudson's Bay Company's men inexperienced in the techniques of inland travel; they lacked equipment also. The canoes which the Indians used to come down to the posts by the Bay were small canoes which seated only two people as a rule. There was no room in such a canoe for an English passenger when the Indians returned after their trade. Nor could the English travel in their own canoes in company with Indians. They lacked the skill to manage canoes, especially in the difficult northern rivers; and neither the birch nor the cedar which were essential for canoe-building grew far enough north to be available. Hostility from the French, reluctance of the Indians to bring Europeans into their own trade areas in the interior, and the puritanical attitude of directors who frowned on any cohabitation with Indian women, were other factors which prevented the English from travelling with Indians to get to their hunting grounds.[3] For on the trail a squaw was not a luxury but a necessity; she took an essential share of the duties of travel, both in the canoe and at the portages.

Notwithstanding these handicaps, it was the English, not the French, who made history by penetrating to the prairies during the period between the Treaty of Ryswick and the Treaty of Utrecht. The French had many advantages, but from Colbert's time onwards the dangers of a dispersed colony were realized, and official policy tended to restrain the explorer and the *coureur*. The initiative was left to ambitious traders such as Duluth, La Salle, Henri Tonti, and La Chesnaye; and their interests were either focussed on the overland route to Hudson Bay or else on the trade to the southwest, taking in Michigan, Detroit, and the Mississippi. Even Duluth, with a permit from La Barre to trade over the height of land from Lake Superior to Lake Nipigon, granted on the ground that he would oppose the Hudson's Bay Company, was diverted to the Mississippi.[4] Though the Jesuits had been able to delineate the north shore of Lake Superior as early as 1670-71, the French were if anything more inaccurate in their geographical notions than the English.[5] At about 1686-88 they assumed that there was a direct river connection between Lake Nipigon and the mouth of the Nelson River, and although by the time of the Treaty of Ryswick the French had a reasonably accurate knowledge of the courses of the Nelson and the Hayes rivers, and of their route from the Bay to within striking distance of Lake Winnipeg, French interest in this hinterland did not awaken as long as they had Fort Bourbon (York Fort) in their possession. Until the Treaty of Utrecht forced them to acknowledge English ownership of that post, they hoped to get coat beaver by the maritime approach, and until 1713 they neglected overland travel and contented themselves with the meagre and spasmodic trade which their post by the Bay afforded.

The English, contrary to expectation, had by the time of Utrecht acquired a clear first-hand account of the route from the mouth of the Nelson River to Lake Winnipeg and from Lake Winnipeg westwards by the Saskatchewan River. For this they were indebted to the first great English inland traveller, Henry Kelsey.

The "Boy Kelsey" marks a great innovation in that he had been recruited as an apprentice to the Hudson's Bay Company in 1684.[6] The English would train their own men and would produce the skills required in the Bay; and in 1687, at the age of seventeen, Kelsey distinguished himself by making a winter journey from York Fort to the Severn River. Since there were few men who could even attempt such a jouney, it was natural that in 1688 he should have been named as a member of the small party which was sent to set up a further post in the Churchill River.[7] That post was meant mainly to develop a trade in oil from the white whale, but it was accidentally burned down in 1690 and was then abandoned. At this time the English,

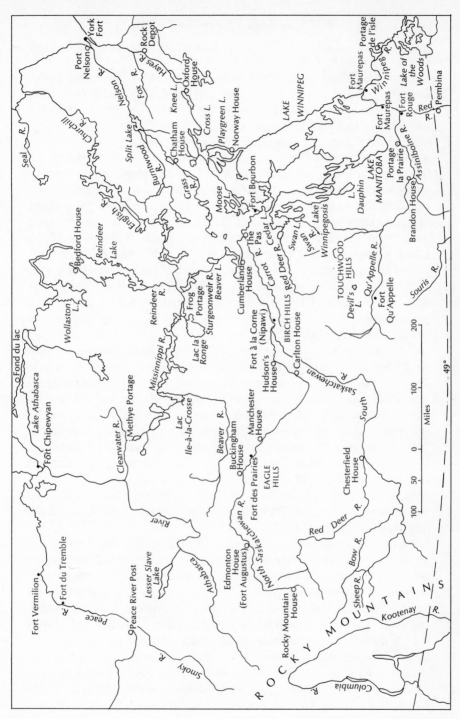

Northwest to the Rockies

with only York Fort in their possession, were anxious to explore to the west and the north rather than to follow the Nelson River to the south, and after the failure of their first post at Churchill the Governor, George Geyer, was told to explore up the west coast of the Bay, northwards from Churchill, to open up a great river formerly known as the Buffalo River but now renamed the Dering River after Sir Edward Dering, Deputy Governor of the Company.[8] The Dering River might perhaps lead to a Northwest Passage; it would more probably lead to "Considerable Traffick . . . from the Northerne Indians."[9] Kelsey had already played his part in the search for the Dering River and for the northern Indians. Although he was young he had become known as "a very active Lad Delighting in Indians Company being never better pleased than when hee is Travelling amongst them."[10] In 1688 he had been put ashore about sixty miles north of the mouth of the Churchill River and travelled north with an Indian companion along the shore for a fortnight in search of the northern Indians, to bring them in to trade at the new post. The Buffalo River was also in part their objective, and his Indian companion maintained that if they had been put ashore at the Buffalo River they would have found the northern Indians —who were in fact Eskimos.[11]

Kelsey's companion proved a weak and timid traveller, afraid the Eskimos would hear them talking and not anxious to penetrate into their country. They covered about one hundred and fifty miles before they began to retrace their steps, but they did not get to the Buffalo River, nor did they see any "northern Indians." Kelsey did, however, see some "Buffilo," and he shot two of them.[12] He was the first white man to see this animal and to leave a description; he found it an "ill-shapen beast" but did not record his opinion of its meat. On his return to Churchill he took five companions (one of them a Canadian, "Ely Gramer" or Elias Grimard) by boat back to his point of departure to rescue some stores which he had left there when he had been first put ashore. On his second return to Churchill he found the little post destroyed by fire.

At this stage Kelsey "had a mind to go for England," but he was still at York Fort in 1690, when the rivers coming down from the south took priority over the coast running north. Governor Geyer then arranged to send an envoy, travelling with the "captain" of the Assinipoets, as the Indians returned from trade at York. These Assinipoets were the Assiniboines, of whom one branch inhabited the plains to the south and west of Lake Winnipeg, another branch the area north and west, round Cedar Lake (Lake Bourbon), making contact with the Crees around the lower Saskatchewan.[13] Kelsey went inland with the leader of the latter branch in 1690. In this he was given precedence over the four Canadian servants of the Company, including young Groseilliers, who had come over to the English when their post in the Nelson River had been taken by Radisson in 1684. They were not trusted and though sent on expeditions from the posts they never went far; in 1690 an expedition under Grimard and young Groseilliers did not get above two hundred miles from York.[14]

Kelsey's journey was meant "to discover and bring to a Commerce the Naywatame poets," the Gros Ventres of the main Saskatchewan and the South Saskatchewan territories. His account of his journey is not easy to follow on a map, but he certainly proceeded to a point about six hundred miles inland from York Fort, past five lakes and thirty-three portages, probably to The Pas on the Saskatchewan. There he was on the borders of the Assiniboine territory, and he took possession in the name of his masters, calling the point on the river Dering's Point. The Indians were at war, and though he managed to bring them to a peace, as soon as his back was turned the "Home Indians" turned on the Gros Ventres and avenged their old grudges on them. The "Home Indians" were the Crees who already frequented the posts by the Bay, who enjoyed the advantages of European arms while the Gros Ventres used only bows and arrows, and who acted the part of middlemen for the trade of the Gros Ventres.

In September 1690 Kelsey turned south and west from Dering's Point, to spend the winter on the plains. He returned to Dering's Point in the spring of 1691, sending an account of his journey and of conditions inland to Governor Geyer by means of Indians who were going to trade at York Fort. Geyer in his turn used the Indians as they went back inland to send a small consignment of luxuries for Kelsey, and in July 1691 Kelsey set off up the Saskatchewan, following the Gros Ventres to their own lands. They had brought their trade down to Dering's Point, but owing to shortage of food had been unable to delay their return until Kelsey could accompany them.[15]

From Kelsey's narrative it is not possible to tell exactly where he went, nor even how he travelled. Probably he was travelling with a band of Assiniboines and sharing a canoe with some of them. Avoiding the main current of the Saskatchewan by using side streams and portages, he came to a point just downstream from what was later to be the site of Cumberland House, where he cached some powder and tobacco, some knives, fishing nets, and other small articles, before setting off on foot across "heavy mossy going" into the valley of the Carrot River, to reach the lands to the south of the Saskatchewan. There, resting and hunting moose[16] for food, he met a deputation of strange Indians, anxious to get him to go back to the area of the Red Deer River and the upper Assiniboine, where he had spent some part of the previous winter. The Assiniboines of the Woods, of that territory, were greatly afraid of the Crees, and Kelsey was warmly welcomed on his return. Again he met Indians coming from further south, also anxious that he should visit them. Their news was that the Gros Ventres had killed some Cree women and had then fled. So Kelsey continued southwards, through grassland with clumps of birch and poplar, until he came to the prairies proper—a plain covered with "short Round sticky grass." Buffalo were numerous and the Indians killed them easily, surrounding them as they grazed.[17]

As Kelsey travelled across the prairies he was continually trying to establish contact with the Assiniboines of the Hills, the Mountain Poets; and the Indians with whom he was travelling were constantly trying to get him to go to war with them against the Crees. But his mission was to secure peace, and concentration on the hunting of beaver, and he refused to supply them with guns for warfare. He continued southwards and after three weeks at last met the "Mountain Poets"; and them also he had to persuade not to go on the warpath.

Accurate information about the inland territories was, of course, what Kelsey had gone to seek. But the Hudson's Bay men knew in general terms that their "Home Indians," the Crees who brought in most of the furs which were traded at the Bay, kept other Indians away from the posts partly because of tribal animosities, partly because they were shrewd enough to want to keep other Indians away from the contact of European buyers. It was Kelsey's mission to preach peace, and when, for example, he found that the Gros Ventres were under threat from the Assiniboines, he told the latter "that they must Imploy their time in Catching of beavour for that will be better liked on then killing their Enemies when they come to the Factory. Neither was I sent there for to kill any Indians but to make peace with as many as I could." In the face of this, the Assiniboines wanted to know why Kelsey should be so concerned with the Gros Ventres since they did not know the use of canoes and could not, in any case, come to trade at the Bay. Nevertheless, the Gros Ventres were promised that the English would protect them from their enemies, and their chief promised Kelsey that in the spring he would meet him at Dering's Point and would then come down to the Bay with him.

When the report of his journey had been taken to London, the Committee there accepted the conclusion that Kelsey had done much to improve the output of furs "in keeping the Indians from warring one with another, that they may have the more time to look after their trade and bring larger quantities of Furrs and other Trade with them to the factory."[18] They accepted also that, although he had not secured an ideal solution in preventing the Indians from going to war, at least he had achieved something in making it clear that if the inland tribes would make direct contact with the Company's posts they could counteract the possession of European arms by the "Home Indians." For at his arrival he noted that the Gros

Ventres knew "No use of Better than their wooden Bows," but when his persuasions proved useless and warfare broke out again, he reported that they were beginning to face their enemies "And with our English guns do make them flie."

Having met his "Mountain Poets," Kelsey travelled southwards with them "into the woods it being all peplar and birch and high Champion land." He was probably approaching the Touchwood Hills, and from this point he began to move northwards in the general direction of Lake Nipawi, hoping to meet the Gros Ventres again. He came up with them after about one hundred and thirty miles of travel, in early September 1691; and again he had hard work to prevent the Assiniboines from attacking them. The Gros Ventres he found friendly but poverty-stricken, and he does not seem to have stayed long with them although his movements during the following winter are quite unaccounted for. He probably wandered in company with the Assiniboines over the prairies, hunting buffalo and perhaps furs, and returned to Dering's Point in the spring of 1692. Then, despite the fact that the Crees had once more attacked the Gros Ventres, he made his way back to York Fort, bringing with him "a good fleet of Indians."

Obscure as Kelsey's narrative may be, the Hudson's Bay Company now had in its service a man who had first-hand and accurate knowledge of the prairies, of the way to get there from York Fort, and of the lives and needs of the Indians who lived there and who enjoyed a choice between trading to the French of Canada or to the English of Hudson Bay. He was welcomed in London, was rewarded and retained in the service, and was sent back to the Bay. But though there can be no reasonable doubt that the English company had promoted Kelsey's journey and had received his report, they showed so little response to the information which he brought that for years it was plausibly maintained that the whole episode was no more than an escapade by a truant boy who had run away to live with Indians so as to escape the hardships at York Fort and who had uncovered nothing of any importance.[19] This version of Kelsey's journey gained currency because the Company so far suppressed their information that within a few years they even seem to have forgotten it themselves. Kelsey's narrative was not in the end discovered in the archives of the Company but among the private papers of an eighteenth-century critic of the Company, who used the Kelsey episode as the basis for an attack on it, on the assumption that Kelsey had made his journey as a private venture, in revolt against the Company's official policy. There can, however, be no reasonable doubt that the journey was organized and approved by the Company.[20]

Since it was defending its privileges, the Company can hardly be blamed for not divulging the account of Kelsey's journey. Its failure to follow up the journey on its own account is equally understandable, for the difficulties in the way of sending trading expeditions inland remained unsolved. There were no canoes and few canoemen, and it remained the English policy to entice Indians to trade at the Bay rather than to send traders inland with European goods. The centralized and closely controlled habits of the English trade also emphasized the attractions of such a policy, for the inland trader naturally worked far more independently than the man in the fort by the shore. The policy of drawing down the Indians to trade was adopted for sound enough reasons, and it was not departed from for the best part of a century after Kelsey had "discovered the prairies."

The English henceforth knew that there were vast areas at the back of their territory, suitable for fur hunting. They had some detailed knowledge, too, of the way in which the rivers ran up to the back of the French trade area. But apart from this basic understanding, Kelsey's contribution was put into cold storage. This was the more acceptable because during the period immediately following this episode the English company, like the French, was trading in a glutted market and was seeking alternatives to beaver. The English sought their remedy in a trade in virgin copper, of which Indian rumour gave hopes. Somewhere on the northwest coast of the Bay lay a copper mine which would bring great wealth. English attention was therefore diverted away from the prairies and was focussed on the Churchill River. This would be an outpost in the direction of the rumoured copper mine and would help in maritime exploration which might result both in the discovery of the mine and in the opening up of a sea passage to the west.

Kelsey's Journal makes no mention of French traders or of Indians trading from the prairies towards the French settlements, although his journey followed close after the French trader de Noyon had travelled up to Rainy Lake, had stayed the winter there and had established a trade with the Assiniboines in 1688.[21] Kelsey may well have heard nothing of de Noyon's visit, for French contacts with this region had almost been forgotten by 1695, when Tonti again travelled among the Assiniboines. Although the French certainly knew the route to Rainy Lake and although occasional French traders reached the Assiniboines, these Indians seem to have forgotten the approach from Canada, and their trade went almost exclusively to Hudson Bay. For this Kelsey himself was to some extent responsible; the superiority of English ironware and woollens helped, and the English showed their control of the hinterland. Whereas in 1688 the Governor of York Fort was told to lure into his post the "straggling French" who picked up beaver from Indians, in 1690 he was told that any Frenchman found "trading or stragling within the Limitts of our Territories" was to be arrested and sent to England.[22]

The way in which the trade of the Lake Winnipeg-Saskatchewan-prairies area ran toward the Bay was also helped by French efforts to restrain their *coureurs*. But it must be accepted that a fugitive French trade undoubtedly continued, and Frenchmen were steadily improving their knowledge and making themselves familiar with the route to the prairies. By 1715 it was reckoned that about a hundred had evaded the controls, had gone beyond Michilimackinac, and were out towards the Mississippi.[23] By the time that the Treaty of Utrecht enforced the restoration of York Fort to the English, the French were able to set out the main outlines of the river system of Lake Winnipeg and of the north. The surrender of their post on the Bay stimulated fresh activity, and in 1716 the Assiniboines who came to York reported that they were able to take their trade to Lake Winnipeg, where there were several settlements of *coureurs*.[24]

This indicated a revindication of the traditional Canadian outlook, of the notion of Canada as the Kingdom of the Great River which would lead past the barriers and into the northern and western country beyond. It was also a sign that a post by the Bay had not solved the troubles of the Canadian economy or of the French fur trade. If anything, it had complicated the situation although the *Compagnie du Nord* had made an arrangement with the financier Oudiette by which his monopoly of the trade of Canada had been merged with the *Compagnie's* monopoly of the trade from Hudson Bay—an arrangement which still stood when Oudiette handed over his position as *fermier-général* in 1687.[25] Iberville in 1694 made his arrangements for the capture of York Fort and the subsequent exploitation of the fur trade direct with the French government.[26] Already the current *fermier*, Louis Guiges, was unable to dispose of the furs on hand and the whole problem was the subject of fierce bargaining in which the proposal to set up a *Nouvelle Compagnie* of *habitants* was again under review.[27] In the end Guiges, despite his protestations, secured control of the trade for a further twelve years, in 1697, and then sold out his concession in 1699.[28]

This was just the time at which the furs got from Fort Bourbon (Nelson River) began to affect the French market. Neither the *fermier* nor the *Compagnie du Nord* had been willing to accept responsibility for putting these furs on the market, and Iberville had himself undertaken this commitment.[29] The overall glut of beaver caused the *fermier* such difficulty that in 1700 he was content to sell out the remaining ten years of his monopoly to a *Compagnie de Canada* which was in fact composed of *habitants*, on condition that they took off his hands the vast accumulation of furs and made themselves responsible for payment of the *Quart* on which the revenues of Canada depended.[30] The *Compagnie de Canada* still had the fine furs from the Bay to rival its own product, and it gladly took over the responsibility for Fort Bourbon when Iberville's grant ran out in 1700.[31]

Apart from the impossibility of securing shipping to exploit the sea-borne access to the furs of the Northwest, the *Compagnie de Canada* found the costs of the Bay trade insupportable. By 1705-6 the *Compagnie* had mortgaged its credit to secure supplies from France on Letters of Credit for which the backing was the huge collection of furs which year by year was deteriorating in value as it rotted in store.[32] The actual trade from Fort Bourbon declined after the first burst, as war conditions and lack of ship-ping added to the difficulties of the French fur trade. From 1708 onwards Fort Bourbon was indeed under the command of an able trader, Nicholas Jérémie; but he was unable to reach his post in that year, and after his arrival no further French ship was able to make the voyage until the war was over. Nevertheless, the first shipment of furs had its effect, and by the time the terms for the Treaty of Utrecht were under discussion it appeared that the only result of Iberville's capture of York Fort had been to emphasize the failure of the Canadian fur trade and to bring the whole Canadian economy and administration into hazard.

Most of these difficulties were inescapable. The French could not neglect their southern interests and concentrate exclusively on the north; they could not control the *coureurs*; and they could not secure shipping or goods during the war. The habits of their trade also differed from those of the English, in conformity with these conditioning factors. Short of guns and ironware, blankets and heavy woollens, the *coureurs* made harder bargains in such goods; for example, they were alleged to get five beaver for a trade gun while the English got only two.[33] The statement must be suspect since the English "Standard" as set by Radisson demanded twelve beaver for a "musket" and the "Double Standard" adopted by the English traders had to balance out advantages in one bargain against losses in another. The only thing which is certain, since this statement emanated from information supplied by Indians, is that the Indians were well aware of the value of having two buyers whom they could play off against each other. On the whole the French traded harder but accompanied their bargains by the giving of presents—often of a dram—and this pattern of trade fitted in well with the supply systems on which the two nations based their trade. At the time of Utrecht Governor de Vaudreuil reckoned that the only article which the Indians preferred to be of French manufacture was gun-powder. They greatly favoured the gaily-coloured English blankets, and so important an article of trade were these that the French even bought supplies in London as soon as the peace made this possible. A constant trade was run from the New England colonies to Canada in such goods, and acts to prevent such supplies from reaching French traders were passed at New York in 1720, 1722, and again in 1724, while the New York merchants maintained that the Indian trade could only be carried on by French traders using English strouds and other goods (largely woollens). They argued that as long as the French were able to supply the Indians it was useless for the English to try to get the furs; but much was gained when, at least, the English supplied the goods which went in exchange.[34]

During the war of the Spanish Succession, when the only post left in English hands had been at Albany, there had been endless rumours that the French would attack that post, and in 1709 they actually brought a force of about a hundred men overland from Canada to do so. The defences held, but the rumours continued; and as the war ended and the French set to work to reorganize their trade, the Bottom of the Bay was, if anything, more under threat than the Lake Winnipeg area and the trade from thence to York Fort.[35]

The Treaty of Utrecht formally and, as it proved, finally acknowledged the English right to the Bay, which had been "restored" to the English, not merely "ceded." So it had been acknowledged that the English claim ran back to right of prior discovery.[36] It remained, however, to draw the boundary between Rupert's Land and Canada. At the time of the Treaty a rough boundary was accepted, running along the line of the watershed; closer definition was to be achieved later, and the English claim for damages inflicted during times of peace was also to be discussed and agreed. But it soon became clear that neither of these points would be at all easy to settle. The English hoped to secure a boundary running from Cape Perdrix on the east coast of Labrador to Lake Mistassini and then westwards along the 49th parallel, but no progress towards an agreement had been achieved by 1719, and by that time a new vigour was beginning to be felt in the French trade.[37] While the merchants of Montreal were telling their governor that the fur trade would have to be abandoned if the English post at Albany could not be taken over, they had set up their own post at the headwaters of the Albany River—perhaps even two posts—where they were not more than a week's travel from the English post.[38] The English had to accept that "now is the time to oblige the Indians," and they managed to keep their end going to such an extent that in 1717 forty canoes of "French Indians," and in 1719 even the "captain of the French Indians," among others, came down, lured by the better supplies of English goods.[39]

This rivalry was played out on commercial terms, and it was the English ability to attract Indians to trade that counted. Their diplomatic pleas that the French should be kept south of the 49th parallel, and so ousted from their position at the head of the Albany River, achieved nothing. On the contrary, the French were revising their notions of "restoring" the Bayside to England, pointing out that since it was the English practice to stay by the shore the boundary should lie between Albany and the French post at Lake Nemiscau. It should then follow a similar line, midway between the French post at Abitibi and the English post at Moose, and to the west it should come to a point on the coast where Fort Bourbon would confront the English post of York Fort in the Nelson River.[40] This was a very different boundary from the line along the height of land which the English wanted; it was supported by arguments drawn from early contacts of Breton fishermen with Acadia and Canada. It was argued that the English had always been chiefly interested in a Northwest Passage and that until recently they had shown no interest either in settlement or in trade. For France, it was not necessary that settlements should have been established throughout the territory; to have conducted a trade, and to have made settlements in the most appropriate places, would be adequate.[41] By insisting on a "restoration" of territories which rightly belonged to them, the English appeared to have cut considerably into the territory which they might have claimed by right of conquest and cession. A boundary along the height of land, according to these arguments, would not be included within anything which could be called "restoration."

As this argument developed, the French diplomats spun out negotiations while French traders steadily encroached on the trade of the English posts at the Bottom of the Bay. By 1723 it was reported that "woodrunners" were within a few days of the English post and were not only spoiling the trade by paying high prices and making the Indians lazy and greedy, but also threatening them with rumours of large bands of hostile Indians who would come to destroy Albany and all who traded there. The Assiniboines were, as always, harassed by the Sioux as they came to trade; Frenchmen were reporting to be sharing in the raids, and when the Hudson's Bay men offered the Crees and Assiniboines guns, tobacco, and even brandy, to help them against the Sioux, the gifts were rejected with scorn. The only acceptable help would be that the English should either prevent the French from helping the Sioux or that they should assist their own allies in the same way.[42]

Despite its internal difficulties, therefore, the fur trade continued to be the main preoccupation of the Canadians and to show an ability to survive despite over-production and declining prices. Moreover, although Kelsey's journey might well have given the advantage to the English, and the English had a notion of the river and lake system at the back of their posts which was surprisingly accurate, they had not sent anyone inland for any distance except Kelsey; they had let their advantage slip from them. They were perhaps better informed of the approach to Lake Winnipeg from the north than the French. But certainly the French made better use of the route up to Rainy Lake than did the English. For the territory between the French posts and the Bottom of the Bay the French had a knowledge which the English could not challenge.

Kelsey himself, captured by Iberville at York Fort in 1697, had returned to England and had been sent out to Albany in 1698. He was then sent with a frigate to the Eastmain, in the hope that he might open up the mica deposits at Slude River. He expected to repeat this expedition in 1705, but the ship from England was so late in arriving that the expedition was cancelled, and Kelsey spent the winter "lying out" and living, Indian fashion, by hunting—as did a few other members of the Albany garrison who were anxious to escape from the regimentation of the post and who were skilled enough to live that way.[43] This was a significant example of the growing competence of the English servants, but it did not lead to penetration of the hinterland of Albany. Nor did the events of the next year, when Kelsey took a sloop from Albany to the Eastmain River; nor those of the last year of the war, when he again "lay abroad" with Indians rather than be cooped up in the post. He had added considerably to knowledge of the coastal areas, had taken part in many slooping voyages and, like many other Hudson's Bay men, had acquired the title of "captain" as a result of the constant use of ships to explore the Bay and its coasts. But even Henry Kelsey had not penetrated into the hinterland from the Bottom of the Bay.

CHAPTER 5

The *Postes du Nord*

French predominance in the years which followed the treaty of Utrecht was achieved despite the length and difficulty of the route which the French must use, and despite constant Indian warfare. The area south from Lake Winnipeg, round Rainy Lake and Lake of the Woods, was the only way by which they could approach the area of Lake Winnipeg and the lower Saskatchewan. It was a hotly contested borderland over which the Sioux, the Chippewas (the Ojibwas), the Crees, and the Assiniboines all had claims. Firearms became available from both English and French sources and although the French trader La Noue (like Kelsey) tried to get the Indians to cease fighting and to concentrate on hunting, he failed to prevent the Sioux from attacking the Crees at Kaministikwia and at Rainy Lake; in fact he lost the trust of his Indian allies when it seemed that he was merely leading them to slaughter by their implacable foes.[1] Situated in territory which was constantly fought over, Kaministikwia remained an outpost with a garrison of about forty men,[2] while Rainy Lake was used merely as a rendezvous for the hardy *coureurs* who continued to trade to that area despite La Noue's failure. Ability to live with Indians counted for much, and the *coureurs'* influence was felt in the Bayside posts. In 1728, for example, the Chief Factor at York Fort feared that all his Indians would resort to the French settlement which, he reported, "is not above four Days paddling from the Great Lake that feeds this River"—by which he probably meant a French post at Lake of the Woods, southeast from Lake Winnipeg.[3]

In 1728, and again in 1730, the Sioux fell upon the Assiniboines as they came north to trade; they certainly used French firearms, and French *coureurs* were reported to be with them on their raids. But although the western English posts were under constant threat, from 1713 up to 1731 their trade prospered. By contrast, at the Bottom of the Bay the threat was so strong that in 1730 the London Committee resolved that it was "of absolute Necessity . . . to Erect a Fort and Factory at Moose." This site had been abandoned since 1686; any trade done there would certainly be at the expense of Albany, but, said the Committee, "that matters not as long as the furs come home at the last." The post at Moose would be well sited to draw trade away from the French; and trade at the Bottom of the Bay was above all else competitive.[4]

As against the unremitting opposition of French *coureurs* at the Bottom of the Bay, the comparative immunity of the western posts continued until 1732, when the returns from York Fort diminished from 52,000 made-beaver to 37,000.[5] Behind the change lay the fact that Pierre Gaultier de Varennes, Sieur de la Vérendrye, had taken control of the *postes du nord*.

La Vérendrye had fought through the War of the Spanish Succession, and had dabbled in the fur trade at his estate on the St Maurice after his return to Canada. In 1727 he had secured the office of Commandant of the *postes du nord*; and Kaministikwia was the centre of his dominion, with Nipigon and Michipicoten as outposts northeast towards the Bottom of the Bay and with Rainy Lake and Lake of the Woods leading on towards York Fort and the Churchill River. He was never able to overlook the financial commitments of the fur trade, for he needed revenue. Exploration was, however, important to him and to those who supported his claims, and La Vérendrye's career was constantly interrupted by the opposing demands of exploration and of trade—the more so since the trade was expected to pay for voyages of discovery to which he was committed.

The French belief in a Sea of the West had been partly responsible for the expedition of La Noue to Rainy Lake, and for subsequent development at Rainy Lake. But the original belief, derived from Verezzano, strengthened by Cartier, Champlain, and their successors, that the Western Sea lay within a reasonable distance from the Atlantic coast, had yielded to the conviction that they would first reach an inland sea, not the ocean itself; and that a navigable waterway would lead from this Western Sea to the Pacific Ocean. By the time of the Treaty of Utrecht, even this modification had been revised, and the great school of French geographers led by Claude and William de l'Isle had followed La Salle and Tonti in emphasizing the importance of the Mississippi and of access to a Sea of the South rather than to a Sea of the West. The problem occupied statesmen and merchants alike.[6] The claims of the Missisippi were debated in the *Académie Française*, in the *Académie des Inscriptions*, in the *Académie des Sciences*; and the change in outlook ultimately drew Iberville away from Hudson Bay to Louisiana. But although Louisiana was established by a sea-borne expedition, the first approaches were from Montreal, and Michilimackinac was the focal point from which the French departed.

So when Father Pierre Charlevoix was sent out in 1720 to report on the best route to the Sea of the West, he made his way to Michilimackinac and there spoke to La Noue himself before making his way to Lake Michigan, to the Mississippi, and so down to the sea. His report stated that the Sea of the West lay west or southwest of Lake of the Woods, in about the fiftieth parallel. He urged further exploration to discover the sources of the Mississippi, for Indian report alleged that the source of the great river lay within easy paddling distance of the Sea of the West.[7] The "Sea" was, of course, Lake Winnipeg; and although Charlevoix emphasized the approach from this area to the Mississippi and the south, it was equally the starting point for access to the west and the north.

The first result of Charlevoix' mission was the establishment of Fort Beauharnois, a fur post and a mission post combined, among the Sioux. The post, at Lake Pepin on the Mississippi, was intended to pacify the Sioux and to stimulate further exploration, but it could only be approached through lands controlled by the Foxes, who opposed the French. The French were therefore forced to abandon the post, in 1730, until they had subdued the Foxes, which they did in the next year.

The setback at Fort Beauharnois turned some of the French effort away from the Mississippi, and when the post was re-established in 1731 it was to secure a passage through the lands of the Foxes to trade with the Crees and the Assiniboines. This was the "undertaking of the Sieur de la Vérendrye," specifically told that he would need to pass through the lands of the Crees and the Assiniboines to discover the Sea of the West.[8]

As La Vérendrye took command of the *postes du nord* in 1731, therefore, he found that there remained the traditional French outlook towards the Mississippi and the south, and that alongside this ran the equally traditional outlook towards Kaministikwia, but leading northwards either to Michipicoten and Moose or else towards Nipigon and Albany. A third way, from Kaministikwia westwards to Rainy Lake, Lake of the Woods, and Lake Winnipeg, was considerably less important and less developed. But it allowed the arguments derived from the fur trade and the arguments derived from the Sea of the West to be brought together in a way not possible in either of the other directions. For the approach to the Mississippi ran southwards and away from the territories which produced the coat beaver which was in demand, while the routes northwards from Lake Superior, though they ran to good beaver country, did nothing to help the search for the Sea of the West. La Vérendrye could not afford to lose sight of the realities of the fur trade; nor was he allowed to forget the search for the Western Sea. Efforts to balance these two interests brought him into trouble even before he entered upon his command. The Report on the state of Canada of 1730 alleged that he and his officers were intent only on the profits of the fur trade, which were considerable, while La Vérendrye himself maintained that since the Sioux barred advance from the Mississippi to the Sea of the West the object could best be achieved by penetrating from the north shore of Lake Superior to the area of Rainy Lake. He followed up this view by suggesting that the French would achieve their object by advancing westwards from Lake Winnipeg along the route of the Saskatchewan.

By 1728-29 La Vérendrye knew that Lake Winnipeg drained north into Hudson Bay, not westwards into some unknown sea. But he knew that the notion of a great river leading westwards from Lake Winnipeg was a necessary part of any scheme to push the French fur trade westwards from the Lake Superior basin. If a search for the Sea of the West could be included, he might hope for support even when he concluded his memorandum by urging that a post must be set up on Lake Winnipeg, so that the English might be forestalled and Canada might get a great increase in the fur trade. There was good reason to fear that any post set up with these ideas in mind would "degenerate into a mere business of fur trading" and would contribute little to exploration, especially since La Vérendrye's memorandum was accompanied by letters from the Governor and the Intendant in which they explained that any post on Lake Winnipeg would have the fur trade as its prime object and that exploration would come under consideration only when a trade to pay the costs of the posts had been developed.[9] As the correspondence continued it became clear that the Canadians, Governor, Intendant, and Commandant of the *postes du nord* alike, assumed that the costs of such a post would be paid from the profits of the trade, while further exploration ought to receive a separate subsidy from the French government. But the French government assumed that further exploration was the condition on which permission to establish a post was given and that voyages would be paid for from the profits of the trade, involving no further expenses for government.

Much of this passed over the head of La Vérendrye in 1731 as he made his way up to Michilimackinac and by the north shore of Lake Superior to the mouth of the Pigeon River. His party consisted of fifty men and one missionary, and from Michilimackinac he wrote to the Minister Maurepas to explain his purpose "to carry the name and arms of His Majesty into a vast stretch of countries hitherto unknown, to enlarge the colony and increase its commerce." He asked for a five years' grant of the *postes du nord*, to cover the expenses which he had incurred, saying that he would also use them as bases for further expansion. In this proposal La Vérendrye abandoned the notion of rapid but unorganized penetration which characterized the journeys of the *coureurs* and the missionaries.[10] He advocated instead a policy which would depend on a series of posts which would open up avenues of penetration and serve as bases for advance. Such ideas were certainly not new in the history of Canada; but they took on a new significance as Le Vérendrye used this system to give to the French an effective control of Lake Winnipeg, of the rivers which ran north from the lake to the Bay, and of the great river which fed the lake, the Saskatchewan, coming down from the west.

La Vérendrye's letter came from the midst of a voyage which, according to the custom of the French trade, had been outfitted on credit. Both the men who were with him and the outfitters who had supplied him were to be paid in full only at the end of the voyage, after the furs had been sold. The route to be followed was also known to the fur trade. From the north shore of Lake Superior, the breakout through the Shield was to be along the Pigeon River, and since the mouth of that river was dangerous, a bay to the south was used as a harbour; and a portage about nine miles long (Grand Portage) was to be used to get canoes and goods on to the Pigeon River higher up. But although the Grand Portage and the Pigeon River were known, there was little accurate information available. Indian report said that it was but ten days' paddling from Lake Winnipeg to the Sea of the West, and it was not realized that there was a distance of about five hundred miles between Lake Superior and Lake Winnipeg. La Vérendrye's men were soon disillusioned. It took them two months, from June 8 to August 26, to get from Montreal to Grand Portage. They then refused to face the Grand Portage and enforced a stop at the foot of the portage for the winter.

La Vérendrye had come up against one of the lasting difficulties in running a fur trade from Montreal. It was almost impossible to make the whole journey from Montreal through Lake Superior into the "Upper Country" with loaded canoes in the course of a normal summer. A staging post was needed, and La Vérendrye had chosen the most suitable place, at Kaministikwia, the nearest post to the point where the Grand Rapid led up from the basin of Lake Superior into the Shield, where five hundred miles of difficult country had to be crossed before Lake Winnipeg could be reached.[11] For these reasons Grand Portage remained a vital centre as long as the fur trade was conducted from Montreal. But La Vérendrye incurred censure for stopping there. Maurepas noted that it "would appear susceptible of the suspicion of self-interest; we know that beaver is plentiful in those quarters and the attractions of that peltry may well have been the principal reason for his wintering there."[12]

Certainly La Vérendrye could not afford to neglect trade; but while his main party remained at Grand Portage, in late August 1731 he sent one of his sons and his nephew, the Sieur de la Jemeraye, into the Shield to set up an advanced post at Rainy Lake. The outpost had to be strong enough for defence; and the fact that their routes ran through country in which every post had to be defensible added considerably to the costs of any French approach to the prairies. Skill and understanding partly offset such disadvantages. La Jemeraye, for example, built Fort St Pierre near the outfall of the Rainy River into Rainy Lake, where there was an abundant fishery (which brought considerable bands of Indians together) and a plentiful supply of wild rice. He had, however, to contend with the quarrels of the Indians, and the Crees and the Assiniboines rejected his invitations to trade. He prevailed on the Monsonis to give up the warpath and devote themselves to the hunt, but they were neither powerful nor numerous. His trade was therefore disappointing; but La Vérendrye sent it down to Montreal and brought up another year's supplies, determined to build a series of posts reaching into the Lake Winnipeg area. He planned a post at Lake of the Woods and another at Lake Winnipeg itself for 1732, and he set out from Kaministikwia to carry out these proposals in June of that year.[13]

Preparing for a continuous trade, he spent time and effort on improving the portages for future use. He assumed that his position in the trade would be secured to him; but a letter from Maurepas was already on its way, emphasizing that his first duty was to seek for the Sea of the West. The search for profits must not take precedence over exploration, though Maurepas was categorical in saying that the Crown could do no more than provide presents for the Indians among whom the explorers would have to travel.

La Vérendrye's actions in 1732 left some doubt whether he and the Minister were seeing eye to eye. He thought it unwise to take his main party further than Lake of the Woods. There he built a substantial post, Fort St Charles, and stayed for the winter. Fish and wild rice were plentiful; the soil was fertile; and Indian report was that living at Lake Winnipeg would be hard. Again, as he and his main party halted, he sent ahead a party under his nephew and one of his sons. They stopped short of Lake Winnipeg, but from the account of the winter's proceedings and from a map which he sent to Governor Beauharnois, it is clear that La Vérendrye now accepted that the Mississippi was the River of the West of the French tradition and that it flowed southwards and should be reached from the Assiniboine. He also accepted that Lake Winnipeg did not drain southwards or westwards but north towards Hudson Bay and that this gave access to the back country of the English posts. He was confident that the friendly relations which he had established with the Crees and the Monsonis would enable him to draw off the trade from the English.[14]

This was not new. The *coureurs* had for long worked on these lines, and they were ahead of La Vérendrye in 1732. At any time from 1727-28 onwards, the England trade at York Fort was under threat from the *coureurs*, and in 1732, when he had stopped at Lake of the Woods and his advance party had stopped short of Lake Winnipeg, the *coureurs* had brought about a notable decline in the trade of York Fort.[15] Three canoes of them were on Lake Winnipeg itself, working "to the most noted places where the Indians resorts" and threatening to make war on them if they traded to the English. La Vérendrye did not emulate the *coureurs* in such deliberate opposition; as Maurepas refused to advance funds for exploration but yet insisted that exploration must take place, in his search for trade and revenue he turned to the north. His efforts to bring the Crees and Monsonis to more industrious fur hunting were not entirely successful, but his dependence on them grew to such an extent that in 1734 he sanctioned their adoption of his eldest son, to go on the warpath with them against the Sioux. Thereby he bound his allies to the French trade; but he alienated the enemies of those allies and turned them into a permanent barrier to French advance.[16]

Secure in the alliance which he had thus concluded, La Vérendrye returned to Kaministikwia and so to Montreal,[17] leaving his second son to consolidate the friendship by setting up the small post of Fort Maurepas on the Maurepas River (which at that time was called the Red River). His posts now gave him some control of the fur trade as far north and west as Lake Winnipeg; but he had not personally gone further than Lake of the Woods, which the *coureurs* had long known. Though he had certainly inflicted hardships on the English posts, he had not achieved solvency for himself, still less for Canada. Above all, he had almost nothing to show which could be called an advance towards the Sea of the West, and against that consideration success as a fur-trader or as a rival of the English would count against him, not in his favour.

Maurepas was still insistent that La Vérendrye must prosecute his exploration, and must do so at his own expense. To ease the situation Governor Beauharnois took advantage of La Vérendrye's presence in Montreal during the winter 1734-35 to arrange that a syndicate of merchants should be responsible for the trading aspects of westwards expansion, paying for licences which would furnish revenue for the costs of exploration and for presents to Indians. The arrangement had little attraction for La Vérendrye as he made his way back to his posts in the spring of 1735, and he seems never to have faltered in his belief that the solution of his problems lay in the pacification of the Indians, the stabilization of his posts so as to create long-term confidence, and the subsequent development of trade.

The laden canoes which the merchants sent up under their licences got no further than Kaministikwia before winter; but La Vérendrye got to Fort St Charles at Lake of the Woods and spent the winter there exploring a new route to Fort Maurepas at the southern end of Lake Winnipeg. This route ran westwards from Lake of the Woods and then north. It lay south of the route previously used and would be of value when southern exploration came to be undertaken. But as the explorers came back to Lake of the Woods in the spring of 1736, La Jemeraye, second-in-command to the leader, died on the journey.[18] Desperate remedies for the lack of goods caused by the stoppage of the canoes at Kaministikwia were under discussion. Any journey to pick up supplies from Kaministikwia would have to be made in strength, for the Sioux were on the warpath. But it could not be made by too strong a party for fear of weakening the garrison of Fort St Charles.

Early in June therefore La Vérendrye sent off twenty-one men, well armed and commanded by his eldest son. The Jesuit Père Aulneau went with them, for the Jesuits were eager to extend their missions, and they felt disillusioned at the way in which the fur trade seemed to preoccupy La Vérendrye and his family. First news of the fate of this party came to Fort St Charles by an independent trader who had met with a Sioux war party about twenty-five miles from Fort St Charles. The incident is interesting as showing that independent traders worked so far afield; but the next arrival was a merchant bringing a couple of canoes from Grand Portage, and he had seen nothing of the French party. Knowing that the Sioux were out, La Vérendrye sent out a search party which found the corpses of all the Frenchmen on an island which since that day has been called Massacre Island. There were no survivors. From their positions, the French seemed to have been cut down as they sat at a council with the Sioux. They were not a day's journey from the fort, and they seemed to have been shadowed on the trail from the moment of their departure. The massacre may well have diverted the Sioux from an attack on the fort itself. It was the expression of a deep hostility, due to the way in which the French had armed the Crees and the Monsonis and had allowed La Vérendrye's son to go on the warpath with these tribes against the Sioux.[19]

The massacre, following on the death of La Jemeraye, greatly weakened La Vérendrye's party and underlined the dangers of the Indian alliances which he and the French traditionally followed. Even their system of giving presents to Indians had dangers when the canoes did not arrive and the presents could not be made. Further exploration certainly could not be undertaken in 1736. Yet during the winter 1736-37 La Vérendrye himself went to Fort Maurepas and there gathered much information about Lake Winnipeg, about the Saskatchewan River flowing into the lake from the west, and about the region to the north of the lake. He gave another son to live with the Crees at the northern end of the lake, and he promised the Assiniboines that he would build a post at the Forks of the Red River.

In return the Assiniboines agreed to act as emissaries to the Mandans, a sedentary people practising agriculture and living in considerable comfort in large villages on the middle waters of the Missouri. These were a people about whom many legends had gathered. They were reputed to be white-complexioned and to wear long beards; and if it should prove true that the Missouri led to the Sea of the West and that its upper waters were commanded by the Mandan villages, then the Mandan villages and the River of the Mandans (as the Missouri was called) lay in La Vérendrye's path. The friendship of the Mandans would be essential if he was to use the Missouri as a route to the Sea of the West; and in 1734 the Assiniboines had brought him an invitation to visit the Mandan villages. He had at that time delayed, since his affairs demanded his presence in Montreal, and in 1737 he again delayed, telling the Assiniboines to say that a post would be built in 1738 at the Forks of the Red River (as he had already agreed with them) and that they must bring the Mandans to trade there. They were to tell the Mandans to come to the post with their horses—which may perhaps be taken to show that La Vérendrye was seriously planning an overland journey and was organizing transport.

Such delays left Maurepas more convinced than ever that the beaver trade was uppermost in La Vérendrye's mind; and since La Vérendrye felt compelled to go to Quebec in the summer of 1737 to secure adequate supplies, instead of pushing out to the west and south, there could be no denying that trade was exceedingly important. Obsession with the fur trade, however, would at least have made La Vérendrye an expansionist, though perhaps he might not have expanded fast enough or in the required direction. But at this time it is possible that he was not even primarily a fur-trader but was above all a colonizer.[20] His constant desire to set up defensible posts supports this view; and his posts were encouraged to feed their men on local produce and to develop gardens and crops. His care for an improved transport system, his work on portages and his search for alternative routes, all indicate a settled rather than an expanding system. The missionaries whom he took with him would fit in with such a policy since the long-term conclusion of such men was that permanent conversion to Christianity must entail abandonment of a wandering way of life and acceptance of steady work, agriculture, and settled habitations. The missionaries in fact achieved little, and the policy of maintaining peace between the tribes was doomed to failure. But whether La Vérendrye based his plans on a series of fur-posts or on a string of small settlements, he meant to consolidate before he indulged in further expansion. Perhaps a distinction between fur-posts and agricultural settlements is in itself too fine, for the fur-trader needed to live off the country, and the agriculturist, in the Canadian tradition, turned to the fur trade during the winter months. Explorers, such as La Vérendrye was expected to be, had both to secure their food and to get money for their journeys.

In fact, La Vérendrye could not transport all the furs that he had traded to Quebec in 1737. He was met by a warning from Governor Beauharnois that he must search for the Western Sea and that further visits to Lower Canada were not acceptable. He agreed that he would make a voyage to the Mandan villages, and he got back to Fort Maurepas by September 22. Fort Rouge was established as a trade post at the Forks of the Red and the Assiniboine rivers, and he was able to set off up the Assiniboine before the river froze. Somewhere in the vicinity of the present Portage la Prairie he set up a small post, Fort la Reine. It stood astride the road which the Assinboines would take to reach Lake Manitoba and so to take their furs by the Nelson and Hayes rivers to the English on Hudson Bay. The little fort was well sited for the fur trade rivalry against the English, but it could also be maintained that it lay on the road to the Mandan villages, the Missouri, and the Western Sea.

In mid-October 1738 La Vérendrye left Fort la Reine on foot, going south by west to Pembina Mountain and then on to Turtle Mountain. His party consisted of twenty-two white men and about thirty Indians, and from Turtle Mountain onwards they were joined by a large party of Assiniboines. As a result, when he reached the Mandan villages towards the end of November, his party was so large as to cause alarm. Only his personal adroitness ensured that his entry into the villages should be peaceful and, indeed, impressive. Nevertheless, the Mandans were frightened of the Assiniboines and spread a rumour that the Sioux were at hand in order to get rid of them. The interpreter decamped along with the Assiniboines, and since La Vérendrye had already been robbed of the goods which he intended for presents, he decided he could do little more and that he also should withdraw. Before doing so, however, he sent a small party to a Mandan village on the banks of the River of the West. This, they discovered, was a river which ran southwest by south, and there were reports of men similar to the French living at its mouth.[21]

So much was already known about the Missouri. La Vérendrye's search for the River of the West was no more than perfunctory, and he seems to have lost whatever enthusiasm he ever had for this project during his journey to the Mandan villages. Confirmation that the river ran southwards was not the only disappointment which he met there; the Mandans proved to be little different from other Indians, they wore only buffalo robes and a loin cloth, and though their women indeed proved to have fair hair and skins (at least by comparison with other Indians) and they grew corn and other crops and stored their provisions, the voyage had proved too arduous for the explorers to expect that the route would ever provide easy access to the River and the Sea of the West. The experience confirmed his conviction that he should turn north, not south.

The English traders on Hudson Bay were already feeling the effects of La Vérendrye's three posts in the Lake Winnipeg area (Fort Rouge, Fort la Reine, and Fort Maurepas), and when he returned to Fort la Reine in March 1739, to concentrate his efforts to the northwards, the interruption of trade was serious. But the French effort was not exclusively directed to the northern trade even after the disappointment of the 1738-39 expedition to the Mandans. A party was sent to explore the Saskatchewan in 1739; and in 1740 as La Vérendrye himself once more went down to Quebec he left his son Pierre to continue exploration, in the hope that he might make contact with the horsed Indians who came to trade with the Mandans and persuade them to guide him to the Great Sea from which they were reputed to come. At that time Pierre de la Vérendrye made little mark, but in a later memorandum he claimed that although the horsed Indians did not come to trade in 1741, he made his way with two Frenchmen to a point at which he was within reach of two Spanish forts.[22] This confirmed that the River of the Mandans or the River of the West was the Missouri and that it led from the Mandan villages south to the Gulf of Mexico. If anything was needed to turn La Vérendrye's attention to the north and west, this knowledge would have done so.

On his return from Quebec in 1741 he was again pledged to press on with exploration; and he carried out his obligation in his own way. As Pierre returned from his journey to the Mandans he was sent to establish a new post on Lake Dauphin, at the mouth of the Mossy River, where it would command the waterways west of Lake Winnipeg and the trade which came from that direction.[23] At the same time La Vérendrye built his first post on the northwest shore of Lake Winnipeg, sited so as to control both the Saskatchewan at its mouth and the materials for making canoes which would be required for taking trade down the rivers to the Bay. For, as Kelsey had discovered, the mouth of the Saskatchewan was a focal point for trade from the prairies to the Bay, and still more so for trade from the areas to the west and north. There or thereabouts the flotillas of canoes were made and assembled, and there many of the furs changed hands, coming into the possession of the Indians who acted the part of middlemen and took them down to the English posts.

The French moves were well planned and based on a growing knowledge of the routes by which furs reached the European traders. But the Sioux and the Crees were still at war as La Vérendrye got back from Quebec in 1741, and he was forced to settle down at Fort la Reine on the Assiniboine and to send his sons on such explorations as seemed necessary. They could accomplish nothing until the spring of 1742, but then two of his sons began a truly remarkable voyage.[24] Starting from Fort la Reine, they first visited the Mandan villages and then spent the summer and winter, until March 1743, in search of the horsed Indians. They went in a southwesterly direction, and on their homewards journey, at the end of March 1743, they buried a leaden plate which has since been dug up and which establishes that they were then on the site of the present city of Pierre, South Dakota. From the internal evidence of their narrative it can be estimated that they must have been in the lands dominated by the Snake tribe and that the point at which they had turned for home was at the foot of the Rockies. They thought that they had reached the "Mountains of Bright Stones," with the Western Sea beyond, and this would also lead to the conclusion that they had penetrated across the prairies to the Rockies. They had quite certainly crossed the prairies; and in so doing they had reached the conclusion that further exploration in that direction would be profitless.

Henceforth the La Vérendrye family made little pretence at searching for the Sea of the West. But from a map put together in 1750 it appears that by that date they knew the Saskatchewan up to the Forks of that river, and they knew the connection with Hudson Bay by way of the Rivière des Cristinaux and the Rivière Bourbon—the Churchill and the Nelson. In 1748 they set up Fort Bourbon on the south shore of Lake Bourbon, now called Cedar Lake, where the Saskatchewan flows in from the west. They were concentrating on the supply centres upon which the English posts depended, and they had got control of the strategic area round Lake Winnipeg, Lake Manitoba, and Lake Winnipegosis. They had not entirely prevented the prairie Indians from going down to trade at the Bay; nor had their exploits enabled La Vérendrye to meet his creditors, to whom he owed at least 50,000 livres by 1742. He had certainly challenged English pretensions to provide the only trading outlet for the tribes of the prairies and the Northwest; but he had done very little indeed to placate Maurepas by effective exploration towards the Sea of the West.

By 1742 even La Vérendrye began to weary of the struggle. At his own request he was replaced as commandant of the *postes du nord*. His successor, Nicolas-Joseph de Noyelles, was expected to maintain friendly relations with the Sioux and to persuade them to make raids on the English trade, so that in effect the policy which La Vérendrye had been upbraided for pursuing was carried on. But de Noyelles resigned in 1749 and La Vérendrye, whose achievements had received some of the recognition which they deserved, was again appointed to command the "Posts of the Western Sea" in 1749. The recognition came too late, for he died at Montreal in December 1749, on his way to take up his appointment and to continue the exploration of the west.

In applying (in vain) for his father's post, the Chevalier de la Vérendrye revealed that by the time of his father's death the family aimed to set out from Lake Bourbon (Cedar Lake) and to follow the Saskatchewan up to the Rockies, there to build a post.[25] They accepted the Saskatchewan as a better avenue of approach than the Missouri, and they knew that the Saskatchewan would lead them into the mountains, to a height of land beyond which would lie a route to the Sea of the West. The difficulties were not minimized. From their journey of 1742-43 the Frenchmen knew something of the distances and the hardships involved in travel across the prairies, and they reckoned that it would take them two years to reach the height of land and to build their post.

Though La Vérendrye had at last achieved some sort of recognition from the French government, his sons were not allowed to succeed to the command for which they had been trained. But their outlook was adopted, and in 1750 a French party was sent up to The Pas on the Saskatchewan, to follow that river to the Rockies in the spring of 1751. A short-lived post, Fort la Jonquière, was then set up somewhere on the upper reaches of the Saskatchewan, but whether on the north branch or on the south branch is not clear. Then, in 1753, the Commandant of the Posts of the West, the Chevalier de la Corne, set up Fort la Corne, or Fort St Louis des Prairies, near the Forks of the Saskatchewan, consolidating French control over the Saskatchewan and of the river system which brought trade down from the west.

Under La Vérendrye's successors, as during his period in office, the frontier of the French expansion lay with traders licensed by the Commandant of the Posts. They were the "woodrunners" of whom the English journals spoke, living with Indians, often accompanied on their travels by a full-blooded squaw, competitive and individualistic, in strong contrast with the regimentation of the English traders; and the element of competition introduced into the fur trade by the traders from Canada had far-reaching effects. Though the Indians do not seem to have become acquisitive in the European sense of that word, they were hard bargainers. They did not, in general, try to accumulate wealth either as a capital to aid in production or as a hoard to be treasured. If their immediate requirement was for a gun and four pounds of powder they lost interest and ceased to hunt and trade or even to bring to market the skins which they had, when they had satisfied those requirements. Yet they were acutely aware of variations in price and quality and would undertake long journeys to secure better bargains. When they thought they were being unjustly treated they would refuse to trade at all even if their requirements were still unsatisfied. In such circumstances the French posts on the southern outskirts of Hudson Bay, and still more the woodrunners who spread out from those posts, permeated the whole trade with the spirit of competition. Prices fluctuated considerably. The Indians were in control; they were able to get arms to carry on their wars and were made confident that they had powerful allies to support them.

So, as the great climacteric of the colonial wars of the eighteenth century dawned, the French had recovered the priority which Kelsey had given to the English. Their dominance in the basin of the Saskatchewan and in the Lake Winnipeg area was forcing the English to forego their privileges and to forsake their principles. The English also must carry their goods up to the Winnipeg area, up the Saskatchewan, across the prairies and into the Northwest, if they wanted to dispute French control. The English would have to take their trade to the Indians in their habitations.

CHAPTER 6

Churchill River,
Exploration, and the
Northwest Passage

While La Vérendrye and his sons were consolidating and expanding the French hold on the inland territories, Albany was thought to be sufficient to carry on the whole of the English trade from the Bottom of the Bay. That post alone produced more than enough furs to satisfy the London market. In accordance with procedure established by Kelsey, an annual slooping voyage (sometimes interrupted) sufficed to get furs from the Eastmain, and it was not until 1724 that a small house was erected at the Slude River, still dependent on an annual slooping voyage from Albany. From the Slude River came a considerable trade in martens, so that it was on the whole complementary to Albany, and the little post greatly encouraged the Indians by remaining open through the winter.

English expansion to the Slude River, such as it was, was due to a desire to trade; it had little or no impetus towards exploration, for the Eastmain coast was already known, and there was no incentive to go inland. The post at Moose was re-established for different reasons; but still with no incentive to go inland. On the contrary, the object was to make it easier for the Indians to bring their furs down, even at the cost of cutting the volume of trade at Albany. The Indians who came down the Moose River to trade at Albany found the last part of the journey, along the coast, the most unattractive part of the whole trip, with no fowl or fish to sustain them, subject to sea-weather in their frail canoes. There was an obvious danger that this trade might be lost to the French unless the coastal journey could be avoided by allowing the Indians to trade in the Moose River. Nevertheless it was 1727 before the London Committee gave serious thought to building again at Moose. The Albany post-master had anticipated them by sending over a reconnaissance party. Then in 1729 a decision was made, and in 1730 building materials were sent out, with the advice that the site of the old post (destroyed by the French in 1693) seemed attractive and with Captain Christopher Middleton to advise on the final choice of site.

The new post at Moose was accepted as being "in the mouth of an enemy," given a garrison of thirty men, and sited for defence by Middleton. But once it had been set up, the relative safety of the mouth of the Moose River and its ease of navigation gave it advantages over Albany, and direct shipments from England to Moose began to be made.

While French encirclement drove the English to build stronger posts at the Bottom of the Bay, the more distant threat to the western posts had, initially, the same effect. A rebuilding of York Fort was put in hand in 1723; stone-faced bastions were erected, and "great guns" were sent out, so that by 1729-30 it was reckoned that York was immune from any attack by small arms or from the land. But lack of timber or of good stone seemed to make it impossible to build a fort on the Hayes River which could face an attack from the sea, or indeed which could be made reasonably comfortable. Attention was therefore all the more easily diverted to other projects, especially to efforts to use the Churchill River as a base for further exploration up the coast, and for penetration to the Saskatchewan.

As James Knight took possession of York Fort in accordance with the terms agreed at Utrecht, he was given the twin tasks of furthering discovery and of increasing trade. In the early years of his command his attention turned southwards rather than to the north, towards land journeys rather than to maritime exploration; eventually he turned towards sea-borne exploration to the north in search of the Straits of Anian. His first move, after he had caustically enumerated the difficulties which the French had bequeathed to him, was to send one of his men, William Stewart, to bring an end to hostilities between the Crees and the Chipewyans, and to get the latter to bring their furs down to York. Although Stewart's guide was a Chipewyan woman, his party contained some Crees, and they attacked the first party of Chipewyans whom they met, so that his journey was not a complete success. Yet he travelled across the Barren Lands to the north and west of the Nelson River, and it is probable that he went some eight hundred miles from York Fort and reached the country east of the Slave River and south of Great Slave Lake. This was Chipewyan country, and he brought back with him ten young men from that tribe, to impress them and to train them as ambassadors to open up a regular trade.

Stewart's journey was in itself a magnificent feat of travel. It brought the English into direct contact with the Indians of the Great Slave Lake area when the French were still reaching out from Montreal towards the Pigeon River and the lands to the south of Lake Winnipeg. Moreover, by breaking the Cree control over the trade of York Fort, Stewart stirred them to much greater activity. They began to give accounts of a great fur-bearing lake and river which lay beyond the headwaters of the Churchill River. This was Athabasca Lake and River, and since they made their journeys without white companions, as a trade with Athabasca developed the Crees secured for themselves the role of middlemen.[1]

From these moves to stimulate trade in the south and the northwest, from the territories bordering on the French and from Great Slave Lake and Athabasca, came a determination to set up a post on the Churchill River; and in 1717 Stewart was sent to choose a site, to be followed later in the year by Knight himself. Knight also had the full support of the London Committee, who ordered the ship *Hudson's Bay* to sail direct to Churchill in 1717 and to winter there if Knight thought it necessary—which he did not.[2] In addition to sending Stewart ahead to fix a site for a post, he had also sent a young apprentice, Richard Norton, to make "a great Sweep to the Southward of the West." It is not clear exactly where Norton went, for he was not trained in survey and his chief memory of his journey was of the terrifying difficulties. But he certainly met the Chipewyans, and he established a peace to the westwards of Churchill which lasted for many years and which enabled the Indians of Great Slave Lake and Athabasca to bring their trade down to the English posts.[3] In due course the friendly relations so established enabled the English to return inland with the Indians and to penetrate to those areas themselves.

While Richard Norton went on his great sweep to the southwest, Knight moved over from York Fort to Churchill. The early history of settlement there had not been encouraging. The Danish explorer Jens Munck had met with stark tragedy when he tried to winter in 1619-20. "When the Dean Capt. Monk wintred at Churchill River," wrote Knight, "he lost above 100 men by his not having time to build Winter setting in so soon upon him." Kelsey, now second in command to Knight, had known the post at Churchill which the Company set up when English attention had been attracted to the river in 1686-87.[4] It had been destroyed by fire, and had not served either to bring on a whale fishery or to enable the English to make contact with the "northern Indians." Kelsey's memory was gilded by the passage of time, and Knight was most disappointed when he saw the site. Misfortune followed, too, when the Chipewyans whom Stewart had brought back to York Fort were sent to winter near Churchill so as to get them away from the Crees, and were massacred by the Eskimos there.[5] Then the *Hudson's Bay* in 1715, after getting within sight of York Fort, failed to make port and took her precious cargo back to England, so that Knight was extremely short of goods and even had to send his sloop over to Albany to get emergency supplies. Nevertheless, in 1717 a defensible post with four bastions and palisades was in occupation at Churchill, and Indians from the north came in to trade in the first year.[6]

The "northern Indians" brought not only furs but rumours of a great supply of natural copper, pure metal, lying at the mouth of a river to the north; and of other yellow metal, perhaps gold, which was brought down to the coast of the "West Seas" by another great river. Knight had, in fact, been given information both of the Coppermine River and of the Mackenzie, and since he was obsessed by precious metals the rumours had a great effect on him. But although the Indian reports influenced him considerably, Knight read the signs in his own way. Whereas the Indians had come to Churchill overland and insisted that there was no way of getting to their territories by sea, Knight was convinced that a sea route must be somewhere, and that when he had sailed to the "West Seas" into which the second reported river (the Mackenzie) flowed, he would have discovered the Northwest Passage; and he would not have been far wrong.

Knight was already an old man. But he spent the next winter in London, convincing the Committee of his views and securing virtual independence for the prosecution of a search for the copper mine, the gold-mine, and the Straits of Anian. In 1719 he brought back the *Albany* frigate and the *Discovery* sloop, with orders that they were not to go to any post south of 64° except in distress and that they were to be under Knight's orders for exploration north of that latitude. This would have forbidden a call even at Churchill. But the Committee had decided to continue and even to augment that post, which was to be substantially built and to be called Prince of Wales Fort. It would serve to open trade to the south and to the northwest, towards Athabasca and Great Slave Lake and back to Lake Winnipeg; and it would combat the French in a way which would override the possibility "whether it may not be a means to lessen the trade at York Fort." [7] Churchill also would act as a base for exploration by sea to the north.

This much James Knight had achieved. But of him and his ships nothing more was heard after they left England in June 1719. Their fate was unknown until in 1722 Captain Scroggs in the *Whalebone* sloop (with Richard Norton aboard as interpreter) sailed north from Churchill on a voyage of discovery. The *Whalebone* was soon back, having found the remains of the two ships, and having concluded that "Every Man was killed by the Eskemoes." [8] The story of the disaster was never discovered in detail. But the shock, and its results on English policy, were clear from the moment the news was known. Maritime expansion to the north was abandoned. Slooping voyages were indeed continued, but they were aimed at increases in the annual trade, not at great discoveries. Kelsey, who had succeeded Knight in command at York Fort, himself sailed north on a slooping voyage in 1719, and in 1720 he sent the *Prosperous* on a similar voyage. Both were unproductive, but in 1721 Richard Norton came to Churchill with a strong band of "northern Indians"—probably Eskimos—who said that they knew the copper mine, and that it lay at a great distance to the north. [9] If the metal was going to be profitable, it had to be got in bulk, which meant

that it must be reached by sea "and not to come Creeping by Land."
Accordingly, in 1721 Kelsey took Norton aboard the *Prosperous*, together
with some of the "northern Indians" as guides, to seek the mine. They were
back at Churchill within a month or so; but there was "no farther Discovery made" by the time Kelsey was recalled to London in 1722.[10]

The London Committee encouraged voyages to the north in search of
trade but, after the disaster of Knight's expedition, discouraged Kelsey
from serious exploration; in particular it forbade him to winter in the north
so that he could not make full use of the season of open water.[11] His successor, Thomas Macklish, an experienced trader and traveller, had in his
time made a canoe journey inland from Albany. But his experience committed him to opposition to the French in the south rather than to exploration in the north of his territories. He was not convinced that Churchill
brought in any trade which would not otherwise have gone to York, and
when in 1724 Richard Norton reported that there was no way to the copper
mine by sea, "it being all a frozen Sea," and that it would take three years
to make a journey overland to the mine and back, Macklish decided to give
up the search for the mine and to concentrate on the fur trade. The London
Committee accepted the conclusion in 1725.[12] But trading sloops were still
to be sent north from Churchill, and that post grew in status and began to
receive its own separate shipments from London, no longer involved with
those for York Fort.

The slooping voyages from Churchill were falling into a routine in which
they merely traded up to Marble Island and back. Hopes of reaching the
copper mine were dim. But "Discovery to the Northwards" was still an
active issue and in 1725 one of the Hudson's Bay Company's servants,
Captain Christopher Middleton, prepared a paper for the Royal Society (of
which he later became a Fellow) on the Variation of the Magnetic Needle
in northern waters. Middleton was a trained professional sailor, distinct
from the many so-called Captains, such as Kelsey, whose title is a tribute
to their competence in small-boat sailing in the Bay and to the importance
of slooping in the economy of the English posts. Middleton had been prevented by a personal quarrel with the captain from going north on the
Whalebone when that ship discovered the remains of Knight's expedition.
But he had taught navigation to some of the men who made that voyage,
and he closely questioned them on their return to Churchill. He contributed a scientific and active mind, and a personal rectitude and persistence,
which sustained interest in exploration when the Company itself lacked
incentive, and which ultimately provoked a determined, if fruitless, effort
to discover the Northwest Passage.

That effort did not come for many years, and it did not come under the
lead of the Hudson's Bay Company but as a challenge to its claims. In the

meantime the influence of Churchill spread to the south. James Knight had from the start decided that circumstances warranted a departure from the rigid English Standard of Trade; he ordered that the trader at Churchill must "trade larger" and give "better pennyworths" than could be got at York, and although this discrimination probably drew away trade from York—and was certainly suspected of so doing—it did much to establish the trade of Churchill. From 1721 onwards great fleets of Missinipi Indians came to trade there, from "the Great Water that lies at the head of this River," that is, from Lake Winnipeg and the area to which La Vérendrye and his sons were penetrating.[13]

It was inevitable that the traders at York Fort should complain, and that they should ascribe to competition from Churchill all the falling-off in their business. But much of their trouble came from French competition in the headwaters of the Nelson and the Hayes rivers; and much of the trade which came in to Churchill came from the Barren Lands and from the Saskatchewan, using the Churchill River as its route to the post. Despite the complaints of York Fort the trade which developed at Churchill was considered to be trade won from the French.[14] It was certainly open to French threats as the *postes du nord* were organized into an effective system and as the woodrunners spread out ahead of the posts. But the French posts lay far off from Churchill, and there seemed little danger of an attack from overland, such as had to be reckoned with at the Bottom of the Bay. The danger at Churchill was either that the post might be starved of trade by reason of French control of the upper reaches of the rivers, or that a sea-borne attack might overwhelm it. So in 1730-31 the Committee decided to replace Knight's post at Munck's Point with a great stone fort at "Eskimay Point," where it would command the entrance to the river.[15] As craftsmen, barges and horses, plans and models were sent out, the imposing solidity of the fort which took shape was a reflection of the determination of the English to maintain their hold on the Churchill River and on the access to the prairies and to the northern wastes and waters which the post there commanded.

Determined though the English might be, their policy was neither expansive nor attractive when compared with that of the French. It was still based on the conviction that the Indians should be drawn down to trade at the Bay, and the great fort which was taking shape in itself emphasized this negative approach. With four bastions ten feet high, connected by curtains along which ran boarded runways for guns, and a five-foot parapet pierced for gunports, eighteen cannon mounted and ready for use, and a magazine with walls five feet thick and a vault of stone, Churchill was the citadel of English defence in the north—so much so that when the War of the Austrian Succession had broken out the Committee decided that the shipping, the trade, and the Indians of York Fort should be transferred to the more easily defensible post, in 1741. Though plans were then put in hand for a rebuilding of York, more cannon, men, and supplies were sent to Churchill, and that post remained at once the avenue to the Northwest and the bastion of English defence.

It was, however, 1749 before the Committee thought that the great stone fort was defensible. The War of the Austrian Succession was then over, but English policy remained unchanged. The French must be prevented from acquiring influence over the Indians who came north to trade by the Bay. But it was not accepted that the best way to do this was by establishing English posts inland. The Company was confident that it had fulfilled its function when it had supplied its customers, made a fair return to its proprietors, and defended its interests against rivals, whether they were English or French. More should not be expected, especially since the government itself was so indifferent to the interior and so reluctant to dispute French claims that during the period of British predominance which followed after Utrecht it failed to secure a definition of the boundary.

The romantic and expansive enthusiasm which had led James Knight to establish his post at Churchill had, by 1749, been replaced by a sturdy and unimaginative commercialism which, without stimulating penetration to the south, nevertheless concentrated English attention in that direction. This approach was matched by the Indians. Constantly assessing prices and quality, they claimed that they could only get past the French and come to market at the Bay by stealth; but they also claimed that the French were "the Shop that they can Market cheapest at."[16] The London Committee concluded that their own goods were superior, with the possible exception of gunpowder, but that the French got great advantage from their being "in the place with the Indians where they Catch their Furs and so Saves them the Trouble of a long journey." The French terrorized the Indians to some extent; and their trade was continuous and could be relied on, whereas the whole of the English system was completely thrown out of gear in the years when, for whatever reason, the ship from England failed to arrive.[17] Such a failure would be all the more serious since the Indians would already have made a long journey to the Bay before they discovered that there were no supplies available for them, and would be faced with an equally arduous return to their hunting grounds.

European supplies were necessities, not luxuries, for the Indians who traded to the Bay, and to many times that number of Indians living inland. Within a decade of their becoming acquainted with European goods, tribe after tribe became utterly dependent on regular European supplies. The bow and arrow went out of use, and the Indian starved if he did not own a serviceable gun, powder, and shot; and in his tribal wars he was even more dependent on European arms. Steel traps replaced wooden ones more slowly. But by 1743 it was reported that the Indians who traded to York Fort were completely dependent on the annual arrival of a ship from England. They had not developed any artisan talent, either for replacing or for repairing European equipment; and as soon as information on this aspect of Indian life becomes available it is evident that by the middle of the eighteenth century a far-reaching and complex Indian system of trade had carried this dependence right up to the foot of the Rockies.[18]

Within this trade system the French had a great advantage in their flexibility. The English tried from time to time to get information about the rates at which the French traded, but could only conclude that "the Indians are so perfidious that no two will agree." The Indians were undoubtedly always anxious to emphasize the bargains which could be got from rival traders, but the variety of their reports derives as much from the flexibility of French methods as from Indian perfidy. When, for example, the English ship failed to arrive and the English were short of goods, the "French Canady" traders would be able to "trade harder" for several years, until the reputation of the English had been re-established and the hard dealing of the French had driven the Indians to seek alternatives.[19] The French could also profit from the Indians' mood of the moment; and this was a great advantage in that it was accepted that they "don't mind little measure providing they can live and have but little trouble." The conclusion that the English goods were better was therefore little to the point. It was the Indians' desires which mattered; and although they had easily accepted dependence on Europeans for the necessities of their lives, they were often as strongly affected by luxuries as by necessities. So brandy on the one hand and Brazil tobacco on the other proved as valuable in attracting trade as good guns or powder. It was of no importance that English traders found French trade-brandy "Hot fiery stuff and very disagreeable to taste"; and of very little significance that a whole series of proclamations had forbidden the *coureurs* to trade brandy for furs. The Indians would make efforts for the sake of brandy which they would not make for more essential goods, and the *coureurs* evaded the ban. "They trade no brandy but make presents of enough to make them Drunk," it was reported; and the only English answer was hopefully to insist that kindly treatment, absolute fairness, and encouragement were the best answers to the mixture of force and cajolery which the French used.[20]

Habits of trade were greatly affected by these considerations, which by allowing the French to make their best trade with comparatively light goods, to some extent offset the distances which they had to travel. So much did each nation fall into a pattern that by 1750 the Hudson's Bay Company was able to inform the Lords of Trade that, notwithstanding the ceaseless inroads of the woodrunners, since the Treaty of Utrecht the French had never attempted to navigate in the Bay, to make any settlements on the coast, or to carry on any trade there. This was perhaps comforting; but in effect it meant that the French had adopted a role in which they carried light goods inland and traded only for the light and valuable furs. The English supplied the Indians with heavy and bulky goods and took the heavy, and less valuable, furs.[21] That there were Indians who accepted the task of carrying the bulky furs to the Bayside, and of carrying the heavy English goods back inland, reveals how an Indian trade system had developed as a complement to the European traders. They had two European nations to play off against each other; and though they complained that the French would "intercept the Trade by force if they cannot have it otherwise," they made no effective protest.[22]

To a large extent the two European systems were complementary; so much was this accepted that it was even suggested that the two nations should help each other in their trade. The French governor of Fort Bourbon, for example, proposed to the English master of York Fort that they should help each other in "un petit Comerce Cachez," supplying each other with the trade goods of their respective countries and arranging which furs each should take. The suggestion brought out the basic difference between the two methods; for while the Frenchman would have been free to carry out his part in such an arrangement, to the Englishman the very idea was wrong and unacceptable, and he would in any case have been unable to carry it into effect. He therefore answered that "My principals are too Generous to leave room for any temptation of that nature to operate on their Servants, if yours are different I'm sorry for it."[23]

Such an arrangement would have done little to mitigate the rivalry. English, French, and Indians alike all did their utmost to profit from the competitive system, loudly though they deplored it in public utterances. In the rivalry there was an inevitable tendency to multiply posts; but an increase in the number of posts did not necessarily bring a comparable increase in the volume of trade; nor could this be so while the Indians ceased to exert themselves as soon as their essential needs had been supplied. Posts set up to combat the rival nation easily became rivals for the nearby posts of the same nation or company. The traders were therefore explicit in saying that York's trade had gone to Churchill, and in the result the two posts between them did not produce as much beaver as York alone had traded prior to 1731. But national rivalry in the fur trade meant that competition between posts could not be accepted as reason for relaxation. The Canadians did their utmost to convince their ministers that their only hope lay in the forcible suppression of the English posts, while the English traders reported that "its the French that is our Chiefest Obstical, they encreasing more than ever."[24]

National rivalry, concerned with exploration, with the discovery of the Passage and with the opening of routes to new territories, seemed to emerge most clearly in the development of the *postes du nord* and expansion towards Lake Winnipeg and the prairies. The new English post at Churchill, with its incentive to northern navigation and its approach to Athabasca and Great Slave Lake, and then with its great stone defences, seemed to take priority in the English programme and to emphasize the maritime and defensive nature of that programme.

But the furs from the Bottom of the Bay played a large part in the trade of the English company in the period after the Treaty of Utrecht, and rivalry there was close and intimate in a way not to be found at York or Churchill. The English posts lay at the end of the easiest and best known approach-route from Canada. French spies hovered round the English, two French houses were reported "near the head of Albany River" with a third near at hand, there was a rumour that an armed attack on the outpost at Eastmain was imminent, and Albany itself seemed likely to be taken by force. Woodrunners skirmished round the post, interrupting the Indians, and when in 1724 the loss of the ship of the year made the English short of goods their discomfort was increased by the report that large bands of Mohawks were coming north to massacre all Indians who traded to the English posts.[25]

The Mohawk attack never took place, but the Master of Albany, Joseph Isbester, decided that his trade would never be safe as long as the woodrunners controlled the headwaters of the Albany River. Breaking traditional English policy, he decided to go inland himself and to set up a post on the upper reaches of the river. Even his "Home Indians" were under French influence and were only bringing down enough furs, of poor quality, to pay for a debauch on the plantation. Although his own post was badly off both for goods and for servants, in 1743 he went inland up the river and set up the small post of Henley House, about a hundred and twenty miles from the sea, near the strategic junction of the east and west branches of the Albany River. An abandoned French post, which the Indians said would soon be rebuilt, lay at "the very part that all Cannoes must pass that Come Down to Albany Fort," and Isbester's expedition added greatly to English first-hand knowledge of both the realities of travel inland and the geographical background of the trade which came down to the Bay.[26]

In the situation which had developed by 1743, either the Indians would trade their furs to anyone who had penetrated inland, or they would hand them over to any Indian middleman who would take them down to the Bay. The English must therefore penetrate to the upper waters of the rivers if they wanted direct access to the hunting Indians. But such a journey would be beyond the capacity of the ordinary servants of the English company, although the journey from Henley House back to the coast took only three days. The London Committee decided that, although Henley House should be accepted as a *fait accompli*, its function should be to act as a display centre with a small selection of English goods, which would encourage the Indians to continue on down to the Bay and, if necessary, would protect them against intimidation as they came to trade at the English posts. On these terms the Committee were prepared to accept Henley House. They seemed, nevertheless, unwilling to seek confrontation with the French, and they ordered that if Henley House seemed to be in any danger of capture it should be abandoned.[27]

There were different views about the results of the establishment of Henley House. Trade at Albany increased, and this was ascribed to the outpost. But the increase at Albany was accompanied by decrease elsewhere. The trade of Moose was immediately affected, and on analysis the London Committee decided that Henley had injured the Company's trade, especially since the French immediately set up a rival post in the vicinity and the Indians demanded that the English give a full supply of trade goods to Henley and carry their trade inland in the fullest sense, during both winter and summer. This the Committee refused. But they did not withdraw from Henley; it was accepted, still in a limited role, as a means of drawing the Indians down to the Bay and of getting them past the cordons of the French.[28]

This episode took place during a period of open war between France and England, and the Hudson's Bay Company sent out guard ships and cannon, and endless unrealistic military instructions for the defence of the posts. It was assumed that any attack would have to come overland since the English held command of the seas; and although an overland attack did not seem very likely, constant caution was urged, and the policy of "making Settlements, higher up the Rivers in better Climates" was also accepted. Henley House remained as a challenge to the French, and even after peace had been arranged the French were regarded as "Enemies to the Company peace or War," for they were "Slie Suttle and artfull to perfaction."[29]

Limited as its task might be, Henley would require English servants to winter inland as a regular routine, and the new situation soon revealed difficulties. There was inevitably a tendency for the inland trader to indulge in private trade and to vary prices in a way which accorded better with French than with English tradition; and, released from the discipline of the post, men and masters alike were prone to "sottishness and ill behaviour."[30]

The problems of inland posts went deep. English servants were unhandy in canoes and were often too elderly and too set in their ways for such journeys. The men themselves, moreover, resented the hardships involved, and as late as 1751 nineteen men at Albany refused the duty, and only five could be found willing to go inland.[31] The inability of the English to live alongside the Indians in the same way as the French soon became evident and brought about the abandonment of Henley in the spring of 1755. Through the winter the Master had had two Indian women "at Bed and Board," and the other men had also had their "squaws" about the post. Familiarity, however, stopped short at the point at which the Indian men expected to be made free of the post and its supplies, and the Captain of the Home Indians, his two sons and his son-in-law, surprised the English, murdered them all, and pillaged the post. Some "upland Indians" in the French allegiance were reported to have assisted in the pillage, but the outstanding element in the grisly tragedy is that the English were quite unable to manage their relations with the Indians once the barriers of aloofness had been broken down.[32]

The pillage of Henley immediately had important results. The Master of Albany seized the Captain of the Home Indians and his sons, convened a court composed of all his men, condemned the Indians to death, and executed them. There was no doubt of the Indians' guilt, for they were not particularly ashamed or alarmed; they confessed, and maintained that they should have been given complete freedom of the post, French fashion. The London Committee were chiefly concerned over the question whether such forcible action might not prevent other Indians, among whom the spoil had probably been widely distributed, from coming to trade with the English. Therefore, while an expedition went to complete the destruction of the post in order to prevent it from falling into French hands, the London Committee ordered that the post should be rebuilt as the only means of recovering the lost trade.

That the incident should cause the London Committee to change their attitude was significant, but more important aspects seem to have attracted little attention. When the Master of Albany tried the Indians for murder he was at a loss as to procedure but convinced that it was necessary to impose the rule of law, and equally convinced that he had powers to do what he intended, under the Charter of the Hudson's Bay Company. Little attention though this aspect of the Henley House massacre received, it meant that the sovereignty of the English Crown over the interior territories of Rupert's Land was vindicated in the rough-and-ready trial of these Indians.

Despite orders from London, Henley House was not immediately rebuilt. Men were not available, and the ship of 1756 arrived too late. Volunteers were augmented in 1757 by men sent out from England under contract for this task, and a party was sent up-river. But they could not manage their canoes and had to return. The episode reveals that not five of all the English servants could be trusted in a canoe and that materials for canoe-making were not available so far north as Albany. The canoes which had been used for the first venture to Henley, and which had subsequently served for provisioning it, had been the result of special forethought, and now the English decided that they must make and master plank-built, flat-bottomed boats to maintain a post inland. They would be easier to handle, and they would carry the bulky English goods better than northern canoes. A boat had been put together for this purpose at Albany in 1746, and though boats also had their limitations (as when in 1757 there was not enough water in the Albany River), yet over the years boats almost completely replaced canoes for the journeys to Henley.[33]

Even with boats to ease their problems, the English did not manage to get off an expedition to refound Henley House until 1759. A post of sorts was then erected, but in little more than a fortnight it was overrun by a mixed party of French and Indians. The best account (by a French woodrunner) enumerates three Indians and twenty Frenchmen and says that they came from Michilimackinac.[34] This second overthrow of the English attempt to set up a post inland was French in origin and execution. It was not the enticement of Indians which was now at issue but an outspoken national rivalry, a clash of claims to the interior. The Seven Years' War had brought this national rivalry to a head, and the interior of Canada was accepted by both France and England as a major subject of dispute.

Though Henley House was one of the first casualties as the national rivalry emerged, more serious ambitions—to open up the northwest lands and perhaps even to open up a Northwest Passage—were involved. It had already become a common charge that the purpose of seeking for a Passage and the discovery of the Straits of Anian had been allowed to lapse since James Knight's expedition, and that the great fort at Churchill was devoted only to protecting trade. But the trade of that post was in part with Eskimos, normally conducted by slooping voyages which had familiarized the English with much of the western coast of the Bay. Churchill denoted something of an expansive policy, too, in that the rumours of the copper mine, and of an overland route by which it might be reached, persisted. Such possibilities were kept under constant review; and the way in which the trade of Churchill arrived from the south by way of the Churchill River meant that the traders at Churchill were constantly accumulating information about the Lake Winnipeg area, from which the Saskatchewan led away west across the prairies. The post felt the impact of French expansion under La Vérendrye and his successors, and although the defences were designed to withstand a naval attack, the interests of the traders turned inland rather than to the sea. As trade fell off in the middle years of the eighteenth century, the traders had no hesitation in ascribing their plight to the woodrunners who lowered the Standard of Trade, offered meretricious French goods on credit and, in the last resort, seized the Indians and took their furs by force. The distances which separated Churchill and York Fort from the bases from which the woodrunners operated were greater than at the Bottom of the Bay, but the results in drawing the English to venture inland, and even to establish posts on the upper waters of their rivers, were the same.

Churchill, moreover, was only one part of the English defence system. At Albany and Moose also the men were kept on watch, guns and gunners were sent out, and the costs of defence added significantly to the balance sheets and weighted judgement against other expenses such as those entailed in inland voyages. At times it seemed that the "deluges" which flooded the plantation at Albany as the river melted, and the difficulties of navigation in the river mouth, would lead to the depot's being sited at Charlton Island. But in 1720 orders were given for Albany to be rebuilt, and by 1722 the new post was declared ready to resist any attack, with its "great guns" sited in flankers and then, after the dangers of floods in the marsh had been demonstrated, concentrated in a separate battery overlooking the river. York Fort was rebuilt and furnished with heavy defences at the same time, and the building of the new post at Moose had the same purpose—to oppose the French. There the same internal dangers which brought about the end of the first Henley House were encountered; for Moose was destroyed by fire during a period of "Debochery" on Christmas Day, 1735.

At some English posts the overland approach by the French might appear easy, at others more difficult; but the problem remained the same. The French were steadily gaining command of the upper waters of the rivers which ran north to the Bay while the English were concentrating their efforts on sea defences. The English were not geared to inland penetration, and although the Hudson's Bay Company had looked long and critically at this problem on many occasions, the official answer was still the same. The English must stay in their great posts, must prepare them for defence against sea-borne or overland attack, and must draw down the Indians to trade. By the middle of the eighteenth century the reiterated policy was being derided as the "Sleep by the Frozen Sea," and as the great bastions of Churchill Fort slowly rose to exemplify the policy, it roused strong criticism.

The Ulster official, Arthur Dobbs, in turn High Sheriff of County Antrim, Member of the Irish Parliament, Engineer-in-Chief and Surveyor-General of Ireland, a reputable economist and historian, first began to take the Hudson's Bay Company's policy in hand about 1730. He then began to compile an historical abstract of voyages of exploration in the Bay and to conclude from it that a Northwest Passage was a practicable possibility. In collecting information about previous voyages, he was passed from the Admiralty to the Governor of the Hudson's Bay Company and was by him assured that the Company would certainly have discovered the Passage if such a Passage existed. He was also given a disheartening account of the failure of James Knight's expedition and of the lesson which the Company had drawn from it—that further maritime exploration northwards from Churchill must be useless.[35]

Unconvinced, Dobbs secured access to the Company's Charter. This document was jealously guarded, for it raised delicate problems in law, and it depended on an acceptance of the royal prerogative which the Company had itself done something to jeopardize by seeking parliamentary approval. But Dobbs discovered a copy in the Plantation Office and convinced himself that the land and privileges had been granted in return for the duty of seeking for the Passage. The text of the Charter makes it clear that these privileges had been granted for services which had already been rendered in searching for the Passage, not for the continuance of those services. But in 1735 members of the Company themselves did not know what the terms were, or what they implied. Dobbs was thus able to impugn the Company for neglect of its duty and for squandering a national asset while the French made important advances. This was the time during which the French were extending westwards under La Vérendrye and were talking with calculated vagueness about the Sea of the West. But although there was an element of deliberate self-deception in the French approach, there was also a deep conviction that a Sea of the West existed in some form or other and that beyond it lay a passage to the western ocean. The French geographers, administrators, and fur-traders were, moreover, convinced that sooner or later their English rivals would take advantage of the position in Hudson's Bay which they had secured at the Treaty of Utrecht and would use their posts there as points of departure to continue their search for a western passage; as indeed James Knight had done immediately after the Treaty.[36]

Between acceptance of the national interest in combating French ambitions and fears that their Charter might prove vulnerable, the Hudson's Bay committee yielded to Dobbs's persuasions and permitted the annual voyages northwards from Churchill to become more enterprising. Dobbs wanted the sloop to go as far north as Roe's Welcome, where an observation of the tide might show discrepancy between the tide coming from the west and that coming from the east. This, if established, would prove that at some place a flow of water had broken through into the Welcome from the west, and so that a passage lay somewhere there, awaiting discovery. The Hudson's Bay Company went further even than Dobbs and ordered that in 1736 eight or ten Indian families should be taken north on the sloop and set up as a hunting community which would wander over the land and bring in reports. The ship from England was, however, lost in the ice in 1736. So in 1737 two sloops were ordered north from Churchill to Roe's Welcome, after which they were to go as far north as they could. But the sloops had already set forth before the orders from England arrived, and their experience merely added to the discouragement; Captain Napper, in command of one of the two sloops, died at Whale Cove, the voyage was abandoned, and the sloops made their way straight back to Churchill, to report that the west coast of the Bay was difficult and dangerous, that there were no navigable rivers leading west, and that the prospects for trade were negligible.

A further voyage was sent north from Churchill in 1738. But its purpose was merely to fulfil a promise to the Eskimos and to get them to come down to Churchill in later years. The search for the Passage had virtually been abandoned, and the Company was trying to establish Indian habits of concentration on fur hunting and regular visits to Churchill for trade. Dobbs, however, insisted that so far nothing had been observed which was incompatible with the tides in Roe's Welcome coming from two different directions and so denoting the existence of a passage. His doubts were shared by Christopher Middleton who, since his quarrel with Captain Scroggs of the *Whalebone* in 1722, had won the confidence of the Hudson's Bay Company as well as the respect of the Royal Society, of which he became a Fellow in 1736. He had been consulted during the discussions with Dobbs, and he made a detailed study of the problem which led him to conclude that a Northwest Passage existed. He was still employed by the Company, and he offered to lead a discovery expedition. The offer was rejected. But Middleton had access to the Company's documents, and he was the intermediary in the discussions with Dobbs. He was at Churchill in 1737 when the sloops got back from their northern voyage, and he questioned the crews closely, concluding that no one among them was qualified to investigate the problem and that, despite their adverse report, the chances for the existence of a passage were as good as ever.

On his return to London in 1737 Middleton communicated these conclusions to Dobbs; and his ability to use the Company's papers at this time probably explains why the narrative of Scroggs's journey in the *Whalebone* disappeared and why Kelsey's account of his travels on the prairies also vanished, to come to light eventually among Dobbs's papers in Northern Ireland. Both men were by now set on pursuing the search for a passage and were prepared to defy the Company if necessary. They maintained close co-operation, and they turned to the Admiralty in an attempt to set on foot an exploring expedition which could not be controlled by the Company. The outbreak of the War of Jenkins's Ear in 1739 brought something of a setback, but as the British government became aware of the explorations of Vitus Bering and of the possibilities of opening up trade with the Pacific coast of Asia, neither the government nor the Hudson's Bay Company could be indifferent to the sort of proposal which Middleton and Dobbs were making. In 1740 the Admiralty started Anson off on his voyage round the world, and the Hudson's Bay Company began to show interest in the interior of Labrador and to order that details of its territories, and of voyages made by its servants, should not be divulged to the outside world. This would have circumscribed Middleton; but he had left the Company's service in 1741 when he had been given command of a naval expedition to "find out a Passage to the South Sea, China and the East Indies."

The Furnace and the Discovery left the Thames under Middleton's command in June 1741. He must have known that he would have to winter in the Bay, and the Admiralty had arranged that Middleton should do nothing to harm the Company's trade and that the Company should assist him if he should be brought into real distress or in danger of the loss of his ships. William Moor, captain of the Discovery, was also a former Hudson's Bay man, and so was Middleton's surgeon. Past experience drove them straight to Churchill, to demand hospitality and to upset both the discipline and the economy of the post. Middleton's men suffered heavily from scurvy and from too lavish a distribution of spirits, and although he managed to add five of the Company's men and two "northern Indians" to his crews, his ships were in a desperate state as they set off in late June 1742. Still, the shelter which the post had given him had without doubt saved him from worse trouble, he managed to get along with James Isham who commanded Churchill for the Company, and he forbade his men to trade with the Indians and even confiscated some trade goods which had been shipped aboard his vessels.

Badly equipped for his task though he was, in the summer of 1742 Middleton managed to navigate up to 66° north and to enter the large inlet which was his objective. He soon concluded that this could not be a passage, and named it the Wager River. His observations convinced him that there was no passage between the Wager River and Churchill and that if any passage should exist further to the north it could not be clear of ice for more than a week in any year.[37] These conclusions were eventually justified. But Arthur Dobbs claimed that Middleton must have been bribed by the Company and that the way in which he had stopped private trade at Churchill was proof of his connivance.

A pamphlet war brought the whole problem before the public.[38] The Hudson's Bay Company and its Charter, the achievements of the French, the theory of the Northwest Passage, and the history of the search for it, all were brought under scrutiny. Dobbs seemed to accept Middleton's conviction that any passage which might be discovered would be made useless by ice; but he turned his attention to the south and urged a search southwards from Churchill by the Nelson or the Churchill River, and then west overland. The change of front brought him into more outspoken hostility to the French, who were pursuing exactly this line of approach; and it led to a challenge to the Hudson's Bay Company, which barred overland exploration even more effectively than it did maritime voyages. Dobbs concluded that the Charter must be challenged and disproved, the trade must be thrown open to any English merchant, settlement must follow trade, and exploration must rely on the knowledge and initiative which would ensue from such free enterprise.

Middleton, knowing conditions in the north better than Dobbs, and conscious that the Hudson's Bay Company was always ready to develop where such expectation of profit existed as would be necessary to attract free merchants, could not agree that access to the trade of the Bay would open up a new interest in discovery. He had found the Hudson's Bay men helpful, experienced, and realistic; and though his care for the Company's trading rights had brought an accusation that he must have been bribed, he was vindicated at a Court of Enquiry set up by the Admiralty. This entailed that the Admiralty accepted his conclusion that there was no passage between Churchill and the Wager River and that any passage north of that would be of no practical value.

Dobbs had already shifted his ground and begun to argue that the way to the Pacific must lie by river to the south from Churchill or York, and then westwards overland. In this he was encouraged by the evidence of a woodrunner, Joseph la France, who had come over to the English; and Dobbs was able to sustain a weighty case in favour of the establishment of posts in the interior. Above all he sought control of the area round Lake Winnipeg and the lower reaches of the Saskatchewan. This brought a new challenge to the Hudson's Bay Company and its Charter, and the Company itself accepted at least the negative aspects as maritime exploration northwards from Churchill was less emphasized. In 1744 it suspended the annual slooping voyage from Churchill—under the pretext that the outbreak of war with France made it doubly dangerous.

The change from a maritime to an overland search for the Passage was, however, against the English tradition, and when in 1745 Dobbs presented a petition to Parliament seeking support for a search for a passage, a Committee of the Whole House of Commons declared itself in terms which clearly envisaged that the search should be maritime, not overland. Since the Admiralty, like Middleton and (though he would not admit it) Dobbs himself, were reasonably convinced that a maritime passage of any commercial value was unlikely, encouragement took the form of offering a reward of £20,000 to anyone who should discover the Passage. The heavy costs of organizing an expedition were thus thrown upon private persons, and the Exchequer would be called upon only when success had been achieved. The reward was large enough to enable Dobbs to get together a "North West Committee" and to send off two ships, the *Dobbs* and the *California*, in 1746. Their instructions involved a deliberate challenge to the Hudson's Bay Company, since they were specifically instructed to trade with any Eskimos whom they might meet, and to do so at better rates than the Company paid.

Again, former servants of the Company had to provide the ships' captains. William Moor commanded the *Dobbs*; he had been with Middleton in 1741 and was a former mate of the Company's ships. The *California* was under Francis Smith, who had commanded many slooping voyages north from Churchill. Again, also, the Company ordered that, although trade must be protected, the discovery ships must be given help if they were in danger. Owing to the war with France, and to the need for convoy, the Company's ships and the explorers were forced to sail up the north sea together, under the protection of a naval sloop commanded by Middleton! Again the explorers made straight for a Company's post for winter shelter. At York Fort, as Middleton had done at Churchill, they met James Isham in command. He had been checked for the treatment which he had accorded to Middleton, and though he could not refuse all hospitality, he was not likely to overreach himself in favour of the explorers on this occasion. He put them in log tents at some distance from his own men and treated them with the minimum courtesy. He felt no personal sympathy for them, such as he had felt for Middleton; he regarded them as perverse supporters of a view which was wrong in itself but which they were too ignorant to be able to prove or to disprove, too ignorant even to be able to assess the evidence which they were going to seek. The two former Hudson's Bay captains, the wife of Francis Smith, and the literary supercargo, Henry Ellis, were all equally unwelcome and troublesome to him, and the nearest he came to cordiality was when he bade them farewell in June 1747 and sent them north on their exploration.

Ignorant though they might be, the two captains had considerable experience of summer navigation in the Bay. They took their ships up the west coast and into Wager Inlet. This they explored, to find that "our hitherto imagined Strait ended in two small unnavigable Rivers"—as, in general terms, Middleton had predicted. Middleton's further conclusion, than any passage north of the Wager River would be valueless, was implicitly accepted when the captains turned down the suggestion of the supercargo, Henry Ellis, that a passage might yet be found in Repulse Bay to the northwards. The ships were turned for home.

The *Dobbs* and the *California* had achieved nothing, but this could not be accepted by Arthur Dobbs and his North West Committee. They mounted a direct challenge to the Hudson's Bay Company with a petition that their North West Committee should be incorporated into a company, with ownership of all lands which they might discover and the right to exclusive trade in those lands for a period of years. The petition went to the Privy Council in January 1748 and was sent to the Law Officers of the Crown for the legal problems to be investigated. It rested on a plea that the Charter of the Hudson's Bay Company should be invalidated because the Company had not fulfilled the conditions that it should search for the Northwest Passage and should set up a colony in its lands; it had even opposed British attempts to settle, while allowing the French to take possession of its lands. The question was sufficiently open for the Law Officers to advise a test case so that the Company's legal position might be ascertained. But the recent expeditions had respected the Company's claims, and no test case could be brought unless a future expedition should infringe them and the Company should then bring a case to court. This would involve the expense of another expedition, to defy the claims and bring on a case. The North West Committee would not face such expenditure.

Dobbs therefore turned from the law courts to the legislature. He won support from a number of influential merchants and prepared a petition to Parliament. But the merchants revealed how little was known about the actual situation and how much their support was part of a general movement against privilege and monopoly, when they refused to sign the petition unless Parliament would give them the freedom of access which they sought. This could not be guaranteed. For though there is no evidence that the Hudson's Bay Company was able to organize an effective lobby, there was a general feeling that the lands under discussion were not only vast but barren, and unsuitable for anything but the fur trade. From the example of France it was clear that the fur trade was a business which was particularly vulnerable to over-production. It was also clear that the Hudson's Bay Company, whatever its defects, could adequately supply the London market at prices which even allowed English hatters to develop an export industry, and that they would undertake the costs of defending the vast and largely unknown lands which had been granted to them, at least so far as the fur trade seemed to be under threat. It was clear, too, that the question of a Northwest Passage had been settled so far as any practical interests of the British government or people were involved. Even Arthur Dobbs could not give the assurances which the merchants sought, and he at last gave up the contest and left the struggle against the Company to "some more happy Adventurer." He had spent eighteen years in pursuit of the Northwest Passage and had ended with proposals to explore and to settle the Northwest Territory.

Arthur Dobbs's departure from the scene did not mean the end of the story. As he went he threw into the arena two pamphlets, the *Short View of the Countries and Trade carried on by the Company in Hudson's Bay*, and the *Short Narrative and Justification of the Proceedings of the Committee appointed by the Adventurers to prosecute the Discovery of the Passage to the Western Ocean of America*. They came when the British Parliament was concerned with problems of an organized trade system and of the part which chartered companies should play in such a system. The Hudson's Bay Company, its claims and its achievements, were bound to come under scrutiny; and in March 1749 the House of Commons set up a Committee to enquire into "the state of the countries adjoining to Hudson's Bay and of the trade carried on there." The result was a full Parliamentary Report, with much first-hand evidence, which is equally valuable as a revelation of the prevailing ignorance of these territories and as showing how shrewd a grasp of conditions the traders had.

When the evidence had been presented to the House of Commons it was soon accepted that the territory was such as to make it doubtful if any interests of the British people were being neglected by the use to which the privileges of the Company were put, and that there was no case for challenging the strong legal position of the Company on grounds of neglect of trade or of settlement. Rumours of an interloping expedition which would provoke a test case still persisted, but no interloper appeared in the Bay. The Hudson's Bay Company had been vindicated in its legal status and in its contention that the best way to exploit its privileges was to leave the hinterland to the Indians and to entice them down to trade by the Bay.

The difficulties in taking trade goods inland in any quantity were accepted as making inland posts almost impossible for the English. They must be costly, and only the Indians would profit if competitive trade were carried up to the headwaters of the rivers which ran north to the Bay. Nothing more was justified than occasional explorations to ascertain the background of the trade and to demonstrate the goods which would be traded to Indians who themselves made the journey to the posts. More would only give to the Indians all the advantages of a competitive trade brought to their doorstep. Thoughtful men who knew the facts agreed with Middleton and James Isham (neither of whom was an uncritical supporter of the Company) that the Company's critics were ignorant both of the immediate problems of penetration from the Bay to the interior and of the underlying realities. The Company's policy, they said, was the only justifiable policy so long as the French held Canada. "Thier is a Great many Difficultys wou'd attend having a Setlement up that River, which they have not a presant Idea of," wrote Isham, "for the trade that is at York fort, and Churchill would be obstructed by such a Setlement, which would not advance or Enlarge the trade more then itt's at presant—unless the French was Dislodged from the Great Lake or Little Sea so called: which is not practicible whilst Canada is in their possession." [39]

CHAPTER 7

The English on the Prairies

The episode of Arthur Dobbs and the Parliamentary Enquiry brought out information which had hitherto not been generally available—indeed, which had not been appreciated within the Hudson's Bay Company itself. At a time when the concepts of a closed imperial economic system were undergoing serious reappraisal, the outcome was almost bound to be that, although the privileges of the Company were vindicated, the policy which had been described as the "Sleep by the Frozen Sea" was severely criticized and in part amended. Although many of the critics could be shown to be unreliable and prejudiced, during the second half of the eighteenth century the Company was aware that it was liable to challenge and that it might be neglecting opportunities.

Many of the arguments which had been raised against the Company were legal and constitutional. Practical criticism rose from allegations that the Company was inept and rigid in its trade, that it did not explore its territory or do anything to secure it for the British allegiance, and that it neglected all resources except the fur trade. Much of such criticism inevitably came from former servants of the Company, of whom the most notable was Joseph Robson, a mason who had been employed to build the fortifications at Churchill, had spent fifteen years in the Bay, and had published an *Account of Six Years Residence in Hudson's Bay*. It was he who treated the voyage of Henry Kelsey as the escapade of a troublesome boy who had run away to live with Indians so as to escape discipline, and he was equally misleading in other respects. He stated, for example, that the Company's traders never gave credit to Indians; but credit was an accepted part of the English system, and though their system did not have the flexibility of the French, it became clear during the Enquiry that the English had established a reliable relationship with their Indians, and that they were not so dominated by unrealistic rules as was claimed.

The Enquiry brought out evidence that the rigid Standard of Trade was not always kept but that each trader varied his prices according to his circumstances, so that he normally got an "overplus" which allowed him to raise prices for scarce furs or to give presents to Indians and entice them to his post. Trade was maintained on a local Standard, accounts were kept according to a London Standard, and the discrepancy within this "Double Standard" gave the "overplus," to be flexibly used.

The Enquiry revealed also that the English had maintained close relations with the "Home Guard" Indians attached to their posts but not in permanent residence on the plantations, who hunted for the posts, controlled the "goose marshes" which allowed the ice-houses to be filled with enough frozen carcases to last through the winter, and kept trade with the interior as much under their own control as they could. So far, there had been little effort to bring English and Indians together in religion or in social life; but the mingling of the blood had begun and James Isham (who should have known, for his son Charles Isham was a noted half-breed) wrote of the merits of the sons of English fathers and Indian mothers. There is no evidence at this time of any Englishman going off to live in the woods as the French did. But there is ample evidence of men climbing out from the posts to spend nights with Indians on the plantations. Robson told the Enquiry that "an Indian will gladly lend his wife to an Englishman for a bottle of brandy," and a handful of half-breeds was able to hunt and to travel with Indians, to manage canoes, and to take furs; they could also take orders, keep some sort of accounts, and make intelligible reports of the journeys which they undertook.

If the Enquiry revealed that criticism of the Company on the ground of rigidity was not always justified, it revealed that failure to explore, and failure to develop resources other than the fur trade, were not entirely justifiable charges either. In the period after the Enquiry the Company showed its reaction to criticism by pushing forward in the Eastmain and Slude River area. Some knowledge of a mica (or slude) mine on the Eastmain had come down from the earliest days of the Company, and settlement at the Slude River had been attempted from 1684 onwards.[1] The project was never taken very seriously; and though a German miner was sent out in 1701 and though Kelsey spent much of his time on the Eastmain, little was achieved. Macklish, however, reported that he had spent eleven winters on the Eastmain and that he had journals of voyages northwards from the Slude River; at least it is clear that he was capable of travelling with Indians.[2] Interest was renewed in the period after Utrecht, a post was erected to act as a permanent base and to make contact with the Eastmain more independent of sloops from Albany, and the Indians coming up from the south (from an area covered by woodrunners) were welcomed. A reasonable trade was built up, but not until 1740 were proposals in hand for drawing trade from the north rather than from the south. Then rumours of three great lakes in the hinterland began to be analysed.[3] A voyage of discovery along the Eastmain coast was organized in 1744, but the two sloops which were engaged went as far north as 56° 30′ without seeing anything to rouse comment. A fresh expedition was ordered for 1748, but this was on the eve of the Parliamentary Enquiry, and attention was directed to mineral deposits rather than to the sober realities of the fur trade.[4]

In the circumstances of 1748-49 it was inevitable that the Company should try to keep any information of the Eastmain to itself. Three Welsh miners were sent out in 1749, a new post was planned, a cargo of low-grade ore was sent to England, and a building for erection at Richmond in the Gulf of Hazard was got ready at Albany, to be erected in 1750. Then the miners were moved to the Little Whale River, where they enjoyed themselves in idleness until in 1751 the mine there was abandoned. The post was still entirely dependent on Albany for supplies and food, beaver was scarce, and the search for minerals had failed.[5] There was, however, still hope that furs might be got from the interior of Labrador, and in 1752 efforts were made to organize an expedition to explore there. Nothing happened, but the interest which the Company was showing in the Labrador Peninsula stood it in good stead when the Lords of Trade set up an enquiry, and a proposal was put forward that a separate company should be chartered for trade to Labrador. The Hudson's Bay Company could easily reply that it had spent considerable sums to open up the country but that it was a barren waste with few people, few furs, and little of anything which would repay investment.[6]

The Company, however, now had a considerable investment to recover, and so it maintained an interest in the peninsula, especially after a party of Nascopie Indians had been got down to trade at Richmond. They were sent back to their hunting grounds with presents in the hope that they would divert trade from the Atlantic coast. They never came again to trade but their visit added to the arguments for maintaining Richmond.

By the 1750's the main reason for persisting in an Eastmain establishment was the whale fishery, for at certain seasons the Little Whale River was so full of whales that the Indians had only to make a commotion to prevent them from going out of the river on the ebb tide and then walk about among the stranded beasts and kill them at leisure. Nothing was required except large numbers of Indians—but that meant generous treatment and plenty of brandy. The Indians who came in to do this work were soon debauched and unreliable; and even more difficult than the Indians were the Eskimos. Shy and elusive, they avoided direct contact with the English and were not even able to speak with them. They came over to the coast from Knapp's Island and haunted the outpost at the Little Whale

River, shadowing its hunting parties without venturing to make contact until eventually some were given presents which they accepted. Several were then taken into the post, two were even sent up to Richmond, and confidence so far outran discretion that an occasion arose on which all the men at the Little Whale River went out on their business, leaving an apprentice boy alone in the post with two Eskimos. The men returned to find the post ransacked and the boy gone, with the Eskimos. They withdrew to the main post at Richmond, and when some Eskimos appeared there, two were made hostages for the safe return of the apprentice. Adequate precautions were still not taken, and the Eskimos soon seized guns and began a fight for their freedom. They were shot; and it then became known that the boy had been killed as soon as he had been captured.[7]

The London Committee did not accept the "massacre" of 1754 as proof of failure, nor agree to abandon the post at Richmond, until 1759. But all work was at a standstill. As at Henley, ineptitude had left the English with no hold on the Eastmain as they came up to the confrontation with the French in the Seven Years' War. Henley and Richmond had proved to be failures, and at the Bottom of the Bay incentive had died down.

But there remained a continuing desire to expand from Churchill to the north and the west, and this policy was much strengthened when in 1752 Ferdinand Jacobs was made master of that post. He had twenty years of experience behind him, since he had come out to the Bay as an apprentice; and though he obeyed the Committee and pushed on with the fortification of Churchill, he also managed each year to send a sloop northwards to search out a large river, the *Kish-stack-ewen*, which was reported to run westwards a great distance into the country from somewhere between 61° and 64° north. Jacobs was convinced that a great river, perhaps even a strait, existed; but the outlet was not found until 1760.[8] Then the *Churchill* sloop sailed about a hundred miles up the river and reported that it could not be a strait which would lead to the Northwest Passage, though it was a river which would lead into the heart of the country.

Kish-stack-ewen, Bowden's Inlet, or Chesterfield Inlet, was then called the Grand River, and the voyage of 1760 would seem to have closed the argument as to whether it might be a strait leading to a passage. But in 1762 the *Churchill* sloop was again sent, accompanied by a smaller vessel which made its way two hundred and thirty miles up the river, to report that it ended in a lake with no outlet to the west. This in effect ended the efforts to find a passage in the eighteenth century. A few unimportant voyages were subsequently sent north; Whale Cove and Marble Island became reasonably familiar; but no serious expedition or significant discoveries mark the last decades of the century.

Though Ferdinand Jacobs and his successor in command at Churchill

(Moses Norton, half-breed son of the Richard Norton who had been responsible for the early attempts to reach the copper mine) were greatly taken
up with maritime exploration to the northward, they were forced to give
much of their attention to Churchill's trade from the south and west. The
Indians from Athabasca failed to come down from 1755 onwards, trade fell
off badly, and the masters had to think of missions to the interior and the
enticement of Indians down to trade. They had to face both the tradition
that Churchill's role should be slooping expeditions to the northward and
the fact that the Churchill River was a devious and unsatisfactory route
inland. It was, however, acceptable and even necessary that the upland
Indians must be made aware of the attractions which Churchill could offer
them. But it was not yet acceptable that posts inland could be justified.

The argument, generally accepted by the English until after 1770, that
in the long run inland posts would merely take trade to Indians who would
otherwise bring their furs to the posts by the Bay, applied to both York
Fort and Churchill. Logically, it applied to Henley House and to Richmond
also, and even to the new post at Moose; but precedents had been established there.

York Fort shared many of the disadvantages of Churchill, for the Nelson
River also became difficult, full of shoals, falls, and narrow channels, within
about forty miles of its mouth. But York had little concern with exploration
to the north, and James Isham as its master was a steady advocate of sending men inland. In the end he urged that a post to maintain English interests
should be sited at Cumberland Lake, that being the point at which the
routes to York and to Churchill converged. Concerned to counteract French
influence, Isham was certain that "if Factories were higher up . . . they
would bring Goods to the Lower Factories," and he argued that not only
the fur trade was involved. By sending explorers southwards and then
westwards the long-desired copper mine might be brought under British
control; and he had under his command a number of competent servants
and of English half-breeds who were willing to make journeys inland. The
London Committee was not quite convinced by Isham. He had recommended an outpost at the Severn River on the basis of an inadequate survey
and of a false rumour that the French had a house there; and he seemed
too open to the persuasions of Indians who wanted a post on every river.[9]

Though his venture at Severn proved profitable, when Isham moderately
suggested that "if a proper person were sent a great way up into the
Country with presents to the Indians it may be a means of drawing down
many of the Natives to Trade," he was merely emphasizing traditional
policy, and was told to choose a suitable person and send him inland.[10] He
showed great sense in the choice of Anthony Henday, a labourer and net-
maker at York Fort, and a one-time smuggler too. But that meant little in

the eighteenth century, when half of the tea drunk in England was smuggled past the customs. Henday had already shown ability to travel with Indians, and he had performed a useful service in measuring the distances up the Hayes River to the Fox River and Split Lake and then back down the Nelson River to York Fort. A bold and enterprising man, he volunteered for inland travel rather than spend his days in the routine of the post, and he was sent off in June 1754.[11]

Henday proved better at travelling with Indians than at setting his experiences out on paper, and his journal was severely edited because his method of travel was that of the woodrunners. He went with Indians, and he travelled in company with an Indian woman whom he uncompromisingly called his "bed fellow" and who, in addition, performed all those functions on the trail and at the portages which made an Indian squaw so invaluable. The original of his journal has not survived. A bowdlerized edition was produced by Isham, whose own "Indian wife" had incurred censure and made him keenly aware of the Committee's susceptibilities; and two other versions later came to hand from the pen of the literate and interested Master of Severn, Andrew Graham.[12]

Henday was to travel with a band of Crees who would take him up to the Saskatchewan and would there hand him over to a band of Earchthinues, members of a tribe of Indians who used the horse—the Blackfeet.[13] The horsed Indians lived and hunted away to the westwards and never came down to the Bay.

Travelling up the Hayes River and then across country to the Nelson River, Henday and his Indian companions came by way of the Fox River to Cross Lake and then to Moose Lake and the Saskatchewan. They went westwards up that river and then south to Saskeram Lake and by the Carrot River to the prairies. Here they left their canoes and marched southwest by west, hunting the red deer until they turned west to strike the south branch of the Saskatchewan somewhere in the vicinity of the modern city of Saskatoon.[14] Crossing the south branch, they moved northwest across the prairies until they came to the north branch and then followed it for about a hundred miles across what Henday called the "Muscuty Plains." He had met a band of Assiniboines, but he found that the Earchthinues were elusive, probably because the buffalo which they would be hunting at the end of August had taken a turn to the northwest. Henday and his Indians were now a band of four hundred, but they found plenty of small game, and berries and fruit were plentiful too. Before they came up with the buffalo herds they met a band of Eagle Indians who had never before seen a European, and they changed from the northwest course which they had hitherto followed, to cross the prairies in a southwesterly direction. This brought them, in the second week of September, to the great buffalo herds, "grazing like English cattle." Henday was the first Englishman to describe the hunt, with the beasts "so numerous obliged to make them sheer out of our way" and the Indians so skilled in the hunt that they could afford to take only the tongue or the hump and could leave the rest of the carcase for the wolves.

Henday was perhaps covering ground which the sons of La Vérendrye had crossed; more likely he was the first white man there. Certainly he was the pioneer in the competition of French and English traders for the furs of the Indians of the upper reaches of the Saskatchewan and the lower slopes of the Rockies. The buffalo hunt was carried out with bows and arrows, a sure sign that the influence of trade with Europeans had not yet penetrated to the western prairies.

Living in plenty, Henday and his friends travelled southwest by west until the end of September. They were then near the Red Deer River of Alberta, and there at last they met the Earchthinues, seven tents of Blood Indians, mounted on horseback, who came to visit Henday on October 1. He established friendly relations with them and rode with them for another fortnight, sometimes through "buffalo in great droves," until he came to the main camp of the Blackfeet, under their Great Leader, south of the Red Deer River, in the vicinity of the former town of Balermo. There were about two hundred tents, arranged with notable orderliness. Food was plentiful, and the horses were an impressive sight. But although Henday was welcomed he could not persuade the Blackfeet to travel down to the Bay to trade. For one thing, they lived on a meat diet and could not stomach the fish on which they would have to subsist during the long canoe journey; for another, they had not mastered the art of travelling in canoes. They did indeed promise to meet Henday again in the spring. But he was not hopeful that he would manage to get them down to the Bay.

Parting from the Blackfeet, Henday and his Indians moved off west-southwest, hunting for food in an improvident way and making no preparation for the winter, still less for the trade on which European supplies for the following year would depend. At the end of October they turned a little to the north, and towards the end of November Henday reached his most westerly point, 114° west, in latitude 51° 50' north. [15] This was a point from which the Rockies would have been visible, but Henday does not mention the fact, and the omission is interesting in view of the preoccupation of London with the search for a passage and the reaction which would have been caused by the revelation that such a barrier as the Rockies lay across the path of any overland expedition. But the precise significance of the omission cannot be estimated in ignorance of Henday's reasons—or the reasons of the post-masters who edited his journal.

This part of Henday's journal revealed that beaver and otter were numerous and easily taken in the region of Banff and Calgary, where he then was, and that the Indians of that area did not themselves bring their furs down to the Bay, nor even to the lower Saskatchewan. Wandering bands of Indians such as that with which Henday was travelling had developed a role as intermediaries, trading supplies of European goods to the Blackfeet and others, and taking their furs to the Europeans. The pattern became clear to Henday during the winter and spring as he failed to persuade his Indians to hunt for the trade and as he saw them begin their preparations for securing the hunts of the equestrian and other inland tribes by bartering the worn European equipment which they had themselves used through the winter.

Henday began to turn eastwards again in December 1754, making slowly for the north branch of the Saskatchewan, which he reached on March 3, as the ice was beginning to melt. Bear, buffalo, and deer were still hunted, and as the Indians began to make canoes for their journey down-river the camps were scenes of revelry. On St. George's Day, April 23, the ice in the river broke, and on the 28th Henday embarked in his canoe and made thirty-four miles down-stream. The flotilla with which he was travelling had grown to over sixty canoes by the time that he reached the French post at Fort la Corne on May 23. They were well loaded with furs despite their laziness during winter and spring, for they had again met the Blackfeet, who had traded furs for used guns, kettles, hatchets and knives, and hardly any of these articles were left. But the Blackfeet again refused to come down to trade at the Bay.

As they passed the French traders at La Corne, and then again at The Pas, Henday found liberal supplies of brandy available, and the French took heavy toll of the prime furs. Nevertheless, more canoes joined the flotilla every day, and when he arrived at York Fort on June 20, 1755, Henday brought with him a great wealth of furs. He had been away for just on a year and had travelled over a thousand miles, to the foot of the Rockies. If anything was needed to show that the prosperity of the English posts by the Bay depended on access to Indians of the far interior, he had provided the evidence.

In general, this was a conclusion which had already been accepted. But Henday underlined three weighty arguments, all leading to the decision that the traditional English policy of "drawing down" the Indians to trade would not work any more. He had first-hand evidence that the hunting Indians would not be "drawn down"; the Blackfeet had shown that, and on his return journey Henday had seen that they were able to get what European goods they needed without facing the hazards of the journey. He had also seen that there was a powerful Indian opposition to any policy of "drawing down" the Blackfeet. The Crees and the Assiniboines were well organized to act as middlemen, and they got a comfortable living by so doing. Henday had tried to get his own Indians to persuade the Blackfeet to make the journey to the Bay, but they remained silent since, as he wrote, "if they could be brought down to trade, the others would be obliged to trap their own Furs; which at present two thirds of them do not."[16] Lastly, Henday had revealed the grip which the French traders now had upon transport routes. On his outward journey he had found them settled at The Pas, where the younger La Vérendrye had built a post in 1748. During his wanderings Henday had often felt that although Indians "in the French interest" accepted his presents, nevertheless they would go with their trade to the French posts, and his premonitions proved true on his return journey. He was much impressed with the competence of the French traders both at La Corne and at The Pas. They had mastered "several Languages to perfection," and he commented on their mixture of familiarity and of mastery in dealing with Indians. In his view only the English monopoly of Brazil tobacco (due to friendly relations with Portugal) enticed any Indians down to the Bay; and if the French could supply that commodity they would cut off the English trade completely.

This was probably an overstatement, though not entirely unjustified. The Indians who came down to the Bay were traders, and skilful enough within their own conventions. They knew that they had to market the mixed produce of the winter's hunts of inland tribes over whom they had little control. Many furs were not of prime quality, but the French, with their attenuated transport system, could not afford transport costs on heavy and inferior furs. Henday merely observed that the French posts took many of the prime furs from the Indians as they passed on their way to the Bay; the reason was outside his brief—that none but prime furs could carry the costs of transportation to Europe by way of the Grand Portage, Lake Superior, the Ottawa River, and Montreal. The result was already known to the English. The heavy furs which the French refused formed a high proportion of those which were brought to the English posts. The conventions of this trade fitted in with Indian habits, and Henday further reported that many Indians whose furs the French had refused to take made no further effort to trade for themselves but handed their furs over to intermediaries, to act as their factors in taking them down to the English posts.

In his narrative Henday set out the physical problems and the possibilities of trade between the English posts by the Bay and the Assiniboines and the Blackfeet, who hunted the prairies and the Rockies. In his account of the trading system through which the furs came down to the Bay he brought forward strong arguments for English posts in the inland territories. But although the Hudson's Bay Committee were well pleased with his expurgated journal, and voted him a gratuity of £20, they did not accept the conclusion that the English must now build trading houses on the Saskat-chewan and on the prairies. Instead they concluded that, although bold and skilful travellers such as Henday might make inland journeys, it would not be possible to maintain a post inland from York because within four days' paddling from the coast the Nelson River ran shoal and could not be navigated by any but the smallest canoe.[17]

This was a decision based on the difficulties of the Nelson River, not on basic principles of trade or on an absolute refusal to build posts in the interior. Indeed, at that time, in 1755 as war with France seemed inevitable, the Committee decided to maintain Henley House and to build another outpost from Albany, further inland.[18] Even for the Saskatchewan and the prairies, where conditions were against inland settlement, Henday was sent off on another journey within a week of his return to York. He had a white companion this time, the ill-fated William Grover. But Grover was "jaded" before he had got ten miles up the Steel River, and the expedition was called off.[19]

Whatever the wishes of the London Committee, when Henday was sent out again in 1756 James Isham instructed him to make a note of a place which he had chosen on his first journey as a promising site for a post. This was some five hundred miles inland, and obviously Henday had discussed with Isham the need for an English post near the Forks of the Saskatchewan, rivalling the French post of La Corne. But Henday had suffered so much on his great journey that he did not complete this expedition, and it was not until 1759 that he set off to visit the Blackfeet once more. He went in com-pany with five canoes of Blackfeet, "Bloody Indians," who in spite of their protestations had managed the journey to the Bay in 1758. He also had a renegade French woodrunner with him, and another experienced English traveller, Joseph Smith.[20]

With another Englishman, Joseph Waggoner—they were known as "the two Josephs"—Smith had in 1756 made his way up the Hayes River to Lake Winnipeg, to Cedar Lake, and then south to the Assiniboine. They had conducted a profitable trade in rivalry with French traders who had no powder for the Indians and were short of other goods; the outbreak of war had interrupted trade between France and Canada.[21] In the spring of 1757 the two Josephs had journeyed to the Swan River, had built canoes and come down to York Fort by way of Oxford Lake and Knee Lake. They had carried the influence of English trade well to the south of Lake Winnipeg, into territory controlled by the French; and they had mastered the route which led at once to the Red River and the Assiniboine and to the Saskatchewan and the western lands which that river laid open. In 1757 they returned swiftly to Lake Winnipeg and then went through Lake Winnipegosis to Lake Manitoba and the Assiniboine. There they had met the Assiniboines and witnessed their way of hunting the buffalo ("boffler," as they called them) by driving them into a pound and slaughtering them. When they returned to York Fort in June 1757 the two Josephs brought with them fifty-seven canoes loaded with furs. The Indians who had accompanied them to the Bay in 1757 were sent back inland accompanied by another English servant, Isaac Batt. They took also a half-breed boy with them, and Joseph Smith went back to that area to carry on the rivalry with the French.[22]

As the struggle with France came to a head, therefore, the English were spreading their influence inland, mainly from York Fort. They were acquiring knowledge of the routes and conditions, were profiting from the difficulties which the war had brought to the woodrunners and to the French posts, and, above all, they were becoming more adventurous. The powerful combination of Henday and Joseph Smith was sent inland in 1759, their destination the foothills of the Rockies, the far end of the known routes for the French as for the English. It was of some significance that the two Englishmen were able to continue on their journey when their renegade French companion went lame and returned to York Fort; and though no journal of their voyage has survived, Henday and Smith were away until June 1760, when they brought down a flotilla of sixty-one well-laden canoes.[23] It may be safely assumed that they achieved their purpose.

The trade of York Fort was greatly improved by these expeditions, especially as the war made it increasingly hard for French traders to get supplies. For example, Indians from the Sturgeon River area, bordering on the north branch of the Saskatchewan and Swan Lake, began to come down to York in increasing numbers. But alongside this success at York must be set a steady decline in the trade of Churchill. This was all the more remarkable because that post was under the vigorous command of Moses Norton who, after a year of temporary command in 1759-60, managed the post from 1762 until his death in 1773. His predecessor at Churchill, Ferdinand Jacobs, had accepted the need to send men inland to counter the French (and was to take a formative part in the southern thrust when he had transferred to the command at York Fort). Jacobs had been responsible for sending William Grover inland from York in 1759, to seek out the Athabasca Indians who had failed to come down to trade in 1758. It was an unfortunate venture, for Grover's companion, a "very Honest Good Leading Indian," went sick only twenty-four miles from the post. Grover turned back and was at Churchill again within three days; the Indian quickly recovered and resumed his journey! But next year Norton was able to welcome at Churchill a party of Indians who had never previously made the journey, and they were followed by Indians who had never seen a European, let alone a factory.[24]

From 1762 the trade of Churchill improved steadily. Though William

Grover had failed and though the Churchill River had not answered as an approach to the interior, the French had failed to satisfy their Indians, and this failure had coincided, most fortunately, with a change in English policy and ability. While the two Josephs and their companions were showing the "Upland Indians" the advantages of trading with the English, the French were losing their bases in Montreal and Quebec, were losing their ability to supply the Indians, and, despite their threats and boasts, were losing the confidence of many of their allies.

Not all the English expeditions were successful, but they continued in a succession which marked a shift in policy and which was in clear contrast to the way in which even the better French traders were forced to desert their Indians during these years. In 1761 Joseph Waggoner noted (as he conducted sixty-five canoes of "Upland Indians" down to trade) that the two French houses on the Saskatchewan, La Corne and The Pas, were deserted.[25] These were key positions. Their abandonment meant that while Wolfe and his troops were capturing Canada, the two Josephs and their companions, following in the footsteps of Anthony Henday, were taking possession of the prairies up to the foot of the Rockies.

CHAPTER 8

The Pedlars from Canada

At the Parliamentary Enquiry of 1749 James Isham had said that it would not pay the British to set up posts inland unless the French were dislodged from the area of Lake Winnipeg, and that this was impossible as long as Canada remained in their possession. In this he was thinking in terms of national rivalry, not of geography; and when the French had been driven from Canada, the relative merits of an approach to the inland beaver meadows and buffalo plains from Montreal and from Hudson Bay remained an open question. It had been a historical accident that the two routes should have fallen into the possession of rival nations; when both routes were placed under British control a conflict between the partisans of the two approaches remained, and, if anything, the bitterness of the opposition increased.

The route from Montreal to the prairies lay in the hands of British subjects after the Peace of Paris. They had supplies of goods, markets, and claims to military protection, equal to those the Hudson's Bay Company enjoyed. Even before the definitive treaty had been signed there were indications of new rivals, using the old routes; and the new "interlopers" were more vigorous and unscrupulous than the French had been. The masters of the Hudson's Bay Company's posts quickly warned that they were being opposed by "Interlopers who will be more Destructive to our Trade than the French was." Fur-trade rivalry in the Northwest would henceforth be conducted between the Company and other British citizens, not French nationals, and between the two groups would lie the chartered privileges of the Company and the geographical merits and demerits of the routes which they used.

The Charter of the Company had survived the attacks of Arthur Dobbs, but exclusive corporations were in disrepute at a time when the doctrines of free trade were gaining general assent. Even the Royal Prerogative, on which the Charter rested, was under discussion, and the area which the

Company might claim was also ill defined. In the period after the Treaty of Utrecht, and again after Aix-la-Chapelle, satisfactory boundaries for Rupert's Land had not been agreed upon with the French; since nothing had seemed to be at stake except the fur trade and since little was known of the geography of the boundary regions, while the Company itself was insistent that possession of the land in a European sense was not necessary so long as the Indians could be "drawn down" to trade, the British diplomatists had not pressed for decisions. With considerable authority the English traders maintained that the Indians directed the flow of trade, and they were "altogether a wandering people" who were not to be coerced or parcelled out by European powers. They traded where they wished, and boundaries allocated by Europeans had little significance and could not, in any case, be accurately set out.

It is not, therefore, surprising that the southern boundary of Rupert's Land occupied little attention as British statesmen drew up the Treaty of Paris. When Canada was transferred to British rule the boundary would become a domestic problem, between two groups of British subjects. But since the French of Canada then became "New Subjects" of the British king, privileged in their laws, their language, and their religion, rather than subject to discrimination, they were in a strong position to challenge the Company's claims. This position was greatly strengthened by the attitude of the Indians.

Although the Iroquois had taken part in the war on the British side, the Hurons and the Ottawas, who commanded the routes to the west and the north, remained allies of the French. The *postes du nord* had indeed been ceded to the British in 1760. But the loyalties of the western Indians counted for more than the failure of the French government, and though Major Rogers and his Rangers managed to secure Detroit, Miamis, and Ouiatanon in 1760, the posts at Michilimackinac, Ste Marie, Green Bay, and St Joseph remained in French hands until 1761. The English when they came were not even fur-traders but soldiers, engaged in the task of "pacifying" the Indians, men fully convinced that the Indians should never be given presents or "bribes" for friendly behaviour, but should be punished if they caused trouble.[1]

Both while the *postes du nord* remained in their possession and after they had been officially taken over by the English, the French traders continued to maintain relations with their Indians, and in 1761 the Hudson's Bay Company's Committee got information of the state of affairs in the interior from a French renegade who brought some Sturgeon River Indians to trade at Albany. He brought a report that Michilimackinac still served as a great emporium for the northern trade, while Ste Marie was still outfitting traders for the Mississippi.[2] The Chippewas and other tribes, trading to these posts, firmly rejected any notion that they had been captured with their lands. "Englishmen," said the chief of the Chippewas, "although you have conquered the French, you have not yet conquered us";[3] and though an Indian rising was avoided in 1761 and again in 1762, the Great Conspiracy of Pontiac broke out in 1763, with the powerful tribe of the Ottawas leading a movement to drive the British out from all the posts. When the Conspiracy had been crushed, the military (with General Amherst as Commander-in-Chief) were convinced that only fear would wean the Indians from their inborn treachery and would make traders or settlers safe in the Indian lands.

British views were also coloured by geographical ignorance, by hostility to chartered corporations, by doctrines of freedom of trade, and by reluctance to accept the costs of defending and administering the apparently valueless territories which had been ceded. Although it had cost so much to conquer, Canada was almost thrown back to France, and the arrangements for its rule were made in a period when the objective of statesmen was the establishment of an empire of trade but not of governance.[4] Enlightened interest in non-European peoples, and the beginnings of the humanitarianism which marked the end of the eighteenth century, played their parts in the formulation of a policy which, if based on ignorance, was nevertheless enlightened in intention. It was ordered that a "new policy" for Indian lands should be adopted, extending to the lands which had been ceded at the Peace the practices which had been followed during the war. The "new policy" rested on the view that it would be dangerous to grant lands for European settlement which might "interfere with the Indians bordering them." It was in part based on a desire to reserve adequate lands for the Indians; this arose both from humanitarian convictions and from the argument that they must be preserved in their hunting way of life if they were to produce the furs which enabled them to buy the British manufactures which they needed. The desire to preserve large areas for the Indians was also supported because it was thought dangerous to allow the spread westwards of a numerically weak colonial society. Adopted as early as 1761, the "new Indian policy" was extended when the French possessions came under consideration.[5] Under Lord Shelburne at the Board of Trade, the new policy emerged as a plan to preserve for the Indians a vast tract of land in the region of the Great Lakes, which should be open for trade but not for settlement. Neither Canadian rule nor the rule of the British colonies was to be extended to this territory; authority would be vested in superintendents for Indian affairs, supported by the military. Acute disagreement arose over the withdrawal of such a reservation from the jurisdiction of the government which was to be set up in Canada. Egremont, as Secretary of State, strongly supported the extension of Canadian rule to the borders of

Rupert's Land on the one hand and to the Mississippi on the other; Shelburne at the Board of Trade urged that these lands must be separated off from Canada if only because the fur trade of these vast but as yet unknown regions (which had never hitherto been under Canadian rule) must not be directed to Canada to the detriment of the Hudson's Bay Company and of the New England fur-traders.

Both Shelburne and Egremont were out of the way—the one resigned, the other dead—when the Proclamation of October 7, 1763, declared that all lands not already surrendered by Indian tribes were reserved to them, no further private purchases of land could be made from Indians, and any white man who settled on Indian lands was to be removed. West of the Appalachians no further grants of land for settlement were to be made, and it was deemed "justice and humanity as well as sound policy" that the areas so reserved should be "left under Your Majesty's immediate Protection to the Indian Tribes for their hunting grounds." Thus the fur trade, and the market for selling English manufactures to the Indians, were to be preserved; the Indians were to be maintained in their natural ways of life, and the costs of organized government were to be avoided.[6] Within these conditions there was to be complete freedom of trade. Subject to their obtaining a licence from the Governor-General and to their observing the restrictions ordered, "New Subjects" and "Old Subjects" alike would have free access to the Indian trade. No charge would be made for licences, but trade would be allowed only at certain points, at which controls would be enforced.

When details of the "Imperial Plan" for the Indian trade (of which the Proclamation of October 7, 1763, was the embodiment) were worked out, it was estimated that a revenue of about £20,000 a year was required; and when the Board of Trade had decided that it would not do to raise this sum by a tax on the fur trade, the alternative adopted was the Stamp Act, with all its baleful consequences. In the meantime the fur-traders and the colonial governments showed that the "Imperial Plan" was unworkable. The traders from Montreal protested against all the features of the plan, the licences, inspections, restrictions to established posts, vetoes on expansion towards the south and the Mississippi, edicts against forcible collection of debts from Indians, price regulations, and corruption of officials. Memoranda multiplied, and they reveal that the merchants of Montreal quickly became predominantly non-French. Some were English, many Scottish; an important few came from the American colonies. They exercised considerable power, and they maintained the barrister, Fowler Walker, to represent them in London. The Governor of Quebec, General Murray, described them as "these Licentious Fanaticks Trading here"; they accused him of brutal violence, and secured his replacement by Sir Guy Carleton, who proved more sympathetic.[7] They combined to put their case, but they were marked individualists. Their strength may be judged by their success in getting rid of General Murray and in achieving the reduction of the import duty on beaver brought into England to a penny a skin, in 1765.

Their manipulations reveal that many "Old Subjects" of the Crown had followed the troops north during the war and had begun to participate in the fur trade even before terms of peace were settled. They used the French routes westwards from Montreal, employed the woodrunners, and adopted the French attitude towards the Indians and to the trade. The French, though they were given the same rights as the English, for the most part either ceased to trade independently or turned from the Grand Portage and the Northwest and devoted most of their energies to the southern trade, to Detroit, the Illinois, and the Mississippi. Those French Canadians who remained in the northwest trade tended (though not completely) to become woodrunners, or subordinate partners of the merchants who outfitted them. For example, in 1761 a partnership consisting of Forrest Oakes, James Goddard, and William Grant (all of them new arrivals in Canada and of New England origin) began to call itself the N. W. Société; its first (and only) venture was to outfit a Frenchman, La Fleur, for trade at Michilimackinac.[8] Within a similar partnership the elder Alexander Henry went up to Michilimackinac in 1761, got involved in the Conspiracy of Pontiac, and barely escaped with his life. Henry had come up to Montreal from Albany and Oswego as a supply-merchant provisioning the British army, and in 1761 he entered a partnership with the French trader, Etienne Cadotte. They reached Michilimackinac ahead of the troops who were supposed to reduce it to submission, and they found several other traders already there.

Many men who followed the British troops into Canada and took to the fur trade there achieved lasting success—Alexander Henry himself, Forrest Oakes, Bostwick, Tracy, Goddard, and the Jew, Ezekiah Solomons—and two reputable and durable concerns soon emerged. One was under control of the three brothers Frobisher, the other under Isaac Todd and James McGill. They had all come from the southern fur trade, working from Lake Michigan and Detroit rather than from the Grand Portage; and they had all made fortunes and could command credit before they began to trade from Montreal. Above all, they knew the English market both for the purchase of goods and for the sale of furs. This was important for the survival of the Canadian economy at a time when France was unable to supply goods, especially heavy woollens, and when the administrative chaos which produced the French Revolution enmeshed the fur trade along with the domestic industry of France.

The licences, which were issued under the terms of the Proclamation of October 7, 1763, and the subsequent Regulations of June 1764, do not survive as a complete series, and it is also clear that not all who traded to the west secured licences. But, making all allowances, it is certain that the supplies going into the west were small in amount. If trade went well, from sixty to a hundred canoes might be brought down to trade, and the annual trade fair at Montreal remained a populous and colourful spectacle. But the numbers who went off to winter with the Indians remained limited. In 1767, for example, only seven canoes were licensed for trade in the Northwest—one Englishman to trade at Grand Portage, one garrison officer, and five Frenchmen who had financial backing from Englishmen. In all, one hundred and twenty-one canoes were licensed to trade out from Michilimackinac in that year, taking goods to the value of almost £40,000. The greater part of this went to the Illinois, the Mississippi, Lake Michigan, and the Southwest, while only fourteen canoes, with goods valued at £5,117 10s. 7d., were licensed to go "by Lake Superior to the N'-West."[9] Even allowing for unlicensed traders, this was not a strong threat to the Hudson's Bay men.

But the trading habits of the Indians meant that, as long as there was competition, the Indians would control the trade; and the habits of the traders themselves ensured that competition should be fully exploited. It was normal and quite reputable to entice an Indian to part with skins which were already pledged to another trader, and fraud and trickery were commonplace. Traders found that any kind of competition upset prices over immense distances and made it impossible to trade by standards based on costs of production and of transport.

The pattern of the Indian trade which developed from the "new policy" should, in theory, hardly have affected the Hudson's Bay Company at all, for the Company's territories and privileges were exempted from the proclamations. But it was not to be expected that the vigorous "Pedlars" who were linking up the markets of London with the skills of Montreal should respect the Company's privileges and claims; nor, indeed, that they would accept the controls which embodied the new system. They evaded the licensing laws, secured the replacement of Murray by Carleton and, having got a friend in office, exploited his friendship to the full. The particular regulation against which they objected was that which confined trade to posts, where it could be controlled. French and English alike opposed this, saying that it would drive the Indians to trade with the French and the Spaniards who came up the Mississippi from the south, and would divert the fur trade of the St Lawrence to the Gulf of Florida.[10] With Carleton in power, the Montreal traders got permission to trade in the villages north and west of the Great Lakes, so that this restriction no longer applied to the Northwest trade. Already there was an organized system of evasion in practice and Major Rogers, in command at Michilimackinac, organized journeys under James Carver and James Tute to seek trade in the west, perhaps even to reach China by way of the prairies; he also set on foot a drive to extend the fur trade of Michilimackinac to the area of the Assiniboine and the Saskatchewan. These were areas in which the delimitations of Rupert's Land and the rights of the Hudson's Bay Company, as well as the geographical advantages of the transport system from the posts by the Bay, were disputed by the traders from Canada.

The first point for decision was the restriction on trading in the Indian villages. By 1767 evasion was so general that there seemed no sensible course except to make the regulations conform to facts.[11] Accordingly, in 1768 it was decided that the colonial legislatures would be the best judges of what their several situations would require and that regulation should be left to them. Local pressures could now triumph over the paternalism of Westminster, and settlers and traders could invade the Indian reservation; the effect was not the less serious because Hillsborough, when he took office as Secretary of State for the Colonies in 1768, emphasized the need to care for Indians, to establish definite and permanent boundaries for their reservations, and to prevent infiltration of settlers into the reserved lands. Colonial governors and legislatures were in no position to resist pressure, and though the Treaty of Fort Stanwix of 1768 forbade white settlement beyond the frontier then agreed, the shift of responsibility to the colonial legislatures and governors meant that the firm frontier and the Indian reservation which had been features of the New Indian Policy had been abandoned. In fact, the fur trade south of the Ohio was left open to traders from the southern colonies, Virginia, Maryland, Georgia, and Carolina. The rest of the Indian country was partitioned among the other colonies, Pennsylvania taking control of the Ohio, New York taking the trade of the Iroquois south of Lake Erie, and Canada taking the great fur-bearing areas and routes of the north and west.

Thus, while New York was supposed to control Niagara and Detroit, Sault Ste Marie and Michilimackinac and the whole area of the Great Lakes were placed under Canada. But the colonial governors had no revenue allocated to this purpose, and effective control of the fur trade which ran south from the Great Lakes, as well as that to the north, was soon assumed by Canada. Nothing was achieved by attempts to agree on a policy acceptable to all the colonies, and it proved impossible to find any ground for agreement between Quebec and New York. "The interests of the two Provinces in regard to the Indian Trade differ too widely, to expect they will ever perfectly agree on general Regulations for carrying it on," wrote the Lieutenant-Governor of Quebec.[12]

As Canada's sphere of control was enlarged, Canadian traders, whether of French or of English origin, found fresh opportunities. Abandonment of

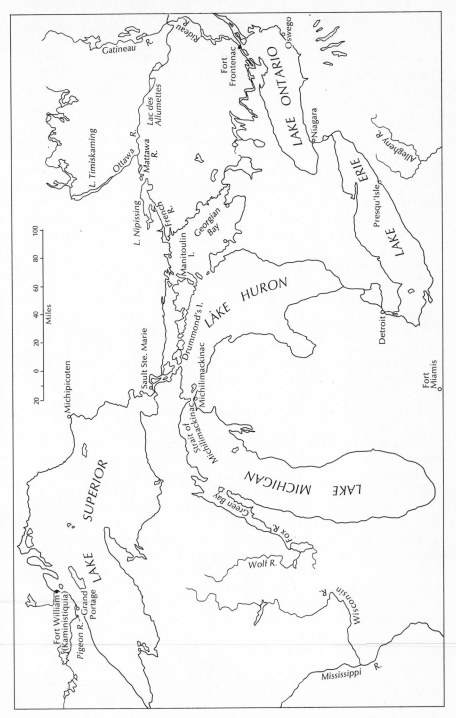

The Great Lakes

the system of licences also benefited them greatly since the long journey to Lake Superior, and so to the southwest or the northwest as the case might be, could not be completed out and back in one year and would not fit a system of annual licences. The length of their route also meant that they were forced to trade for food as they went, and so they could not accept the rule that all trade must be confined to posts. When freed from the controls of the "imperial system" the Canadians showed great vigour, organizing a shipping system for their goods on the Great Lakes and turning Sault Ste Marie into a wealthy rendezvous. The traders profited by their friendship with Carleton and his desire to "enlarge our Commerce to the utmost," and secured the "same Liberty of Trading up the Rivers" as the French had formerly enjoyed.[13] By April 1768 Hillsborough was faced with a choice between throwing the fur trade open to all or else providing revenue for enforcement of regulations. The colonial governors had shown their inability to provide for enforcement and Hillsborough chose the easy course, declaring the fur trade open to all and abandoning the licence system.[14]

The petitions which led up to this step and the evidence of the licences themselves show that no great number of merchants was in a position to take advantage of this freedom to trade. There were, for example, only fifty-seven signatures to a petition to Governor Carleton in September 1766. But a mercantile oligarchy of fifty-seven merchants is not negligible either in local politics or in local finance. The "Pedlars from Quebec," as the Hudson's Bay men called them, had won a charter of liberty; and it was inevitable that they would challenge the Company's privileges in Rupert's Land.

The threat was all the more dangerous because it came at a time when the Hudson's Bay Company was unable to send its own men inland; the initiative given by Kelsey, and more recently by Henday and the two Josephs and their companions, had slipped away. In 1761 Indians reported that the French had deserted their inland posts; but York Fort, which in 1759 had been able to send four men inland in three different directions, was unable to send in a single man in 1762.[15] Henday himself had been allowed to come home, the two Josephs, Isaac Batt, and George Potts had all been discharged, and the team of inland voyagers had to be recreated when in 1763 the Company turned to seize the opportunities which the capture of Canada offered. Then Smith, Waggoner, and Batt were re-engaged while new men were recruited expressly for the purpose of inland travel. Old and new, they were illiterate, and the value of their journeys is difficult to assess. It is not even clear exactly where they went. Not until a French deserter, Louis Primeau, was recruited in 1765, did the Company manage an effective opposition to the vigorous Pedlars. Then in 1766 Primeau and five other men were sent inland from York Fort, Primeau to the Churchill River, the others to the north and the south branch of the Saskatchewan, to the Sturgeon River, and to Alberta's Red Deer River.[16] They spread the area of the Company's trade and greatly increased its volume, though they brought little information about the Canadian traders since they did not move far enough south to make contact with them.

But in 1767, on their return from a similar series of journeys, the "inland traders" reported that "French" goods were in use on the Saskatchewan and that "French" trade was reviving. This, of course, was really "English" trade, run for the most part by "Old Subjects" of the Crown even when the active traders were "New Subjects." It used trade goods of English origin. In 1768 it was reported that on the Saskatchewan a "French" house had been established under François le Blanc, with twelve Frenchmen under his command. They were dispensing presents freely, and they spoke of trade goods coming up from Montreal and of the folly of alienating the woodrunners by friendship with the Hudson's Bay men.[17] The English had by then recovered something of their impetus, and they managed to secure a fair proportion of the trade. But the Indians again had two markets available, and they made the most of their position.

Indian wars were alleged as a cause when trade returns fell off at the Bottom of the Bay and when the trade of York declined in 1768. But Ferdinand Jacobs and the other experienced traders knew that the real cause was that the "French" were with the Indians in the places where they caught the furs. Competition was general, and its effects spread far beyond the limits to which the traders penetrated. But competition was not one-sided. The "English" traders also posed a threat to the "Pedlars," who felt the pressure particularly in the focal area of Lake Winnipeg and its rivers.

The springboard for the next "English" push was not York Fort or Churchill but the small outpost at the Severn River. The master there, Andrew Graham, an outstanding naturalist and collector, was also a keen-minded strategist. In 1767 he chose William Tomison and sent him inland, still to carry out the traditional task of bringing the Indians down to trade by the Bay. At Lake Winnipeg Tomison found the Indians awaiting the arrival of the "French," who had gone down to Grand Portage to bring up more goods.[18] Tomison's arrival before the "French" had returned emphasized the superiority of the approach-route from the Bay. But there were two "French" houses on the Red River, and reports of three more to the west; and during the winter a further "French" post was set up at The Pas on the Saskatchewan. Tomison's evidence strongly reinforced that which Jacobs was getting at York Fort from the men whom he was sending inland, and Jacobs's conclusion was that the old policy must be abandoned. Instead of solitary emissaries, instructed not to trade but merely to draw the Indians down to the Bay, a party of about fifteen men "with a Carefull

Prudent man to Command them" must be sent to build posts at the most convenient places and to trade as the "French" did. Recognizing that nothing could make it easy to build and maintain canoes at the posts by the Bay, he suggested (as Isbester had done for the upkeep of Henley House) shallow-draft boats to get the necessary goods inland.[19]

It took more than a full year for Jacobs's suggestion to reach London, to be considered there, and for orders and goods to reach the Bay. In the meantime resistance to the Pedlars took shape in the re-establishment in 1766 of Henley House; but that post was still to be subordinate to Albany and was still to trade at a harsher standard than that which the Indians would enjoy if they made the journey down to the Bay.[20] The old principle was reaffirmed. But the dogma had lost its value, and by 1770 Henley was equipped as a trade post, the traditional view preserved only in the instruction that trade was to be avoided there except in case of urgent necessity.[21] Reluctance to change policy, derived from the disasters at Henley and from fears that inland masters would compete with the posts by the Bay, would indulge in private trade, and would take to women and to drink, is also evident in the reaction to Jacobs's proposals. Conceding the need to depart from established policy and accepting the merits of an inland post, the Committee ordered that only a limited selection of goods should be sent inland, preferred the use of canoes to boats, and made no arrangements for manning a post if it should be established.[22] The instructions arrived too late in 1769 for Jacobs to do anything about them that year.

Pedlars were by then reported to be everywhere through the Company's territories. In particular James Finlay, an Englishman from Montreal, was reported to be at Nipawi, near the Forks of the Saskatchewan. This might well be the post containing twelve men which had been reported in 1768; and just as William Tomison had then reported three other posts to the west, so now Jacobs was informed that there were three other "French" posts in the region. The Pedlars were boasting that they would come all the way to the Bay to trade whenever they wished, and Finlay declared that the order of 1768, because it abandoned the system of licences, had set the trade free. He challenged the Company, or anyone else, to exclude him from trade in Rupert's Land.[23] While rumours abounded of the Pedlars lining every creek, stopping Indians by force, and even killing some to prevent them from trading to the Bay, many of the Hudson's Bay men wanted to meet force with force and to "remove those thieves off your Land." But the London Committee were reluctant to provoke legal controversy about the validity of the Charter, and so, although the Company's canoes were plundered in 1768 and again in 1769, the men were forbidden to use force.

The Pedlars were as much in opposition to each other as to the Company's men, and they demonstrated a great variety of approaches and organizations. While Finlay was a powerful and well-equipped merchant, Thomas Corry was a skilled and experienced trader, but with little financial strength. When in 1770 he set up a post at Cedar Lake he had the partnership of Todd and McGill behind him, to finance him and to take the furs which he traded.[24] In 1771 he was at Cedar Lake again, doing a fine trade and well sited to intercept Indians on their way from Lake Winnipegosis and Cedar Lake to the Bay. But two of Corry's men deserted to York Factory in 1772; they were followed down to the Bay by a letter from Corry, to suggest that he and the Hudson's Bay men might work together, they mending the Indians' guns and helping to recover property which, he maintained, the deserters had stolen. He had won the friendship of the Indians, but at the cost of so much debauchery that they had made their worst hunt for years. The leading Indian had drunk so much brandy that he was useless; but Corry intended to take him to Grand Portage "to Drinke two or three Caskes." The letter itself was written from a scene of "Confusion with two hundred Drunken Vilions about me," from Corry's post as The Pas.[25] The deserters, and the Hudson's Bay men who had been inland, rounded out the picture, saying that Corry's was "a decent kind of house" which he was preparing to improve and that he had with him thirty men whom he had brought in from Grand Portage.

Behind such traders lay powerful combinations of merchants and supply-houses. The trade goods used by Corry were procured from England by an organization headed by Chief Justice Walker, who broke bulk at Quebec and sent the goods to a partnership of two Frenchmen, Blondeau and Keshew, at Montreal. That partnership sent the goods up to Michilimackinac, to the order of another partnership consisting of Isaac Todd, George McBeath, and two "Indian traders" of whom one was Corry himself, the other being John Erskine, who managed a little post upstream on the Saskatchewan from Corry. There may have been yet a third "Indian trader" attached to the partnership. From Michilimackinac the goods were brought through Lake Superior to Kaministikwia and the Grand Portage in canoes forty feet long, with crews of seven men. It took ten days and a considerable organization to get the goods over the Grand Portage and then, using smaller northern canoes, they were taken to the Saskatchewan by way of Rainy Lake, Lake of the Woods, and Lake Winnipeg. The journey from the Grand Portage to The Pas, and so to the Northwest, would take as much as six weeks, and involved over a hundred and thirty carrying places.[26]

Compared with the simple expedient of "drawing down" the Indians to the Bay, the difficulties of such a route are obvious. But the system yielded profits, and it drove the Pedlars ever further into the Northwest. It also diminished the volume of trade by the Bay, and it culled off the finest and lightest furs. It made far heavier demands on the men than did the Hudson's Bay system; and this was a consideration which the Company could not overlook when it seemed impossible that any number of the Company's servants could meet the requirements of such a technique. It was, also, possible to meet Canadian competition simply by buying Canadian furs in Montreal or Quebec and then controlling their appearance on the London market. The Company gave serious consideration to this possibility and to the possibility of employing Canadian servants[27] before it reached its conclusion, in 1769, that the posts by the Bay must still be paramount, but that the minimum trading commitment was to be undertaken inland.[28]

The information which led to this decision was gloomy. The Pedlars were "swarming" up-country, and the harshness with which they traded was offset by the generosity with which they gave credit and supplied spirits. They were not only absorbing the trade; they were making the Indians indolent and insolent. The numbers who lived by trading rather than by hunting had greatly increased since Henday had reported on this feature, and consequently the Canadian traders were spreading rapidly westwards as they tried to get past the trading Indians and to deal with the hunting Indians. The only cheerful aspect was that the Pedlars often lost control of the Indians as they drove their trade too hard. The Pedlars' canoes were plundered in 1769, and in 1770 both their upper and their lower houses at The Pas were deserted.[29]

This reaction by the Indians seemed to underline the conclusion that the Pedlars should be left to create their own difficulties, on top of those which their long approach-route entailed. They lacked any central organization which could give them the advantages of bulk-purchase or of bulk-selling, they were split by competition at every stage of their trade, and since they relied on the vigour and hardihood of their Indian traders they often suffered from the complementary qualities of indiscipline and irresponsibility. The way in which the Pedlars conducted their trade certainly seemed to the Hudson's Bay Committee to be insecure and dangerous. But the situation which had developed by 1770 was not that which the Company had expected as a consequence of the British taking possession of Canada. So far was the result from easing the burden of French competition that it was becoming increasingly apparent that the only answer to the uncompromising rivalry with which the "Old Subjects" of the Crown had taken over the fur trade of Canada must be to take the Company's trade also to the Indians in the places where they caught their furs.

CHAPTER 9

Trading Posts Inland:
Cumberland House

Though the traders by the Bay felt convinced that they would have to go inland, the Committee in London still hoped that the troubles into which the Pedlars ran, and the comparative instability of their financial structure, would cause their trade to collapse. The reports and opinions of the masters of the posts, moreover, were seldom clear; local knowledge went with local prejudice; ignorance and special pleading filled the memoranda in favour of carrying the Company's trade inland. The argument would need to be put clearly and convincingly if the traditional English policy was to be changed—unless profits declined; and the Company was paying a steady 10 per cent dividend through these years.[1]

The case for establishing trading posts inland was at last effectively presented when Andrew Graham took command at York Fort. There he had under him Edward Umfreville, a "pretty accountant" who had already done well at Severn, also an advocate of inland trading. Together, in 1772, they submitted a memorandum which went far to change policy. When Graham had sent William Tomison inland from the Severn River in 1767 he had been told that the Pedlars were overrunning Rupert's Land. Like Ferdinand Jacobs at York Fort, he saw no remedy but forcible ejection; but this was forbidden by the London Committee. Jacobs's plans for a post inland, using boats as a means of transport, met half-hearted support and he, though very ready to "remove those thieves off your Land,"[2] was not sure that there was much to be said for an inland post which was merely a place "to live in quietly and Encourage the Indians to come to Trade."[3]

Graham shared these feelings and had sent Tomison inland for a second journey to the Saskatchewan, which had again proved discouraging. Tomison's information tied in with reports from William Pink, James Allen, and James Dearing, who had been sent up-country from York Fort. The Pedlars were "swarming" (though in truth there cannot have been more than a score of them); they were interrupting trade to the Bay, and they were making the Indians of Lake Winnipeg, Cedar Lake, and the Saskatchewan idle and dangerous. Graham maintained that sending men inland "must be of some service",[4] but the defects of the system so far used were apparent, and when in 1772 Jacobs went on leave and Graham took command at York Fort, he gave his attention to a plan for avoiding the defects of inland trading. All would depend on a young lively master, who should have at his disposal two canoes and fourteen men.[5] For master, Graham suggested either Thomas Hutchins, a competent accountant and clerk, or Samuel Hearne, a former naval officer with a capacity for accurate surveying and description.

While his suggestion was being sent to London, Graham put preparations in hand. Since all must depend on accurate information, he decided to send inland Matthew Cocking, who "readily offered himself" when approached. Cocking had served the company as a writer and had been made second-in-command at York Fort in 1765. He had experience of face-to-face trading with Indians, and he had real ability and honesty. Though his instruments failed him, and he had little skill as a surveyor, his *Journal of a Journey Inland with the Natives* is clear, well written, and informative. He set off from York Fort towards the end of June, 1772, and made for The Pas on the Saskatchewan by way of Knee Lake, Cross Lake, and Moose Lake.[6] From The Pas he went up the Saskatchewan and then through Saskeram to the Forks of the Saskatchewan, to the Eagle Hills and the great plains to the southwest. There, as Henday had done before him, Cocking met horsed Indian tribes, this time the Gros Ventres; and like Henday, he failed to persuade them to come to trade at the Bay, for they still could not manage canoes and they still disliked the prospect of a fish diet as they travelled. He also found it impossible to convince the Indians that the Company would not set up trading establishments inland. Knowing the way in which the Pedlars traded inland, and that some of the Company's men were notorious traders, the Indians refused to believe Cocking when he insisted that he was not there to trade. Cocking himself argued that, since the Pedlars often established strong personal ties with Indians inland, there was little likelihood that the Company could cut in on them except by similar practices. Every year in which the Pedlars alone traded in the interior diminished the chances of drawing Indians down to the Bay.

Although Cocking was a competent penman, his journal, like that of Henday, was edited by Andrew Graham before it was sent to London. There are considerable differences between Cocking's own narrative and the version of his journal which became known to the general public through the compilation of Graham's *Observations on Hudson's Bay*, especially where the "French Canadians" are concerned. In the printed versions Cocking is made to remark on the "warm side" which the Indians had to the "French"; but in fact he noted that the Indians plundered the "French" and kept them in fear. Yet he concluded that the Indians would trade to the Bay only if the Pedlars failed them; the sole remedy was to build an inland settlement, and he concluded his narrative with an appendix of "Thoughts on making a Settlement Inland." Cocking realized that the Company's "inlanders," especially the French renegade, Louis Primeau, were abusing their freedom; they were notorious private traders, and were building up ill-feeling against the Company while several had private arrangements with Pedlars. A Hudson's Bay house on the Saskatchewan was necessary; and it would have to be kept supplied by canoes since boats could not be got past the portages.

Cocking argued, further, that a Hudson's Bay house must be at The Pas, or even higher up, since the Pedlars could reach that far up the Saskatchewan and they must be outdistanced. Though troubled by sickness, he had reached the Birch Hills, where he discarded his canoe, in forty-five days; and he reckoned that in a normal year this could be done in twenty days from the Bay. This gave the Hudson's Bay men an enormous advantage over the Pedlars, and Cocking argued that they ought always to be able to keep their posts a little farther up the Saskatchewan than their rivals. He noted the number and the strength of the Pedlars' posts, and he reported on their trading methods. On his way inland he found their posts deserted—at The Pas, higher up the Saskatchewan where a Canadian (Franceways: François) had traded in 1768-69, and further on where he had traded subsequently; it was not until midwinter that he found Franceways at the middle house, at Nipawi. Franceways then had five canoes of goods with him, and there were three more canoes up-stream from The Pas; down-stream were four more canoes belonging to Pedlars; there were four north, on the route to York Factory, and several others in places all the way to the Grand Portage. Cocking observed Corry's trading methods at Cedar Lake, and he concluded that the great advantage which the Pedlars had over the Hudson's Bay men was that their Standards of Trade were flexible. Gifts, and especially drams, were "above all Perswasion" attractive to the Indians. Cocking found one Pedlar, William Bruce, who had come into the northern trade from the Mississippi and the south, anxious to do a deal with him, and he was not unduly depressed. He saw the Pedlars being plundered and put upon, and he felt that the Company could be as attractive as any Pedlar. But a completely new approach, and a determination to make a trading settlement inland, would be necessary.

If further arguments had been needed, Cocking's *Journal* would have provided the Hudson's Bay Committee with reasons for establishing a trading post inland. In fact, they had made up their minds before they received his *Journal*. In May 1773 they instructed Ferdinand Jacobs that, in view of the way in which the Pedlars had intercepted the Indians, they would establish a trading house near The Pas on the Saskatchewan. Seventeen extra men were sent out for the purpose, and an assortment of trading goods. For transportation the Committee relied on Andrew Graham's report that he had ordered two of the large Indian canoes to be sent down from inland. They hoped to get more of such canoes as the project developed. The Instructions of 1773 were clear; a log hut was to be built, and the expedition was to trade furs which the Indians brought in.[7]

The Committee fully expected that Matthew Cocking would be sent inland once more, but they decided that Samuel Hearne should be master of the inland post. Hearne had served in the Royal Navy from the age of eleven until, in 1766 at the age of twenty-one, he had taken employment with the Company. He had been appointed to Churchill, where the half-breed Moses Norton was in command and where the search for the copper mine and for the Northwest Passage (heritages from Moses Norton's father Richard) still dominated policy.[8] Moses Norton himself had been on the northern voyages of 1761, 1762, 1763, and 1764, and had sailed up Bowden's Inlet until it was clear that it was not a Northwest Passage. By the end of 1764 he was "Certain and Shure that there is no Passage into the Western Ocean in this Hudson's Bay."[9] Norton then continued normal slooping voyages northwards from Churchill, and Samuel Hearne as mate of the sloop learned much about northern navigation.

Norton's ambition to reach the copper mine (of whose existence, somewhere, there could be no reasonable doubt, so constant and explicit were the Indian reports) at this time began to take the shape of an overland journey in company with Indians. To make such an expedition possible he would first have to overcome opposition between those he called the "Northern Indians" (the Chipewyans) and those he called the "Far Indians" (the Dogribs). A few Dogribs had come in to trade at Churchill in 1766, and Norton was so well aware of the trading function which the "Northern Indians" had developed that he wrote that "the Northern Indians will rather be a Hinderance to their coming to the fort than otherwise, in order to keep that Monopoly in their Power as much as they can." In 1768 Norton himself went to London. He took with him a large piece of copper which two of his Chipewyan chiefs had brought in, explaining that the copper mine river lay "far to the northward where the sun don't set."[10]

London was then much affected by the publication of a book, The American Traveller, in which Alexander Cluny alleged (quite wrongly) that he had himself picked up large lumps of virgin copper in the north. Between Norton and Cluny, the Committee resolved that Norton would improve their trade by exploring as far north as 70°, and they agreed that a party should be sent under Samuel Hearne on an inland journey. The change from slooping voyages to an inland journey was the result of Moses Norton's persuasions. The choice of Hearne was a tribute to his ability as a surveyor.

Hearne was to take possession of any land which offered chances of profit, he was to survey his course accurately and to leave marks on the shore so that if his search for the copper mine should be successful the copper could be got out by sea. Above all, he was to make a detailed report of his journey. He was to take presents but was not to engage in trade; and he was not to hold out hopes that a post would ever be established in the far north. Churchill would be able to manage all the trade which could be got from that source.

When he set off from Churchill in November 1769, Hearne was prepared for a journey of up to two years. He took surveying instruments, some ammunition, some iron tools, a little tobacco, a few knives to give away as presents, and very little clothing or reserve equipment. But his first journey lasted little more than a month. On December 11 he was back at Churchill, mortified and ready to suffer the disappointment of the Governor. His Indians had proved unreliable, and they did not know the country to which they were taking him in a northwesterly direction. Eventually they deserted him altogether and Hearne, with the two Englishmen and the small party of Home Guard Indians who had accompanied him, found his way back.

In February 1770 Hearne was off again, this time with no white companions and accompanied only by two Home Guards and three Northern Indians. But by mid-March game was scarce, and Hearne and his companions settled by a lake, to live on fish. Not until towards the end of May did they move off northwestwards again; then, in fine weather but impeded by soft snow and with no shelter as they crossed the Barren Ground, they reached the Kazan River, from which point they sent a message back to Churchill by an Indian party which was going down to trade. At the Kazan River, Hearne found the Northern Indians spearing deer as they crossed the river, and he was able to recruit his strength and his supplies. But by the end of July he knew that he could not get to the mouth of the Coppermine River before winter and that he had therefore better spend the winter in company with his Indians and make a determined thrust for the river in the spring. He began wandering to and fro, hunting for the pot, in company with Indians. Deer abounded, but when he broke his quadrant on August 12 he decided that he could not make a report which would have any value. So, plundered of most of his goods, including his gun, he made his way back to Churchill again.

By good fortune, as Hearne was wandering back to the fort, he fell in with the great Indian leader Matonabbee on September 20, 1771. Matonabbee was a Chipewyan who had reported news of the copper mine in 1767, and Hearne had been especially instructed to find this chief if he could. Matonabbee fed and clothed Hearne, and took him back to Churchill, delighted to learn that the Englishman would make a further effort and anxious to go with him.

By now Hearne was an experienced northern traveller. But he was nothing of a trader, and he resented the Indians' assumption that he must have come among them to trade; for trade was not in view, and indeed he had no goods for that purpose. Exploration rather than trade was again the object when Moses Norton sent him off once more, in company with Matonabbee, after only twelve days at the fort. Again he took only his personal equipment and travelled as an Indian. As they took up their course, it became clear that Matonabbee was directing the expedition, and he proved to be a most remarkable Indian, as much devoted to opening up the copper mine as the whites were themselves. In December 1771 he took Hearne off from Churchill and soon revealed that his intention was to move steadily westwards and only to change course north when the longitude of the copper mine had been reached. In this way he would be sure of deer and other food during the winter and could then follow the deer north in the early summer. The plan had great advantages over the straightforward approach to the Northwest which Hearne had previously followed, although it would not keep in view the western coast of Hudson Bay and the possibility of bringing shipping to the mine to take out the ore. It would avoid the rough, inhospitable land over which Hearne's previous journeys had taken him.

It was the middle of April, 1772, before the party began to turn north; they then carried wood and birchrind to make canoes in the barren and treeless north, to run down the river of the copper mine to its mouth, and to furnish their tents as they crossed the Barren Lands. As they went north they were joined by a party of over two hundred Indians whose sole purpose was to murder any Eskimos who might be met. Hearne's revulsion from this bloodthirsty suggestion was so ill received that he was obliged to acquiesce. The party struck Coppermine River on July 13, but found it a sore disappointment. Nevertheless, they travelled down-stream with little trouble, to a point about thirty miles from its mouth. It was then obvious that this was no great river up which seagoing vessels could sail, to take raw copper, or ore, out in bulk; it was barely navigable by canoes.

Hearne's disappointment at this conclusion was turned to sheer revulsion when the Indians surprised a camp of Eskimos and massacred them in their tents, with their women and children. The grisly episode is still commemorated by the name of Bloody Falls on the Coppermine River. Upset by this shock, Hearne made so cursory a survey of the mouth of the river that commentators have wondered whether he concluded his journey down to the mouth. His narrative states that he did so, that he erected a mark there, and that he took possession for the Hudson's Bay Company. Despite his preoccupations, Hearne's description of the copper mine was definitive. Where he had been led to expect hills entirely composed of virgin copper, he had to spend several hours to find a single specimen in the "jungle of rocks and gravel." This was a fine piece of copper, but it made a mockery of the expectations of the copper mine which had been roused by Indian rumour. Nevertheless, Hearne had done what he set out to do. He had put an end to disputes concerning a Northwest Passage, for at the mouth of the Coppermine he was too far north for any commercial route to be practicable, and he had not crossed any passage on the way north; he had seen the mouth of the Coppermine, and he brought back a valuable sample of the copper.

Hearne's route on his return to Churchill cannot be accurately traced, for he had broken his watch, and he had lost his quadrant. He was led back to Churchill by way of Great Slave Lake and Slave River, a long detour during which he was "foot-foundered" for the first time. At Great Slave Lake he emerged from the "jumble of rocks and hills," the Barren Lands of the north, into a fine level country, well supplied with buffalo, moose, beaver, martens, and other animals. He was in the country of the Slaves, whom he called the Athapascows, and he wandered in this country until March 1773, to reach Churchill after an absence of eighteen months and twenty-three days, on June 30, 1773.

With the minimum of equipment, living with Indians and travelling their way, Hearne had accomplished a great feat of exploration. He was competent to set out a convincing and informative narrative, and both the geographical information and his descriptions of Indians and their ways were invaluable. Comparing the "Northern Indians" with those to the south, he noted that they did not trade furs for brandy although they would drink it as a gift; but they required firm handling since they were morose and covetous, and strangers to the very notion of gratitude. Yet they were, he thought, the mildest Indians whom the Company had to deal with, always sensible and never violent. With so much buffalo and other meat, they would never need to hunt furs for the purpose of trading. Indeed, the Company would profit little by drawing such people down to trade; it would be better to get their furs by means of intermediary tribes who would buy up the small surpluses and bring them to the posts. Hearne was not, however, entirely consistent in this view, and at a later stage in his journal he deprecated the "yearly traders" who brought down the furs from the Dogribs and other northern tribes and thought that the Chipewyans made it their business to prevent direct trade with the more distant Indians.

When the journal, and the maps which Hearne had made on his third, successful, journey reached London in the fall of 1773, they came on the heels of a memorandum from Graham, reasserting his belief in a trading post inland. The accumulated evidence from the Company's "inlanders," which had led Graham and Umfreville to put in their requisition for the supplies necessary for a post, had been greatly strengthened by the statements which the Canadian deserter John Cole had made to them. This New Englander, deserting from Thomas Corry's post at Cedar Lake, had come down to York Fort in the early summer of 1772. He proved unreliable, but he was plausible and well informed. He gave a complete description of the arrangements by which the Pedlars financed their trade, and his information went far to persuade Graham that "nothing will do but the making of a Settlement Inland."[11] The arrival together of Graham's persuasive arguments, backed by the detailed information of John Cole, and the narrative of Hearne's journal, led the Committee to appoint Hearne to command the expedition to set up a post on the Saskatchewan. He had been one of the two men recommended by Graham, and with the proof of his capacity to travel with Indians in their hands, the Committee felt little doubt.

Hearne was ordered to meet the full strength of the Company's "inlanders" and of the deserters from the Pedlars at The Pas on the Saskatchewan. He was to ascertain the precise latitude and longitude of that spot, about which the Committee had heard so much but the exact position of which had never been taken; he was to choose a site for his post, and was to start trading.[12] Though he was attached to Churchill, the expedition was to start from York, and Hearne went there in August 1773, hoping to pick up the two large canoes about which Graham had written. But the canoes had not arrived and Ferdinand Jacobs, now Master at York, decided that the voyage would have to be postponed for a year. The Indians, however, were to be warned of the Company's intentions and were to be asked to prepare canoes for a voyage in 1774. Jacobs assumed that the large canoes would never be got down to the Bay, and he planned the voyage on the assumption that he would have to use the smaller *canots du nord* in which the Indians would bring their normal trade.

Recruiting for Hearne's party proved difficult. Some of the servants refused to go inland, and they were sent home as an example (which was probably what they most desired!). On the whole the men accepted the task dourly and unenthusiastically, and Hearne got together a party of twelve. The expectation was that the Company's ordinary servants would, with experience, prove as good at this work as Canadians and would be far more reliable; Andrew Graham, however, was anxious to recruit Canadians and much less critical of their defects.

Though the English route to the Saskatchewan was shorter than the

journey from Montreal, there was no time to spare. All had to be geared
to the arrival of the ship from England, her unloading, and the departure
of the Indians from the Bay, to return to their winter hunting-grounds.
Even the comparatively brief journey to the Saskatchewan was a race
against time; any delay, to hunt or fish, might mean that the rivers would
be frozen before the expedition reached its destination. As against this,
the Canadians were hampered by their long route, but they travelled
through a country rich in game, where wild rice and Indian corn could
easily be got. Jacobs therefore arranged to give Hearne's men as much food
as he could spare. He even traded tongues, dried meat, bladders of fat and
bundles of "pimmicon," so that they could travel quickly without having
to "hunt their way" inland.[13]

In late June 1774 Hearne set off from York.[14] But the Indians had not
come down to trade in sufficient numbers that year for the whole of his
party to be able to go inland together. No large canoes had come down at
all, and Hearne's men had to travel as passengers in the small *canots du
nord*; they therefore went inland in sections, Hearne and his carpenter,
and Robert Longmoor, setting off on June 21. So great was the advantage
which the Company's route to the Saskatchewan gave that by early September Hearne had chosen a site for his post sixty miles above The Pas, at Pine
Island Lake, and was clearing the land for building. This was to be the
site for Cumberland House, and it is significant that Hearne and his men
had got further up-stream than their normal annual voyages took the
Pedlars. The site itself was of the greatest value for the control of the routes
of the fur trade, for Pine Island Lake was where the Beaver Indians carried
their canoes and their furs over from the Saskatchewan to the northern
rivers. It was well provided with food, and since it lay "in the middle
between Three Tribes" it would be better situated for trade than The Pas.
Pine Island Lake was "the key to an entire system of waterways; westward
lay the route to the Rockies, north to Athabaska, the Peace River country
and the vast unknown beyond Great Slave Lake; east to the Churchill and
the Nelson on the one hand, and Lake Winnipeg and Red River on the
other."[15]

As his party came up, Hearne established Cumberland House[16] on a
footing which would give shelter through the winter. Not all of his men
arrived; one was plundered and abandoned by his Indians; one did not
arrive till the middle of October. Two experienced "inlanders," Isaac Batt
and Charles Price Isham, had been abandoned by their Indians at Cedar
Lake, where Cocking came upon them and decided that he must stay with
them. They therefore crossed into Lake Winnipegosis, and so by way of
Red Deer River and Red Deer Lake to Witch Lake, where they all spent
the winter. Cocking was able to observe the Pedlars during the winter, but

he had equipment which Hearne needed, and he lost Isaac Batt as a deserter to the Canadians.

As Hearne reviewed the outlook for an inland post, he concluded that transportation would be the great problem.[17] "The want of Proper Cannoes" seemed to him the crux of the matter and to impose limitations on the Englishmen's power to explore—unless they would go on foot, as he had gone to the Coppermine; but then they could take no goods with them. He found that no payment or promises would induce Indians to make canoes for the white traders, and at the end of winter he was as dependent on Indians for transportation as he had been at the start. The fact that it was the experienced "inlanders" who failed to reach the post, while the raw hands under competent command managed the journey, may support the suspicions of the "inlanders" which had hitherto played their part in preventing the Company from developing inland trade. The outcome, however, was that Hearne had with him men who were unused to the hard conditions and the short supplies of life inland, and his attempts to impose a rationing system and to get work from them met resistance.

Despite this, Hearne's experience in the Arctic had given him so much knowledge and skill that he spent a reasonably successful winter. In June 1775 he started off from Cumberland with thirty-two canoes of Indians, of which seventeen intended to go all the way to trade at York. He had had no desertions from among his men, and he had managed to maintain relationships with the Pedlars in his vicinity. He was even thinking of expanding to further posts; and in this he was of one mind with the masters by the Bay, who realized that a single post could not be the answer to the problem of inland trading in opposition to the Pedlars.

When the "inlanders" reassembled at York, the decision was that Matthew Cocking should take command at Severn and that Hearne should return to Cumberland. But when the Instructions for 1775 arrived, Hearne was appointed to succeed Moses Norton (who had died) at Churchill, and Cocking appeared to be the fittest man to take command at Cumberland. Hearne had already gone back inland before the ship came with these orders, and he was at Cumberland until October 1775.

Whether Hearne or Cocking was in command made little difference. The Pedlars could be assured that the English had moved into a deliberate and determined opposition on the Saskatchewan. Their answer was to form wider and more durable combinations than those which had hitherto proved adequate. In 1775, for example, the powerful combination of James McGill, Benjamin Frobisher, and Maurice Blondeau secured a joint licence to take twelve canoes and fifty-eight men up from Michilimackinac, while the four groups of traders who had formerly worked in competition on the Saskatchewan agreed to run their trade together. This agreement was only for one year, but it showed the Pedlars' desire to eliminate competition among themselves and to give their trade a broader base. The same motives lay behind the formation of a "North West Company" in 1776.[18]

Such combinations were invaluable in equipping the Pedlars to deal with the opposition which the Hudson's Bay Company was bringing into the Northwest. The individual qualities of the Pedlars were nevertheless given free scope, as may be seen from the part which Peter Pond[19] played at this time. A vigorous and unscrupulous New Englander who had come north to serve with the British army during the Seven Years' War, Peter Pond, as a commissioned officer, twenty years old, had been present at the siege of Montreal. After the peace he had made a trading voyage to the West Indies and had then settled down for a brief period at Milford while his father began to venture in the fur trade. Peter Pond himself entered that trade from Detroit, working to Michilimackinac; and by 1772 he had done well enough to make another trip to the West Indies. His competence and experience in the trade to the south and the Mississippi were well known, and in 1773 he was the active trader in a partnership which sent twelve canoes to the Mississippi. The voyage made him enough money to buy out his partner, and as an independent trader he set out for another voyage. It was not until 1775 that he left the southern trade and took his goods from Michilimackinac to Sault Ste Marie, the Grand Portage, and Lake Winnipeg. He then made his way up to The Pas in company with other Pedlars such as Alexander Henry and two of the Frobisher brothers; and although it was late in October before they reached Cumberland House (where Matthew Cocking was by then in command) they intercepted the trade of that post to the north, to the west, and to the south. For this purpose they made some sort of a syndicate among themselves. The northern approaches were cut off by Alexander Henry and the Frobishers, who went to Beaver Lake; Henry's partner, the Frenchman Cadotte, went westwards to winter on the North Saskatchewan at Fort des Prairies. Other Pedlars also went westwards, and Finlay was already in position up the Saskatchewan. Pond moved a little down-stream, through Cedar Lake and Lake Winnipegosis, to the Mossy River and Lake Dauphin. He was probably not part of the amalgamation which had been formed to oppose the Hudson's Bay post, for he had only two canoes, whereas Henry and Cadotte had eight, Charles Patterson had fourteen, and the Frobishers twenty.

Nevertheless, Pond showed the value of this kind of partnership when in 1776, instead of taking his furs down to Michilimackinac—or perhaps even right down to Montreal—he went only as far as the Grand Portage, picked up his outfit there, and so saved enough time to go back up the Saskatchewan and over the watershed into the Athabasca region before winter set in. This was a period when the trade of Montreal was seriously interrupted by the War of American Independence. The city was captured by the Americans in 1775 and recaptured by the British in 1776. The disturbances to the trading life of Montreal were, however, offset by a fresh influx of "Loyalists" from the New England states. Many of them were men of considerable experience and capital. Among them were Simon McTavish, who was to become the "Marquis" of the Montreal fur trade, and the merchant firm of Phynn and Ellice, which prospered by supplying the Montreal fur-traders and marketing their furs for them. Pond's backer as he picked up his outfit at the Grand Portage in 1776 was probably George McBeath, an experienced fur-trader who was eminently capable of supplying the link with Montreal which Pond needed, and who was engaged in 1776 in negotiations with Simon McTavish which would have allowed him to outfit Pond at Grand Portage.[20] Much of the background to Pond's venture must remain guesswork; but there can be no doubt that great arrangements were taking place at Montreal, at Michilimackinac, and at the Grand Portage, and that Peter Pond wasted little time in taking down his trade returns and was back at the Forks of the Saskatchewan fully equipped and ready to go further afield than the Hudson's Bay men, early in the year.[21]

Pond was not an innovator in this. The Grand Portage had been used for outfitting before 1776; and other Pedlars had pushed further up the Saskatchewan and had already overflowed into the basin of the Churchill River. The Frobisher brothers, Joseph and Thomas, for example, had got almost to Cumberland Lake in 1774, had wintered there with twenty canoes, and had there "pillaged" a Hudson's Bay man. Joseph Hansom had been sent inland in 1773 from Churchill by Moses Norton, by way of the Churchill River to the Sturgeonweir River and Cumberland Lake, to cross over to the Saskatchewan. He wintered with the Frobishers at Cumberland Lake on his return journey, and then, in the spring of 1774, he began to lead his Indians down to Churchill to trade, and was met at Frog Portage— henceforth called Portage du Traite—by Joseph Frobisher who, with a mixture of force and cajolery, stopped the Indians and took their furs from them. The episode has been made much of as an instance of the unscrupulous competence of the Pedlars.[22] Its real significance was that it showed that the Pedlars commanded the routes to Churchill in the same way as they controlled the routes to York, Severn, Albany, and Moose, before Cumberland House had been established and before Peter Pond made his 1776 voyage, outfitted from the Grand Portage.

Pond, then, had done nothing unprecedented in 1776, and indeed others were in the field with him (Louis Primeau, for example, had set up a Pedlars' post at Ile-à-la-Crosse, and James Tute had taken his canoes westwards, to Beaver Lake). In 1777 it became clear that Cumberland House was again surrounded and that the main threat lay in a concentration of thirty-six canoes further up the Saskatchewan than the English post. Peter Pond, Booty Graves (an Englishman), and Bruce were working in a partnership at Fort des Prairies, and during the winter a letter signed jointly by Graves, Charles McCormick, Bruce, Pond, Pangman, Blondeau, and Nicolas Montour bore witness to the sort of loosely formed partnership into which the Pedlars were able to fall. They were at what they called the "Upper Settlement" at the Sturgeonweir River, and were joined in one general concern.[23]

The outcome was that when in May 1778 Pond came down from his "upper post" he found five large canoes of goods, a year's supply still on hand at the end of the season, available as the remains of the trading supplies of this syndicate. Pond had already done much to bring forward the supply base of the Pedlars when he took up his outfit at the Grand Portage instead of at Michilimackinac. Now he took the remains of goods which were on hand at Pine Island Lake and was thereby able to bring his supply base further forward and to set off for Athabasca in the early summer instead of in the late autumn. The surplus seems to have been the produce of the common pool of the Pedlars, and the high quality and large quantity of the furs which had been got from Ile-à-la-Crosse seems to have been the motive which led the Pedlars to pool their resources and to send Pond over the watershed into Athabasca.[24]

The result was an extension of the Pedlars' sphere of operations into the Eldorado of the fur trade—for so Athabasca came to be known. Athabasca was also the starting-point for exploration of the ultimate Northwest; for the breakout from the basin of the Saskatchewan into Athabasca entailed the overcoming of the last geographical obstacle which barred access to the Northwest.

In 1778 the Company's men could do little to rival the moves made by Pond. During the winter 1776-77 Matthew Cocking, serving again at Cumberland House, urged that posts should be set up even further inland. He sent a small party up to the plains, where they wintered in the Eagle Hills, returning to Cumberland in February 1777. They were sent off again, under Robert Longmoor, to stay above the Pedlars on the Saskatchewan until the river broke, to persuade the Indians to go down to York with their furs and to choose a site at which a further outpost might be set up. Other Hudson's Bay men wintered with Indians to the south and to the north; and during that year Cocking brought the returns from Cumberland up to over 6,000 made-beaver.[25] He also spent considerable effort on trying out the different routes to York, in the hope that he might avoid the comparatively long way through Lake Winnipeg. The Sea Lake (Lake Winnipeg) and the Spruce River were the particular objects of his enquiry. When the rivers broke in May 1777 he sent one of his men, Robert Davey, north to Beaver Lake and then to the Churchill River. One of the Frobisher brothers "accompanied" Davey to Beaver Lake, and shadowed him up the Churchill River. Davey got very few furs, and the episode reinforced the argument that rivalry with the Pedlars could be effective only if the posts on the Saskatchewan were further expanded by posts in Athabasca.[26]

This conclusion was accepted by Humphrey Marten, then Chief at York, who ordered that posts should be established further out from Cumberland. This was the only way by which the Company could break through the cordon of Pedlars. Marten hoped that a new outpost, which was to be of temporary structure only and was to be near the buffalo-hunting grounds, would be about four hundred and fifty miles further up the Saskatchewan, and that this would outdistance the Pedlars. Any delay would be dangerous; the onset of winter was always to be borne in mind. But Marten's plans were based on the assumption that Cocking would again be in command of Cumberland and that William Tomison would lead the new venture. Cocking, however, on his arrival at York Fort, decided that a serious rupture would prevent him from making any further journeys. Tomison was therefore given command at Cumberland, and Joseph Hansom (whom Cocking had left in temporary command as he went down to York) was ordered to go up-river. But Hansom read his orders so that he retained command at Cumberland until the following spring, and the new outpost was not set up that year. Robert Longmoor was, however, sent off to the buffalo country, and a further party was sent out to collect materials for making canoes and to kill provisions so that the Company's men could move forward rapidly in the following year. When the river broke in May 1778, five men were sent up to trade above the Pedlars on the Saskatchewan and a further party under Hansom was sent north to trade with Indians from Athabasca.[27]

In all this, the Company was concentrating upon active opposition to the Pedlars, and there was little urge for exploration. The Pedlars had the advantage in numbers of men and in quantities of goods, which they dispensed lavishly. At the end of the season of 1778 William Tomison was despondent; but from the north came news that the Pedlars were in trouble. In the absence of competition they were trading hard with the Indians, were disputing among themselves, and were, many of them, broken down by hardship, riotous living, and disease. Against this, the Company's men traded well; the returns brought from the Athabascan Indians by Hansom were good, and to crown all Robert Longmoor went down to York in 1778 in a canoe which he had made for himself.[28]

While the English achieved such reasonable success inland, at York Humphrey Marten was working on the problem of alternative routes from the posts on the Bay to Cumberland. The route by the Hayes River, the Fox River, and Lake Winnipeg was being improved. So was the alternative by way of the Nelson River, the Grass River, Cranberry Lake, the Sturgeon-weir River, and Sturgeon Lake. This was useful work, but it did not match the imaginative innovation by which Peter Pond had taken the remains of the other Pedlars' trade goods and had set off back inland without return-ing to his base. There was, however, great determination in many of the English servants; in 1778 Robert Longmoor promised that he would go as far inland as any of the Canadians; and Humphrey Marten instructed him to do so.

By 1778 the English Company had a body of men who knew how to travel and who were determined and resourceful in their opposition to the Pedlars. But the Company's equipment was less appropriate than that of its rivals. Not only were there difficulties over canoe-making and canoe-management—difficulties which were only beginning to be overcome. There were also problems of selecting and of packaging goods for the long journeys. The English goods were still heavier and clumsier than those of the Cana-dians, and although the English government's attempts to tie in the economy of the West Indies with that of Canada were bringing rum to the fur trade, to replace much of the brandy which the French had used with such effect, rum was available to Pedlars and to Hudson's Bay men alike, and there was nothing to choose between them in this respect. For the rest, ineptitudes (such as a lack of oilskins to protect the bales of goods as they went inland) were discouraging but were not prohibitive. Transportation and the supplies of men and of goods were the only limitations on the quantities of furs which either side could secure.

Minor inefficiencies prevented Longmoor from setting off from Cumber-land to settle higher up-river until September 1778. He was then caught by ice and was only able to reach the Pedlars' "middle settlement." There he found three syndicates of Pedlars, in opposition to each other as well as to him, and although personal relationships were not unreasonable, trading opposition was implacable. The Indians were prevented by force from trad-ing and were generously supplied with rum and tobacco. Against a hundred men under the Pedlars' command, Longmoor had but twelve. The signifi-cance of this is in terms of status and as a demonstration of the Pedlars' knowledge of the country and of their ability to get large numbers of men and overwhelming quantities of goods over their difficult route to the upper waters of the Saskatchewan.[29]

The rivalry which Longmoor had to meet was indeed intimidating. But the Pedlars were making troubles for themselves. During the winter they traded so hard that in the spring of 1779 the Indians murdered two of their servants and drove them from their middle settlement. Longmoor, feeling that he had more friends among the Indians than the Pedlars could boast, stayed at his post and demonstrated the differences in the two trading ventures' relations with the Indians.

The way in which the Indians controlled the situation was shown clearly in the following year. In the fall of 1779 Tomison accompanied Longmoor up-river and at last built the outpost of Hudson House. This did not out-distance the Pedlars but was about fourteen miles lower down the river than the post which Longmoor himself had previously occupied. The Pedlars soon surrounded it and built alongside; and Pedlar Holmes and others showed their hostility and their ability to cajole, bully, and debauch the Indians. Holmes brought up thirty sledge-loads of goods, and his "saucy pride" made him a formidable opponent. Nevertheless, Longmoor main-tained his position and secured a valuable trade in the spring of 1780. The Indians, however, were not to be neglected in such a three-cornered rivalry; they refused to trade meat except for brandy, and since Longmoor had very little spirits he faced great difficulty in getting food for his outward journey and in getting canoes built. The Indians also raided the Company's post in an attempt to get guns; for the Pedlars, knowing the extent to which they had lost the confidence of the Indians, had refused to trade any weapons. The cause of trouble was the harsh treatment meted out, and the suspicions aroused, by the Pedlars. But the Hudson's Bay men also felt the hostility, and in 1781 the Indians went so far as to burn off the prairie round all the posts, so as to scare the game away from the white men.[30]

Nevertheless it was assumed, with justification, that by 1781 the English were established on the Saskatchewan and that the Indians would maintain them there in their own interests. Rivalry was now to extend to the Rockies and to Athabasca, where Peter Pond was interrupting the trade which would normally have come down to Churchill; and arrangements were in hand to counteract this further advance. Longmoor was to winter on the upper reaches of the Saskatchewan, to collect food and canoes for a further journey, and to be ready to start as soon as the ice melted in 1782.

This plan was made impossible by two events. The burning of the plains by the Indians made it impossible to collect food for the journey; Longmoor and his four chosen companions had to winter out and could not even be kept going as residents at Hudson House. Then a great smallpox epidemic struck the Indians. This had probably come up from the south, from the Mississippi by contact with the Snake Indians. The "plaguey disorder" first appeared among the Indians of Hudson House in October, and at Cumber-land House in December 1781. The Hudson's Bay men ascribed it to the ammunition which the Pedlars gave out, so that the Indians could indulge their tribal enmities and could go to fight the Snakes, to catch the disease from them. The smallpox epidemic of 1781-82 must be a classic instance of the immunity of Europeans and the vulnerability of non-Europeans to certain diseases. By the end of the eighteenth century smallpox had begun to lose its terrors for most of the populations of Europe. Only one of the Company's servants caught the disease, the half-breed Charles Isham; and he recovered. The Indians, in contrast, died almost by whole tribes. Families lay unburied in their tents while the few survivors fled, to spread the disease. Hudson House was kept open through the summer months instead of being closed down and used merely as a winter outpost; for the Indians on the plains still had furs which they had been unable to bring in. But Longmoor was driven back from the plains, and the plan to send him to Athabasca was postponed.[31] It was as much as the inland posts could do to take care of their sick Indians and to maintain their own position during the winter of 1782 and the spring of 1783; and during that time they received no reinforcement and, indeed, no news, from the posts on the Bay.

The capture of Canada from the French had been the starting-point for the invasion of the Northwest by the Pedlars from Montreal. They were assuming the mantle of their French predecessors and companions, travelling by way of the St Lawrence and the overland routes. Nevertheless when, in 1782, the French made their last attempt to interrupt the English control of the furs of the Northwest, it was by a sea-borne raid into Hudson's Bay. As allies of the American colonists in the War of American Independence, the French had shown themselves anxious to reassert French influence, especially in the West Indies. A great naval attack on Jamaica had ended when the British Admiral Rodney brought the Comte de Grasse to action at the Battle of the Saints and won a notable victory. After the battle some twenty-six French ships were dispersed along the American coast and were reinforced by a fleet of eight Spanish ships. This could have threatened the English command of the seas; but the concentration was dispersed on minor projects, among which was the plan to send three ships, under command of the Comte de Lapérouse, to destroy the English fur-posts in the Bay.[32]

This project had long been planned and had been several times revised, and in 1781 it was accepted that York and Severn, and even the great stone fort at Churchill, could be captured and destroyed by a naval expedition. Behind this lay some hope that the French fur trade might be re-established.[33] The plan fell aptly into the designs for using dispersed French forces after the Battle of the Saints had been fought and lost. Lapérouse then took aboard two hundred and fifty troops and forty gunners who had been destined for service in Jamaica, and appeared with the 74-gun *Sceptre* and two 36-gun frigates, the *Astrée* and the *Engageante*, off the mouth of the Churchill River in high summer 1782—probably early in August, although there is some dispute as to the actual date.[34]

Samuel Hearne was then Governor of Churchill, but he had only thirty-nine men under his command, and when the French had deceived him by sailing under English colours (a quite legitimate device) until they had managed to land their men and their guns, he had little hope of effective resistance. In fact, he surrendered after the briefest of parleys and without making any conditions for himself, his men, or his employers' goods. This fits in well with the character which he had shown when, on his travels, he had been robbed and abused by Indians. With all his great fortitude as a traveller, Samuel Hearne was nothing of a fighting man. As Governor he evoked little valour from his men, and the whole episode is marked by the lack of offensive spirit shown by the English. Men hired merely to trade and to travel could not, perhaps, be expected to stand to their guns in the face of an attack by professional European soldiers. In any case, Hearne's men were too few even to man the guns of the fort.

Nevertheless when Hearne, having surrendered, was taken aboard the French ships, he may well have had misgivings. The soldiers and sailors were packed so close and were so badly provisioned that they were lousy and were suffering two or three deaths a day from scurvy. Even the dram of brandy at each meal did not counteract a diet of "about two ozs Beef or Pork a day or a few beans boiled in a little fresh water together with some maggoty biscuit almost capable to walk itself."[35] Lapérouse tried to destroy the English fort, and this again may have given Hearne some doubts, for the stonework proved too substantial. The French burned the gun carriages, spiked the guns, blew breaches in the walls, and set fire to the buildings at several points.

The destruction of Churchill must inevitably have lowered the status of the English in the eyes of the Indians. This was serious; but when Lapérouse took Hearne and the other prisoners aboard and moved over to York he was attacking the supply base for the inland posts. It was late in August before the French got to the Hayes River, for the Hudson's Bay men refused to pilot them. As the French came in sight a sloop took aboard the furs of the year, slipped out from the river (with Matthew Cocking aboard), and set out for London. Violent weather was in part responsible for the French delay, but the respite was not enough for Humphrey Marten to put his "fort" in any posture for defence. It was built only of wood and Marten, like Hearne, surrendered at the first demand. He managed better than Hearne in that he secured terms in which the lives and the private property of the English garrison were guaranteed to them.[36]

Although the French so easily took the English posts, they had no time ashore in which to refresh themselves and to recover from the scurvy or from the ship's typhus from which (since their men were lousy) they almost certainly suffered. If they were to make their way out from the Bay before ice closed the Strait they had no time to lose. Accordingly, having set fire to the wooden buildings and destroyed York in a way which had not been possible at Churchill, Lapérouse got his troops aboard on September 1 and set sail for Europe. Eventually he reached Cadiz, with four hundred sick on board his own ship and after suffering seventy deaths from scurvy. But he reckoned that the venture had been a success since the Hudson's Bay Company had lost so much that it must surrender its charter and discontinue its trade; and he reckoned that, since the trade to the Bay could only be managed by a company, the English trade would cease.[37]

In this Lapérouse was more optimistic than some of his contemporaries and companions. The Indians had already come to trade at York, and indeed their furs had been shipped to England before the French took possession; and the outfits and goods for the next year's trade had been sent inland. The impact of the smallpox epidemic was therefore already known, as were the other difficulties from which the Hudson's Bay men were suffering in the interior. In their conversations with the Hudson's Bay men, the French had been so impressed with the way in which the Indians depended on regular supplies of European goods—especially of powder and guns—that they left a supply of lead and of gunpowder outside York, to help the Indians through their troubles. The inland posts therefore survived; they were already supplied with much of their goods, and the men remained at their duties. The great harm which they suffered was the blow to their prestige, and the destruction of the posts by the Bay both contributed to this and made their supply system difficult and uncertain. It was serious, too, when such well-known and experienced traders as Samuel Hearne and Humphrey Marten were taken off as prisoners. So much was this the case that Hearne's old travelling companion, the great chief Matonabbee, committed suicide when he heard of his capture.

Hearne himself was then enjoying the hospitality of the French aboard their ships and was so impressive that Lapérouse returned to him the manuscript of his account of his journey to the Arctic on condition that he should publish it. The French were in no position to estimate the damage which they had done, and since they were unable to maintain their position, the irruption of Lapérouse and his ships could have lasting importance only if (as he hoped) it deterred the Hudson's Bay Company from making good the damage and continuing the trade. The Company estimated that the furs captured at Churchill were worth £14,000 or more, and this was a serious loss.[38] But they were strangely philosophical over the whole affair. They refrained from upbraiding either Hearne or Marten for surrendering their posts, they reappointed them both without demur, and in 1783 they sent them out once more. The furs which had been safely got home from York, together with those from the Bottom of the Bay, proved adequate for the market under war conditions, and the sales of January and March 1783 were satisfactory. The Committee seem never to have contemplated that abandonment of the trade which the French and their American supporters had at times envisaged.

It is indeed true that dividends were suspended in 1783 for the first time since 1718, but orders were sent that the garrisons should return to their places, the posts should be restored, and over one hundred and twenty men should be allotted to service in the "Grand North."

CHAPTER 10

The Invasion of Athabasca

The dramatic raid by Lapérouse focussed attention on York and Churchill. But the interests of both English and Canadian fur-traders were as much concerned with the Bottom of the Bay as with posts further west, and the territory at the back of the posts at the Bottom of the Bay almost assumed more importance than the posts themselves. Each of the inland territories at this time was given its own title, the "*Petit Nord*" describing the lands at the back of the Bottom of the Bay, the "Grand North" the lands at the back of Churchill, York, and Severn; and as the Hudson's Bay Committee re-planned policy in the winter of 1784-85, the *Petit Nord* received equal attention with the Grand North. There the threat from Lapérouse had been met by a decision to drill and arm the men (and even to put them into a uniform of sorts) and to place the major post at Albany in a posture of defence. This was a brave decision, but it entailed the abandonment of all the outposts, which by that date were beginning to show signs of effective penetration by the English into the hinterland.

After the cession of Canada, in 1763, the men at the Bottom of the Bay proved unwilling to go inland, trained leaders were lacking, and resettlement of the pioneer post at Henley could not be put in hand until the summer of 1766, to be completed in 1768 "in spite of the most inveterate malice and Envy of your Honors most undutifull Servants."[1] Decisions in 1768 and again in 1770 entailed that Henley should merely help the Indians on their way down to trade at the Bayside and should not be made a trading post itself. This was partly due to difficulties in transporting goods inland, for the river ran shoal at times, boats could not be used, and canoes carried little cargo. But once Henley had been established, the suggestion that Indians should make the further journey down to the Bay was taken by them as "a deceit"; moreover, it brought the Hudson's Bay men into rivalry with the Pedlars on their own ground and on their own terms.[2] At inland posts opportunities for private trade and for "clandestine proceedings" were many, and the Hudson's Bay men found themselves involved not only in the results of their own misconduct towards Indians but in those of the Pedlars' misdoings as well. Brandy was the eternal cry of the Indians, and when they turned to abuse the Canadian traders they threatened the Hudson's Bay men also.[3]

Nevertheless, Henley was re-established, and it proved to be the springboard for advance into the *Petit Nord*. There, as on the Saskatchewan and in the Grand North, the Hudson's Bay men slowly realized that they could contain the Canadians only by pushing forward their own frontier. So, in 1773, proposals were put forward that Henley should be made into a major trading post, and in 1775 Edward Jarvis (an active young man, and a surgeon whose competence in reporting on the routes which he travelled was greater than that of the normal Hudson's Bay employee) began to explore the territory between the Bottom of the Bay and Lake Superior. Overcoming the opposition of the Indians who, as he noted, were "averse to our making any discovery or settlement where the Pedlars are, because they find it more beneficial to have two places of opposite interests to resort to," in 1775 he penetrated up the Albany River to Missinaibi Lake and then returned to Moose; in 1776 he reached Michipicoten on Lake Superior.[4] He reported that the Pedlars were badly housed and could easily be opposed; and he advocated that Henley should be used as a starting-point for penetration into their territory.

These views were implemented in 1777, when Gloucester House was set up, almost two hundred and fifty miles south of Henley. The English were feeling their way towards Lake Superior, partly in rivalry with the Pedlars, partly in a search for the coarser beaver pelts from the south, which were in demand on the London market as new processes in the fur and felting industries developed.[5] The policy of southwards penetration was carried further when, in 1776-77, another surgeon, Thomas Atkinson, was sent out by the combined efforts of Moose and Albany to build a post on the west branch of the Moose River (known as the Missinaibi River). This was Wapiscogamy House; reinforced and rebuilt in 1781, it was then called Brunswick House and was transferred in 1791 to a more favourable position on Brunswick Lake.[6]

The London Committee had accepted a policy of moves "towards Quebec," and the post-masters at the Bottom of the Bay supported that policy. At Moose yet another surgeon was in command, with some fifteen years of experience as a surgeon and an Indian trader—Eusebius Bacchus Kitchin. For him the Abitibi River was the line of approach to Moose for the Indians, and French hostility on the Abitibi needed counteraction. His plans to make a settlement at Abitibi came to nothing, for although in 1774 he sent John Thomas to explore the Abitibi River, and in 1777 sent him to establish a post actually on Lake Superior, Thomas was held up on Lake Missinaibi, where the Indians refused to supply him with food and drove him back to spend the winter at Wapiscogamy-Brunswick House. The Indian refusal to supply Missinaibi with food entailed its abandonment in 1780, and the Indians then burned the post. Brunswick-Wapiscogamy therefore was the furthest which the Hudson's Bay men reached towards Lake Superior at this time, and the need to maintain and even to rebuild the posts at the Bottom of the Bay made such demands that nothing more could be achieved. Nevertheless the policy of expanding inland from the Bottom of the Bay was clear (the Nottaway River in its turn had been explored by canoe in 1772 and in 1773) and while the traders were anxious to outfront the "Quebec Runnagates," the London Committee was pressing for surveys of the territory and for estimates of distances, with notes on the supply-system which would be involved in maintaining posts inland.

The fact that so many of the English were one-time surgeons, turned traders, was something of an advantage. But they were not trained surveyors, and in 1778 the Hudson's Bay Company turned to the great London charity school of Christ's Hospital in search of apprentices and clerks who could be trained into professional surveyors. They had an advantage in that William Wales, an astronomer who had been sent to Churchill in 1768-69 to observe the transit of Venus from that spot, was a master at Christ's Hospital. The request for three "Inland Surveyors" from Christ's Hospital, however, produced in the first place a nomination from Wales of "a Person skilled in Mathematicks" who did not come from that school. This was Philip Turnor, who was aged twenty-six when he was engaged by the Company in 1778,[7] to go out to York Factory as a full-time surveyor.

After a brief period at York, Turnor was sent to the Saskatchewan to survey the position of Cumberland House and of its outpost, Hudson House. He was then to be sent by an inland route—"through the Lakes inland"— if it should prove practicable, to Moose and Albany, to survey the routes and distances, and the posts at the Bottom of the Bay. From the start of his career in the Northwest Turnor showed a capacity for travel which was almost equal to his ability in making surveys and in drawing maps; he arrived at Cumberland in October 1778, spent the winter there and then marched almost three hundred miles on the ice of the river to Hudson House, where he was stopped by the resentment of the Indians at the treatment which the Canadians had given them at the Upper Settlement. In the summer of 1779 he returned to York and then went by sloop to Severn and to Moose. From Moose he walked to Albany, and in the spring of 1780 he made a journey on snow-shoes of about one hundred and fifty miles to Henley House, although he suffered from snow-blindness on the way and arrived "foot-foundered." He had intended to continue on to the new outpost at Gloucester House, but he was forced to rest up and to return to Albany. Later in the year he was able to get up to Gloucester House, and 'he then made a careful survey of the route. After a journey overland from Moose to Albany and back, he set out in 1781 to survey the shores of James Bay. He was back in Moose again at the end of that winter, and then went by canoe up the Moose River to Wapiscogamy House and from Wapisco-gamy on to Michipicoten; on his return he compiled a further survey of this route, all the way from Michipicoten down to Moose. He failed in an attempt to reach the Canadians' settlement on Lake Abitibi towards the end of 1781, and again in June 1782, when his canoe was swamped in the Abitibi River; but he re-equipped himself and in that year reached Abitibi and mapped the route to the settlement there.

The work of surveying and route-finding on which Turnor was engaged in the country "towards Quebec" kept him there during the smallpox epi-demic of 1781-82 and the French invasion of 1782. It might well have been interrupted by either of these disasters, and still more by the destruction of Henley House by fire in January 1782; for Henley was still the springboard for English expansion into the *Petit Nord*. But the rebuilding of Henley was taken almost as a matter of course, and Turnor, as the only skilled drafts-man available, drew plans for a new post. He then went on his successful journey to Abitibi and, having virtually completed his tasks as a surveyor, was drawn into the fur trade by appointment as Master at Wapiscogamy, which he had rebuilt and had named Brunswick House by March 1783, when news came to him of the destruction of York and Churchill by the French. The sturdy decision of the Masters of Moose and Albany, that Albany should be defended, entailed a decision that the rebuilding of Hen-ley should not be put in hand; and since Henley was the post from which Gloucester House was maintained, Gloucester had to be abandoned. Turnor was also ordered to close his new post at Brunswick House, and the Eastmain post and that at Rupert River (which were sharing in the expansion of English influence) were drawn in and the men were taken back to Moose. In fact, Turnor was sick with gout and rheumatism and did not abandon Brunswick until the winter was over. When in June 1783 he made his way down to Moose, taking his furs and his goods with him, it was already clear that the war with the United States was over, and with it any further danger from the French; Turnor was quickly sent back, to find Brunswick still in good order and to resume the flow of trade.

The maintenance of Brunswick was a good omen; but as a result of the decisions taken in 1782 English penetration "towards Quebec" had to be started again in 1783. Nevertheless the work of the previous decade meant that the Hudson's Bay men were mastering the techniques of travel by canoe and by snow-shoe while they were experimenting with boats and bateaux as means of taking cargoes inland. With Turnor and his pupils available, the Hudson's Bay men had clearer information than the Canadians on which to base their decisions. But their policy was framed at a distance from actuality, whereas the Montreal traders enjoyed much greater flexibility, and the opportunism of an individual trader (such as Peter Pond) could lead to unplanned developments, not all of which were successful.

As had been shown in their instructions that Turnor should, if possible, travel from Cumberland House to Moose and Albany by "the Lakes inland," the Hudson's Bay Committee were concerned to define their frontier to the south. They were aware of the returns which the Canadians got both from the Saskatchewan and the territories to the Northwest (reached from Lake Superior, the Grand Portage, and Lake Winnipeg) and from what they called the "Fire Country." This area, never clearly defined, was accepted as the land north and west from Grand Portage, an area in which the London Committee desired "to gain a thorough knowledge of the Country and of the Natives; and the best method of procuring Country Provisions which would lessen the Carriage of European Victuals." The "Fire Country" was at times equated to the "Barren Lands," to the "Meadow Country" of Cumberland House, and to what the Indians called the "Muscuty Plains."[8] From this territory the Company hoped to get buffalo, moose, and deer in great plenty and so to ease the English provision problem; and the "Fire Country" was particularly important because policy was being shaped against the probable outcome of the Treaty of Versailles, which was defining the frontier with the newly independent United States of America.

The capture of Canada, and subsequent legislation, had led to a great development in the fur trade from Canada; and the Quebec Act of 1774[9] confirmed the Montreal traders' advantages when it extended the jurisdiction of Quebec to the area of the Great Lakes. The Grand Portage, the Ohio River, and the upper reaches of the Mississippi all lay under the distant and ineffective jurisdiction of Quebec, and traders who set out from Montreal enjoyed the access to these areas which the regime created. This extension of the jurisdiction of Quebec was achieved largely because the states of New York and Connecticut were reluctant to assume responsibility for distant, uninhabited, and inaccessible territories in the period during which the English plan for a great Indian reserve had been undermined. American interests were non-existent in the key area round Grand Portage at the time of the achievement of American independence, but at the Peace of Versailles Lord Shelburne accepted a frontier from Lake Superior by the Pigeon River to the northwest angle of Lake of the Woods and then by the forty-ninth parallel to the Mississippi. This ceded to the Americans a great area between the Ohio and the Mississippi which was covered by fur-traders who worked from Montreal and by no one else, was garrisoned by British troops stationed in the "Western Posts" (Detroit, Michilimackinac, Oswego, Niagara, and Presqu'isle), and was neither settled nor administered by men who would now come under American orders. The terms of the treaty were vague, geographical knowledge was sketchy, and the forty-ninth parallel would not lead to the Mississippi. Moreover, the newly-established United States were reluctant to undertake either defence or government of western lands. The date at which the British garrisons of the Western Posts must be withdrawn was thus left open, and British subjects were left free to travel and to trade along the boundary and in the territories adjacent to it.[10]

Notwithstanding the treaty, therefore, the Grand Portage remained in British hands; and Montreal traders continued to use Michilimackinac as a means of access to the southwest and to lands which, according to the treaty, must one day become American. This southwestern trade was considerable, reaching totals of £184,000 in 1782 and £226,000 in 1783 for goods taken up for trade; and trade from Michilimackinac steadily increased, drawing furs from the Illinois and even from Louisiana. Well-established and profitable, the southern trade maintained a powerful group of traders who kept up a constant campaign for amendment of the treaty, revision of the boundary with America, and retention in English hands of the means of access both to the rivers which flowed south and to the Grand Portage, the Pigeon River, and the established route from Lake Superior to Lake Winnipeg and the Saskatchewan. The United States steadily refused to cede territory, and so the Montreal traders worked against a threat that, when the Americans felt strong enough to vindicate their rights, access to Lake Winnipeg and the Northwest might be barred, and the all-important Grand Portage would lie on the American side of the frontier.[11]

The Hudson's Bay Committee consequently expected that the Canadians would suffer from the boundary outlined at the Treaty of Versailles, and in their exploration of the "Fire Country" between Lake Superior and Lake Winnipeg they were anticipating a move by them. For the Montreal traders would have to revise their whole transportation system if the Grand Portage and the Pigeon River were taken from them by the treaty, and they were in search of alternative routes. As it became clear that diplomatic intervention was unlikely to prevent American control of the area which was so essential to them, the Canadians hired the former Hudson's Bay man, Edward Umfreville, who had assisted Andrew Graham in planning the advance of the English posts to the Saskatchewan. He had been captured by Lapérouse, but on his release he fell out with the Committee over his salary and entered into the service of the Montreal traders. He was now sent with a French-Canadian companion to plot a new route into the

Northwest, striking north from Lake Superior to Lake Nipigon before the American frontier was reached.[12] This would take the men from Montreal deeper into the "Fire Country" but would be a longer and more arduous route than that by the Grand Portage; and since the Canadians managed to retain access to the Grand Portage, the Lake Nipigon route was never made of great use.

Umfreville himself was then sent to the outpost of the Montreal traders farthest up the Saskatchewan, and from there he made unsuccessful overtures for further employment by the Hudson's Bay Company. Here he was still "in the Fire Country," and although he was certainly in what would have been considered part of the Grand North, he conducted a correspondence with Edward Jarvis, Chief at Albany, and with the Master of Gloucester House on the Albany River;[13] both posts were not in the *Grand* but in the *Petit Nord*. The lesson was clear—that the Fire Country, the plains, and the territory between Lake Superior and Lake Winnipeg and their extension to east and to west, formed a channel between the two major areas; the broad distinctions were not absolute but relative; there were common problems all the way from Athabasca to the Eastmain, and common means of communication and access. Umfreville emphasized the importance of the area between the Bay and the Great Lakes, between the Saskatchewan with its routes to the Northwest, and the Bottom of the Bay with its approach to the Eastmain and to Abitibi. He showed his Hudson's Bay friends that the "Provision trade" from the "Fire Country" was vital to the Pedlars' approach to Athabasca, and the Hudson's Bay men accepted his conclusion.

Thus not only were Henley, Brunswick, and Gloucester House set going once more, and Eastmain rebuilt on a larger scale, but the thrust towards Abitibi was again undertaken, and Turnor was again employed for the task of expansion and route-finding. The post at the mouth of the Severn River (which had been abandoned during the French raid) was also re-established and although the Indians had again shown the control which they exercised by refusing to trade at Henley during the year 1783-84, confidence was high when in June 1784 Turnor and ten men set off "towards Abitibi." He had trouble, first with his boats (which he had to leave on the journey), then with his canoes (which he had to abandon and to build afresh). As a result he was unable to get to Abitibi Lake in 1784 and spent the winter in a log tent at the junction of the Abitibi and Frederick House rivers. However, in the spring of 1785 he moved on and built the post of Frederick House, where he remained in command for the winter of 1785-86, in close rivalry with the Canadians until, in 1787, he set out on a survey of their posts around Lake Abitibi and opened the route south to Lake Timiskaming. Here he was certainly outside any territory which might be called Rupert's Land or held to be under the Charter of the Hudson's Bay Company, for he had crossed the watershed and was in the basin of the Ottawa River. This ended a period in Turnor's service, for he was brought home to London, to perfect his maps and surveys.

While Turnor worked south from Moose, a parallel English thrust had gone forward from Albany, with a move towards Lake Nipigon in 1784 and the establishment of Osnaburgh on Lake St Joseph in 1786. While the Hudson's Bay Company's Committee wanted to push their frontier to the south, at least up to the height of land, they also wanted to avoid the heavy costs and the static outlook which went with fixed posts and to achieve something of the mobility and flexibility which characterized the Montreal men. Many small posts were to be preferred to a handful of stable forts, and the problems of food supply were to be given almost as much attention as the problems of trade. The Hudson's Bay Company was being forced to learn how to live and move under northern inland conditions. The post at Osnaburgh, for example, was to be only a temporary post, the master of which would exert himself to "make the Canadians' trade precarious and hard to get." Osnaburgh was so far south that it produced many offers from Canadians to desert to the English Company, and it drove a wedge into the territory of Montreal; it was established from Albany by way of the Albany River, but it might equally well have fallen into the sphere of Severn or even of York.[14]

As mobility and the interdependence of fur-trading posts with supply depots and country provisions became accepted, the last quarter of the eighteenth century saw a definite change of policy on the part of the English company. All the northern territories were knit together in one comprehensive plan for penetration, provisioning, and fur trading. The heart of the system lay around Lake Winnipeg. From there ran the routes to Lake Superior and the south by way of Grand Portage; to the Petit Nord and the Bottom of the Bay; and to the Grand North and the newly opened territories of the Northwest. The area was also the centre of the provision-country, with wild rice to supplement the buffalo and deer of the prairies. From Abitibi to Athabasca the northern territories were becoming accepted as a unified problem, with the "Fire Country" and the provision trade as common factors. The Company was coming to terms with the northern environment on the fringes of which it had traded for a century.

As it faced this expansion of its interests, the Hudson's Bay Company paid particular attention to transportation. A Superintendent of Boats was appointed to get goods up to Henley, and that post assumed increasing importance as a supply depot for the outposts "towards Quebec." Despite the facility with which the Canadians undersold the Hudson's Bay men and granted easier credit, and the setback which had inevitably followed the abandonment of their posts, the English had firmly re-established the *Petit Nord* by 1787, and their position was strengthened by a flow of renegades from the Pedlars' service.

The reaction of the English in the *Petit Nord* was based on Moose and Albany. In the Grand North the first move must be to re-establish York and Churchill; Severn, which should normally have been dependent on York, had already been re-established from the Bottom of the Bay. Humphrey Marten and Samuel Hearne were sent back to their posts with houses "in frame" from England, ready to be set up. It was a good move to send back the same post-masters, for prestige was at stake. At York Marten found a party of starving Indians awaiting his arrival in the ruins of the old fort, and he discovered also that William Tomison, having come down from Cumberland, had waited as long as he dared for the arrival of the ship from England and had then set off to winter inland. Tomison and his men, at Cumberland and at Hudson House, survived the winter largely by trading furs to the Canadians for food and supplies, but in the summer of 1784 they brought down a substantial trade to York once more.

Whereas the trade at York by 1784 showed a vitality derived from its inland settlements, at Churchill trade depended on Indians who brought their furs down to the fort and who came for the most part from Athabasca and from the area north of the Saskatchewan. There the capture of Samuel Hearne counted for much, the death of Matonabbee perhaps for more; during the whole season of 1784 no upland Indians came to Churchill.[15] It was reported that they were either dead or had gone to the Canadians with their furs. A glance at the map makes it clear that the trade of Churchill was particularly vulnerable as the Montreal men advanced up the Saskatchewan and over the watershed into Athabasca. For although Churchill had been founded by James Knight especially in order to establish contact with Indians from Athabasca, there was no direct river connection between the mouth of the Churchill River and Lake Athabasca and the district north of that lake. That the rivers of the north froze earlier and melted later than those of the south entailed that an approach to Athabasca by the comparatively direct route of Seal River, Wollaston Lake, and Fond du Lac was available for a more limited period in each year than the more southern and lengthy route which was used by Indians who came from Athabasca to trade by the Bay. They normally travelled south by the Little Athabasca River to the Clearwater River, over Portage la Loche (or Methy Portage) south to Ile-à-la-Crosse and by the Missinipi River (or upper Churchill River) to Lac la Ronge, and so over Frog Portage (or Portage du Traite) into the Churchill River. By the time they arrived at the headwaters of the Churchill River, the ice would be gone from it, and they could travel down to the Bay with little trouble. But the deep southward swing involved, while it gave better conditions and a longer season, also brought the Chipewyans and the other Athabascan Indians into contact with the Canadians, who often took the better part of their furs from them.

It was therefore not surprising that the trade at Churchill, and at York also, suffered severely, especially since the end of the War of American Independence witnessed great reorganizations among the traders from Canada—reorganizations which coincided with, and were to some extent due to, the realization that their trade must derive increasingly from the great Eldorado of Athabasca.

Peter Pond's expedition into Athabasca in 1778, outfitted for this journey from the remains of trade goods left on hand at the end of a winter's trade, had followed the route of other Pedlars (the Frobishers and Louis Primeau). But he had been able to travel further and to trade better. By the time he got back to Cumberland House in 1779, the Hudson's Bay men reported that he was much distressed for want of food. But he had made a magnificent trade, and he had revealed the fabulous wealth which might be got from Athabasca once a supply system could be organized to support regular journeys into that territory. Pond had probably crossed Portage la Loche and had carried on his trade about thirty miles from the entrance of the Athabasca River into Lake Athabasca.[16] Here he had crossed the watershed into a system draining to the Arctic Ocean. Hitherto he had been trespassing, for while the Hudson's Bay men would enjoy equal rights with other British subjects in trading south of the Hudson Bay watershed (but would have no privileges there), the Pedlars were infringing the Company's Charter when they crossed the height of land and entered Rupert's Land.

The difficulties caused by the War of American Independence, together with the prospects of a great enlargement of trade if financial backing could be organized, between them led to closer integration of the fur-traders of Montreal. As Peter Pond came out with his furs in 1779, an organization which could meet both the requirements of trade and of politics appeared when a formal "North West Company" was organized, divided into sixteen shares which would be held by nine different partnerships. The coverage of this "company" was considerable, ranging from Montreal business men such as Isaac Todd and James McGill, Simon McTavish, Forrest Oakes, and Lawrence Ermatinger, to Michilimackinac traders such as George McBeath, and genuine travelling traders such as the brothers Frobisher, Booty Graves Holmes, John Ross, Stephen Waden, and Peter Pond himself.[17]

The "company" was dissolved at the end of the year. But in the meantime the syndicate which had outfitted Peter Pond for his journey into Athabasca sent the Swiss trader Stephen Waden (himself a partner in the "North West Company") to winter at Lac la Ronge, to bring out the furs·which belonged to them and which Pond had been unable to bring out with him in 1779.

Pond himself did not go back to Athabasca again until 1780, and then he went as the envoy of the great firms—the Ellices, the Frobishers, the Mc-Gills, and Simon McTavish—who had in that year formed a second "North West Company." The Indians were troublesome in that year and little trade was secured. But Pond went again into Athabasca as the agent of the "North West Company" in 1781-82, and there he came up against Waden, who was still acting on behalf of the smaller men who were not members of the great concern. Some sort of quarrel arose between Pond and Waden —the details were never precisely elucidated—and in the clash Waden was killed. Pond was suspected of a brutal murder; and it would not have been out of character.[18]

The result was that the smaller traders were dealt a severe blow while the great partnership of the "North West Company" was forced to close its ranks in view of the adverse publicity which Pond had brought upon it. This episode took place as the peace with the United States underlined the importance of a united "lobby" of Canadian fur-traders in order to bring pressure to bear on Governor Haldimand and on the statesmen at West-minster. The threat that the key point of their trade route, at Grand Portage, might be denied to them by the United States, and the prospects and the dangers revealed by Peter Pond, between them drove the Montreal traders to the formation of a powerful and lasting group.

The North West Company formed during the winter of 1783-84[19] was to combine the resources of the traders, again divided into sixteen shares, for a period of at least five years. Authority lay with the great Montreal merchants, the brothers Benjamin and Joseph Frobisher, and Simon Mc-Tavish. A number of important traders—Isaac Todd, the brothers McGill, and Charles Patterson, were still enjoying access to the Mississippi and to the south, and they were content to take no share at this juncture in the Northwest trade. Pond himself was offered one share, but he refused to participate, preferring to join the more active but smaller traders, who were already beginning to feel the weight of the Montreal merchants' con-trol. He went to Montreal in 1784 in an attempt to found a rival company, but instead he took up the share which was still open to him in the great North West Company. This was a more formal and more powerful North West Company than the earlier partnerships which had carried that title. But it was not a chartered corporation, it had no rights which were not open to every citizen, and it was not a limited liability company. It was a form of multiple partnership which would have been described in those days as a "common-law company." The general management of the company's affairs lay with the brothers Frobisher and with Simon McTavish; and the trade which they controlled was considerable. It was reckoned to amount to about £100,000 sterling a year, and that was almost a half of the total trade of Quebec.

Although the North West Company, as formed during the winter of 1783–84, had no peculiar privileges, it had vast power; and it was convinced that trade to the Northwest could be developed only in monopoly conditions. Its views were large and ambitious; its influence and its concepts were on a national scale, far removed from anything which the name of Pedlars would denote. Peter Pond, when he had joined the Company, exemplified its far-flung interests and ambitions. Exchanges of views with Indians in Athabasca had given him a hazy, but fundamentally correct, notion of the Slave and Mackenzie rivers, leading north to the Arctic.[20] He was in error in thinking that from the mouth of the river which would lead to the Arctic it would be easy to sail into the Pacific, but he asked for the support of Governor Haldimand for the North West Company to explore north from Athabasca Lake to the north Pacific Ocean. This was part of a campaign to portray the North West Company as a vigorous exploring body, resisting American influence across the continent and anxious to take a leading part in that search for a passage to the Pacific which was receiving encouragement from the British Admiralty and which had resulted in the voyages of exploration of Captain Cook. Pond received no official government support; but he was sent again into Athabasca by the North West Company in 1785, and in 1786 he made his way north to Great Slave Lake. There he set up Fort Resolution and even ventured further north, to the mouth of the Yellowknife River, where Fort Providence was later set up.

Pond had pushed the trade of the North West Company into the territory of the Chipewyan and Slave Indians, who in normal times would have taken their furs down to York and to Churchill. Those posts were recovering with difficulty from smallpox and the French invasion, and the Nor'westers' ascendancy appears from the fact that the shipments of furs from Quebec and Montreal to the London market then ranged between £165,000 and £242,000 a year, while the Hudson's Bay Company's shipments totalled only about £30,000.[21] There was an obvious need for the English to take up the challenge of the North West Company. But it was not from Hudson's Bay Company men that Pond met opposition in Athabasca. His rivals there were other traders from Montreal.

There had been many active traders who had not been included in the great partnership formed in 1783-84, or who had not accepted the status granted to them in that arrangement. They could do little unless they could find some substantial merchant or banking firm which would supply them with imported trade goods on credit and which would take their furs to sell on the London market. The North West Company, however, while it had been unable to include many such men, had also been unable to find a place for the powerful merchant company of Finlay and Gregory. In 1783 that company had received a new impetus when Finlay retired and Norman McLeod took his place as a partner. Gregory, McLeod and Company then provided the financial backing and the business organization which was needed by the traders left out of the North West Company; and the firm of Gregory, McLeod and Company sent John Ross, who had opposed the English on the Saskatchewan as far back as 1777 and who had been included in the North West Company of 1779 but not in that of 1783-84, to compete in Athabasca with the redoubtable Peter Pond. Once more Pond got into "a scuffle," and Ross was killed, again in circumstances which made it seem not impossible that Pond had murdered his competitor.[22]

The death of Ross was but one incident in the bitter rivalry between uncompromising men, working far from any effective jurisdiction. The whole of the Northwest was involved in the severest struggle it had ever known, and the rivalry between the two groups of Canadian traders far outweighed any opposition from the Hudson's Bay men. Convinced monopolists as they were, the great managers of the North West Company therefore took the logical step of reorganizing their partnership in 1787 so as to included Gregory, McLeod and Company[23] and to offer participation to the traders who had served under them. So from 1787 onwards the North West Company of Montreal controlled virtually the whole fur-trading capacity of Canada, organized to exploit the Northwest by using the route by the Grand Portage and the Saskatchewan. Peter Pond was included, as was young Alexander Mackenzie, trained in Gregory's office and already experienced as an Indian trader on the English River, at the back of Churchill. Authority, and a predominant block of the shares, lay with the two firms of Joseph Frobisher and Simon McTavish; their joint firm of McTavish, Frobisher and Company acted as the agent for the North West Company, to purchase supplies and to market furs, and Simon McTavish steadily gained that control which in the end was to earn him the title of the "Marquis."

If anything was required to explain the decline in the trade of Churchill, these amalgamations and the competence of the Montreal traders would suffice. Their outlook may be seen in the way in which they sent Alexander Mackenzie into Athabasca, where he learned from Peter Pond those views of exploration to the Arctic and the Pacific which he later implemented. Their success may be explained by their skill in placing the Northwest fur trade on a two-year cycle by the movement of trade goods to Grand Portage, to exchange for the furs brought down by the inland traders, "the wintering partners." They combined ability to exploit market conditions in London (which the English company also possessed) with a knowledge of moving, trading, and living in the Northwest which the men of the Hudson's Bay Company were only beginning to learn. Until the Hudson's Bay Company matched the French Canadian *voyageur* with the Orkney boatman, the canoe with the York boat, the "wintering partner," or *bourgeois*, with the "inland master," it could not match the Canadian company. The Nor'-westers boasted a mastery of the rivers, forests, and prairies of the Northwest which the English could not challenge; and this in turn bred a pride and determination which were invaluable.

The Hudson's Bay Company's reaction came more slowly in the west than at the Bottom of the Bay. This may have been due to local leadership; for at the Bottom of the Bay the chiefs had decided to resist the French, whereas Hearne and Marten had yielded their well-built posts. Turnor also was available at the Bottom of the Bay, much taken up with the moves "towards Quebec." For the Grand North, as for the *Petit Nord*, the Hudson's Bay Committee needed better surveys and more accurate information than the individualistic Canadians required. Consequently their methods were slower. In 1785 they decided that Robert Longmoor must explore the Churchill River and report on sites at which houses might be built. He was to take with him a competent surveyor, the apprentice George Charles, recruited from the Grey Coat School in London. Samuel Hearne, however, decided that, notwithstanding orders, the best route for opposition to the Montreal traders was that which he had followed when he had established Cumberland House—from York to Cedar Lake and then up-stream; not from Churchill by way of the Churchill River. He therefore sent Longmoor to the Saskatchewan, there to set up Manchester House. George Charles was sent with Malchom Ross, one of the best travellers in the Company's service. These two also made their way to Cumberland House, but they went by the Churchill River and then portaged into the basin of the Saskatchewan. Ross and Longmoor both found numbers of small and mobile opposition posts throughout the country, penetrating down to within a couple of days' travel of the Bayside.[24]

The London Committee derived much information from these journeys, and the establishment of Manchester House in the heart of the Pedlars' country was a considerable achievement. When Malchom Ross returned to York Fort he brought down Indians to trade who had never been there before. But he had not penetrated into Athabasca, as the Committee had hoped, and it was clear by 1786 that effective rivalry with the growing power of the North West Company must be directed from inland, and that the age-old assumption that the Bayside posts were the centres of command must be revised. In 1786 a new policy of mobility, and of emphasis on the inland posts, was therefore adopted; Osnaburgh was then established at Lake St Joseph, for example, the Committee ordering that this must be only a temporary post, with mobility implied in the order that its Master should get as near to the Canadians as possible. Henley and Gloucester were to be mobile in the same way and, taking a leaf from the Pedlars' book, the Committee ordered log tents to replace the more stable square-built posts. In 1785, as Hearne was ordered to send Longmoor to chart the Churchill River, Humphrey Marten at York was told that the inland trade should be his first consideration and that sixty-five out of his eighty-five men must be sent inland.[25]

This tendency was confirmed in 1786, when Marten retired. Formal command was then transferred to the inland posts as William Tomison was made Chief at York, to reside inland. He was given power to allocate men and goods to the inland posts at his discretion, while a Resident at York was to be subservient to him whenever he should be present. The main duty of the Resident, and indeed of York, was to supply the demands of the inland posts.[26] The inland trade was to be pushed on with the greatest vigour; and the immediate result was a notable increase in the trade of York.

Hearne was allowed to retire in 1787, and Churchill also was made subservient to the development of the inland trade. At the Bottom of the Bay there was no one of Longmoor's or Tomison's stature to take command of the situation from inland; but there the Hudson's Bay Company appeared in a better light, and several competent traders deserted from the Montreal concerns and were taken into the Company's employment. One of these, Germain Maugenest, who claimed to have invented the Hudson's Bay Point Blanket and who had been concerned with exploration to the south, was made second-in-command at Moose in 1787, while at the same time he was made Master of the new post of New Brunswick House on Brunswick Lake.[27] The arrangement did not give the predominance to the inland posts achieved by the appointment of Tomison at York, but it gave the inland traders a substantial voice. The Eastmain trade was at the same time strengthened and reorganized; an inland post was established at Rupert's House, and the eastern coast of Hudson Bay was explored in the hope of finding a passage to the Atlantic which would exempt shipping from the difficult and arduous northern passage through Hudson Strait.

The Canadians taken into English employment at this time brought valuable qualities as travellers and as Indian traders, although some of them also brought an independence of outlook which could not easily be reconciled to the English system. Typical of such recruits was Donald Mackay, who had been in correspondence with Turnor when the latter was at Abitibi and who joined the English at Nipigon in 1789. Mackay was a violent and energetic traveller, full of ideas which varied from the wild and eccentric to the shrewd and imaginative. He proposed to the Company that a route should be established north from Michilimackinac (to which the Hudson's Bay men had equal rights of access with the Pedlars), and he promised to establish four posts in the area of Lake Nipigon within five years.[28] His acceptance by the Company was evidence of a desire to counter the Canadians in the "Fire Country," to organize a provision trade which would make possible an inland transportation system comparable with that of the Montreal men, to push south to the height of land, and to compete in the market for the beaver of the south.

The Committee had taken Samuel Hearne to task for his conclusion that the best way to Athabasca was by the Saskatchewan and not by the apparently more direct route of the Churchill River. But when they perused the (illiterate) journal sent in by Malchom Ross, they decided to send Charles Price Isham (an English half-breed well used to travel in the north) from York to Cedar Lake, and so to the Swan River. There he was to make canoes and to take them up to Cumberland and was then to form part of an expedition to follow the Nor'westers into Athabasca. This meant going up to Peter Pond's outpost at Fort Providence on Great Slave Lake. The death of the Chief Trader at Cumberland, a competent surveyor who was to have led the expedition north, prevented this plan from being put into execution; but the enthusiasm for exploring and for surveying was such that in this year Thomas Stayner set out from Cumberland in the direction of the Rockies. At the same time the Committee ordered that the "Back of Churchill" should be explored. They had records of Hearne's journey to the mouth of the Coppermine, and they were anxious to know details of "Dubawnt or Slave Lake," confusing the two.

As a further incentive to exploration, Philip Turnor was sent out from England again in 1789 and was given command at Cumberland, where he took in hand the planning of the expedition to the north. During the winter 1789-90, while he was in command at Cumberland, he trained David Thompson, a young apprentice who was destined to play a great part in the surveying of North America, in survey work. When Thompson broke his leg and was unable to participate, another man with a great future as a surveyor, Peter Fidler, was trained for the task. Turnor made some useful preliminary explorations of the route to Athabasca during the winter 1790-91, and again in 1791-92. He saw the Nor'westers as they brought their furs out from Athabasca, and in particular he exchanged views with Alexander Mackenzie as the latter came out in 1790, and learned of the journey down the Mackenzie River to the Arctic Ocean which Mackenzie had just completed. Turnor commented that since the Nor'wester did not seem able to make observations he could not be precisely certain where he had been.

After spending the winter of 1787-88 in company with Peter Pond at Pond's "Old Establishment" on Lake Athabasca, Mackenzie had accepted the convictions of the old trader and, when Pond went out from Athabasca in 1788, Mackenzie was eager to maintain Athabasca both for the sake of its furs and as a base from which an expedition to the Arctic (and perhaps to the Pacific) might be launched. He would have behind him the great strength of the North West Company as it had been reorganized in 1787, and he would also have the provision system used by that company. The outstanding merit of this system was the way in which the abundant buffalo meat of the prairies was used for pounding into pemmican; and pemmican made it possible to organize the transport of men and goods over vast distances without delay, since the "brigades" lived on pemmican as they travelled. Mackenzie had reorganized the trade of Athabasca under the control of a new and imposing establishment at Fort Chipewyan on Lake Athabasca, had handed the business over to his cousin, Roderick Mackenzie, and had then set off with a small party in June 1789, down the Slave River to Great Slave Lake. There he had been held up by ice and had spent much time searching for the outlet of the Mackenzie River from the north end of Great Slave Lake; for the outlet runs from an extreme westerly inlet, not from the north shore, as might have been expected. Having found his river, he reached its mouth on July 10. Although this must have been a disappointment to him since he concluded that he had probably arrived at the "Hyperborean Sea" when he had hoped to reach the Pacific, nevertheless Mackenzie had completed an epic journey and had in effect achieved that break-through to western tidal waters which two and a half centuries of northern exploration had sought in vain. Mackenzie's conclusions, however, supported the views of Middleton, reached half a century earlier. He had shown that there could not be any passage south of the mouth of the Mackenzie, and that any passage to the north, if such should exist, would have no practical value since the sea was "eternally covered with ice." [29]

Mackenzie's voyage, like Peter Pond's earlier memoranda, was meant to emphasize the importance of the North West Company in opening up the British part of North America. But the British government was not at that time greatly concerned to discover new areas over which to extend its rule; the search was for routes which would bring British merchants into profitable contact with the peoples of the east, not for new realms to conquer, to govern, and to defend. Mackenzie held that the North West Company should support exploration "from the hope that if they succeed in penetrating to the Ocean, Government may be induced to grant them a Charter and Exclusive Right in the lucrative Furr trade in those parts." Having failed to reach the ocean, they could not hope for the exclusive right. Mackenzie's voyage was therefore as much of a disappointment to the Company as to him, and when he came out to the meeting of the partners at the Grand Portage in 1790, he found himself given very little attention.

Mackenzie had met Turnor on several occasions, not only as he went down to the Grand Portage in 1790, and Mackenzie's views on Turnor's lack of pemmican and other equipment for exploring, which the Nor'westers took for granted, were as strong as were Turnor's views of Mackenzie's lack of surveying skill. Turnor's ambitions were "heartily laughed at by the Canadian gents"; but he got some valuable hints from them. For example, he was told by Mackenzie himself that he would not be able to collect his food as he went from Ile-à-la-Crosse over Portage la Loche and down the Athabasca River to Lake Athabasca; and when he set off on his northern journey he therefore went by a longer route—by Swan Lake to the Clear-water—reaching Lake Athabasca in late June 1791. Turnor was greatly impressed by Fort Chipewyan, already famous as the "Grand Magazine of Athabasca." He reported that Athabasca was "the bulwark of the Canadian Company," with something like 20,000 made-beaver in fine skins taken from that territory each year by the Nor'westers; and he was certain that the Hudson's Bay Company could not maintain any posts there unless at least one subsidiary post could be established on the Peace River, whose duty it would be to provide meat and pemmican for the posts in Athabasca. Otherwise any post would be entirely dependent on fish to be got from Athabasca Lake, and that would not enable the brigades of canoes to travel, although it might enable the posts to subsist through the winters.[30] Turnor had seen and had appreciated the methods which the Canadian company used in the exploitation of the Northwest.

At this time Turnor promulgated a thesis that all discovery in Canada must start from inland and proceed down-stream on the rivers. Explorers would then never have to choose which branch of a river to take; they would be on streams which would steadily grow in size and which would certainly lead them to the sea. He argued that he could start from Athabasca and could find a direct way to the coast, either by the Nelson River to York or by the Churchill to Churchill. But when he continued his journey from Lake Athabasca to Great Slave Lake he could hear no report of any river to the north of that lake except the Mackenzie. He therefore spent the winter on Lake Athabasca, intending to renew his exploration in 1792; and there he and his men were able to watch the Nor'westers' methods of trading and to conclude that the Indians would welcome the Hudson's Bay men as an alternative to the Nor'westers. When the Chipewyans from the Slave River asked for one of his men to winter with them, Turnor sent Peter Fidler, who delighted the Indians and spent a most successful winter.

In the end, Turnor went out to York Factory in 1792 by the established route past Ile-à-la-Crosse, over Portage la Loche and so to Cumberland House. Starting from Lake Athabasca on May 9, he arrived at York on July 17. He was well prepared to go inland once more and to continue exploration in Athabasca, but the Inland Master, Tomison, obsessed by the importance of the Saskatchewan and Cumberland, proved unwilling to foster establishments to the north of Cumberland. Frustrated and unable to carry through his proposals for the crucial area to the north of Cumberland, Turnor returned to England, to work on his maps and to write up his experiences.[31]

Limited though his outlook might be, in the area of the Saskatchewan Tomison was a vigorous and successful Inland Master. In 1786 he had presided over the establishment of Manchester House on the north branch of the Saskatchewan, and of the South Branch House which was replaced by Carlton House in 1794. Both Cumberland and Hudson House were rebuilt, while another outpost, Buckingham House, was also built upstream from Cumberland. His views were broad and imaginative, and he was particularly aware of the need to organize provisions and transport if the inland posts were to rival the Nor'westers. In 1794, therefore, he ordered the construction of Gordon House, later known as the Rock Depot, up the Hill River one hundred and twenty miles inland from York Factory.[32] Up to that point the river contained no falls or obstructions which would prevent boats from being used to get goods up. At the Rock both boat and cargo had to be carried over a barrier in the stream, and there were some thirty carrying places in the two hundred and seventy miles or so which lay between the Rock and Lake Winnipeg. It was therefore desirable to use smaller boats above the Rock than below it, or even canoes; and the Rock became the depot to which goods were transported at leisure from York, there to be stored until the appropriate time for their further transport inland by craft which did not have to make the whole journey down to tidal water and back.

From the first year of its use, the Rock Depot saved over a week in transportation of goods to the upper Saskatchewan. With this advantage Tomison was able in 1795 to go past Buckingham House, there to leave the river and to travel overland due west, to rejoin the river and to build on the north bank at what came to be called Edmonton House, where the Nor'westers already had their Fort Augustus.[33] In all of this Tomison was devoting his energy to what Turnor would have called the "southern trade." But he had advanced English trade to within striking distance of the Rockies.

While the Inland Master was thus diverted from exploring Athabasca, the Resident at York Factory had his preoccupations too. Joseph Colen, greatly taken up with rebuilding his post, devoted much of his trading attention to what David Thompson called the "muskrat country." For Thompson this was a territory extending about three hundred miles south from the shores of Hudson Bay, characterized by the "granite and other siliceous Rocks" which formed it, by the swamps which marked it, and by the absence of trees.[34] This was an area bounded on the south side by the Great Shield of Canada and extending from the coast of Labrador to the chain of lakes which led from Lake Superior to Lake Athabasca and Great Slave Lake. For Colen the muskrat country between the Nelson River and the Churchill River was of great interest, an area in which his Home Guard Crees roamed, and through which there might be found a short route to Athabasca by way of Split Lake and the Burntwood River and Lake. The route, however, was a comparatively unimportant consideration; Colen's main trouble was that the Nor'westers had invaded the area in strength after the reorganization of their company in 1787 and that their lavish methods of trade secured skins which would otherwise have come to York.

With both Colen and Turnor anxious to find a more direct way to Athabasca than that offered by Lake Winnipeg and the Saskatchewan, the London Committee showed their interest when in 1790 they engaged a naval captain, Charles Duncan, to command the *Churchill* sloop and to explore in her from Churchill northwards. The Committee were inspired by the "very indistinct account that has been received of the recent Peregrinations of *Peter Pond* and the *Canadian Traders* to Slave Lake,"[35] but their own notions were still hazy and their plans unrealistic.

Duncan sailed from the Orkneys in 1790; but the *Churchill* sloop proved inadequate for his purposes. He returned to Churchill in 1791 and stayed in the Bay through 1792, but, face to face with his problems, he concluded that the Hudson's Bay men on the spot had more realistic notions than either their detractors or their employers would have allowed. He was forced to return before he could decide whether the Seal River, part of which he explored, would lead to a shorter route to the west, because he had not mastered the skills of nothern travel.

While the grand plan under Duncan faltered, Colen found the Nor'westers closing in on his post and was forced to thrust outwards to combat them. In 1790 he founded a post at Split Lake, and in 1791 a further post at Chatham House. As Turnor came out from his voyage to Athabasca he was persuaded to explore the Nelson River up to Chatham House during the summer of 1792, and he then heard Indian reports that the Burntwood River, branching off southwestwards from Split Lake, might be the most direct approach to Athabasca, leading over a portage to the upper waters of the Churchill River, from where Reindeer River and Lake, and Wollaston Lake, would lead to the extreme eastern end of Lake Athabasca—the goal on which Turnor's thoughts were concentrated. Alternatively, it might be possible to go by the Burntwood to the upper Churchill and then by that river (the Missinipi River) to Ile-à-la-Crosse and so by the known route of the Clearwater River to the great lake. These possibilities needed investigation, and David Thompson (now fully recovered) and Malchom Ross were chosen for the purpose.

The two men were ideally suited for the task, and that they were available is in itself a tribute to the change in outlook from that which Robson had derided as the "sleep by the Frozen Sea." But they were diverted to other activities and could not be sent to the Burntwood Carrying Place, and so to the Churchill River, until 1795. There they wintered, and in 1796, while Ross went down to York, Thompson completed an epic journey to Lake Athabasca. Accompanied only by two young Chipewyans, he had almost no equipment, and no provisions for the journey. He had to make his own canoe, and his chief dependence was on a fishing net. When he reached Lake Athabasca he lost his canoe and his gear in a fall and was resigned to death. But he was rescued by an Indian family and eventually returned to meet Ross.

The woeful inadequacy of the equipment and preparations with which Thompson had been sent on this journey stands in stark contrast to the methods of the Nor'westers. Nothing but his own determination made the journey possible. Some of his troubles were due to misfortune; but the route was in any case difficult to the point of impossibility. In particular it was impossible under the Hudson's Bay régime of hunting and fishing on the march. Thompson, with a streak of sheer obstinacy in his character, refused to accept the forbidding difficulties. With Ross, who had come up from York with supplies and food, he built Bedford House on Reindeer Lake and spent a miserable winter there, hunting, fishing, and compiling notes on the flora and fauna.[36] They were easily the first Hudson's Bay men in those parts, and their explorations and their reports were invaluable. But the Nor'westers' advantage was revealed when, in the spring of 1797, David Thompson made his way to the nearest North West post—that under Alexander Fraser at the outlet of Reindeer Lake—and there entered the service of the North West Company.

Just as Mackenzie's journey to the "Hyperborean Sea" had left the disconcerting conclusion that there could be no passage south of the Mackenzie's mouth, and that any passage to the north would be useless, but had combined this negative verdict with an important positive achievement, so did Thompson's exploration of the Burntwood route to Athabasca. Accurately surveying as he went, he made it clear that the route would save many miles of travel; but he had also made it clear that it would be too difficult, dangerous, and sparsely peopled to be of any practical value. If something of the Nor'westers' methods of provisioning and travel could be adopted, the route might be made tolerable, and this may perhaps explain to some extent why Thompson threw in his lot with the Nor'westers. For he maintained that the Burntwood route should be developed, whereas the

Hudson's Bay men rejected it out of hand at that time, to toy with it later when, in the early years of the nineteenth century, they had accepted some of the Nor'westers' methods.

David Thompson took with him the skills which he had acquired, and married them with the vigour and the competence of the North West Company. At the same time Alexander Mackenzie, possibly as a result of his conversations with Turnor, realized the defects in his own techniques as an explorer. He intended to continue with his search for a passage to the Western Ocean, and to equip himself for the task he came to England, to master the surveying skills in which he felt himself deficient.

While the Hudson's Bay men were engaged in the pedestrian, if exhausting, task of exploring a better route from the Bay to Athabasca, Mackenzie fulfilled the Nor'westers' desire to find a way to the shores of the Pacific, overland from Canada. Returning from England with a competence in surveying added to his great ability as a traveller, he had gone back to his old point of departure, at Fort Chipewyan on Lake Athabasca. Preparations had already been put in hand to further the journey which he proposed, and the Nor'westers had established posts at Vermilion Falls, at Fort du Tremble, and at the Smoky River to help him up to the headwaters of the Peace River. He set off from Fort Chipewyan in October 1792, built a small house just above the mouth of the Smoky River, and spent the winter there, to set off again in May 1793. He had seven Canadians and two Indians with him, and they tracked their canoe up through Peace River Canyon to the Forks of the Finlay and Parsnip rivers. There Mackenzie followed the Parsnip up to its source on the height of land and was then guided overland to the Great River, as he called it, and so down-stream to the Forks of the Fraser.

In his leaky and worn-out canoe Mackenzie travelled southwest, on down the Fraser. It was a desperate journey, for the Fraser is a constant danger; and he found that the Indians of the western slopes of the Rockies were numerous and threatening in a way in which the scattered bands of the east were not. Early in July 1793 even Mackenzie was ready to abandon the dangerous river, and he struck off overland to reach the Bella Coola River. Only his great strength and determination kept his party going, but at last he led his men, in canoes provided by the Indians of Bella Coola, down to salt water at North Bentinck Arm. Here he narrowly missed meeting Vancouver's *Discovery* and Broughton's *Chatham*, exploring from west to east in search of the Passage and charting large areas of the Pacific coast. But he met with hostility from Indians whom the sailors had offended, and so he continued quickly down to the open sea. There he left the classically simple inscription, written on a rock by the shore in a mixture of vermilion and grease—"Alexander Mackenzie, from Canada, by land, the twenty-second of July, one thousand seven hundred and ninety-three."

Mackenzie made his return journey to Peace River in thirty-three days. He was then thirty years old and had ended his career as an explorer. His triumph was a triumph of determination over difficulties; but it was something more. It was the triumph of an idea—the idea that somewhere an overland passage to the Pacific must exist, and that the North West Company must discover it, must exploit it, and use it as evidence of their competence and of their public spirit, to secure from the British government that monopoly of the fur trade which lay at the centre of their planning.

Much of this took years to appear. At the time the direct and uncomplicated desire to find the overland route to the west coast was the most apparent feature of the great exploit; and the immediate result was that Mackenzie himself, and the North West Company, appeared in ever more glamorous colours. Their ability to organize and support voyages of discovery stood in sharp contrast to the neglect and the lack of equipment from which Thompson had suffered in his journey to Lake Athabasca. Mackenzie had laid out a way from Montreal to the Pacific, and so on to China. While Athabasca was still the ultimate goal for the Hudson's Bay men, it seemed likely to become merely a stage on the way to the foot of the Rockies for the Nor'westers. Dedicated as he was to his task of surveying, David Thompson must have felt to the full the attractions of serving in such a company. Between them, he and Mackenzie gave to the Nor'westers a technical competence to match their vigour and determination. The powerful organization of the North West Company had, by the end of the eighteenth century, given to its men an ability to reach, and to live in, the lands from Quebec to the Bottom of the Bay, from Lake Winnipeg to the Muskrat Country, and from the upper Saskatchewan to Athabasca and to the foot of the Rockies. Less effective in their provisioning and travel techniques but more accurate in their knowledge and in their reports, the Hudson's Bay men had done much to exploit the advantages which access to the shores of the Bay had given to them, and had, in effect, carried out the instructions given when it had first been decided that competitive trade must be undertaken on the Saskatchewan—to go as far as the Canadians. Between the two companies, the fur-traders had crossed the prairies, had entered the Northwest, and had approached the Rockies. Their efforts were co-ordinated with renewed purpose by the British Admiralty, seeking again the Passage to the Western Sea.

CHAPTER 11

The North West Company
and the Red River Colony

As the Revolutionary and Napoleonic Wars in Europe began to upset the patterns of trade through the world, both the Hudson's Bay Company and the North West Company were busy pressing their services on the British government, anxious to further the national objective of achieving some new route to the Pacific—if only their privileges could be confirmed and extended. Both companies felt the impact of these wars, but it was the Hudson's Bay Company which appeared to suffer the more. By 1805-6 the situation was clearly outlined, and the relative strength of the two concerns could be estimated. By that date the Hudson's Bay Company, affected by the war conditions, rising prices for trade goods, diminished returns in furs, and obstructed markets in Europe, was obviously in trouble. In 1801 the annual dividend had been dropped from a steady 6 per cent per annum to 4 per cent. By 1806 a payment of 4 per cent was still maintained, but the yearly trade did not justify this. In 1806 the British government was told that the Company's stock had steadily depreciated and that the gross profit had diminished. The Company was compelled to sell its investments and to negotiate a substantial loan from the Bank of England; by 1808 it was seeking (in vain) for government support for a further loan. By that time the Committee were explaining that they had not sold a single fur for export since 1806 and that they had three years' stocks on hand.[1] Apart from their troubles with the export market, their great difficulty lay in the remoteness of their control over their traders. They had, however, a good reputation in the City of London and could raise money on credit. Their large shareholders were not dependent on the Company for day-to-day income but were prepared to advance money and support the Company, and they had at their back their Charter with its territorial and trading rights.

Their posts too were in good heart, and even when the Company had to pass its dividend in 1809, this was done with the consoling phrase that "the

Affairs of the Company at their Factories and Settlements in Hudson's Bay continue to prosper."[2] This was an honest enough reflection; after rising to 94,000 made-beaver in 1801 the returns had declined to 63,000 in 1803; but they rose again to almost 70,000 by 1805, and as far as the fur returns were concerned the Company was justified in its quiet confidence.[3] "We do not expect returns equal to those of our more powerful Opponents but we ought to receive such returns as are adequate to the quantity of goods you are annually supplied with," the Committee told the traders.[4]

The posts inland and at the Bayside were of course not without their troubles. They were bound to share in the consequences of the ill-treatment which the Nor'westers at times dealt out to the Indians; their post at South Branch House was destroyed in 1792 by Indians whom the Nor'westers had abused, and in 1793 Manchester House was pillaged of its arms, so that in the next year South Branch House could again be overrun, three of the Hudson's Bay men killed, and the Indian women and children attached to the post massacred. The danger rose from the confident assertiveness of the Nor'westers being found alongside the trustful unpreparedness of the Hudson's Bay men.[5] Despite such troubles, the urge to explore the Company's territories, to take trade inland, and in particular to find a better route to Athabasca, remained. In 1793 Peter Fidler explored the Seal River and pronounced it an admirable route inland from Churchill, in which flat-bottomed boats could be used. He was then diverted to other tasks, and exploration from Churchill came under William Auld, another surgeon turned trader, who in 1794 tried to establish an inland post up the Churchill River. Little was achieved, although in 1795 Auld was made "Inland Trader" for Churchill. In fact neither York Factory nor Churchill produced an effective opposition to the North West Company in Athabasca until 1802, when Peter Fidler returned there.

In the meantime the Hudson's Bay men had followed the Nor'westers into areas from which they got furs, pemmican, and wild rice—the area of the Swan River, the Assiniboine, and the Red River, south of Lake Winnipeg and Lake Manitoba. Here the Hudson's Bay men might come either from York Factory or from the Bottom of the Bay, and they were as much in opposition to each other as to the North West Company. Despite the Committee's pressure for good understanding among all its posts, internal rivalry could not be avoided, especially when such a man as Donald MacKay (in his heart despising the Hudson's Bay men with whom he served) was sent up to that area from Albany. Donald MacKay and his brother John fought the North West Company in the Lake Nipigon-Rainy Lake area with blustering irascibility; the provision trade was vital although the fur returns from that area had never been significant. By 1796, when Donald MacKay was sent down to York Factory, the English Company had a post at Rainy Lake, one at Portage de l'Isle, and one at Lake of the Woods; they also had a provisions depot of sorts at Bas de la Rivière at the foot of Lake Winnipeg, and another at Brandon House on the Assiniboine. They had moved into the Nor'westers' provision department; and although they were not opening up new territory they were making the Rainy Lake district so well known that in 1795 there were twenty-one posts on the Assiniboine alone, and all the managements involved—Hudson's Bay, North West Company, and independent traders—fully understood the territory.

The Hudson's Bay Committee concluded that their posts were thriving; but in comparison with the North West Company their business was small, their enterprise negligible. In 1795, for example, the North West Company controlled eleven-fourteenths of the fur trade of Canada, the Hudson's Bay Company two-fourteenths, and independent traders one-fourteenth. Later, in 1800, the Hudson's Bay Company imported into England £38,463 worth of furs, whereas the Nor'westers imported £144,300 worth.[6]

When the amalgamation of 1787 had brought Gregory, McLeod and Company into the North West Company, the average trade for the next six years came to about £72,000 a year. The Nor'westers' predominance in trade was equalled by their personal pre-eminence over most of the Hudson's Bay men; for within the North West Company there had grown the feeling that they were an *élite*, adventurous, hardy, and purposeful. The distances to be covered, and the area from which trade was to be drawn, were vast; and a magnificent and efficient system was evolved to deal with the trade. Goods bought in London (but often made in Lancashire or Yorkshire) would be sorted and parcelled in Quebec and got up to Montreal by the time the St Lawrence was free of ice, each spring. From Lachine Rapids the goods would be taken up the Ottawa River and so to Sault Ste Marie. For their journey through Lake Superior the North West Company had in 1790 provided two ships, to which was added a seventy-five-ton ship in 1793, with sloops on Lake Huron, Lake Erie, and Lake Michigan. The goods would go by ship to the foot of the Grand Portage, be allotted to the posts, packed into the comparatively small *canots du nord* which would take them and the winterers (who worked from Grand Portage onwards, as distinct from the *mangeurs de lard* who managed the transport system up to the Grand Portage), and would be dispersed throughout the Northwest. The annual meeting at Grand Portage was a brief period of festivity and of intense activity. The furs would be appraised by the partners and the agents, plans would be agreed and policy accepted, accounts would be rendered, and the business for the ensuing year would be organized. Altogether the North West Company under this system employed something like 1,120 canoemen and 35 guides, and the cost of such a labour-force was considerable even though the *voyageurs* spent most of their wages at the Company's store.[7]

By keen business methods and great hardihood the Nor'westers overcame most of the disadvantages of the long route to the Northwest—and Alexander Mackenzie reckoned that from Montreal to Lake Athabasca was 2,750 miles and that there was a further 1,540 to the mouth of the Mackenzie. But this did not mean that all depended on the hardihood of the *voyageurs* and the winterers. The ability of Simon McTavish and the agents in Montreal was as much the distinguishing mark of the partnership as the strength of any winterer; and the competence of McTavish, Fraser and Company in London also counted for much.

The amalgamation of 1787 was modified in 1790 by an agreement whose chief difference from that of 1787 was that it began with a clause that "McTavish, Frobisher and Coy shall do all the business of the concern at Montreal and import the goods necessary for the supplies."[8] Increasingly, the strength of the North West Company was directed by the fine intelligence of Simon McTavish; but in so far as Simon McTavish increased his grip, there was less scope for other men to find satisfying careers within the Company. Accordingly, from the start of the revised partnership, as early as 1791, it became clear that John McGill, Isaac Todd, Alexander Henry, and others who normally traded southwest from Detroit, were feeling excluded from trade to the Northwest. Rivalry must be expected, and in September 1792 a new formal agreement was sent up to the Grand Portage, by which Todd, McGill and Company, Forsyth, Richardson and Company, Alexander Henry and Company, and Grant, Campion and Company, all agreed with the North West Company that they would further each other's trade and would not interfere with each other's Indians in the Upper Country. This agreement gave the great North West Company an outer fringe of friendly rivals, all anxious to use the services of McTavish, Frobisher and Company and of McTavish, Fraser and Company, as agents either in Montreal or in London. The power and the wealth of the agents consequently rose by comparison with the strength of the wintering partners of the concern. The agents, furthermore, confirmed their strength and their joint purpose, by new deeds of partnership in 1792.[9]

As ever, the closer the great concern drew together, the more determined were those who were not included to challenge its control. The brothers Peter and David Grant, in particular, took their trade up to the Assiniboine, an area in which the Nor'westers could tolerate no rivalry. Competition upset the Indians, increased the price of canoes and the wages of canoemen, and led to a series of incidents.

The difficulties of the North West Company came to a head in 1794, as the boundary with the United States was at last definitively settled in Jay's

Treaty. Access to the western posts, to Lake Michigan, Chicago, and Detroit was now interrupted. Important Montreal firms, such as McGill, Todd and Company, or Forsyth, Richardson and Company, who traded from the Grand Portage to the southwest in the same way as the Nor'westers traded to the Northwest, were forced in the next decade to review their positions and either to abandon their Canadian character and adopt an American background or to abandon the southwest trade and transfer their interests to the Northwest.[10] Outwardly the interests of these great Canadian fur-traders were secured by Jay's Treaty since it was then agreed that both British and American subjects could trade on either side of the frontier and could travel on the rivers on both sides of the boundary and on the Mississippi. But from this time forward Canadian traders were always in danger from discrimination directed "to drive the British Indian traders from the American territory by every species of vexation." Further competition in the Northwest was inevitable, and though the combinations in which these merchants merged were short-lived, they were none the less competent.

In the years immediately following Jay's Treaty the Nor'westers were faced with a new opposition, of which Forsyth, Richardson and Company and Grant, Campion and Company were the two most powerful groups. Both were moving out from the southwest trade and into the Northwest. In 1795 therefore the North West Company reorganized.[11] The precise terms of the contract then made are not available, but it is clear that the agents had to combat both the winterers, who thought that the agents got a disproportionate share of the profits, and the southern traders who wished to enter the northern trade. The revised agreement of 1795 left Simon McTavish in control and brought his nephew, William McGillivray, into a commanding position in the Montreal house. But though the winterers led by Alexander Mackenzie secured several shares, terms satisfying to the new North West partners could not be agreed on. In the end the great firm of Todd, McGill and Company decided to remain in the southwest trade and did not join the North West partnership. The equally important firm of Forsyth, Richardson and Company found the terms offered unacceptable. They, and the firms of John Mure of Quebec; Parker, Gerrard and Ogilvy and Company; Phynn, Inglis and Company; and Leith, Jamieson and Company were all outside the new North West agreement, to finance and organize free traders. These were serious rivals in Canada in 1795, to add to competition with the Hudson's Bay Company and to dispute the North West Company's plans for monopoly.

Perhaps the most dangerous sign of the weakness of the 1795 agreement was that the winterers, protesting against the predominance of the agents, had found a spokesman in Alexander Mackenzie. He was bound by the agreement of 1790 to remain in the Company until 1799, but it was increasingly evident that he would gladly support a rival concern and that such a concern could easily be formed. His support of the winterers against the agents, and his personal stature, led the agents to take him away from contact with the winterers, and he spent 1798 and the first part of 1799 as representative of the Company in New York, negotiating with John Jacob Astor and other Americans for agreements by which the North West Company might evade the East India Company's monopoly of trade to China by shipping furs into the United States, and then to China as American produce. The experience in New York was frustrating for Mackenzie, but it left him with an even stronger resolution to secure access for Canadian traders to the Pacific and the Far East, coupled with a determination to escape from the controls of the agents, who were engaging in devious, and unsuccessful, arrangements with the Americans. When Mackenzie left the concern in 1799 on the expiration of his agreement and found his way to London, he had got "an entire ascendancy over the young men," and there was already in the field a well-organized opposition to the North West Company. In 1797 the firm of Forsyth, Richardson and Company had begun to organize the uncommitted winterers, and in 1798 they had formed a partnership with Leith, Jamieson and Company and with a group of six winterers. This new combination had difficulties both in recruiting men and in getting its goods inland; and it was by no means closely united. But Simon McTavish and his nephew William McGillivray had become so predominant in the North West Company when Joseph Frobisher resigned in 1798 that the "New North West Company" (as the Hudson's Bay men called it) was able to carry opposition right into Athabasca, and in 1800 Mackenzie himself joined this partnership.[12]

The New North West Company had already begun to be called the XY Company—a name derived from the markings on its bales of goods, to distinguish them from those of the North West Company—and from 1800 onwards it was from time to time called Sir Alexander Mackenzie and Company. Mackenzie was a person of consequence, both in Canada and in England, especially after the publication in 1801 of his *Voyages from Montreal on the River St Lawrence through the Continent of North America to the Frozen and Pacific Oceans*. The book included an account of the rise and condition of the Canadian fur trade, and it gave Mackenzie the ear of many politicians as well as earning him his knighthood in 1802. His views included the formation of a comprehensive Fur and Fishery Company which would develop the whole resources of Canada and would override the privileges of the Hudson's Bay Company, shipping its goods in through the Bay, not through the long route from Montreal to the Grand Portage and so north. With his conviction of the importance of access to the Pacific coast and his experience of the China trade as run through New

York, he embraced the whole concept in a world-wide view of markets and supplies. But he failed to win over the cabinet ministers who fêted him. He wanted three posts to be established on the Pacific coast—at Nootka Sound on Vancouver Island, at the mouth of the Columbia River (the future site of Astoria), and in Sea Otter Harbour. Not only were the privileges of the Hudson's Bay Company to be absorbed in the Fur and Fishery Company which Mackenzie had in mind, but the exclusive privileges of the East India Company and of the South Sea Company were also to be co-ordinated. This could only make sense on the assumption that the Old and the New North West Companies were also amalgamated and that the whole vast imperial project would become one concern. This was the preliminary on which Lord Hobart, as Colonial Secretary, insisted.[13]

But Simon McTavish regarded the establishment of the XY Company as a defiance of himself and his regime, and he had reconstituted the Old Concern with the express purpose of fighting the XY Company for control of the fur trade of Canada. The reorganization entailed concessions to the wintering partners, but it confirmed the power of the Marquis and of his nephew, giving them a close-knit body of supporters pledged to buy their goods and to market their furs through the agents' houses; and it expressly took into account proposals to extend posts "to other and more distant parts in the Northwest, towards the Rocky Mountain and beyond it." [14]

As part of its plans, the Old Concern bought the fishing and trading rights of the King's Posts, as they had survived from the French régime. The concession brought them legitimately to Lake Mistassini, at the head-waters of the Rupert River, and gave them a new status in the fur country at the back of the Bottom of the Bay. At the same time they challenged the chartered rights of the Hudson's Bay Company to an exclusive approach to the Bay by sea. In 1803 they sent their ship, the *Eddystone*, into the Bay, and set up a base on Charlton Island and a trading post on the Moose River.[15] The personal and political success of Mackenzie in London had more effect in this direction than did the direct challenge from the Old Concern. For the voyage of the *Eddystone* and the attempt to set up posts in the Bay both failed simply because the Indians maintained their attachment to the English posts. The Hudson's Bay Committee ordered the capture of the *Eddystone*, but the intransigent "North West spirit" (as it was getting to be called) produced such defiance from the partner in command, Angus Shaw, that the attack was called off. By 1807, nevertheless, the Nor'westers had withdrawn their ship, and their posts at Charlton Island, Hannah Bay, and Hayes Island in the Moose River. They had simply failed to establish a trade.

In their orders the London Committee had stated that their principal concern was "our Opponents assuming a Right to send Vessels of any kind into the Bay"; but the Company was uncertain of the validity of its Charter. The Committee concluded that "If any serious consequences should arise from our Quarrels and Disputes it would be very difficult to find redress here even on application to Government."[16] Mackenzie's moves had sapped the confidence with which they would otherwise have met the inroads of the Old Concern.

The Committee, watching the steady growth in power of the Canadians, realized that Athabasca was the centre not only of the geo-political schemes which were being advanced but also of the fur-trade profits which would have to pay for such plans. They therefore ordered their traders to establish themselves in Athabasca. In 1800 they told their Chief Factor at York that he was to rival the Canadians there and that Athabasca could support ten times the number of men who were being sent there each year. In pursuit of this objective Peter Fidler was brought back into Athabasca once more; in 1800 he journeyed up the south branch of the Saskatchewan to build Chesterfield House, and in 1802 he crossed Portage la Loche and built the first Hudson's Bay post in Athabasca itself, at Nottingham House on the lake. Here Fidler was close alongside the great North West emporium of Fort Chipewyan, and his blustering opponents took full advantage of their strength.[17] Nevertheless, Fidler had taken the Company's trade into Athabasca on a permanent footing; and since he had been taught by Turnor he was able to send his maps to England, to help in drawing up the Arrowsmith maps which were at that time beginning to make the outlines of the Northwest Territories known.

The condition for an establishment in Athabasca which Turnor had set out had been that a subsidiary post on the Peace River would be necessary, to supply meat and other provender so that the men in Athabasca would not have to live exclusively on fish. Fidler tried to build such a post in 1802, but although his main post at Nottingham House was maintained, the Nor'westers forced the abandonment of the Peace River post and the men on Lake Athabasca were hard put to it to keep themselves alive. Even for their journeys down to the coast they had to subsist on dried fish. This was quiet, almost unimaginative, competence according to a set pattern. There was nothing in it to challenge comparison with the explosive assertiveness of either the Old Concern or the XY Company; nor were the personalities involved comparable with Simon McTavish, William McGillivray, or Alexander Mackenzie.

It is therefore not surprising that during these years attention was focussed on the bitter rivalry between the two Canadian companies rather than on the challenge which each of them offered to the Hudson's Bay Company; and that each of the Canadian concerns confidently assumed that the Hudson's Bay Company could without question be absorbed by whichever of the Canadian partnerships should emerge triumphant. The London agent for the XY Company was Edward Ellice, partner in the firm of Phynn, Ellice and Company; Alexander Mackenzie set him to work to buy controlling shares in the Hudson's Bay Company. Such control, at the ruling price of the shares, might have been bought for about £103,000.[18] The Old Concern was equally alive to the possibility of making an "accommodation" with the Hudson's Bay Company and of securing by arrangement the right to use the Bay route which it was at the same time declaring was open to any British subject. Duncan McGillivray, another nephew of Simon McTavish, was in London in 1804, trying to negotiate arrangements which would give the Old Concern the facilities which they sought. The Hudson's Bay men first took legal advice to assure themselves that the rights over which discussion was hovering were indeed legally valid. Their lawyers assured them that, although the right of exclusive trade might be disputed as granting a monopoly which would be contrary to British law, nevertheless the grant of territory would stand any challenge.[19] The Committee were, in consequence, so anxious to avoid a legal confrontation which might invalidate the grant of exclusive trade that they appeared uncertain and lacking in confidence, and both the Canadian concerns were confident that at any time they could get from the Hudson's Bay Company a right of transit across its territories. This would give access to the Rockies, and to the Pacific beyond, more cheaply and quickly than any other route would make possible; and it would take their trade out from dependence on the Kaministikwia-Grand Portage area and from the threat of American discrimination.

While it slowly became apparent that such expectations would not be fulfilled since the Hudson's Bay men would cling to what they thought was theirs by right, the fur trade was ravaged by the most uncompromising hostility in the whole history of that adventurous business. Since the trade had fallen into English hands, French brandy had been largely replaced by "Fiery Double distilled Rum" as the produce of the West Indian sugar trade became available to British subjects. In two years the quantity of spirits taken into the Indian country was more than doubled, from 10,098 gallons in 1800 to 16,299 gallons taken in by the North West Company and over 5,000 gallons taken in by the XY Company in 1803. The Indians were not only spoiled and debauched, they were bullied and abused as well.[20] But trade declined. Disputes over furs and over Indian loyalties at times led to murder, and in August 1803 the situation had reached such a state that the British Parliament passed the Canada Jurisdiction Act, which empowered the Governor or Lieutenant-Governor of Lower Canada to nominate Justices of the Peace for the Indian Territories with authority to commit men to be brought down to Lower Canada, there to be dealt with in the courts of law for offences committed in the Upper Country. As events were to prove, this would allow fur-traders who had secured appointments as Justices of the Peace to drag out their rivals in trade, in an arbitrary and irresponsible way, to stand trial.[21] But the Act was in itself an honest effort to mitigate the violence which had arisen from the rivalry between the two North West Companies.

By 1803 the bitterness of this rivalry was such that even Alexander Mackenzie, much as he disliked McTavish and the McGillivrays, was feeling that some arrangement should be reached; and when in July 1804 Simon McTavish died and the hostilities arising from his personal predominance were removed, the Old and the New North West Companies were amalgamated.[22] By the arrangement then made, the trade of the two concerns was to be handled by a company of a hundred shares, of which seventy-five were to go to the Old Concern and twenty-five to the New. The North West Company now got strength from both the McGillivrays and from Sir Alexander Mackenzie, both from the London agencies of McTavish, Frazer and Company and from Phynn, Inglis and Company, both from the Montreal agencies of McTavish, Frobisher and Company and from Forsyth, Richardson and Company. It had the posts of both the companies dispersed through Athabasca, up the Peace River, and up to the foot of the Rockies. So powerful was the new concern that the agreement expressly provided for the contingency of the Hudson's Bay Company selling its rights, or at least granting the right of transit through its territories which the Nor'-westers had been seeking.

Despite the personal ascendancy of Mackenzie, the Old Concern predominated in the North West Company as set up in 1804. This was a reflection of the position which it held in trade; for while in 1802 it was reckoned that the Old Concern and the New controlled about equal sums in capital, the Old Concern employed about three times as many men as the New, and managed a proportionate amount of trade. The explanation was that although a number of winterers had supported Sir Alexander Mackenzie and had rebelled against the control of Simon McTavish, yet they were bound to the Old Concern by agreements, and McTavish and McGillivray had held them to their contracts and prevented them from being employed by the XY Company.[23] Some of its strength the Old Concern spent in reorganizing its transportation system, intent on getting its goods up to the focal point at the foot of the Grand Portage. A canal was built on the Canadian side of Sault Ste Marie in 1798 and, in order to avoid possible dangers from the redefinition of the American frontier, in the same year the old French route northwards from Lake Superior was again explored, taking the *voyageurs* through Kaministikwia. It took three years to make the route effective, but in 1801 Kaministikwia was in use as the headquarters of the Old Concern, forty miles north of the Grand Portage and indisputably on the Canadian side of the frontier. Not until 1803 was the headquarters completed, with its great hall, its houses, sheds, and canoe-wharves. Later the establishment was to be called Fort William in honour of William McGillivray and was to be the meeting-place for the annual assembly of agents and winterers of the reorganized North West Company.

The first such meeting (for the Old Concern only) was marked by the admission into partnership of the one-time Hudson's Bay surveyor, David Thompson; and the use which the North West Company made of his talents is ample evidence of the determination to expand and to dominate the whole trade of Canada which drove the Nor'westers on.

Since he had joined the North West Company in 1797-98, Thompson had been used to survey the boundary with the United States and to ascertain whether the North West Company's posts stood on one side or the other of the frontier. From Grand Portage he had gone down the Rainy River to Lake Winnipeg and to the Swan River. Here he had turned south to the lower Assiniboine, the headwaters of the Missouri, and the Mandan villages which the La Vérendrye family had opened up. Thompson made it clear that the Missouri and all the villages on it lay within the United States. He then returned to the Assiniboine, followed that river to its Forks, and so ran south on the Red River to Pembina. This post also, he decided, was on United States territory. Thompson then moved up the Red Lake River to Red Lake and, abandoning his canoe at that point, made his way to Turtle Lake, which he decided was the headwater of the Mississippi River. To within a few miles he was correct in this; but he was more completely accurate in showing that when the diplomats in 1783 had drawn the frontier from the northwest corner of Lake of the Woods to the sources of the Mississippi they had given to the United States many hundreds of square miles of territory which had so far been opened up only by Canadian fur-traders and which were still a source of lucrative trade. Thompson then continued east from Turtle Lake and the sources of the Mississippi to strike the western end of Lake Superior, to continue on, surveying the south shore of the great lake and to reach Sault Ste Marie in May 1798. There he met the agents of the North West Company, coming up to the annual meeting at the Grand Portage, and they directed him to continue his survey of the lake by travelling round the eastern and northern shores. So, by the time he had arrived at Grand Portage, he had not only surveyed Lake Superior but he had defined the American boundary line as far as it concerned the fur trade.[24]

The boundary would affect the North West Company more than had been hoped. The result was to turn Simon McTavish more towards Athabasca and towards the Pacific, away from the south. Thompson was there-

Le Bison, an engraving done after the sketch by Georges Louis Leclerc, comte de Buffon, in his Histoire Naturelle.

Fort William, 1866, from a watercolour by W. Armstrong.

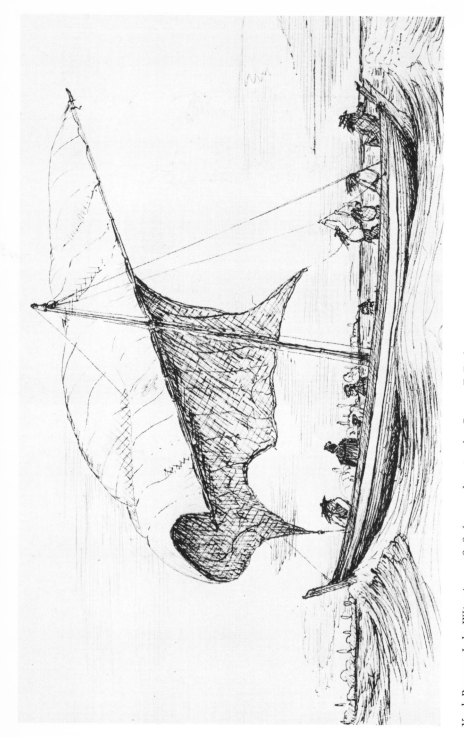

York Boat on Lake Winnipeg, 1848, from a drawing by George E. Finlay.

Alexander Mackenzie, from an engraving by T. Lawrence.

The Buffalo Hunt (or The Indians of the Prairies) from a
painting by George Catlin, 1830's.

Sir George Simpson, from an engraving after Stephen Pearce.

Doctor John McLoughlin.

Edmonton, From Point Below Wesleyan Mission, December, 1871.

fore sent to survey the upper Saskatchewan, to Beaver Lake, the Churchill River, Ile-à-la-Crosse and Athabasca, after which, in 1799, he moved north and west, surveying to Lesser Slave Lake in the one direction and to Rocky Mountain House on the Saskatchewan, in the other. In 1800 he was sent back to Rocky Mountain House, for the North West Company was preparing to cross the mountains. He wintered 1800–1801 at Rocky Mountain House, but before he settled down he completed a great southern tour to the Red Deer River and then to the Bow River, two tributaries of the south branch of the Saskatchewan. The route discovered by Alexander Mackenzie was already authenticated, but it was too difficult; Thompson's task was to seek an easier and more southerly route, by which a constant flow of trade to the Pacific coast and so to China might be maintained.

The centre of this project was Rocky Mountain House, which had been set up in 1799; the chief protagonist was Duncan McGillivray. While David Thompson worked south from Rocky Mountain House towards the Red Deer River and the Bow River, McGillivray explored northwards into the valley of the Athabasca River, and in spring 1801 he sent Thompson up the Saskatchewan, along the Sheep River until the mountains made further progress impossible. Both to the north and to the south of Rocky Mountain House, Kootenay Indians were met with, who had been driven over the mountains by tribal warfare and by their search for contact with white traders, and Thompson had sent two French *voyageurs* back in company with the Kootenay bands whom he had met in the south. In 1801 McGillivray made his way over the Rockies by White Man's Pass to a branch of the Kootenay River (henceforth known as McGillivray's River) and to Kootenay Lake.[25] He would probably never have reached the Pacific coast if he had pushed on; but he had managed to cross the Rockies, and he was convinced that the route which he had followed, or any other route, would be valueless if the approach-journey from the Atlantic seaboard had to be made by the St Lawrence, the Grand Portage, and the Saskatchewan. For the purpose which Duncan McGillivray had in view, development of Canadian trade on the Pacific coast, the right to use Hudson Bay was essential.

The newly united North West Company underwrote Duncan McGillivray's views at its first general meeting at Kaministikwia in 1805 when the Company agreed to offer up to £2,000 a year to the Hudson's Bay Company for the right to ship goods through the Bay, on condition that actual trade by the Bayside should be left to the Hudson's Bay men.[26] McGillivray himself went to London to try to carry this negotiation through, while the North West Company set to work to discover a way across the Rockies which would tie on to this concession, if it could be secured.

Simon Fraser and John Stuart were sent to seek a way by the Peace River and the Parsnip River to the headwaters of the Fraser River. In preparation, in 1805 Simon Fraser went up the Peace River, up Parsnip and Pack rivers to McLeod Lake, to build a post there before he returned down the Peace River, leaving James McDougall in charge. During the winter Mc-Dougall traded some furs of superlative quality, and he also went overland, across the height of land, from McLeod Lake to Stuart Lake. In the following spring Fraser and Stuart came up from Rocky Mountain House and also reached Stuart Lake. Their progress was, however, slow, for they had to build canoes at McLeod Lake, and they suffered from shortage of food and had to hunt and fish as they went. They therefore contented themselves with building a post on Stuart Lake and then dispersed to hunt, with the intention of meeting and travelling down-river to the ocean.

Frazer thought that at Stuart Lake he was on the Columbia River. But he and his men were unable to collect enough food for the journey; they therefore spent the winter of 1806-7 building yet another trade post, and it was spring 1808 before Fraser, reinforced by a couple of canoes which brought up food and goods, was able to build Fort George at the Forks of the Fraser and Nechako Rivers and to set off down the Fraser. The five posts which he had by then established were the beginnings of the wealthy fur department which came to be called New Caledonia. But the trade from that district, good though it was, could not pay transit costs. To get the furs out at any profit they must be taken westwards to the Pacific, not east to the Atlantic. Fraser's purpose was in any case clear; but the wealth in furs which he had discovered added to the urgency of his task.

As they set off, Fraser's party consisted of two officers and nineteen men; and the difficulties which they met almost overwhelmed them. The Fraser proved to be completely unsuitable for canoe travel for much of its length—as, indeed, Alexander Mackenzie had concluded. Fraser and his party survived the whirlpools, they rode the current down the canyon of the Fraser, they carried their canoes over portages of rock so rough and sharp that their shoes were destroyed. Fraser's description of the journey was terse and terrifying: "I scarcely ever saw anything so dreary and dangerous in any country, whatever way I turned my eyes, mountains upon mountains whose summits are covered with eternal snow close the gloomy scene." He reached tidal water on July 1, 1808, and it was only as he was able to ascertain the point at which the river entered the ocean that he realized that he could not be upon the Columbia.[27] His route would not, in any case, have suited the fur trade. But as he travelled he heard of other white men on the river, for the North West Company had not pinned all its hopes on Fraser. At the same meeting at which the partners had decided to bid for the Hudson's Bay route and to send Fraser over the Rockies, they had also ordered David Thompson to direct his great skill and his capacity for travel to this purpose.

While Duncan McGillivray, Stuart, and Fraser had been probing for a route over the Rockies, Thompson had been sent to the Muskrat Country, and had been working in the district at the back of Churchill. He then spent the winter of 1806-7 at Rocky Mountain House preparing for a journey across the mountains while Jacko Finlay, a half-breed, was sent ahead from Rocky Mountain House up the north branch of the Saskatchewan to build a post at which provisions might be collected and where a party might rest and prepare for the further journey. Finlay was also to prepare canoes in which Thompson and the main party might travel down-stream on the western slopes of the Rockies when once they had reached rivers which ran that way.

In his preparatory moves Thompson found that to cross the Rockies he would either have to disarm the suspicions or to counteract the hostility of the Indians; for the penetration of white fur-traders into the mountains was vigorously opposed by the Piegans. These Indians had been worsted in their wars with the Snake Indians because the Snakes had traded guns from the whites, and their own weapons were still only bows and arrows and occasionally lances. The Piegans in their turn learned to use the white man's weapons and were determined that the Kootenay and other mountain tribes must be kept apart from the white traders and their guns.[28] In addition, Thompson had a deep dislike of the way in which the fur trade spread the use of alcohol among the Indians—which he carried even to the extent of rejoicing when spirits were spilled away through defective casks. The Piegans barred his way, and he had to wait until they wandered off to the south, into United States territory. He then seized his chance to move west. But he found that Jacko Finlay's work was valueless; his canoes were cranky, his post was badly sited and was abandoned. Thompson, using horses which he had traded, nevertheless moved into the mountains to the Kootenay Plain near the sources of the Saskatchewan and then over the height of land to the headwaters of the Columbia. He did not immediately press on towards the ocean but built loghouses—the Kootenay post—and put them in readiness for defence against the Indians. His position was strong enough to command respect, but in the spring of 1807 he left Kootenay House and moved all his equipment up to Lake Windermere, over McGillivray's Portage to McGillivray's River, down which he travelled to Kootenay Bottoms in the modern state of Idaho. He had reached this point by mid-May 1808, but once more he did not press on to the ocean. Travelling largely by horseback and overland, he made his way back, met his family, and travelled with them down the Saskatchewan to Rainy River House. He then went back to Kootenay House to spend the winter, and in the spring of 1809 (once more instead of pressing on to the coast) he brought his furs out to the Saskatchewan. He returned to the Rockies in the high summer of that year and began to travel down the Kootenay River, but gave up as winter set in. Returning up the Pack River, he reached Pend d'Oreille Lake, built Kullyspell House there and began a trade which brought in considerable quantities of furs and which brought arms to the Kootenay and other western tribes, thereby making access to the Rockies even more difficult for himself and his successors as the Piegans increased their hostility.

The hostility of the Piegans made it desirable that Thompson should avoid their territory. He tried the Pend d'Oreille River, came back to Kullyspell House, returned from there to the Kootenay River, and then went back to spend the winter 1809-10 at a new post which he built, Salish House, about a hundred miles up-river from Kullyspell House. In 1810 he tried the Pend d'Oreille River again but found it "a terrible cataract" and reconciled himself reluctantly to using the Kootenay River, despite the fact that it ran through Piegan territory. Again, however, he did not immediately embark on his project but returned eastwards. He was back at Fort Augustus on the Saskatchewan in June and arrived at Rainy Lake in July 1810. There he found urgent orders from the North West partners, stimulated into frantic activity by news that the American Fur Company had been formed by John Jacob Astor to take over the fur trade of the west.

Thompson's orders allowed no further delay. He reached Rocky Mountain House late in September 1810, and after two or three weeks for recuperation and preparation set off to accomplish his mission. The opposition of the Piegans made Howse Pass and what Thompson called "the defiles of the Saskatchewan River" impossible, and he turned north towards the Athabasca River, which he reached towards the end of November. Forced to abandon his horses and to continue on snowshoes, with his goods on sledges hauled by dogs, he went, in the depths of winter, up past the Athabasca glacier; by January 10 he had crossed the height of land and had only a descent to the west to make. In a week he reached the Boat Encampment, and by January 26 he was on the Columbia itself. The route which he had followed was arduous and terrifying, and it entailed a detour to the north which might have been avoided if he had gone from Rocky Mountain House directly through Howse Pass; but it was well known to several of his party, and he was able to send men back over the mountains with letters and to bring supplies and provisions forward. His men, however, were exhausted and dispirited. He therefore returned to the Boat Encampment, built shelters, waited for better weather, and began to make canoes. By the middle of April 1811 he had a cedar-plank canoe, twenty-five feet long. But he could get only three men who would venture on with him.

Accordingly, instead of proceeding down the Columbia River towards the ocean, Thompson once more turned back, following the Columbia upstream, south from its forks with the Canoe River, up to the Kootenay area.

Here he was already known, and he hoped to recruit a few "free hunters," Iroquois or half-breeds who knew the country. He made his way up to the sources of the Columbia, then over McGillivray's Portage to the Kootenay River. From the Kootenay he went across country to the Salish River and so down-stream to Salish House. Here he built a canoe and followed the turbulent and dangerous Salish River, flooded by melting snow, down to the Long Carrying Place, where he was met by a party which had come from Spokane House over the Mountains, to help him with the portage which he would have to make to get back on the Columbia again. He stayed briefly at Spokane House and then completed his portage, to join the Columbia at Kettle Falls on June 18. Again he had to build a canoe, which he managed with great difficulty, using cedar wood; and on July 3 he at last set off with five French Canadians, two Iroquois guides, and two Indian interpreters.

The Columbia was not an easy river to travel in the sort of canoe which Thompson had. But he went past the Forks with the Snake River, marking out a site for a post there. He began to hear Indian rumours of a ship at the mouth of the river, and after carrying his canoe over the Dalles of the Columbia and over the Cascades, on July 13, 1811, he came to Point Vancouver. He had travelled the Columbia to the sea and had placed at the disposal of the North West Company that route to the Pacific which it had sought since its creation in 1804. The coast which he reached had already been surveyed by British naval expeditions, but access by land from Canada was what the North West Company wanted; Thompson had given it to them.[29]

Nevertheless, as Thompson came to his long-sought "full view of the Pacific Ocean" at Tongue Point on July 15, he there found that John Jacob Astor's men had already established the trading post of Astoria. The outlet to the ocean for the route which Thompson had pioneered lay in American hands. The Astorians had come by sea from Boston, the first arrivals from Astor's double attempt to establish an American fur trade on the Pacific coast, one party coming to the mouth of the Columbia by sea, the other overland. Though Thompson derided the equipment and the achievement of the Astorians—and most of their traders were former employees of the North West Company itself—nevertheless their presence at Astoria meant that, unless some significant change could be manoeuvred, Thompson had arrived too late. The War of 1812 with America in fact gave the North West Company its chance to take possession of Astoria. But the six years, from 1805 to 1811, which David Thompson had taken to establish a way across the Rockies, were irretrievably lost, and the North West Company had forfeited the initiative in Pacific trade.

The six years taken to cross the Rockies were also years in which the North West Company, despite its aggressive management, also failed to open up the way to the Rockies through the Hudson's Bay Company's territories. Worse, it saw the firm entrenchment of the Hudson's Bay Company in the heart of the existing North West transport system, in and around Lake Winnipeg. This was contrary to expectation and was due almost entirely to a small group of men who, without previous experience of the problems involved, ranged themselves on the side of the Company and its chartered rights. The challenge to the Charter, which had developed from the sending of the *Eddystone* to the Bay by the Old North West Company, had led to a search for legal opinion, and both the Hudson's Bay Company and its opponents were aware that a great weight of legal learning would support the view that the grant of propriety of the land was legal, whatever might be the validity of the grant of exclusive trade. The extent to which such a grant of land would support the Company's claims to exercise jurisdiction was a more open question and would probably not be settled until a test case had been fought, to produce a judicial decision. In view of their lawyers' opinions, the Hudson's Bay Committee were themselves unwilling to put this issue to the test. But they met to consider the Nor'westers' proposals, fearing that "the Company's affairs cannot prosper when in competition with the Canadian traders, who respect neither justice nor equity but Commit open acts of violence, unless the Company's Charter should allow them to punish the offenders." [30]

It was therefore in a defensive mood that the Committee began negotiations with Thomas Forsyth, who represented the North West Company, in January 1805. The Nor'westers were on the offensive, claiming the right as British subjects to use the route from York Fort to Athabasca. Although the Hudson's Bay Committee were not in their hearts prepared to challenge this view, nevertheless negotiations dragged on, discussion concentrating on the realistic problems of prices and conditions rather than on legal and constitutional considerations. The Nor'westers, though they wished to threaten the Hudson's Bay men with a challenge to its legal validity, hoped secretly to preserve and substantiate the Charter, to secure possession for themselves, and to use it to exclude all rivals from the territories and the trade. Outright purchase of the assets of the Hudson's Bay Company, including the whole of Rupert's Land and all the posts in it, would on any reasonable valuation certainly have been beyond the capacity even of the reconstituted North West Company, for its capital was fully committed to its existing trade and to plans for expansion. It seemed unlikely therefore that any solution would be reached on these lines; but negotiations dragged on through 1805 and 1806. [31]

As it became clear that control from London, not from Quebec, Montreal, or Kaministikwia, would be an inevitable consequence of the Nor'westers' trade being run under the aegis of the Hudson's Bay Charter, and that the growing practice of the Nor'westers shipping furs to markets other than to London must cease (in particular using the United States as an *entrepôt* through which furs could be shipped to Europe or to China), negotiations ended. In February 1806 the Hudson's Bay men drew off, determined "not to procrastinate a negotiation which we thought could not be completed and which in the end would be ruining ourselves without a doubt or a remedy."[32]

This was courageous in view of the Company's trade at that time. But in view of the other interests involved, of the predominance of the North West Company in trade, and of the importance which it was achieving by combating American pretensions, it is not surprising that the Hudson's Bay Company's appeal to the Treasury for "that temporary Assistance which we cannot ask at any other hands"[33] met with no response.

By the end of 1808 the Hudson's Bay Committee could see no policy open except a temporary withdrawal from the fur trade, and in April 1809 George Wollaston read to the Committee his "Observations on the Trade of the Company."[34] Part of this paper was taken up with the remedies, largely to be adapted from the practices of the Nor'westers, by which the Company might balance its budgets and improve the salaries (and devotion) of its servants. But the main purpose was to advise the Company that in war conditions the fur trade was bound to lose money. However, epoch-making efforts were in hand to develop a timber industry which would lie entirely within the sphere of imperial regulation and would free the Navy from dependence on the Baltic and other European sources of timber which had fallen under Napoleon's control. Any timber industry, it appeared, would be profitable because of the preferential duties which Empire-produced timber would enjoy. This was written in ignorance that the timber resources of Hudson Bay itself are negligible, though this had long been accepted by the traders there. Nevertheless, just south of Moose, and at the Bottom of the Bay, moderate stands of timber could be found within reasonable distance of the sea and, under Wollaston's urgings, the Hudson's Bay Company attempted to develop a timber trade from the territory south of Moose. The venture failed, for technical skill is needed in the selecting, felling, and loading of timber; and the English shipping industry was by 1809 evading Napoleon's Continental System and getting access to the straight-run firs and deals of the Baltic, the traditional source of supply. The Committee ordered a sawmill for Moose and sent what must have been the first steam-engine to be seen in Rupert's Land to drive the saws, in 1812. But no one was capable of erecting or working it.[35]

Wollaston would not have succeeded if he had advocated complete abandonment of the fur trade, for the Hudson's Bay Company had much at stake, and the hope was that with peace in Europe the market would open up once more; the trade would need to be kept going in some form until that date. Wollaston's proposals therefore included a suggestion that the traders' salaries system should be revised so as to make them merely the agents of the Company, not its employees. They would work on a system similar to that of the North West Company's "wintering partners." The idea had been introduced into the English Company when in 1806 William Tomison had been made "Inland Trader" from York. Given no salary, no jurisdiction or influence, he was to recruit his own men to enlarge trade in Athabasca for the Company and was to receive a commission on any trade which he got.[36] The arrangement, accepted by other traders, was a complete innovation for the Hudson's Bay Company, and it showed that there was vitality and purpose still available; and that Athabasca was still in the forefront.

The new outlook fitted in with proposals from a vigorous, imaginative, and colourful North West renegade, Colin Robertson.[37] In 1809 Robertson had made his way from Canada to London to persuade the Hudson's Bay Committee that, like the Nor'westers, it must recruit voyageurs through an agency in Montreal. This he confidently volunteered to manage. Robertson's proposals coincided with the withdrawal of Wollaston and assumption of control by a trio of newcomers to whom his suggestion that the Company should persevere in the fur trade and should challenge the North West Company in Athabasca appealed strongly.

From the end of 1809 the Hudson's Bay Committee was increasingly controlled by Andrew Wedderburn (known as Andrew Wedderburn Colvile from 1814 onwards), a distinguished and competent business man, senior partner in a firm of sugar brokers which had sold rum, sugar, and molasses to the Company for many years. Wedderburn was connected by the marriage of his sisters to two other newcomers. Jean Wedderburn had married Thomas Douglas, fifth Earl of Selkirk, while another sister had married the London merchant, John Halkett. Wedderburn defeated Wollaston's proposals for withdrawal from the fur trade, but he did not accept Robertson's plans for a full-scale attack on Athabasca. Rather he fell back on his own business experience, advocating sound management, careful accountancy, and shrewd buying and selling, always with a view to avoiding waste and peculation. The result was what came to be known as "The Retrenching System," a system whose main elements were economy and care, but which also incorporated a scheme of payment by results which, it was hoped, would make the Hudson's Bay men increase their efforts. Significant economies were rapidly achieved, and despite the continuance of the war, by 1812 the Hudson's Bay Company was showing a small profit. This inevitably affected the spirit in which negotiations with the North West agents were conducted.

The new blood in the Hudson's Bay Committee was due in the first place to Selkirk, who had begun to buy shares in the Company in 1808—at a time when they were selling at a discount of about 40 per cent on the London market and could easily be got. Selkirk's partner, as he began to accumulate shares, was Sir Alexander Mackenzie; but the two men had different objects in view. Mackenzie's object was to secure control at a far lower price than would be needed to buy out the Company, and so to get its privileges and assets for the North West Company at bargain rates. In 1808 Mackenzie had asked the British government for a grant of the exclusive trade on the Pacific coast, coupled with a right of transit through Rupert's Land and with exemptions from the monopoly rights of the East India and of the South Sea Companies. This would have given him the ingredients for the Fur and Fishery Company which he advocated, and he was able to maintain that some such organization of British trade was necessary if American advances were to be countered. But the Board of Trade took no action on his petition. It was at this juncture that Mackenzie began to buy shares in collaboration with Selkirk, and he continued to do so until he realized that their purposes were irreconcilable. Since Selkirk had supplied most of the money for the purchases, when he fell out with Mackenzie he was left in possession of most of the shares which had been bought. This gave him a powerful influence in the Company. The Earl attended his first Court of the Company in November 1809, and when his brothers-in-law bought up the large holding of a retiring committee-man, the family group was able to exercise almost complete control over the Company.[38]

Wedderburn's determination to maintain, and to make a profit from, the fur trade soon manifested itself. Selkirk accepted this, for it was necessary for his purpose that the Hudson's Bay Company should maintain its claims under the Charter and should vindicate them against any challenge from the North West Company. It was to be expected that Selkirk would arouse the opposition of the Nor'westers, and he was already aware that he must expect such opposition to be shown in deeds as well as in words. His ideas revolved round the acceptance of the Hudson's Bay Company's right to the soil of Rupert's Land, and the establishment of an agricultural colony in that territory—at the very point which the Nor'westers regarded as the focus of their provisions and transportation system, the southeast corner of Lake Winnipeg.

The notion of colonizing some part of the Hudson's Bay Company's territories was not new in 1808. Indeed, in the Charter itself there were provisions for a colony to be established and even for the whole direction of the Company to be taken out to such a colony; but the Company had never seriously engaged in colonization. The few women who had found their way to the Bayside had not stayed long, and it was not until late in the eighteenth century that any number of English-born, or Scots-born, Hudson's Bay half-breeds had begun to be available. But in the difficulties of recruiting men during the Napoleonic Wars, the Edinburgh-born doctor William Auld, Chief of the Northern Department of Rupert's Land, was told that he should sign on men from the Western Isles of Scotland for a period of three years' service, after which they would be given a grant of thirty acres of land at Red River. To encourage the Company's servants, a tract of land to the west of Lake Winnipeg was to be set aside for settlement by retired servants, and the Company began to look forward to a colony of useful half-breed settlers from whom it might recruit servants who would rival the Canadian *voyageurs* in their aptitude for the trade. A schoolmaster was sent out in 1807, and the servants themselves began to press the Committee to set aside a tract for colonization.[39] At one time it seemed possible that an agricultural settlement would emerge near Cumberland House on the Saskatchewan rather than in the Red River-Assiniboine area. But hopes of provisioning the fur trade swung the balance, for the Bas de la Rivière district at the southern end of Lake Winnipeg was the most important district for getting provisions for journeys into the Northwest. For this reason, if for no other, the Hudson's Bay projects for settlement at Red

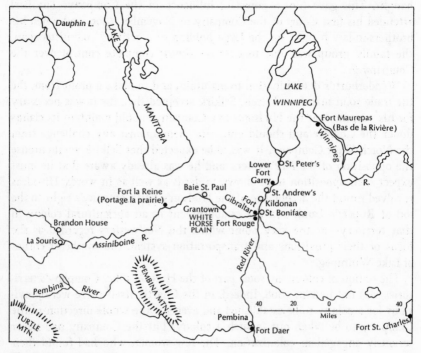

The Red River Region

River were bitterly opposed by the North West Company; and when Selkirk chose this area for the furtherance of his ideas he made it inevitable that he also would meet opposition.

He had previously appeared, as in his relations with Alexander Mackenzie, likely to prove acceptable to the Nor'westers; though what they thought of his ideas was not clear. In fact, his previous career should have made it evident that Selkirk would be a devoted exponent of organized colonization. The evictions in the Highlands, and the changes in the Irish social system which had accompanied the developments in agriculture in the late eighteenth and early nineteenth century, had convinced him that emigration was the only remedy. He had toyed with notions for a settlement in Louisiana, and he had bought land in western New York State. In 1802 he had suggested that the Hudson's Bay Company's lands at Red River should be compulsorily taken over and an Irish colony set up there. The suggestion revealed some basis for common action with the Nor'westers, but the outcome would have been unacceptable to them. The suggestion was not taken up by the Colonial Office, and Selkirk turned his attention to the establishment of settlers in Prince Edward Island and at Baldoon Farm near Lake St Clair in Canada. In this work he visited Montreal in 1804, was entertained by the Nor'westers in the great Beaver Club there, and was accepted by them as almost one of themselves. They expected that his colonization projects would run him into difficulties and thought that his enthusiasm would then wilt.

But Selkirk was more persistent than the Nor'westers allowed, and by 1806 he was more convinced than ever that emigration and the settlement of a colony at the heart of the fur trade (if possible with the support of both the great companies) was essential. At that time it seemed possible that the two companies would unite, and this seemed to make Selkirk's notions more acceptable since, if the Nor'westers managed to get the use of the Bay route, the provision system which centred on Lake Winnipeg would be less vital to them. It was with these ideas in mind that Selkirk began to buy shares in the Company, and as the new management under Wedderburn's direction began to plan the Company's own settlement for retired traders and for the half-breed offspring of employees, in 1810 proposals were formulated which would result in the transfer of a large block of land to Selkirk, for colonization purposes.

Alexander Mackenzie, representing the North West opposition to any such move, and as a considerable shareholder, insisted that such proposals must go before a General Court of the whole Company and could not be settled by the Committee. Accordingly, in February 1811 Wedderburn was instructed to formulate terms, while Mackenzie and the other Nor'westers then in London set to work in a frantic attempt to buy shares which would give them enough votes to negative the proposals. They failed, but they opposed the grant of land at every stage, maintaining with good reason that "it has been found that Colonisation is at all time unfavourable to the fur trade"—a consideration which should have weighed with a fur-trading concern such as the Hudson's Bay Company.[40] While they proclaimed that the grant under discussion would give too much power to Selkirk and would give him an immensely valuable tract of country at the expense of the other shareholders, they also warned him that he would meet the hostility of their company, of men utterly destitute of all moral principle (for so they described themselves and their associates).[41]

The territory under discussion came to be known as Assiniboia, and whatever its significance in the strategy of the fur trade, it proved to be one of the most fertile areas in North America. That the Hudson's Bay Company should have contemplated an agricultural settlement in this area for its own retired servants had not particularly inflamed its disputes with the North West Company; in so far as the Nor'westers were hopeful of securing a majority shareholding, such a settlement would in due course have its uses for them. But when the renewed purposefulness of the Hudson's Bay Company coincided with a determined effort to establish genuine agriculturists at the heart of the North West system, Selkirk's Red River Colony was bound to become completely unacceptable.

CHAPTER 12

The Massacre of Seven Oaks,
the Athabasca Campaign,
and Coalition

The terms of the grant to Selkirk could not fail to arouse great misgivings. The Nor'westers were not silenced until May 30, and the legal deed of transfer was not completed until June 12, 1811. Then the colony of Assiniboia, or Red River Colony, was handed over to Selkirk despite the critics. In return for a token payment of ten shillings he was granted 116,000 square miles of land, equal in fertility to any in North America; an area five times the size of Scotland, bounded on the east by the Winnipeg River from its source to its mouth, and then by a line through Lake Winnipeg, and on the west by a line which was to run from the point at which the 52nd parallel cut the Assiniboine River south to the height of land, which was to be the southern boundary. On the north the grant was bounded by the parallel of $52\frac{1}{2}°$, westwards from Lake Winnipeg to Lake Winnipegosis and from Lake Winnipegosis along the 52nd parallel until it reached the Assiniboine.[1]

The implications of such a grant for the fur trade were clear, quite apart from any fears which the Nor'westers felt about their provisions system. The colony which Selkirk was to establish was to provide the Hudson's Bay Company with two hundred servants a year. The Company was to be allowed to set up trade posts within the colony, and settlers were to be forbidden to take part in the fur trade. Selkirk agreed to provide land for retired servants of the Company, and the Company agreed to provide transportation and equipment, and even seed corn and seed potatoes, for the colony. The Governor whom Selkirk chose was given a commission by the Company so that he might exercise jurisdiction over the settlers by virtue of the authority given in the Company's Charter. Further, to ensure discipline, the settlers whom Selkirk's agents recruited were also signed on as servants of the Company. The Nor'westers may be forgiven for their refusal to distinguish between Selkirk's colony and the Hudson's Bay Company.

Selkirk had already negotiated an agreement with a retired army officer,

Miles Macdonell, to be Governor of his colony and had sent him and other agents recruiting in the Highlands, the Western Isles, and Ireland. The North West Company's agents campaigned to emphasize the difficulties and dangers, and to belittle the prospects, of settlement at Red River. "Even if (the emigrants) escape the scalping knife, they will be subject to constant alarm and terror. Their habitations, their crops, their cattle will be destroyed, and they will find it impossible to exist in the country," wrote Simon McGillivray under the pen-name of "Highlander" in the *Inverness Journal*.[2] Such warnings had their effect, and the utmost which Selkirk's agents could achieve was a hundred and five servants for both the colony and the Company.

Departure from Stornoway in the Hebrides had to be hurried, and essential stores had to be left behind, to prevent the party from melting away as the Nor'westers continued their campaign. Even so, the party did not reach York Factory until September 24, and it was then too late to venture inland or to achieve anything useful at Red River if they did so. Macdonell took his men some twenty miles up the Nelson River, to spend a mutinous and quarrelsome winter on short commons. They could not set out until July 1812, and it was towards the end of August before the advance party of nineteen men reached Red River, and early September before Macdonell took possession of the territory, chose a site for a post two miles from the Nor'westers' Fort Gibraltar, and began to clear the ground. It was too late for his men to get a crop to live through the coming winter, and the Hudson's Bay post at Brandon House could spare little for the settlers. Macdonell decided that his men would have to winter with the buffalo hunters towards Pembina to the south. The alternative was starvation; but the decision confirmed the fears of those who thought that the colony must necessarily interfere with the fur trade.

Such fears were, of course, stimulated by the Hudson's Bay Committee's new approach to the fur trade and adoption of new methods of recruitment and a more active policy. The Company's activities reflected the interests of Selkirk; for in 1810, as the Hudson's Bay men rejected the take-over bids of the Nor'westers, they created two new departments, of Saskatchewan and of Winnipeg.[3] The Winnipeg Department was to be divided into the districts of East and West Winnipeg, the former extending from Pembina to the watershed at the headwaters of the Severn and Albany rivers, the latter including Swan River, Fort Dauphin, and Brandon House, and running from the western branch of the Red River to Cumberland.[4] Both were areas in which a challenge to North West dominance was to be mounted, and in 1811 it was decided that the activities of the Northern and of the Southern Department (centred on York Factory and on Albany respectively) must be maintained but not expanded and that the two new departments must be pushed on. The aim was to recruit tough and well-disciplined servants in Ireland, to place them under separate command, and to use them first to break down North West ascendancy in the Winnipeg-Lake Nipigon country and then on the upper Saskatchewan.[5] Again the Nor'westers could not be expected to differentiate between these moves and the establishment of Selkirk's colony, especially as recruitment for the two projects could not be separated. The Irish servants spent the winter of 1811-12 at Seal Island in a separate establishment from the colonists, but Macdonnell took thirty of them to serve the colony, and the Irish travelled up to Red River in 1812 in company with Macdonnell and the settlers. They also had to rely on the buffalo hunts to get them through the winter of 1812-13. The Irish were then drawn out from the Winnipeg Department and sent west to form a strong post at Ile-à-la-Crosse, to prevent North West bullying and to give the Hudson's Bay traders status with the Indians of Athabasca.

The journey to Red River of Miles Macdonell and of the Irish was difficult beyond description, for they were new to the work, and conditions were particularly hard. Whatever the advantages of the route via Hudson Bay to the prairies for fur-traders, there could be little doubt that it was almost prohibitively difficult for settlers. It would be unlikely (though not impossible) that a party of settlers could get inland in the same summer as they arrived in the Bay; a winter by the frozen sea seemed inevitable, and the prospect of establishing a colony and of opening the prairie under such conditions was not attractive. Yet neither was Selkirk discouraged nor were the Nor'westers hopeful that the natural difficulties would kill the project.

The party under Miles Macdonell had gone inland in four crude boats. This was the only way by which they could get the heavy instruments of agriculture and of settlement up from the Bay to Red River. They could not have managed canoes at all and would have been in danger even as passengers. The problem so revealed brought the Hudson's Bay Company to a review of its transportation system and to emphasis on the replacement of canoes by boats. The depot at the Rock in the Hill River was to be reorganized, other depots were to be set up near Knee Lake and at the Jack River, and a force of Norwegians was to be recruited to build a great central emporium at the depot on the Jack River—the Norway House which was to become the centre of the trading system of the Hudson's Bay Company for the next half century.[6] The Company was forced to reappraisal of transportation largely because maintenance of a colony was even more demanding than maintenance of trading posts in the interior; and that step had been accepted only after much experiment and with serious misgivings.

As part of the program entailed by a colony, the Committee planned a Winter Road which would run from the settlement to York Factory, giving contact with the shipping link to England. The road would use the trade posts and depots as stages where relays of horses (or even of reindeer) would be available. It would run alongside the rivers, and in summer the road would serve the function of portages for river travellers. The project was discussed in detail, and it was thought that when the first stage to Lake Winnipeg had been built the road could then be driven up the Saskatchewan to Cumberland and the upper settlements. Posts should be spaced along the road about three days' journey apart, and the road would not only allow settlements to develop at chosen points but would also mean that the whole territory would be penetrated and developed in a quite new way. In many ways the proposal was out of touch with reality, and nothing came of its broader aspects although eventually it was completed up to Lake Winnipeg in 1827-28. The Committee thought at the time that "it very nearly amounts to bringing the maritime navigation to Lake Winnipeg."[7] Some such improvement in the means of access was indeed essential if a colony at Red River was ever to be established.

In the meantime, difficulty of access was probably all that saved the colony from abandonment, for no news of the troubles of the settlers came through to England after the departure of the ship of 1811. So Selkirk spent the early months of 1812 in Ireland, recruiting a further band of settlers. By mid-June 1812 his agents had a party assembled at Sligo on the west coast of Ireland. Many came from the Highlands of Scotland, and when Selkirk met them he was impressed by their quality. They were about eighty all told, including a handful of families with young children, and he hoped that they would give a stability to his colony which hired servants could never offer. So far was he from either realizing the difficulties which the settlers would encounter or from yielding his position that at this time he ordered that any Nor'wester fishing or hunting within the territory which had been granted should be treated as a poacher would be treated in England. But although he regarded his 1812 settlers as "a very good nest-egg," dissension between the Scots and the Irish, and the stern discipline imposed by Selkirk's nominee, Owen Keveney, provoked a near mutiny on the voyage.[8]

Although the ship of 1812 took exactly the same time on the voyage as the ship of 1811—sixty-one days at sea—she had started a month earlier, and she had sailed from Sligo instead of from the Hebrides. There was, moreover, already a party inland which would have made preparations for the newcomers. So Keveney took his party, including a newborn baby, inland to arrive at Red River on October 27. This was late in the season; but Miles Macdonell was ready to receive them. Fort Daer had been set up, near the Forks of the Red River and the Pembina River and near the pasture grounds of the buffalo. It was also close to the posts of the Hudson's Bay and of the North West companies. There was, however, but scanty accommodation; Fort Daer was little more than a storehouse, and there was little in store, for the wheat harvest had failed. Like the first party of settlers, the immigrants of 1812 were dependent on the buffalo hunters for meat which would enable them to survive the winter. They were helped even by the Nor'westers. But the North West post at Pembina, which had previously been abandoned, was re-established expressly for the purpose of opposing the colonists in the purchase of provisions, and although personal relations might be amicable, the hostility to the colony of the North West Company, as a partnership, remained firm.[9]

The colonists passed an uneasy and uncomfortable winter. They got little active support from the Hudson's Bay men in their posts, and the Nor'westers—whose leader was a cousin, as well as a brother-in-law, of Miles Macdonell—at times appeared to be the more sympathetic group. At York, William Auld resented the authority of Macdonell, regarding the colony as a threat to the Hudson's Bay Company's trade and to the Share of Trade by which the traders were remunerated. He wrote that, if the colony were not completely separated from the Company, the result would be "a ruin as perfect as it will be speedy,"[10] and he obeyed instructions to help the colonists with over-meticulous care and with emphasis on the disparity between the "gloomy superstition of Calvinism" of the Orkney-men and the Scots, and the Roman Catholicism of the Irish.

Auld's personal interests lay in Athabasca; and in an approach to Athabasca from the Churchill River. Ile-à-la-Crosse lay at the centre of his vision, and there the Nor'westers were mustering in strength to displace the Hudson's Bay men. In 1811 they prevented their opponents from getting at the Indians, cut their fishing nets to pieces, hacked down their stockades and impounded their goods. The Hudson's Bay men were driven to abandon their post, and Auld accused two Nor'westers, Samuel Black and John Duncan Campbell, of premeditated murder although they had not actually killed anyone but had merely discharged their guns to intimidate and bluster. The Hudson's Bay Committee accepted Ile-à-la-Crosse as vital, and in 1812 they recalled the Irish from East Winnipeg to form a strong bastion at Ile-à-la-Crosse. The transport system was also reviewed with the object of approaching that post from the Burntwood route into Churchill River. Ile-à-la-Crosse was to be created a separate factory, distinct from Churchill, and the intention of rebutting the Nor'westers there was clear. But although the Committee reiterated the instructions that the Irish should form the main strength of a "Methy Factory" in 1813, they could not be provided with a guide, and Auld sent them back to East Winnipeg after they had been brought down to York Factory. The attempt to recruit Irishmen, to counter North West intimidation, was abandoned.[11]

Whether at this time the Hudson's Bay men saw the colony as an element in the fur trade rivalry or not, the Nor'westers undeniably did so; and it is difficult to accept that this was not clear to the Hudson's Bay men also, when they saw such close interaction as was shown by the transference of the Irish from colony to Company and back again. Selkirk himself, as the Nor'westers proclaimed, was "striking at the very root of the fur trade," and he fully realized that unless the Hudson's Bay Charter could be vindicated, and the Company maintained, his grant and his project would be overcome. A restoration of the Company's trade was necessary, and attention was inevitably directed to the strategic trade areas, the upper Saskatchewan and Athabasca.

At Edmonton Chief Trader James Bird managed affairs for the long period from 1804 to 1816. An expert trader, who was reputed to be the only man who understood the intricacies of the English Standard of Trade and who commanded the loyalty of his men, he maintained his position against the Nor'westers without provoking them,[12] drove up profits, and insisted that Edmonton must be the point of departure for any expedition across the Rockies and that it should also be the starting-point for trade in Athabasca or further north. Edmonton was an outpost from Cumberland, supplied from York Factory and traditionally tied to an approach to Athabasca by way of Moose Portage, Rivière la Biche, and the Athabasca River. This, however, was a way which involved a great detour to the south and west and which could not stand comparison with the normal route from Cumberland to Beaver Lake, Portage du Traite, upper Churchill River (the Missinipi), and Ile-à-la-Crosse. Even the historic route from York Fort to Lake Winnipeg, and so up the Saskatchewan, seemed devious, let alone the further detour to Edmonton which Bird recommended; but Edmonton had access to provisions which no other route could boast.

Athabasca was accepted as essential to any re-formulation of the Hudson's Bay Company's trade and as the source of the prosperity of the Nor'westers. But as yet, in 1811-12, the English had no secure footing there. Fidler had met opposition from Nor'westers whose declared object was to frighten away the Indians and to undermine the Hudson's Bay men. In 1805-6 they were led by Samuel Black, "the most malicious and impudent man I ever saw," who told Fidler "that he did not care a Dam for either me, Mr McKenzie (his own Master at Fort Chipewyan) or both Companies."[13] Fidler was driven to abandon his post in 1806. Planning nevertheless continued. Against the traditional approach from York Factory stood the conviction that the best route to Athabasca would be more northerly; as David Thompson had argued, it should reach Lake Athabasca by Wollaston Lake and Deer Lake, not by Missinipi River, Portage la Loche, and the Clearwater River. The approach might either be from York, following the Nelson River and then using the Burntwood route, or from Churchill by the Churchill River. Alternatively, the route might be even further to the north, by the Seal River from the Bay and so across country to Deer Lake. Unless Thompson's route, in some form or another, was to be followed, Ile-à-la-Crosse must control access to Athabasca. With all this speculation, with rivalry between York and Churchill, and with personal differences between the Chiefs at those places, in practice the route by Cumberland had great advantages and was confirmed by experience. Ile-à-la-Crosse was therefore never denied its importance. Indeed, the great object of the Nor'westers was to secure the right to use the Hudson's Bay route to Lake Winnipeg and then to use the Saskatchewan until they crossed to Beaver Lake, Ile-à-la-Crosse, and Methy Portage, and so to Athabasca.

During the years when the formation of the colony was in the balance the convictions of William Auld led to emphasis on Churchill and the Churchill River. That river in itself was difficult and tortuous, especially for a journey up-stream. From 1806 onwards Fidler had been used to survey this route, and in 1808 the Committee ordered that York should surrender its interests in Athabasca in favour of Churchill, for Fidler had found a new track from the Churchill River into Reindeer Lake.[14] Fidler's discovery proved impracticable, and the predominance of Churchill therefore merely meant that Portage du Traite (Frog Portage) would be reached by the Churchill River instead of by one of the routes from York; it did not diminish the importance attached to Athabasca or to Ile-à-la-Crosse.

Edmonton, and James Bird's notions of using that post as a stage towards Athabasca, were put on one side. But at Edmonton Bird had an experienced and competent explorer and surveyor in Joseph Howse.[15] In 1809 Howse, with ten years of travel behind him, was eager to explore from the north branch of the Saskatchewan up into the Rockies. While David Thompson had been fighting his way over the Rockies, Howse was in 1809 making a preliminary reconnaissance; then, after wintering at Edmonton, in 1810 he set off once more. Where he went is not quite clear (for his journals are missing) but there is little doubt that, with nine servants and some Indians, he crossed the Rockies by the north branch of the Saskatchewan and over what later came to be called Howse Pass. Like Thompson, he then turned up-stream on the Columbia instead of pushing on to the coast, worked up to the Kootenay River and so down to the Flathead River, where he built a house and spent the winter. He travelled to the headwaters of the Missouri, returned to his house at the Flatheads, and came back to the Saskatchewan and so to Edmonton with a good trade in furs in the summer in 1811.[16] Howse had run into Indian tribal wars, and nothing but his ability in handling Indians enabled him to bring out his trade intact. He emerged convinced that the warring tribes of the Rocky Mountains made trade there so dangerous that it was not worth the trouble. The idea of trading into, and even across, the Rocky Mountains was therefore abandoned by the Hudson's Bay Company. Attention was even more concentrated on Athabasca.

Howse's excursion from Edmonton had shown that the Hudson's Bay Company had men who could rival the Nor'westers in their ability to travel, to trade, and to manage Indians. It revealed also that the Company had not that zest for expansion which marked the Nor-westers and that, in the crisis of its affairs, posts which could supply provisions were as important as those which were in good fur country. Red River was without rival for this purpose.

By 1814 the Napoleonic Wars were coming to an end, markets were opening up, and the Hudson's Bay Company was again enjoying prosperity. It had nothing to set against the way in which the Nor'westers had captured Astoria; nor did it enjoy the standing with the British government which that achievement and an ostentatious zeal to guard the American frontier had given to the Nor'westers. But in 1814 the national emergency had passed. This was the period in which the Hudson's Bay Company proposed that Howse should be sent once more across the Rockies and that the Irish should be sent to defy the Nor-westers at Ile-à-la-Crosse. Any thought of concession was put aside, the salary system was revised to galvanize the officers by a share in the profits of trade, and the Nor'westers realized that collapse of the opposition was not to be looked for.

The Nor'westers were well aware of the economics of competition. They were prepared to trade at a loss where there were rivals in the field, both to win over the Indians and to drive the opposition to a losing trade; where they had the whip hand they exploited their advantage and recouped their losses. The Hudson's Bay men therefore concluded that they could not "avoid this Species of Malicious opposition by any partial concession."[17] To make an arrangement in one district would only be to unleash greater strength against themselves elsewhere. Competition must be total. Accordingly, in 1814 the Company decided that it must undertake a vigorous, even an expensive, campaign in Athabasca.

For this, Colin Robertson was at hand and eager for employment.[18] Since his plan to manage a Hudson's Bay agency at Montreal had been rejected, he had got some experience in outfitting for the fur trade, and he had acted as a recruiting agent for Lord Selkirk. He still maintained that the Nor'westers must be opposed by the same kind of men as they employed and that voyageurs must be recruited in Montreal. When he had made his arrangements with the Committee, therefore, he did not sail to the Bay but to Quebec, where he arrived in September 1814. He then set to work to recruit *voyageurs*, and by lavish expenditure of money and charm he got together a brigade of sixteen canoes and set out from Montreal by May 1815.

During the winter in Montreal Robertson had passed back to London some significant rumours. He reported that the Nor'westers were gathering in strength to drive out the settlers from Red River and that they were preparing for an arrangement with the Hudson's Bay Company, thinking they could dictate terms.

The rumour that the Nor'westers were organizing the eviction of the settlers was strongly denied when, questioned by the Colonial Secretary (to whom Selkirk had taken Robertson's report, asking for some measure of "precaution and police"), the Acting Governor of Canada, Sir Gordon Drummond, turned to William McGillivray (now a Legislative Councillor), and accepted his indignant denial of the "shameful accusation."[19] The rumour that an arrangement with the Hudson's Bay Company was pending was as strongly denied by the Hudson's Bay Committee, by this time confident that they need accept an arrangement only on their own terms— which would probably not be acceptable to the Nor'westers. This, however, did not mean that no discussions were afoot.

As he got his expedition together at Lachine in 1815, Robertson should have been free to return to England. But he had no one to whom to hand over command. His first choice as leader, Donald McKenzie, took employment with Astor in the American Fur Company, while his second choice filled him with misgiving. This was John Clarke, like himself a former Nor'wester, but one who had also served in the American Fur Company and who seemed unlikely to have the necessary powers of self discipline. Robertson decided to take the expedition up to Lake Winnipeg himself; there he would meet the Chief Factor of the Hudson's Bay Company and would hand over to him the responsibility of nominating a commander. Before he reached the foot of Lake Winnipeg, however, he met a triumphant brigade of Nor'westers going out to Montreal with Miles Macdonell and several of the colonists. Macdonell was alleged to be a prisoner going to stand trial, as was the Sheriff of the colony, John Spencer. The settlers were going under North West safe conduct, deserting the colony. Hurrying on and meeting the Chief Factor of the Hudson's Bay Company, who had come up from York, Robertson found that the whole colony was on the point of being dispersed by the Nor'westers and the half-breeds of Red River.

Selkirk, in the meantime, knew nothing of this, and though uneasy at reports of lack of discipline and of the difficulties which the settlers had met, had decided to press on. The threat to the frontier implicit in the War of 1812 had so far been used by the North West Company only as an excuse for demonstrating their loyalty and for asking privileges; it now seemed to Selkirk to offer the possibility that troops might be sent from England and that his own men might also perform a public service and win recognition. He approached the Army and the Colonial Office with proposals for sending out a battalion of Fencibles, recruited in the Highlands, for the defence of Red River; and the mounting distress in the Highlands enabled him to secure the services of over a thousand men, women, and children from the Kildonan district of Sutherland, as the nucleus of a frontier defence force. The plan came to nothing; but in June 1813 Selkirk sent out a reinforcement of over ninety people, many of them sturdy young men and mostly from Kildonan. They were a homogeneous group, quite the most promising settlers whom Selkirk had yet sent out. But ship's fever broke out on the voyage, five of them died, and the ship's captain on his arrival in Hudson Bay sailed straight to Churchill instead of putting in to York. At Churchill no preparations for receiving the settlers had been made, their ship ran aground as they tried to sail her out from the Churchill River to York, and they settled down to winter in cabins at Churchill, in some danger from scurvy and from starvation as well as from typhus.[20]

This was a winter in which the settlers already at the colony were forced to depend on the buffalo and on the half-breed hunters, in which dissension spread between the various groups, and in which Miles Macdonell, with his North West relations and his autocratic manner, drew apart from the settlers and from the Hudson's Bay men. There was grave and obvious danger that he would precipitate a crisis by asserting that all the pemmican produced from within the grant of land made to Selkirk came under his control and might, if he wished, be directed to the sole use of the settlers. Selkirk himself had counselled some caution and had warned that "any violent overstretch of authority would be extremely pernicious to our cause."[21] But Macdonell had to make his own decisions, and on January 8, 1814, he published his Pemmican Proclamation.

This proclamation brought to an issue the question of ownership of the soil. It forbade the export from Assiniboia of any provisions, either of meat, grain, or vegetables, procured or raised within that territory. Neither the North West traders nor those of the Hudson's Bay Company, nor any others, were exempt; the colony alone was to enjoy the produce of the district. Provisions diverted to the settlers were indeed to be paid for at the customary rates, but as the North West brigades began to converge on Lake Winnipeg during the early summer, some of them already hungry and all of them dependent on the pemmican of the district to carry the winterers up to their posts, it became clear that the Proclamation would be quite unacceptable.

In rejecting the Proclamation, the fur-traders had full support from the

Métis, alarmed at Selkirk's claim to the land over which they roamed and hunted. For the most part they were descended from North West traders and employees. The North West Company itself ignored the Proclamation, collected its pemmican and refused to surrender it. Miles Macdonell sent to seize a supply from their post at La Souris. Tactlessly, the colony's Sheriff on this occasion was supported by Hudson's Bay Company's men, and the impounded pemmican was then stored at the Company's post at Brandon House. A clash seemed inevitable, but by the end of June a compromise had been reached in which Macdonell gave up all the North West pemmican except two hundred bags, and the Nor'westers agreed to send men to haul oatmeal from York Factory for the use of the settlers. This meant that the settlers would be fed on food which had to be carried across the Atlantic instead of on local produce; and the Nor'westers also secured the concession that they might send such furs as they carried on this trip to England by the Hudson's Bay ship. It is not clear what right Macdonell had to grant such a concession, and the arrangement estranged him further from the settlers who saw the pemmican taken from their grasp, and from the Hudson's Bay traders who obeyed the Proclamation and found themselves at a disadvantage compared with the Nor'westers.[22]

When the first Kildonan settlers arrived at Red River in early July 1814, Macdonell left the colony and went down to York Factory, where he suffered a breakdown. He had already written to Selkirk asking to be relieved of his command. The Kildonan settlers had shown their quality by marching one hundred and fifty miles from Churchill to York across the frozen swamps in the last weeks of winter, so that they were ready to go up-river as soon as the ice gave. Though news had got to London (from Robertson) of the rumours circulating in Montreal that the Nor'westers were planning the dispersal of the colony, at York the future seemed secure as the Kildonan settlers started up-river.

But although the arrangement which had been reached mitigated the worst consequences of the Pemmican Proclamation, when the North West partners met at Fort William they denounced the agreement and arranged that Duncan Cameron should command at Red River and that Alexander Macdonell should go as a clerk whose prime duty it was to marshal the Métis in opposition to the colony. There was no doubt that, in Macdonell's words, their purpose was "to commence open hostilities against the enemy in Red River."[23] Cameron wore army officer's uniform to impress the Métis and the Indians—and, indeed, the settlers—and he carried warrants for the arrest of Miles Macdonell and of John Spencer, Sheriff of the colony.

Before Miles Macdonell, his health restored, returned from York Factory to the colony, Cameron had arrested the Sheriff, and the settlers were being pressed by the Nor'westers to desert the colony and accept transport to the good land which, it was said, would be available in Upper Canada. But the Kildonan people had come up in strength, they had started work on the land, and during the winter 1814-15 they were kept together at the Forks instead of being dispersed in order to get buffalo meat. They were nevertheless subject to temptation, especially as spring came with reports that the Sioux were on the warpath and that the Métis were gathering to overthrow the colony. Much of the danger arose from personal hostility to Miles Macdonell, and in June 1815 he was so persuaded that he was an obstacle to the safety of the colony that he crossed to Fort Gibraltar and surrendered himself to Cameron. Over one hundred and forty settlers were taken out with him in the North West canoes, leaving only about sixty stolid but uneasy families still at Red River.

As Colin Robertson met Macdonell and heard this news, he left his expedition and hurried ahead.[24] The settlers who remained had been assured that, once Macdonell himself gave in, they and their crops should be safe. But the Métis rode down the crops and burned the huts. The settlers, all except four men, took to their boats and set out for Lake Winnipeg, and so for York Factory. Robertson met the fugitives at the north end of Lake Winnipeg, persuaded them to return with him, defied the Métis, and set the colony on its feet once more.

Selkirk had not expected anything so serious as the virtual dispersal of his colony. He had, however, been alarmed at Robertson's warning, had recruited a group of about eighty new settlers for 1815, and in conjunction with the Hudson's Bay Company had appointed a new Governor, Robert Semple, with authority both over the Company's affairs and over the colony.[25] Semple was an American Loyalist, experienced and much travelled although he had never taken any part in the fur trade. A man of determination and standing, he received the large salary of £1,500 a year. The settlers of 1815 came for the most part from Sutherland and were of solid agricultural origin. The voyage to the Bay was smooth and short, and Semple arrived at York Factory on August 27, to learn of the dispersal of the colonists. It was early in November before he arrived at the colony. By then Robertson had so settled affairs that Semple found it difficult to take the threat to the colony as seriously as it deserved. A bountiful harvest had been brought home despite the Métis depredations, all seemed prosperous and stable, and Semple concluded that they "really did too much honour to this Crew in supposing them to be so formidable."

As Robertson, basking in the popularity which he had so thoroughly earned, decided to spend the winter at the colony and to see it really on its feet, John Clarke was got away to Athabasca with the Hudson's Bay expedition which Robertson had recruited in Montreal. Clarke established Fort

Wedderburn on Lake Athabasca, and the first news of the expedition was encouraging.

All promised well, and the winter was the most comfortable which the colony had as yet seen. Semple and Robertson, different though they were in character, got along well enough, and Semple took himself off to the Hudson's Bay posts at Pembina and Brandon House, leaving Robertson at the colony. There Robertson took the initiative in the war of nerves and of ostentation. He raided Fort Gibraltar, recovered some of the colonists' property, seized incriminating documents, and even put Duncan Cameron under arrest. It was not until the spring of 1816 that he and Semple were thrown together and began to differ seriously. Robertson, convinced from letters which he had seized that an attack on the colony was imminent, was aghast at much that Semple did; Semple refused to take Robertson's warnings seriously. Robertson therefore left the colony in June 1816, warning the Governor that ruin was imminent. He was at York Factory, en route for England, when he received news which showed that his alarm had been only too well founded.

The Massacre of Seven Oaks,[26] of which news then came to Robertson, had taken place on June 19. Governor Semple and twenty-one of the settlers were murdered. The remainder were either taken prisoner or escaped by swimming the river.

In May it had been known that a half-breed force was converging on the colony. Brandon House had been plundered, and a Hudson's Bay brigade had been held up and robbed of its furs and pemmican. The Métis were under Cuthbert Grant, a young half-breed whom the Nor'westers had decked out in an army uniform. Early in June two Saulteaux Indians had come in to Semple, to report the danger from the Métis and to offer the Indians' help against them. Semple had refused it; the colonists thus stood alone when on June 19 some thirty-five Métis approached the newly-rebuilt Fort Douglas. Semple rode out to meet them, apparently meaning to proclaim his authority and to order them to disperse. He called for volunteers and took about twenty-six settlers with him, but not the three-pounder field-piece which was the heavy armament of the settlement. His party had no clear instructions, and they were not all armed. The accidental discharge of a gun as the settlers went to meet the Métis was dangerous in itself and could easily have started general shooting. The incident passed off; but when the two groups met at the grove known as Seven Oaks the settlers realized that the Métis were dressed like Indians in warpaint and that there were many more of them than had been thought. The settlers were outnumbered, and the situation was almost bound to end in disaster. When one of the Métis rode up to Semple, and the Governor seized his bridle and the butt of his gun, a shot rang out. Firing became general, Semple went down with a broken hip, and the Métis whooped in. Semple was killed and the massacre became general. That night Archie Macdonald, now in charge of the colony, went to Frog Plain to arrange surrender of Fort Douglas, and on June 22 the remaining settlers left the colony, to go down to Hudson Bay.

The news of the Massacre of Seven Oaks spread, to appal many besides Colin Robertson. He, after all, had read of the threat in the North West letters which he had captured at Fort Gibraltar; others were not so prepared. On the way up from Montreal were three separate parties, each of which was strongly affected by the news. First to get the information was a North West party under Archibald Norman McLeod, a vigorous and uncompromising North West partner who, under the Quebec Act, held power as a magistrate for the Indian country. He had issued the warrants for the arrest of Macdonell and Sheriff Spencer in 1815. McLeod had set out from Montreal so early that he had to fight the ice on the lakes, and as rumours of Robertson's success at Red River grew, he wrote in early June, as he passed through Fort William, to call Indians to rendezvous with him at Red River, to prevent the North West Company from being "imposed upon." McLeod had expected to meet the Métis at the mouth of the Red River, but he was late there and was met instead by the settlers, moving out after the massacre. As magistrate he examined them and then went to the settlement, where he so far identified himself with the Métis that he issued a reward on behalf of the North West Company to some who had taken part. McLeod then went on into Athabasca, to play his part, again as a magistrate, against the Hudson's Bay expedition there.

Second on the scene was Miles Macdonell, who had been liberated from custody in Montreal, re-engaged by Selkirk, and sent ahead with an advance party to act as second in command to Robertson at the settlement. Macdonell was hard on the heels of McLeod when he got the news, and his immediate action was to send back information to the third party which was coming up behind him. This third party was under Selkirk himself, and Macdonell turned back to meet them and to prevent them from running into the trap which he thought lay ahead.

Selkirk was coming up from Montreal in considerable strength and was not inclined to accept defeat, as Macdonell apparently was. He had learned of the mishaps of the previous year, the capture of Macdonell and the dispersal of his settlement, as he set out from England in October 1815, and during the winter 1815-16 he tried to galvanize the Acting Governor, Sir Gordon Drummond, into action against the Nor'westers. He and Lady Selkirk fought the social and political power of William McGillivray, Archibald Norman McLeod, and John Richardson, through the winter in Montreal. The Nor'westers were uneasy, especially at the possibility that some of the partners and many of the winterers might draw out their investment in the concern before it ran into trouble. Selkirk had gone to Montreal with instructions from the Hudson's Bay Committee to discuss terms for an amalgamation (as Robertson had anticipated). But the "arrogance and violence of Mr McGillivray's temper," increased by the triumph of 1815 at Red River, precluded any success, especially since the Nor'westers started from the presumption that their monopoly in Athabasca should be accepted in return for recognition of the Charter.[27] Since Selkirk knew that Robertson's expedition to Athabasca had resulted in Clarke's establishing a Hudson's Bay post at Fort Wedderburn and that Athabasca provided the best profits in the whole fur trade, he never seriously considered renunciation of that district. While negotiations on an amalgamation drifted into troubled waters, Selkirk prepared an imposing expedition which he intended to lead himself to Red River, in 1816. He was greatly encouraged in his purpose by a message from Colin Robertson. The messenger, Jean-Baptiste Lagimonière, had travelled the eighteen hundred miles from Red River to Montreal in the depth of winter, and he brought news that under Robertson the colony was stable and flourishing.

During this winter Selkirk occupied himself in writing his *Sketch of the British Fur Trade in North America, with Observations on the Northwest Company of Montreal*. It was a book which he had started before leaving England, a telling indictment of the Nor'westers and their systematic bullying and bribery. Selkirk challenged the claims of the Nor'westers to the gratitude of the British government for their part in the War of 1812; and he set out in detail the particular case of John Mowat, a Hudson's Bay Company man who had killed Aeneas Macdonell, a North West bully who had seized furs at the Hudson's Bay post at Eagle Lake, terrified the Indians, and finally entered the Hudson's Bay post with drawn sabre and pistols, wounding two men and driving others into the woods. Mowat shot him. He was seized, spent the winter in irons, and in the spring was taken with the post-master and other witnesses to Montreal for trial before a Grand Jury on which several North West partners sat. Mowat was pardoned; but in the meantime he had been severely ill-treated, the business of the post had been interrupted, and the Indians had been intimidated. Selkirk's book did much to undermine the social and political status of the Nor'westers, and it stirred up a pamphlet war[28] in which the chief opponent of Selkirk's case was Rev. Dr. John Strachan, then rector of York, later to become an archdeacon and then a bishop, who attacked Selkirk as an unscrupulous land speculator.

Having impugned the image of the North West Company, Selkirk tried to impress on authority the need for the colony to be given military protection. Drummond would grant no more than that Selkirk might take a body-guard for himself. The body-guard was to have come from the de Meuron Regiment of Swiss and German mercenaries. When the arrangement was revoked on the ground that the regiment was to be dispersed, Selkirk set to work to engage about ninety officers and men, on the condition that if they accompanied him to Red River they should then be offered either a grant of land or a passage to Europe. In all, twelve boatloads of supplies were needed for Selkirk's expedition, and since the de Meurons were not finally discharged until June 4, 1816, they made a late start. Selkirk at that time intended to bring down several partners of the North West Company to stand trial in the courts of Canada for the part which they had played in the arrest of Macdonell and the dispersal of the colony in the previous year.

Hurrying back to give Selkirk news of the Massacre of Seven Oaks, Macdonell met him in the last week of July at Sault Ste Marie. Writing to the newly appointed Governor Sir John Sherbrooke to say that he was certain that evidence about the massacre could be unearthed at Fort William and that he intended to call there, Selkirk hastened on to the rendezvous, where the North West Company was assembled as Selkirk, and his brigade entered the Kaministikwia River, paddled past the fort, and made camp on the opposite shore. The de Meurons were an impressive sight, and Selkirk easily secured the release of four of the colony's officials who were in North West custody. William McGillivray plausibly explained that he had not regarded them as prisoners, but the narratives which they poured out led Selkirk to conclude that the North West Company was culpably responsible for the massacre. On August 13, therefore, he sent two constables over to arrest William McGillivray on a charge of treason and conspiracy and as an accessory to murder. Two of his partners, Kenneth McKenzie and Dr John McLoughlin, were also arrested; and bail was refused.

Selkirk had acted as a magistrate in the Indian Territories, for which he had secured a commission. He had tried to get other justices of the peace in Upper Canada to come forward from Sault Ste Marie when he had realized the probability that legal action against the Nor'westers would be possible. But those whom he approached had excused themselves.

After the arrest of McGillivray and the two other partners, Selkirk's constable (John McNabb, late of the Glengarry Fencibles) was sent over to Fort William to arrest the remaining partners in the concern, with a warrant to search for and to seal their papers. Though there were something like two hundred servants of the North West Company clustered round the gates of the fort, the discipline and confidence of the de Meurons triumphed, and after a short scuffle Selkirk's men took possession. Desks and papers were sealed, and guards were mounted. The headquarters of the North West Company had been taken, the Honourable William McGillivray was in custody, and several partners had been roughly handled and placed under arrest. The North West Company, largely dependent on its own ruthless strength, had suffered a great public humiliation.

The next days were spent by the North West partners in hurried destruction of papers and evidence, by Selkirk and his men in searching the fort. Apart from the possibility that he might uncover evidence that the North West Company was involved in the Massacre of Seven Oaks, Selkirk now controlled supplies which were essential to maintain something like 2,000 men through the winter at their posts in the interior. When, on August 17, McGillivray and the other prisoners were sent down to Montreal to stand their trials, Selkirk seemed in complete control of the situation; and when, three days later, some marked furs, taken by Cuthbert Grant and the Métis from the Hudson's Bay posts in Red River and Qu'Appelle River, were found, the connection between the North West Company and the half-breeds seemed to be proved. The responsibility of the Nor'westers appeared even clearer when a list of half-breeds who had been rewarded for their parts in the massacre, and a further list of those who had as yet to be rewarded, were found; then Daniel McKenzie, a dipsomaniac and unreliable partner of the North West Company, disclosed to Selkirk his knowledge of the part which the concern had played in directing the half-breeds. Selkirk decided not to return to Montreal but to spend the winter in the North West stronghold.

As the hard weather approached, Selkirk and his de Meurons moved into the fort itself, and by the connivance of Daniel McKenzie he took possession of the North West furs and stores under a dubious contract of sale. He discovered further proof of North West complicity in the half-breeds' activities against the colony. But his position was spoiled when one of the canoes going down to Montreal was overset and six prisoners were drowned; and he lost countenance again by refusing to allow pemmican from Red River to be sent to the interior, thereby placing the winterers in grave danger of starvation. He was aware that his actions would look like an arbitrary assumption of complete authority, for which he had only his magistrate's commission to warrant him, and he wrote to Sir John Sherbrooke to request that a commission should be sent to the Upper Country, to report on the situation, to collect evidence, and to make a proper trial possible at a later stage.[29]

At Montreal in the autumn of 1816 the outlook for the Hudson's Bay Company and for Selkirk and his colony was bright. Heavy pressure was brought to bear to secure the appointment of commissioners, and eventually Sherbrooke appointed an Executive Councillor of Lower Canada, William Bachelor Coltman; with him was named a police magistrate of Quebec, John Fletcher. Coltman, with legal training and with a reputation for honesty and common sense, seemed acceptable; Fletcher, fussy, assertive, fuddled, and hostile to what he called the "Selkirkonian system," roused doubts. Although the North West partners easily secured release on bail when they reached Montreal, they lost face when the news of the massacre came through in detail, and still more when an "armada" of ships and canoes which they had prepared for the recapture of Fort William was dispersed by bad weather. All that they achieved was that Dr. Mitchell, a magistrate of Drummond's Island, was prevailed on to issue a warrant for the arrest of Selkirk, and a constable in a single express canoe got through to Fort William and served the warrant in person. Selkirk knew how such arrests had been used merely as a means for getting rivals away from the Upper Country, and the dangers run by those who went down to Montreal in custody, yet he placed himself in the wrong when he refused to surrender to the constable. It was irrelevant that Dr. Mitchell knew nothing of the dispute, that the warrant was not based on any examination of the facts, or that Mitchell could be described as "an old man in his dotage . . . never by any chance sober after mid-day."[30]

The information that Selkirk had resisted lawful arrest was soon communicated to the Colonial Office, and in February 1817 the Colonial Secretary, Earl Bathurst, sent for the Governor of the Hudson's Bay Company, told him that he had ordered the men whom Selkirk had accused to be sent to England for trial, and urged that Selkirk should be ordered home by the Hudson's Bay Company. In vain the Governor pointed out that Selkirk had no official position within the Company. The Colonial Secretary was convinced that Selkirk's schemes were "wild and unpromising," and he was not in a mood to listen to fine distinctions. Bathurst then sent to Canada, on February 11, 1817, a dispatch requiring both companies to restore captured property and to abstain from hostilities, suggesting that Selkirk was opening the way for the United States to gain influence over the Indians, declaring that Selkirk had "rendered himself doubly amenable to the laws" and that it was necessary that the power of the law should be demonstrated "more particularly with respect to Lord Selkirk." An indictment was therefore to be prepared, and "upon a true bill being found against him" he was to be arrested and brought to trial. "Surrounded as Lord Selkirk appears to be by a Military Force which has once already been employed to defeat the execution of legal process," he seemed to Bathurst unlikely to submit to arrest, and force was to be used if necessary.[31] The bias of these instructions cannot be explained simply as the outcome of the reports which the Colonial Office had received from Governor Sherbrooke. The North West Company had made seven communications to the Colonial Office during the previous month, and the dispatch told the Governor that the Colonial Office derived its information not only from himself but from "different quarters." The

Nor'westers may have lost some of their standing at Montreal, but they stood as high as ever at Westminster.

Bathurst's dispatch was, of course, not known to Selkirk as he wintered at Fort William; indeed it only came to his knowledge during the subsequent trials, when it was put into his hands by mistake. The dispatch was followed by the "Prince Regent's Proclamation" on May 1, 1817.[32] This required both sides to refrain from further hostilities and to restore all captured property. The proclamation showed none of the assumption that right lay on the side of the Nor'westers which was so strong a feature of the dispatch, and when it was presented to Selkirk by the commissioners he found it acceptable in itself. This, however, did not happen until late summer 1817, when Coltman had caught up with the Earl, who had left Fort William and arrived at Red River. There he was busy reinvigorating the colony, allotting holdings to churches and schools, and settling many of the problems which remained to be solved. He not only accepted the proclamation, he also had a warrant for his arrest served on him, gave bail for his appearance in the courts, and fulfilled it although the sum set was out of all proportion to that demanded of the North West partners.

Fletcher had been left behind at Fort William, but Coltman's attitude depressed Selkirk. He maintained that the fact that the Nor'westers were accused of complicity in murder, robbery, and arson did not make it legal for Selkirk to take their property and invade their premises; and he accepted the Nor'westers' insistence that restoration of provisions and goods was to them a matter of immediate necessity which could not await the collection of evidence from all over the continent.

As he saw the state of the settlers at Red River, Coltman developed a considerable respect for the colony,[33] so much so that he thought the Indians would wish it to continue. He was also impressed with the fact that during his period of residence Selkirk met the Chiefs of the Crees, the Assiniboines, and the Saulteaux, and concluded with them a form of purchase of Assiniboia which left them content and which at least had the merit of clearing his title to the land as against any claims of the "native-born"—as the Métis were apt to style themselves. As he accepted the notion that a colony at Red River might prove viable and that Selkirk's settlement had at last got its roots down, Coltman began to think that a colony should be administered from Canada, and should be a part of Canada, not the private property of Selkirk, with Canada responsible for defence and law enforcement. He was therefore aghast at Selkirk's suggestion that perhaps the colonists should be moved south into the United States, where they would be immune from further North West attacks; and he was angered when Selkirk returned to Montreal to stand his trial by way of the Missouri, the Mississippi to St Louis, the Wabash, Kentucky, Washington, New

York, and Albany. This seemed merely a pleasure jaunt unless Selkirk was thinking of transferring his settlers, and his allegiance, south of the frontier. In fact Selkirk arrived in Montreal early in 1818 after surrendering to his bail at York (Toronto) and being released until the Quarter Sessions.

There followed a whole series of charges and countercharges, cases being tried in Quebec, in Montreal, and in Toronto, until in the autumn of 1818 the whole business was removed to the courts of Upper Canada and Selkirk was faced with the ruinous costs of getting his witnesses and counsel from Montreal to York. The lawyers of Upper Canada denied the right of barristers of Lower Canada to practise in their courts, and the courts themselves felt the need to take the trials back to their beginnings. Everything would therefore have to be proved once more, and it was doubtful whether indictments originating in Lower Canada could be heard in the Courts of Upper Canada.[34] Connivance, laxity, ignorance and prejudice, disgraced the proceedings, and when, for example, true bills were found against Cuthbert Grant at Montreal on two charges of murder, two of larceny, and nine other charges, he was allowed a trifling bail, and absconded to the interior.[35]

Selkirk, his health failing, never secured a verdict on the major charge held against him, that of resisting arrest on a legal warrant; the case was continuously deferred. As the trials lingered on, the incapacity of the courts became clear. When the transfer to the courts of Upper Canada was decreed, he withdrew to England and then to France. Desperately disillusioned as he was, he had firmly established his colony, and in so doing he had revealed the problems of access, of administration, and of defence which would need solution before settlement of the prairies could be undertaken on a major scale.

Colin Robertson had at last procured a trial and had been acquitted in May 1818. When in 1816 he had learned of the Massacre of Seven Oaks and when he knew that a party of settlers was on its way to York Factory, he had turned back, met them, and led them back to Lake Winnipeg. He had then continued on down to York Factory and taken ship for England. In October, however, his ship was caught by ice, the passengers were distributed among the posts for the winter, and Robertson spent a frustrating time waiting for travel to become possible once more. At the end of the winter of 1816-17 he learned that he would be accused for his raid on Fort Gibraltar, and he also learned of Selkirk's capture of Fort William—a move after his own heart. With spring he made his way overland from Moose to Montreal, arriving in August 1817, anxious to stand trial and clear himself.[36]

Robertson had also heard, on his way from the colony to the Bay, that his expedition into Athabasca had been run into disaster by John Clarke. Though Clarke had shown a truculence equal to that of the Nor'westers, and enormous hardihood, he had not faced the realities of his problem and refused to "drag grease (pemmican) into Athabasca." The consequent starvation had brought ruin. His expedition reached Lake Athabasca in fair shape, and Fort Wedderburn was established there. Further posts were set up at Great Slave Lake, at Lesser Slave Lake, and at Ile-à-la-Crosse. To save provisions Clarke then decided to winter up the Peace River, somewhere in the vicinity of the North West Fort Vermilion. His canoes were halted by starvation at the Loon River, and the Nor'westers used all their power to withdraw all Indians from their path and to prevent them from trading either furs or food. Clarke was forced to pledge his personal property for a meagre supply of food, and his goods were impounded. Sixteen of his men were starved to death, thirteen of them in an attempt to make their way back to Fort Wedderburn. Clarke himself barely survived, living through the winter largely on berries.[37] Even so, he was eager to get back to Athabasca and to renew the struggle; but he was clearly not fit for such a command. In the summer of 1816 the London Committee, unaware of the disaster, was ordering supplies and sending out fresh men and fresh orders for Athabasca; trade there was to be vigorously prosecuted. But with Robertson shut up in the north and no one else available, Clarke led the 1816 expedition in, for the Committee did not yet know of his incompetence.

At Lake Athabasca in the winter of 1816-17, Clarke met Archibald Norman McLeod, the North West Magistrate, who had been using his official position to intimidate the small party which Clarke had left in his posts. Clarke's officers had been imprisoned, and they were released only on condition that they took no further part in trading and that they kept the peace. McLeod completely dominated the situation. He arrested Clarke immediately on his return, and although the Hudson's Bay man was released on security, his trade goods were taken and, having been arrested in the presence of the Indians, he lost their respect. Towards the end of January 1817, the Nor'westers seized Fort Wedderburn completely and again arrested Clarke while they also sent a force up the Peace River to liquidate the small post there, largely designed to get provisions. Although McLeod was acting as a justice of the peace in the Indian Territory—"Yesterday I was a Judge, today I am an Indian Trader"—Clarke was not sent for trial in the courts of Canada but was sent to Lesser Slave Lake and then to other posts in the district. Eventually released at Fort Vermilion in Peace River, he walked to Lake Athabasca, where he was again arrested and sent out to Cumberland. At Cumberland he was again freed, so that in the summer of 1818 he would have been able to take command in Athabasca yet once more.[38]

The Hudson's Bay flag had in the meantime been kept flying in Athabasca by a French employee, a former Nor'wester, François Decoigne. But he resigned in 1818. Therefore, despite some misgivings on both sides, in

March 1818 Robertson agreed to establish the Hudson's Bay position in Athabasca himself.[39] He arrived at Fort Wedderburn, full of his usual infectious enthusiasm, well ahead of the Nor'westers (for whom he had arranged a series of "mischances" at the portages) and in good time to organize his fishery, settle the business of his posts, and get his winter arrangements in hand before his rivals came in.

Significantly, it was at Norway House, the new depot, that Robertson got his expedition together. Norway House was being organized to deal with the transportation both of the colony and the trade and to tie in with the Winter Road. The post was also intended to be a stage on the route to Montreal, with which communication was now accepted as a normal requirement. A small force of Norwegian labourers had been sent out to help in construction in 1814, and with Peter Fidler in charge the depot was built on the west bank of the Nelson River "at the outlet of Lake Winnipeg." It was in use in the summer of 1817, and the post at the Jack River on Playgreen Lake was then abandoned. The buildings were still unfinished, but Norway House immediately became the centre of the transportation system of the Hudson's Bay Company.

Robertson's party was of a size and strength which would have seemed impossible for the Hudson's Bay Company ten years earlier. The notion of pruning an expedition to a size which would be justified by profits had been abandoned. Losses must, if necessary, be accepted in order to maintain a footing. Robertson commanded twenty-six officers, a hundred and sixty men, and twenty-seven canoes. His district included Ile-à-la-Crosse and Lesser Slave Lake, and though some of his men were (as he said) "the Blind, the lame, and the decrepit" and some of his goods were ill chosen, it was nevertheless a powerful force which he led. With almost a month's lead over his rivals, he was able to win the trust of the Indians and to instil confidence into his own men. He knew that he would have to be extravagant and that the system of payment by "Shares of Trade" would make the Hudson's Bay men consider any extravagance as an inroad into their salaries. But he secured "unheard of disaffection and independence" among the Indians by the time the Nor'westers came up, and they found that they had lost "character, reputation and fame." Samuel Black and other North West "hair-pulling heroes," as Robertson called them, were much in evidence, but nothing was achieved until on October 11 Robertson himself was arrested and taken to Fort Chipewyan. There he remained a prisoner for the rest of the winter, but he managed to conduct his correspondence and to supervise his post by means of a cipher; and his opportunities of observing the Nor'westers convinced him that there was much opposition, especially among the winterers, to the lengths to which McGillivray was pushing the partnership in his determination to force Selkirk to abandon the colony. The wintering partners were anxious for their fortunes, and several of them were revolted at the Massacre of Seven Oaks, at other murders which had taken place, and at the sixteen deaths which the "starving system" had brought upon John Clarke's party in Peace River. Though Robertson felt that there was a considerable number whose hopes were pinned on a union with the Hudson's Bay Company, he judged that there would be very few who would stand up to William McGillivray. Robertson was taken out as a prisoner in the spring of 1819, but at Cumberland House he escaped.

The status of the Nor'westers had suffered a heavy blow. Not only had Robertson done much, but the reappearance of John Clarke affected the Indians mightily, for they had seen him taken out as a prisoner in the previous year. Clarke had been sent up the Peace River once more. There he had set up the posts towards the Rockies, in the provision country, which Philip Turnor had warned would be necessary if men were to winter in Athabasca. Colvile House on the Loon River and St Mary's post on the Smoky River were established, and Clarke had recovered the goods which had been sequestered at the Nor'westers' Fort Vermilion. This was a notable and public rebuff to the Nor'westers, and their prestige was completely undermined by the capture of the partners *en bloc*, at he Grand Rapid of the Saskatchewan as they went down from the Upper Country in June 1819.

This "Glorious news" came to Robertson in Cedar Lake as he went down from Cumberland in the Hudson's Bay brigade. The hero of this exploit was William Williams, the new Governor-in-Chief of Rupert's Land, appointed to take over from James Bird. The latter had all the knowledge needed for a successor to Semple, but he lacked the robust decisiveness which the situation demanded, and he was not anxious for the appointment. He was therefore made Governor *pro tempore* while the Committee made other arrangements. They wanted a Governor "of an Enterprising and active mind and whose talents and habits of life are calculated to command obedience and to insure strict discipline," and they found him in Williams, a former ship's captain who had served with the East India Company.

The Grand Rapid of the Saskatchewan had for many years been accepted by the Hudson's Bay people as a focal point at which access to the Upper Country could most easily be controlled. William Williams in 1819 mustered there a force of thirty men, including twenty de Meurons, a small cannon on a barge and another small cannon and two swivel guns at the foot of the Rapid. As the Nor'westers began to arrive from the Upper Country and began to walk down through the woods while their canoes shot the rapids, they were easily captured. By June 23 seven of the partners and a number of men had been taken. Not only was the partnership's capacity to manage its trade destroyed, but a paralyzing blow had been struck at the prestige of the concern. The legality of the arrests, under warrants which Williams had brought from Montreal, supplemented by warrants drawn out by himself as Governor of Rupert's Land, was dubious; but the effect of his action was incontrovertible.[40]

Accompanied by the jubilant Robertson, Williams took his prisoners down to Norway House, to Rock Depot, and so on to York Factory. William McIntosh escaped and so did Benjamin Frobisher, and the triumph was marred when Frobisher died of the hardships which he suffered during his escape. The other partners were sent to England for trial and were there released for lack of a prosecutor. Even had the law on the subject of prosecutions for offences committed outside England, except murder and treason, been clear, great expense would have been involved in taking witnesses from Canada to the United Kingdom, and in 1820 the Hudson's Bay Committee was thinking of making a settlement with the North West Company rather than of driving them to their last ditch by such actions as their new Governor had taken.

Williams was not aware that he would not be fully supported by his Committee. Convinced that Robertson must go back to Athabasca, to show the Indians that the Hudson's Bay men could not be suppressed and that the Nor'westers were the weaker party, he sent him off, sure that he had "gained a complete footing in Athabasca." Once he had shown himself at Fort Wedderburn, Robertson proposed to go on to Peace River and to open up trade across the Rockies in New Caledonia, while he would also organize expansion towards Great Slave Lake and the Mackenzie River. He regarded Ile-à-la-Crosse as the "last ridout" of North West influence, and he appointed John Clarke to that post. During the winter 1819-20 Clarke established a strong post at Ile-à-la-Crosse while Robertson at Colvile House, Peace River, found more Indians than he could trade with.

It was a sign of the times that the North West Company sent its more controversial characters, Peter Skene Ogden, Samuel Black, and John Haldane, up the Peace River into the Rockies and into New Caledonia, out of the way of judicial proceedings. The extremists were in a quandary, and Robertson was following them up hard. He sent an expedition under the French Canadian Ignace Giasson into New Caledonia, and this party crossed the mountains in the spring of 1820 and remained on the western slopes until the fall of that year, trading furs to the limit of their supplies and coming back convinced that there was indeed a good trade to be driven in New Caledonia.[41]

Much of Robertson's plan was not achieved, and by the time that he set out for Canada again in 1820 it had become clear that the Athabasca Department of the Hudson's Bay Company would have to shake off some lethargy and much extravagance before victory over the Nor'westers would be consolidated. The Nor'westers, however, were now also short of food and of goods in New Caledonia and were afraid of the Indians. Whereas the Hudson's Bay men had previously been plagued by the Athabasca Justice, A. N. McLeod, and his warrants, Montreal warrants for the arrest of Black and other North West "heroes" had been sent up together with a properly sworn constable to execute them.

It says much for the way in which the country had been opened up that, during the winter of 1819-20, an Arctic Discovery expedition under the command of Captain John Franklin, manned almost entirely by men to whom arctic travel was new, made its way up to Lake Athabasca, there to demand help from both companies of fur-traders. England itself, moved by some suspicion of Russia, had again taken up the quest for the Northwest Passage, but its search from inland, complementary to that by ships in the northern waters, rested on the fur trade. The general competence in travel may also be seen in the way in which William Williams, a newcomer to the scene, made his way up to Cumberland House and there spent the winter. The exclusive control of the fur-traders was nearing its end; and by 1820 the North West Company was working against the certainty that its partnership agreement must expire in 1821 and against the virtual certainty that the partnership could not be renewed on anything like the current terms. There was a split between the agents and the winterers, and the agents could not even command the loyal support of all the partners. Some, under the lead of Angus Bethune and John McLoughlin, were uneasy at the lengths to which the struggle to uproot the colony had led them and were anxious also to bring some notion of economy into their affairs. As the partners met at Fort William in the summer of 1820, all seemed to turn on success in Athabasca, both because the trade from that district would have to pay for the expenses of the campaign and because it seemed that only by overwhelming failure in Athabasca could the Hudson's Bay Company be convinced that rivalry in the fur trade could not be made to pay and that agreement must be arranged on the Nor'westers' terms.

With Colin Robertson a prisoner, taken in his turn at the Grand Rapid of the Saskatchewan as he came down from Peace River, John Clarke discredited, and François Decoigne resigned, there was no obvious leader for the Hudson's Bay men in Athabasca in 1820. But at this juncture George Simpson appeared on the scene.[42] Shrewd, purposeful, and little troubled by scruples, George Simpson proved to be the man of the moment; and the man of the next half century too. He had behind him twelve years' experience as a sugar broker's clerk in London, a thorough grounding in the disciplines of book-keeping, grammar and arithmetic, derived from a sound education in the parish school at Avoch in Morayshire, and a self-confident independence of judgement. He had, too, a strange mixture of obsequiousness and assertiveness which made him acceptable to his masters and to his followers alike. Psychologists may perhaps trace his characteristics to the fact that he was the illegitimate offspring of a son of the manse, but his origins never troubled George Simpson any more than did the way in which he scattered his own progeny through the territory.[43] He brought great abilities to the Hudson's Bay Company, and he came at a timely moment. When he first crossed the Atlantic in 1820 he was about thirty-five years old, and it says much for the discernment of the city gentry who were managing the Company that they chose him and that they placed such confidence in him even before he had any experience of the fur trade. They appointed him Governor-in-Chief in the event of William Williams being called out to stand trial; if Williams remained free to carry on his duties as Governor he was to use Simpson to the best advantage as an assistant to himself.

A brief stay in Montreal gave Simpson some idea of the hostility between the two companies and of the bitterness which had become part of their struggles. He carried with him, to deliver to the Nor'westers at Fort William, a copy of a dispatch from Bathurst instructing them to keep the peace. This done, he travelled on, past Red River settlement to Norway House. There he met William Williams and accepted the Governor's proposal that he should go inland and take command in Athabasca. Simpson brought to the Northwest at this peculiar juncture all the gifts—and some of the defects—of a first-class English civil servant. He had an amazing capacity for absorbing detail, for shrewd analysis of complex data, for unscrupulous exploitation of other people's ideas and experience, and he had a marked capacity for exhausting work. He travelled up to Athabasca in company with the competent young clerk, Robert Miles, and he later acknowledged his great debt to him; the journal which Simpson dictated on the journey is full of ideas and of knowledge which must have come from the clerk; for to the "greenhorn" it was all new.[44] This was to be typical of Simpson's service and of his ability to take the knowledge of others, enlarge it and fit it into an overall view, and present it effectively.

By the time he reached Fort Wedderburn, Simpson had convinced himself that the key to policy lay in securing a firm footing in Athabasca and in expanding from there to New Caledonia and to the Mackenzie River. He found on his arrival that Fort Wedderburn was in good heart and that the Nor'westers were disunited and despondent. Aware that negotiations for a merger were under way, they were naturally anxious that they should not act so as to render themselves unacceptable if a joint concern should be created. Simpson took complete command of the situation and even turned the tables on the Nor'westers by arresting Simon McGillivray, Jr., on a Montreal warrant. His own men he disciplined, whether they were negro cooks (and he had a negro with him in that capacity !), "half-gentry," or commissioned officers; and he had with him Lieutenant Jonas Oxley, late of the Third West India Regiment.

During his winter in Athabasca [45] Simpson ran across almost every aspect of the fur trade, from drunken Indians and mutinous servants up to intense loyalty despite starvation, and dour endurance of hardship. He learned with astonishing speed, and by the time he came out to Norway House in May and June 1821 he was already as complete a master of the problems of the Canadian fur trade as anyone had ever been. Then, as he ran the Grand Rapid of the Saskatchewan, he met couriers with news which was to give him opportunities which no one had ever previously enjoyed. The two companies had reached a coalition. George Simpson was (though this was not yet arranged) to be the man who would command the resources of both companies and of the whole of the Canadian fur trade. He brought un-rivalled talents to an unprecedented opportunity.

CHAPTER 13

Coalition and Consolidation

Events in the Northwest since 1814 had revealed to England that this vast region could not be left as it was, reluctant although the British government was to acknowledge responsibility in a corner of the globe so little known and so lacking in profit. But American claims to the Columbia and Russian expansion in Alaska now combined with violence in the Northwest itself to necessitate some arrangement that would ensure peace and restore that region to its wonted obscurity. In facing this need the British government sought first to twist together the two lines of advance by which the Canadian and English fur companies had penetrated the Shield and created the fur trade of the far Northwest, to end the rivalry that had begun a century and a half before, and to use the fur-traders as the frontier-guard of British claims and influence.

During the struggle between the North West Company and the Hudson's Bay Company it became clear that the Secretary of State for War and the Colonies, Lord Bathurst, was uneasy at the pretensions of the Hudson's Bay Company, while the Under-Secretary, Henry Goulbourn, was in active sympathy with the Nor'westers and in constant correspondence with them. This did not imply that the Colonial Office accepted the Nor'westers' claims on the government. On the contrary, the Colonial Office was ready to sacrifice the Nor'westers claims to the mouth of the Columbia for the sake of peace with the United States. But although the British government would not fully accept North West Company claims, the Colonial Office showed a distinct leaning towards the Nor'westers in all their disputes with the Hudson's Bay Company. When in 1814 the Hudson's Bay Company submitted reports that the colony at Red River was under threat and asked for a small military force for its defence, Goulbourn refused, and although by 1815 the dispersal of the settlers and the arrest of Miles Macdonell should have led at least to a reappraisal of the situation, Goulbourn again refused.[1] Bathurst at that time regarded the whole business as a commercial quarrel, with both sides equally to blame. He was persuaded to authorize the Acting Governor General of Lower Canada to "furnish such protection and assistance as can be afforded without detriment to His Majesty's service," but he left it to the Acting Governor General to decide whether the Hudson's Bay Company's fears were well grounded and to furnish protection in the event of his considering such action to be necessary. Nothing was done since Goulbourn explained that any action would prejudge the whole issue. Bathurst hoped that the companies would bring their claims before the British courts, while Goulbourn stated that the question must be dealt with in Parliament.[2]

In Canada, William McGillivray had the ear of the Acting Governor General, and Drummond concluded that "if the lives and property of the Earl of Selkirk's settlers are or may be hereafter endangered, that danger will arise principally from the conduct of Mr. Miles Macdonell." He turned to McGillivray and the Nor'westers with "perfect confidence in their candour and liberality of sentiment" and asked whether there was any reason for the Hudson's Bay men or the settlers to require protection.[3] McGillivray indignantly denied the allegation at the very moment when the agents of the North West Company were completing the destruction of the settlers' huts and crops.

In London, at the same time, the Nor'westers were assuring Goulbourn that the charges against them were utterly unfounded, while Drummond told Bathurst that protection for the settlers was "decidedly impracticable."[4] During 1815 the Hudson's Bay Company on two occasions submitted to the Colonial Office proposals for the government of their territories, but no decision could be elicited. As the Massacre of Seven Oaks was being enacted, Goulbourn was informing the Hudson's Bay men that any crimes committed would come to trial in due course, and the whole problem of rights and jurisdiction would come under the cognizance of the courts. He was contemptuous of the folly of sending troops to defend a settlement "so remote from His Majesty's other possessions."[5]

Sir Gordon Drummond gave up his office in May 1816, and news of the Massacre of Seven Oaks came to Montreal in the first weeks of the tenure of the new Governor, Sir John Sherbrooke, who was on terms "of less ingenuous intimacy" with the Nor'westers. Selkirk's recruitment of the de Meurons and his decision that he must himself bring the North West partners to justice and even impound the evidence to be found at Fort William, are the measure of his conviction that there was no hope of governmental intervention.

Confirmation of the news of the massacre, of Selkirk's capture of Fort William and of his purchases of North West goods there (which could be taken as breaking, entering, and larceny) had stirred Sherbrooke to the appointment of commissioners, and so to the collection of evidence which eventually led to a government enquiry and a Parliamentary Blue Book. At the same time, Selkirk's refusal to surrender to the Drummond Island Warrant for his arrest, issued by Dr. Mitchell, set the Colonial Office even more firmly against him and caused Bathurst's dispatch of February 11, 1817.[6] Selkirk was assumed to be so much in the wrong that the case against him hardly required trial. If he could not be arrested, Sherbrooke was to notify Bathurst, who would put the matter to Parliament; and there was an obvious expectation that Selkirk would take the law into his own hands and would make such measures necessary.

In the trials which ensued, Selkirk was prosecuted at the instigation of the Colonial Office; but the indictment against him was unceremoniously thrown out by the Grand Jury. The North West partners were prosecuted at Selkirk's instigation, not as men accused of offences against the peace. Throughout the trials Selkirk and his counsel were bewildered by the animus shown by the Crown officials until, by mistake, Bathurst's dispatch of February 11 was put into Selkirk's hands and he realized that the Colonial Office assumed that he would never quietly submit to the course of justice. When he thus became aware of the official attitude, Selkirk communicated the information to the Hudson's Bay Company; and his brother-in-law John Halkett, the third member of the triumvirate which had taken control of the Hudson's Bay Company's affairs, a trenchant pamphleteer as well as a considerable merchant, wrote to Bathurst a letter which could not be ignored.[7] Halkett inveighed against the general conspiracy and against the stigma on Selkirk. Goulbourn was unmoved, but Selkirk's friends took the question to the Prime Minister, Lord Liverpool, and to the Privy Council; for it was clear that other members of the Cabinet had not been consulted by the Colonial Secretary and that his Under-Secretary had managed the dispute in his own way.

At the same time the Governor and other members of the Hudson's Bay Company demanded an opinion from the Law Officers of the Crown on the Company's powers, reminding Bathurst of the many requests for protection which they had submitted. They protested vigorously against the assumption of the Prince Regent's Proclamation, that both companies were equally at fault, and they asked that Parliament should lay down the boundaries within which the Company's chartered rights held good. Goulbourn, waspishly hoping that the tone of instructions given to their servants by the Hudson's Bay Company did not reflect that of the letter which he had received, still delayed action.[8] It was in the mood engendered by these refusals even to institute an enquiry that the Hudson's Bay Company had recruited William Williams and that he enforced warrants which he had issued as Governor of Rupert's Land and arrested the North West partners at the Grand Rapid of the Saskatchewan. Thereby Williams got possession of a great deal of North West Company correspondence and, taking a leaf from Robertson's book, read it, and revealed the involvement of the North West partners in much of the villainy which had taken place.

The Hudson's Bay Committee were not certain that they could protect Williams from the law; in fact, the counsel whom they consulted was very uneasy. But they took the captured correspondence and forwarded copious extracts to Bathurst, together with other correspondence. Thus at last, in September 1819, Bathurst perused a fully documented narrative of the Hudson's Bay Company's version of the struggle. This was probably the first time that he had become aware that there were two sides to the dispute, and he ordered the compilation of the 1819 Blue Book—the *Papers Relating to the Red River Settlement, 1815-1819*. Then, in February 1820, he sent a formal warning to both companies to instruct their servants to cease hostilities. The Blue Book was brought before Parliament, and the evidence submitted by the Hudson's Bay Company was put before the Privy Council. The North West Company maintained a good front as the evidence gathered. They submitted a statement that they had always pressed for a judicial decision from 1816 onwards, and their agent Edward Ellice was busily trying to buy a dominating block of Hudson's Bay Company shares while he exercised great influence on Goulbourn. The government view was still that there were faults on both sides. It favoured an arrangement between the two companies, with more than a hint that a compromise would be acceptable to government.[9] It is therefore not surprising that, when the two great concerns reached an agreement, the Colonial Office came out strongly in support of the joint concern which emerged.

The Blue Book left no doubt that illegal actions had taken place in the Indian country, and clearly indicated two conclusions. First, competition in the fur trade was "productive of great inconvenience and loss . . . , and also of great injury to the native Indians and other persons."[10] Second, the judicial system must be revised so that when crimes did occur in the Upper Country the criminals could be brought to justice. Elimination of competition and the creation of an effective system for law enforcement were therefore the two objectives of the statute passed in July 1821 "For regulating the Fur Trade and establishing a Criminal and Civil Jurisdiction within certain parts of North America."[11]

The political situation had changed little as the two companies reached their agreement. Goulbourn "in some mysterious but unmistakable way was in cordial touch with Ellice and the Northwesters,"[12] and Ellice now turned all his energies to perpetuating and enlarging the privileges of the Hudson's Bay Company instead of to their destruction. As a Member of Parliament (for Coventry) he was in close touch with the Colonial Office and with the ministers, and he later claimed that he was instrumental in drawing up the terms of the 1821 Act. Parliament accepted the Blue Book's conclusion that competition was disastrous for the fur trade, and the 1821 Act gave the Crown power to grant an exclusive right to the Indian trade in any part of British North America except the two provinces of Canada and the territory of Rupert's Land. This accepted the Hudson's Bay Company's Charter with its grant of exclusive trade in Rupert's Land. In addition, under consideration was the area which came to be known as the North West Territories— Athabasca, the Peace River, the Rockies, New Caledonia, the Mackenzie River, and the Pacific Coast. Government's intention was to grant exclusive rights within these territories, under the 1821 statute, to the new coalition of the companies. But others might come forward with claims, and Ellice, to eliminate any chance of competition, pushed the grant through and got the traders to accept it, in draft form, in December 1821.[13]

The grant was expressly made to remedy the evils "which have arisen from the competition which has heretofore existed"; it conceded the exclusive privilege of trading with Indians in the territories under discussion for twenty-one years from 1821. The grant was free, but the traders were to keep accurate registers of all persons in their employ and were to guarantee that all criminal processes, and any civil process in which the sum at issue exceeded two hundred pounds, should be enforced by legally appointed officers within those territories. They were also invited to submit regulations for managing the fur trade in such a manner as to diminish, and ultimately prevent, the sale or distribution of spirituous liquors to the Indians. In view of the special arrangements for joint occupancy of the territory west of the Rockies, the British traders were not to exclude American citizens from trade in that area; but as against other British subjects they had an exclusive right there.[14]

The Act of 1821 left the fur-traders responsible for keeping the peace in the territories of which the trade was allotted to them. They were themselves responsible for their own employees, and there would be few others in those territories. For strangers, and indeed for their own men if the question should arise, they were to ensure that law officers sent into the territories were allowed to do their duty. Ellice alleged that he had "put in those clauses myself" so that the Crown and the Canadian authorities might have power to appoint justices; but that the powers were not taken up and the territory was left to be governed under the chartered rights of the Hudson's Bay Company.[15]

Important questions about the extension of effective jurisdiction into the North West Territories nevertheless remained unsolved. The Canada Jurisdiction Act of 1803 had allowed justices of the peace, appointed in Canada, to exercise authority in the Indian Territories and had ordered that those arrested upon Canadian warrants should be sent down to the courts of Canada for trial. The system had permitted serious abuses. The fur-traders themselves were the only people who were given authority as justices of the peace; and it was never quite clear whether the Indian Territories included Rupert's Land, or Red River Colony as deriving from Rupert's Land. Although the 1821 Act opened by stating that such doubts should be removed, the Act was unable to effect any substantial change since the basic problem was that of human character. It remained true, after as before the Act, that fur-traders would for many years be the only people involved and the only people who could be empowered to act as justices. The judicial clauses therefore remained of little or no effect; the real achievement was the elimination of competition and of causes for breaches of the peace.

It is significant that the Hudson's Bay Company on the one hand, and William McGillivray, Simon McGillivray, and Edward Ellice (three partners of the North West Company) on the other, should have been named as recipients of the Grant of Exclusive Trade of 1821, made under the Act for Regulating the Fur Trade. They were a coalition and not an amalgamation. Each of the companies was supposed to retain its identity. In the last phase of the negotiations the agents of the North West Company had recovered their authority, and the wintering partners, who had been instrumental in bringing about the collapse of North West resistance, were reduced in status. William McGillivray's desire to penalize both the Hudson's Bay men who had taken active parts against him and the winterers who had led the revolt against the agents, John McLoughlin and Angus Bethune, was vetoed. There was no victimization in the coalition. Only a small number of Nor'westers, including Samuel Black and Peter Skene Ogden, who had gone to great lengths in opposition, were excepted from a general amnesty. The coalition[16] was to last for twenty-one years; and the Licence for Exclusive Trade was timed to begin with the first Outfit under the joint management and to end with the expiry of the coalition.

The coalition was apparently an agreement between equals, and the Nor'westers inevitably tended to dominate by virtue of their vigorous personalities, their knowledge, and their involvement in the trade. Yet the actual terms placed them in a minority. In theory the grant of Exclusive Trade was made to the two companies, and the Hudson's Bay Company and the North West agents made a deed of covenant in which they both agreed to keep the terms of the grant and spent the winter months in working out conditions by which they could implement their privileges. Much effort went into constructing a form of agreement known as the Deed Poll, which adopted something of the North West practice, giving Councils to the traders by which they could participate in the management of the trade; it also regulated the Shares of Trade by which they would be paid.[17] Forty

shares of the profits of the trade were allotted to the traders. Separate
Councils and separate Governors were to be appointed for the Northern
and for the Southern Department, and they were to arrange the business for
each season for their department. Strict measures were at the same time
taken to weed out the idle, the dissipated, and the incompetent, and immediate retirement was offered to several traders who seemed to be at the end
of their useful period of office. The two Governors named under this arrangement were both Hudson's Bay men, William Williams and George Simpson.

To settle immediate problems, Simon McGillivray on behalf of the North
West Company and Nicholas Garry (the only bachelor on the board of the
Hudson's Bay Company) went to Canada in the summer of 1821.[18] There
they were joined by William McGillivray, and in a prolonged session at
Fort William they brought the affairs of the North West Company into
conformity with the new arrangements. The McGillivrays secured most of
the important appointments for former Nor'westers; and there could be
little doubt that the Nor'westers would make the most efficient fur-traders.
Colin Robertson, who survived an attempt by the McGillivrays to oust him
from employment and who got command of Norway House, reported that
"It would appear ... that the N. W. Co. had gained a complete victory and
were dictating to us the terms of capitulation."[19]

Yet the meeting decided to abandon Fort William as a depot for the fur
trade. Since this was what the North West Company had, in a way, been
trying to do for ten years, the decision should have caused little surprise.
But the result was that "the fur trade is for ever lost to Canada."[20] So wrote
William McGillivray. The decision in favour of Hudson's Bay and against
Montreal as the springboard for the fur trade was confirmed when a full
Council of the joint concern was held at Norway House, with the newly
appointed Chief Factors and Traders having their powers and their terms
of service explained to them by George Simpson.

It became apparent that the North West agents had "chalked out" a snug
business for themselves as Montreal agents for the coalition. But although
Simon McGillivray protested that Athabasca should get its supplies from
Montreal and that at least the trade of Lake Huron, Lake Superior, Lake
Michigan, and Timiskaming, should be supplied by that way, the Chief
Factors, led by George Simpson, overcame him and decided that even these
districts should receive their supplies by way of Moose and the Southern
Department of Rupert's Land. The decisions to use the Bayside transport
system were supported by a detailed policy of improving the routes; money
and effort were to go into the portages and tracking places, the Winter
Road was to be pushed on, and a provisions system in Assiniboia was to be
incorporated with the trade of the North West. Once more, the merits of
boats as against canoes were advocated. In all of this George Simpson

profited by his ability to understand and to expound the complicated documents involved. He profited also from the Nor'westers' dislike for William Williams.[21] Garry had to repulse a suggestion that Williams be excluded from the joint concern, but in view of the feeling against him it seemed sensible to make him Governor of the less important Southern Department while Simpson took command of the more potent Northern Department—an arrangement which Garry effected and which Williams accepted.[22]

Though the Nor'westers were able to comfort themselves over the allocations of posts, it could not be overlooked that the agents had been ousted from their "snug business" of bringing in supplies through Montreal. William McGillivray maintained that "we have made no submission—we met and negotiated on equal terms—and rating the N. W. Co. collectively they now hold fifty-five out of a hundred shares." Ellice put his interpretation on the arrangement by claiming that "from the union sprang the present Hudson's Bay Company, which is more in fact a Canadian Company than an English Company in its origin."[23] McGillivray's calculation that the Nor'westers held a majority of the shares could, however, only be justified on the assumption that twenty-five of the forty shares to be enjoyed by the traders would be controlled by Nor'westers. But since the wintering partners had rebelled against the agents, and eighteen of them had given powers of attorney to McLoughlin and Bethune to use against the agents, such a calculation is not justifiable. It would in any case refer only to shares in the profits of the trade, not to control and direction. For this a Board or Joint Committee was set up, with the Governor of the Hudson's Bay Company as Chairman and with two members from each of the concerns. The North West Company named Simon McGillivray and Edward Ellice; the Hudson's Bay Company named Andrew Wedderburn Colvile and Nicholas Garry. The separate core of the Hudson's Bay Company was carefully preserved, and it was considered that its Charter and privileges would emerge intact at the end of the specified period of twenty-one years.[24] The stability of the Hudson's Bay Company was emphasized as the firm of McGillivrays, Thain and Company crashed in bankruptcy, and William McGillivray died in 1825; the North West agents became ordinary shareholders of the Hudson's Bay Company, and the Joint Committee of Management then yielded to the unified control of the Hudson's Bay Committee.[25]

The predominance which the Hudson's Bay Company had in reality secured was confirmed by Simpson's control of the Council which was set up at Norway House, and by his continuous and increasing mastery of the "Empire" which circumstances had thrown into his hands. This was an empire of fur-traders, not of settlers or agriculturists. He gave some indication of his methods and of his outlook during his first winter in office.

Arrangements for the trade were concluded by a formal banquet at York Factory, during which Simpson showed as great a mastery over personalities as he had already shown over documentation. He then spent a couple of months checking, stock-taking, and planning at York before he set out on a winter journey which took him something like fifteen hundred miles, for the most part on snowshoes, round the centre of his domain. From York he went back to Norway House, then through Lake Winnipeg and up the Saskatchewan to Cumberland, to the Swan River and the upper Assiniboine, Fort Qu'Appelle, and Brandon House. He returned to Norway House accompanied by Cuthbert Grant, the leader of the Red River Métis; and he showed his capacity for selecting people when, despite the part which Grant had played in the Massacre of Seven Oaks, he brought him into the colony's service as Warden of the Plains, harnessing his capacity and leadership to the settlement. He also brought the Sioux to order when they threatened to attack the post at Pembina, jeopardizing the buffalo hunt on which the settlement still depended.

Simpson was instructed that the affairs of the colony must be separated off from those of the fur trade but that the concern accepted responsibility for maintaining a shop at Red River and that it retained the right to trade for furs and provisions there. The Company was also to be responsible for the maintenance of law and order in the settlement. Relations between Company and colony promised difficulty from the start, and Simpson as Governor of the Northern Department, working with a Council of fur-traders for whom the colony represented a distant prospect of retirement but an instant drain on resources, was understandably less enthusiastic than the Hudson's Bay members of the joint committee in London, of whom one was a relative of Selkirk and the other a strong supporter of the colony. The problem was revealed by the continuing North West opposition to the colony, set against Garry's insistence on its status, the fact that he brought an Anglican missionary, Rev. John West, to minister to the settlers, and that under his lead the traders at York made a handsome subscription to support a mission to the colony.

For the moment the divergent interests of Company and colony were fused by common enthusiasm, and having started John West off on his mission and seen to the installation of the new Governor of the colony, Alexander Macdonell (whom the settlers called "the Grasshopper Governor" because he did as much damage as the grasshoppers), Simpson and his Council turned to the business of the fur trade; above all to the basic problem of transportation, which occupied much of his time during his early years as Governor. His first journey into Athabasca had given him a knowledge of the route all the way from Montreal to the Northwest and back to Norway House and York, and he had appended a thesis on transportation to his Journal of that winter.[26] His second winter, spent in travelling round the centre of his Northern Department, added greatly to his knowledge; and the Committee supported him in his devotion to this question. In 1822 they approved a plan to explore the route from the Nelson River to the Burntwood Carrying Place and so to Frog Portage and to Athabasca. They also asked for a report on the route to Norway House from York by way of the Nelson River instead of by the Hayes River. This was one of his duties in which Simpson, from the start, allowed enthusiasm to run away with him, and the confidence with which he dictated his first reports on the routes concealed the fact that most of his information was at second hand. Himself an indefatigable traveller who always took great pleasure in breaking records both for speed and for endurance, but who expected others to emulate him, he was apt to think in terms of a light canoe, manned by a picked crew and carrying only the Governor and his secretary, rather than of a normal canoe, heavily laden with goods or furs and manned by the ordinary *voyageur*. The brigades had considerable loads to carry over the portages and often had to feed themselves en route. Accordingly, in 1822 Simpson reported that the Burntwood route had been examined, that it was safe, and that it would save from eighteen to twenty days. He used it in 1824 to make a record-breaking journey to Ile-à-la-Crosse and decided to order the Athabasca brigades to use that route.[27] But he overlooked the difficulties of finding provisions en route and the brevity of the season of open water. In 1825 the Burntwood route quietly vanished from his correspondence. The Nelson River route to Norway House was likewise abandoned because in normal years the river carried too much water in the early summer to make a passage up-stream easy.

As Simpson and his Council tackled these problems they had to give attention to their southern frontier with the Americans, and to the removal from the posts of men and families whom the end of competition had made redundant. For the joint purpose they organized the Bow River Expedition of 1822. The expedition was to set forth from Edmonton, and command was eventually given to Donald Mackenzie, a Nor'wester who had served in the American Fur Company and who had travelled extensively in the Columbia and in the Snake Country. Traditionally, Bow River was a territory from which few furs would be got and in which Piegans and other Plains Indians would be troublesome—for they were not dependent on fur-traders either for food or for equipment, and they had among them American traders who offered competition and who stirred them up against the Canadians. But the North Saskatchewan had been overtrapped during the rivalry of the companies, and there were some eighty men for whom the Bow River Expedition might provide occupation. Yet, despite the enthusiasm with which the project was launched, the result was such that even Simpson was persuaded to abandon Bow River in 1823.[28]

Partly to convince himself of the situation in Bow River, and of the relative merits of the north and south branches of the Saskatchewan, Simpson undertook his second winter tour, to take in Ile-à-la-Crosse, Athabasca, Great Slave Lake, Lesser Slave Lake, the Peace River, the Pembina River, and so back to the Saskatchewan.[29] He was unable to leave York until August 1822, and so could get no further than Ile-à-la-Crosse by open water. There he was held from October 16 until the ice had set, in mid-November. So far he had travelled by light canoe and by a magnificent boat, specially built for use on the Saskatchewan; he now set off on snow-shoes and plodded for the rest of his journey, as far afield as Great Slave Lake and the Peace River and so back to the Saskatchewan at the end of February 1823.

Already Simpson had acquired a unique knowledge of the Northwest, and he was constantly noting improvements which could be made, as well as pondering great strategic decisions. He was such a master of the fur trade as had not previously been seen. But when he went down to York in July 1823, to push his notions through the Council there (and his mastery of "the Councilling business" was already one of his greatest assets) it was agreed that he should go back to Red River and should winter there. In view of the success of Garry's mission, he was shortly followed by another English director, John Halkett, brother-in-law of Selkirk. Halkett came to further the work of giving the colony the amenities of a civilized community. He had always been a firm supporter of the colony and had developed a shrewd skill as a pamphleteer in its defence. It was, however, as an executor of Selkirk's will that he had come to North America in 1821; for he wished to discover whether he could get a legal title to those parts of Assiniboia which lay within American territory. The Selkirk grant had been ignored in the boundary treaty, and Selkirk had given to Halkett his claims to land south of 49° and had urged him to establish a legal title. Halkett spent the winter of 1821-22 in the United States, and concluded that American agriculture was so depressed that there was little point in pressing the legal issue until prosperity came again. Accordingly, the colony's post at Fort Daer should be given up, and Halkett went north with this in view, arriving in the colony in July 1822. In London Simon McGillivray was still working against the colony; since Halkett was on the spot, the London Committee therefore gave him powers to take any necessary action. He journeyed down from Red River to York Fort to meet the ship of the year in 1822 and there got his full instructions from London.[30] As he met Simpson and a temporary Council, it became clear that in some respects the mantle of the Nor'westers had fallen upon George Simpson, whose increasing devotion to the fur trade made it inevitable that he should be wary of the demands of the colony.

The settlers were still dependent on the buffalo hunts for much of their winter provisions, and since buffalo were scarce during the winter of 1822-23, the situation was made precarious by the hostility of the Sioux, which prevented the settlers, and even the half-breeds, from venturing out into the plain in search of the herds. The Sioux, moreover, were anxious to maintain competition in the fur trade, if necessary from an American source. By 1822-23, therefore, Simpson was forced to give the colony some of his attention, for it was clear that for a variety of reasons the colony would challenge the Licence for Exclusive Trade. The settlers, whether they were retired servants, de Meurons, Highlanders, or half-breed hunters, were indifferent to the Company's claims and favoured the petty traders who would offer them an alternative market; and the mission priest, Father Desmoulins, with considerable influence among the Métis, also supported the petty traders.[31] Simpson knew that the petty traders were unlikely to do themselves any good, but "the very rumour of an opposition is sufficient to disorganize the Indians of the most distant establishments in the Country." In London, Colvile and Halkett had a tender regard for the colony and were anxious that the traders should carry goods up from York for the settlers at special rates. Simpson was not the man to affront his masters; but he made a hard bargain on rates, accepting the duty of the Company to supply and to manage a Red River shop while making the point that such a shop could never be expected to cover its costs.[32]

In the meantime a campaign of recruitment in Switzerland had produced a considerable increase in the size of the colony. Many of the Swiss were watchmakers and petty artisans; some had been taken out of jails, workhouses, and madhouses; and some were dangerous and drunken—at least, so Simpson alleged. Discharged Canadian servants also had their defects; and the Governor, Alexander Macdonell, was held in contempt by the settlers, was bad at choosing his advisors, and was lacking in method.[33] Grasshoppers made serious inroads into the crops, and Simpson, feeling that the colony "assumes more the appearance of a receptacle for freebooters and infamous characters of all descriptions than a well-regulated Colony," advised that no more settlers should be sent from Europe, far less from Canada, until the agricultural and food position had been got in hand and until the colony had been provided with a code of laws, with magistrates and a full civil establishment. He felt that then, and only then, a great many servants of the Company, of all ranks, would be willing to build up the colony and would become respectable and useful members of society there. As a fur-trader, in the meantime, he was uneasy, fearing that the costs of administration must be borne by the fur trade and that the colony itself might never achieve economic stability and would remain a perpetual charge on the trade.

To establish some source of revenue apart from agricultural surpluses, Simpson supported the notion of a Buffalo Wool Company. The London Committee also swallowed the specious arguments put forward by John Pritchard and set up the Buffalo Wool Company in 1822. The notion had some merits, but by 1824 mismanagement and personal differences, plus the enormous costs of transportation, had brought the Buffalo Wool Company to the verge of bankruptcy.

It was as Simpson digested these issues that he had to face Halkett and the determination of the London Committee to make something of the colony. Halkett's intructions envisaged a third governor, for the colony, in addition to two Governors for the Departments of Rupert's Land. The Governors of the Northern and the Southern Departments, assisted by any two members of their Councils, could administer justice and exercise the functions of governing bestowed by the Hudson's Bay Company's Charter. The Governor of Assiniboia, with his own Council, would have the same powers within the colony, and was to have a sheriff to assist him. Whenever one of the Company's governors happened to be present in Assiniboia he would take precedence over the Governor of the colony. By these measures the Company would make itself responsible for the maintenance of law and order and for the administration of justice throughout the Northwest; and since the Colonial Office did not think it expedient to set up separate justices under a royal commission, as specified in the Act for Regulating the Fur Trade, the Company's arrangements controlled judicial and adminis-trative developments in the Northwest for the next half century.

As Halkett met a Council of the Northern Department and explained these directions, Captain Andrew Bulger, a brusque former soldier, was appointed Governor of Assiniboia to replace Alexander Macdonell; and Halkett directed the Council's attention to the problems of educating and civilizing the half-breeds, Indians, and children, who were beginning to need attention as hangers-on of the settlement. This was in the Selkirk tradition, and Rev. John West was already at the colony, battling with these problems. The fur trade was not in direct opposition to the colony here, for (as the Bow River Expedition had shown) the fur trade carried a great many men who were not needed when opposition had ceased, and apart from servants there was an "immense number of Women and Children supported at the different Trading Posts, some belonging to men still in the Service and others who have been left by the Fathers unpro-tected and a burden on the Trade."[34] Money was available from the Church Missionary Society for two clergymen, a schoolmaster, and a schoolmistress for the instruction of Indian children and others. The danger was that a concentration of Indians and half-breeds would lead to unlawful conduct. Old servants with large families were also to be brought to Red River, where allotments of twenty to twenty-five acres were to be given to them and where a School of Industry was to be set up. It seemed to the Committee that a Chief Factor or a Chief Trader with a talent for managing people, with proper assistance, would be needed; and they suggested that John Clarke would be the right person.

Though Clarke was ordered to destroy the post at Pembina, which was on American territory, he was also to guard against Americans trading to the colony or anywhere within the Company's lands, and he was to guard against the settlers profiting from American traders while they enjoyed free administration, cheap transport, and low prices from the Company.

As Governor of Assiniboia, Andrew Bulger represented the Committee's view that the colony must be supported by the fur-traders. John Clarke was put in to safeguard the traders' interests, and it was inevitable that the two should clash; at the end of their first year both withdrew from the colony, Bulger to England and Clarke to a new appointment at Swan Lake. Clarke had, however, suppressed the petty traders and had taken their furs, leaving them ruined men, whom Simpson was pleased to use as a means of selling the Company's goods to the settlers. It had been shown that the settlers were entirely dependent on the Company's store and that the petty traders were unable to get supplies from any equally reliable source and could be made instruments for counteracting American traders south of the frontier, to whom furs might be sold and from whom goods might be got. Astor and his American Fur Company looked menacing; but the serious threat to the exclusive trade of the Hudson's Bay Company came from comparatively small traders such as Robert Dixon, who had been bought off by Selkirk in 1816. In 1823 Simpson was forced to take notice of the American, Hercules Dousman, who was offering to supply the settlers and even the Company's store with goods. Against such opposition Simpson simply used the financial strength of the Company. He had no authority to which he could appeal against American traders operating from south of the frontier, nor could he rival them in trade there. He was forced to prevent them from trading on Company's territory by underselling them and by offering better prices for furs to Métis, Indians, and settlers. He had behind him the services of an expert purchasing agency in England, shipment through the Bay, and great financial resources. He was able to keep the Company's shop at Fort Garry plentifully supplied at controlled prices. By 1830 the shop was selling above £7,000 of goods every year, and much of this was used by the settlers to buy furs from Indians who would otherwise have disposed of them to Americans south of the frontier. The settlers then brought the furs to the

Company's store, to finance further purchases. The Americans were thus repulsed without the Company transgressing the frontier and without the legalistic protection of the Licence for Exclusive Trade. Though Clarke had forbidden all retail trading except at the Company's store, in 1823 the Committee reversed this and allowed trade in all goods except furs and leather. This meant that much trade to supply the settlers came up from the United States and in particular that spirits and tobacco tended to be brought to the settlement by that route; for the Company decreed that spirits were to be sold only to servants of the Company, and in limited quantities.[35]

The Company had not tried to retain a monopoly of retail trade, only to make trading in furs unprofitable for external buyers such as the American traders. Indeed, it was anxious to get settlers to undertake the responsibilities of securing stocks and setting up shop to supply the colony. To some extent such traders were deliberately fostered; to some extent the result was unplanned. For to facilitate the development of economic and social stability the Company issued its own banknotes from 1823 onwards, and so for about the next twenty years the Company acted as banker for the private traders and financed their purchases both from Canada and from the United States, as well as from the Company. Under this régime the petty traders of Red River ceased to worry the fur trade and played a significant part in the economic development which the Company regarded as desirable.

But as Clarke was succeeded by Donald Mackenzie and Bulger by Robert Parker Pelly, and as Simpson spent the winter of 1824 in the colony, the outlook remained unpromising despite the official support for the settlers even when they turned to trade. The grasshopper invasions of 1820 and 1821 and the buffalo famine of 1822 were followed by prairie fires in 1823; once more buffalo were scarce. Starvation was just round the corner. When the great flood of 1826 followed, the colony might well have been abandoned, and many of the de Meurons, the Swiss, the Canadians, and the half-breeds were driven to the United States.[36] But the Scots and the Orkneymen remained, and the Company came to their rescue. After the flood the crops were good, a mill was got to work, and fine flour was produced. By 1830 the means of living were abundant, and even Simpson hoped that the colonists would be happy and well supplied. The plains away from the river were well stocked with cattle, the river banks were highly cultivated, abundant fish were taken from the river.

But still the colony was purely agricultural. Living was plentiful, but the people had little paid employment, and although the Company had begun to buy butter and flour, barley and peas, from the settlers, there was little money in circulation. The Buffalo Wool Company was followed by an Experimental Farm, by the Assiniboine Wool Company which pioneered experiments in sheep farming, and by a Tallow Company which brought up cattle from the south and tried to ranch on a large scale. The Company encouraged individuals to make experiments and gave them preferential terms to help launch new ventures which might diversify the economy. Flax and hemp were crops which might be grown by small holders, and the Company provided seed and set up a mill, offering a premium on all flax and hemp grown. The result was over-production followed by general abandonment of these crops when the Company withdrew its subsidies. Sheep had been tried by Selkirk and had shown that they could thrive at Red River; Simpson therefore ordered up a flock from the United States, tried to get ewes and rams from England, and established a company to underwrite the considerable capital expenditure which was involved. But by 1832 the Assiniboine Wool Company abandoned its business. Sheep farming had made a start, however, and some sheep which had been brought up from Fort William throve. When the Company's first Experimental Farm tried to bring up a further flock from Missouri and Kentucky the sheep, driven in difficult conditions for over fifteen hundred miles, died wholesale. Only 251 out of 1,075 reached Red River, and the disaster brought not only sheep farming but the Experimental Farm itself, and even the Governor who had sponsored these costly ventures, into derision. Altogether the Hudson's Bay Company underwrote three Experimental Farms; and the last of the "Three Unfortunate Sisters" at least reinforced the existing sheep and was able to supply the settlers with stock which they needed to improve their flocks.[37]

This was the pattern to which Simpson hoped to work—a pattern in which the Company encouraged prosperous and enterprising individuals to maintain the economic activity which the colony needed. But the climate of Red River proved to be poor for sheep farming, and though something like two thousand sheep were soon grazed there, this was a sheep population sparsely distributed among the settlers. It represented no great woollen industry; what it did represent was a group of settlers competent to take over anything which looked like achieving success.

When the great sheep drive had failed, Simpson and the Company turned to a cattle-ranching industry. Bulls and cows had been shipped out to York and been brought to Red River by boat, and attempts had been made to cross the wild buffalo with domestic cattle. American speculators had driven about three hundred cattle to the colony in 1822, and grazing became profitable. This was, however, a small-holders' by-product, and the Tallow Company was launched in an attempt to turn cattle into a serious industry. It was run on a co-operative basis, and members "subscribed" several hundreds of cattle in 1832. But bad weather proved the dangers of wintering cattle out of doors at Red River, and within two years the herd was sold by auction and the Tallow Company was written off. Once more, some of the settlers showed their ability to take over useful assets, and though the great project was a failure a useful dairy and cattle industry was established with a wide range of ownership. This was a valuable supplement to grain growing.

By the 1830's the settlers were, on the whole, more competent than the experimenters, and not much less enterprising—as was shown by the third Model Farm. In 1837 Simpson, still determined to set the colony on its feet, ordered ewes and rams from England and brought out Captain George Marcus Cary with twenty agriculturists. But the model farmers were unused to conditions in Red River; confusion, lavish expenditure, and optimism overset the experiment, and by 1840 it was clear that the settlers had little or nothing to learn about farming at Red River. By 1843 Simpson reported that the colony was flourishing, crops looked good, cattle and sheep were as thick on the ground as winter fodder allowed, and the Governor had never seen a peasantry so comfortable and so independent in their circumstances.[38] There was a fair trade south, bringing up horses and taking cattle down to the Americans.

As the colony got on its feet, the fur trade tried to withdraw its support. Credit at the Company's store was discontinued in 1832, and the amount of freight which could be brought in for settlers at cheap rates was cut. This helped the development of retail traders, men who could afford to pay cash at the Company's store and could then finance smaller purchases on credit by the mass of the settlers.

It is significant that Rupert's Land, the North West Territory, and the Pacific Coast were not included in the area upon which Lord Durham was to report in 1837. Emigration—and emigration to Canada—was indeed a national concern, but neither Red River Colony nor any other part of the Company's territories attracted the attention either of the British government or of Durham. Agricultural settlement there must be achieved under the aegis of the fur trade, and according to notions which would be acceptable to the fur-traders. The basic problem, therefore, was to establish a suitable relationship between agriculturists and fur-traders.

A place had to be found not only for white traders and white settlers but also for both the Indians and the half-breeds. Normally, when settlers took land from the Indians, the result, as Sir Francis Bond Head had reported in Upper Canada, was "1st. That an attempt to make farmers of the red men has been generally speaking a complete failure. 2nd. That congregating them for the purpose of civilization has implanted many more vices than it has eradicated; and, consequently, 3rd. That the greatest kindness we can perform towards these intelligent, simple-minded people, is to remove and fortify them as much as possible from all communications with the whites."[39] Philanthropy, like friendship, had failed as far as the full-blooded Indians were concerned. For the fur-traders this was acceptable doctrine; their object throughout was to maintain the Indians in their wandering and hunting way of life.

The Métis were a different problem from the Indians. For the most part they preferred some degree of settled life, and they congregated in considerable numbers in and around Red River. As the colony achieved stability, and as the Company learned to assimilate Red River into its system, the Métis, indifferent and often indolent farmers, nevertheless managed to maintain a high standard of living. As Warden of the Plains, Cuthbert Grant was able to control them, and his chief duties were to encourage them to settle on the White Horse Plain and to prevent their conducting an illicit trade in furs—that is, a trade in furs with American dealers. Grant himself farmed sensibly and profitably, and he built a watermill. But like other Métis he set off twice a year on an organized buffalo hunt. As many as fifteen hundred of them would go into the plains for a disciplined but wanton slaughter of the buffalo herds. Sometimes as many as a thousand buffalo would be killed in a single "race"; at times the Métis were so prodigal that they took nothing but the tongues and the humps (the bossues) of the great beasts and left the rest to the wolves. Wasteful as the buffalo hunts were, they were a colourful and exhilarating spectacle. The great pride of the Métis lay in their horses, and their "races" were conducted at a gallop. Great skill was needed, both as a horseman and as a rifleman, to achieve distinction.[40]

The hunts ultimately proved disastrous since they helped to exterminate the great herds of buffalo. But in the middle years of the nineteenth century, when the colony was turning in every direction to discover some means of paying for external purchases, the Métis and their hunts were the one source of cash. They provided the pemmican which the fur trade still needed and which the Company readily bought in almost any quantity. There were indeed years in which all the pemmican was not purchased; but the buffalo hunts provided most of the cash on which the colony depended. The Métis disbursed their gains with such prodigality that they stimulated economic life in a way which was in itself necessary and desirable, however untoward the consequences for the Métis themselves. Most of them squandered the profits of the spring hunt so improvidently that they were forced to undertake a second hunt in the autumn in order to provide for the winter.

On their hunts the Métis crossed freely into American territory. They traded goods and supplies from American stores, giving provisions and furs in return. They underlined the dangers implicit in the frontier; and this, at least, the colony at Red River shared with the Canadian provinces. This was something which Simpson and his Councillors had in common with Lord Durham and his advisers; for both were faced by a United States which, while going through a period of financial crisis, was nevertheless expanding rapidly westwards. Texas had declared its independence of Mexico in 1836 and had applied for admission to the United States in 1837. On this and other questions, relations between Great Britain and the United States were at breaking point. The Maine boundary dispute had been unsettled since the State of Maine had joined the republic in 1820, the Fisheries Convention of 1818 was giving rise to constant incidents, and the rebellions in Lower and Upper Canada led to numerous clashes, of which the looting of a Canadian steamboat, the *Sir Robert Peel*, on the upper St Lawrence by "a band of American pirates" (as Durham called them) was perhaps the outstanding example. Paradoxically, the Loyalists in Upper Canada were partly enraged at American sympathy with French outbreaks in Lower Canada, partly anxious to join the United States as the surest way to swamp the French by Anglo-Saxon blood and institutions. In many points the Durham *Report* set up the United States as an example to be followed, but throughout the *Report* there ran a feeling that Canada should be preserved to maintain British influence on the American continent. For reasons of their own, Simpson and the fur-traders felt the same pressures and reached the same conclusions. But while Simpson was anxious to define the frontier he was equally anxious to deal with American traders wherever it seemed profitable, using them both to supply the colony and to bring in goods for the fur trade itself.

The American trade along the frontier reached its zenith under the direction of Ramsay Crooks, whom John Jacob Astor had put in to manage the American Fur Company, which had absorbed the Columbia Fur Company. At the same time, in 1837, the American frontier advanced to include what in 1849 became the Territory of Minnesota. Before the country could be spoiled for the fur trade, Norman Kittson gave a great impetus to the American trade there, and a regular "cart-line" began to run annually from Red River Colony to Pembina and to St Paul. The answer adopted by Simpson and his councillors was to equip petty traders, who then outbid the Americans and who brought what furs they got to the Company's store. But the annual value of the fur trade to the States had reached about $20,000 by the 1840's, and all along the frontier there was a threat of American competition. It mattered little that individual traders were often unreliable and easily put out of business. Difficult as the Bow River Expedition had proved, nevertheless much of the fur which was traded on the upper Saskatchewan came from south of the frontier, and on at least one notable occasion there was good reason to believe that furs brought in to Edmonton had been plundered by Indians from an American expedition.[41] The Piegans,

the Bloods, and the Blackfoot Indians were made restless by American competition, and in dealing with such rivalry Simpson was prepared to use
almost any help which came to hand. In 1833, at a time when competition
in the Rainy Lake District, at Lake of the Woods, at Whitefish Lake, and at
Swan River was compelling him to "trade close" to put rivals out of business, he managed an arrangement with the American Fur Company by
which the Hudson's Bay Company paid £300 a year in return for a promise
not to interfere with Indians to the north or to the west of Lake Superior.[42]

Throughout the Middle West, the frontier with America had little meaning. But Simpson managed to hold his own by using the independent
traders where possible, by direct underselling, or by buying off his rivals.
At Fort Garry the Company was even able to buy furs for cash across the
counter, and the Americans were making steady losses. But, though by the
1840's Simpson was convinced that in the Lake Superior-Rainy Lake-Lake
Huron area he had silenced the American Fur Company, new influences
began to be felt in that area. A rich vein of copper was struck, a chain of
agricultural settlements grew up, a ship canal was started between Lake
Huron and Lake Superior, and, although the American Fur Company was
under control, a new and powerful rival appeared in the Cleveland Company.[43] This company lasted only from 1840 to 1845, when it was driven
out of business by its losses. Its policy was to found a series of agricultural
settlements supplemented by trading posts. The company operated entirely
on American territory, but it had a post at Pigeon River (Grand Portage)
which drew Indians away from Fort William and forced Simpson to offer
extravagant prices for furs. In this particular struggle it was necessary to
set up an agricultural settlement of his own at Kaministikwia and to
arrange that it should have a Roman Catholic priest.

Where settlement seemed inevitable, Simpson regarded missionary effort
and attempts to civilize the Indians as essential. But neither Simpson nor
the Company accepted attempts to change the Indians' way of life as a
general policy, desirable in itself. Weaning the Indians from their nomadic
way of life was, on the contrary, to be accepted only when it could not be
evaded. For the traders would have agreed with Francis Bond Head that
the "portion of the Indian population which is undergoing the operation
of being civilized" was merely being degraded. "If we attempt to Christianize the Indians, and for that sacred object congregate them in villages of
substantial log-houses," the results would be disastrous. Head concluded
that "it is against his nature to cultivate the soil" and that the Indian should
either retire upon Manitoulin Island, or other reserves in and around Lake
Superior, where conditions for his own kind of life might be maintained, or
should withdraw into the Northwest.[44] Simpson had early given his opinion
that educated Indians were useless both to themselves and to society. But

the Company consistently followed a policy of educating Indian children. In general it was accepted that missionary effort should be confined to posts of settlement, not spread through the backwoods in Jesuit fashion, keeping up with the fur-traders and sometimes outrunning them. "Every mission if successful should be considered the germ of a future village," which might be useless to the fur trade and would probably entail costs for administration and for social and educational work.[45]

A Jesuit mission was nevertheless set up at Abitibi in 1843, Wesleyan missionaries were brought out from London in 1844, and the fur trade found itself faced both with the problems arising from changes in the Indians' way of life and with those deriving from the missionaries, who required transport and other amenities. Jesuits and other Roman Catholics had much greater influence over the Frenchmen and the half-breeds than Protestants, and more determination in approaching the Indians too; but they were not entirely reconciled to the English and Protestant tradition of the Company and could from time to time create difficulties. The Protestant missions, on the other hand, were unfamiliar with Canadian conditions and often out of sympathy with the fur-traders. In particular, Simpson found himself engaged in a long struggle with Rev. James Evans, the leading Wesleyan missionary, who not only disapproved of many of the habits of the traders (including such commonplace habits as that of travelling on Sundays when *en voyage*) but who also wanted to develop cottage manufactures among Indians and other converts. This would have entailed settling the Indians down as agriculturists and artisans and would have meant a substantial interference with the fur trade. It was an active policy, easily distinguishable from the fur-traders' notion of accepting change when it had become inevitable, but of delaying the process as long as possible, and of encouraging the Indians to remain dependent on the hunt.

The traders in Council (led by Simpson) did, however, accept a scheme for an agricultural settlement of Indians at Norway House when, in 1843, they found that Indians who were necessary for the maintenance of that post and for transportation duties were moving to Red River Colony, where they were mere hangers-on and easily became a liability. Accepting Evans's help, they began an agricultural settlement for Indians at the depot[46] which soon justified itself and proved able to supply the fur trade with quantities of potatoes and barley.

The problems of settlement, of missions, of free-traders and of the American frontier, came to a head in 1849. It may perhaps seem strange that Simpson and the fur-traders should still be concerned with these matters at Red River Colony, although it is clear that they would be involved where less accessible parts of their domain were at issue. But in 1836 Selkirk's heirs sold back Assiniboia to the Company,[47] and so what had been a task

undertaken in loyalty to the memory of Selkirk and under the direction of
his friends and relations on the Board became a matter of legal right and
responsibility for the Company. In practice the Governor of the colony
had been an officer of the Company since the departure of Robert Parker
Pelly in 1825, and the reconveyance seemed to make little difference.
Alexander Christie remained Governor and was then followed in 1839 by
the kindly and sympathetic Chief Factor Duncan Finlayson. Under them
the settlers were themselves called more into partnership; the Council of
Assiniboia was increased in 1835, and Bishop Provencher sat there, together with Cuthbert Grant as a representative of Métis opinion and
Andrew McDermot to speak for the merchants. But with all its attempts
to saddle the growing community with responsibility for its own welfare
and to insist only on its own trading privileges, the Company could not
relinquish responsibility for the colony. Hoping to make the colony into
something which could play an important part in the fur trade, it could
not allow authority there to fall into unwilling or incompetent hands. A
distinction between Company and colony, therefore, remained a myth.
When Simpson had spent the winter of 1823-24 at the colony he had done
so under strong pressure from London, where Colvile was insistent that
the fur trade should not oppress the settlement and that Simpson should
devote time to bringing it to order; and the Governor, much as he despised
the weak and ill-affected elements of the colony, then managed to get
something of "a Councilling System" going. Even at that stage there were
rumours that the Company would resume the grant of land; and there was
enough substance in the rumours for the Company to take over the goods
belonging to the Selkirk estate at a valuation. From 1825 onwards the
Company was in virtual control of the colony, and the formal reconveyance
in 1836 could not be expected to excite much interest among the settlers.

But a new Legislative Council was set up, and the colony slowly began
to take control of its own affairs—with the Company only too anxious that
it should do so.[48] The fact that many members of the Legislative Council
were in the employ of the Company did not mean that local government
was being kept as a Company preserve. The colony was being given the
responsibility, rather than the right, of managing its own affairs. But control of local government involved duties on trade goods which might be
brought into the settlement, and this emphasized the divergent interests of
the Company and its store, and of the petty traders with their desire to keep
open a trade route to the Americans, for use when better terms could be
got that way than the Company's store offered. The difficulties were domestic and could be got round by personal sympathy or by cajolery; but a basic
divergence of outlook was there, and even Simpson could not always find a
way round. His attempt to make an arrangement with the American Fur

Company, such as he had made for other districts, failed when the Americans refused his terms. From 1843 onwards the American Fur Company, reorganized by Pierre Chouteau, Jr, and invigorated by the success achieved by Kittson at Pembina, secured many of the furs which might have come in to Fort Garry. Petty traders, Métis, Indians, and agriculturists were all involved, and the Company's efforts to stop such trade merely made it evident that serious opposition would be met if the private trade in furs were consistently interrupted. In such a quandary the Company doubled its efforts to place on other shoulders the responsibility for enforcing the law in the settlement. If an appeal to the Parliamentary Licence for Exclusive Trade should become necessary, a legal verdict would inevitably support the Company. But there was much to be said for ensuring that the Company did not appear in such a case both as plaintiff and judge. This possibility added to the pressure to separate the government of the colony from the control of the Company.

By 1849 the Red River settlement had a population of over 5,000. The settlers were split into three recognizable communities—the Scottish colony at Kildonan, the French and Métis colonies of the Upper Settlement and the White Horse Plain, and the Scottish and Orcadian half-breed colony of St Paul's (or the Middle Settlement) and St Andrew's (or the Lower Settlement). Just above the delta of Red River was a settlement of Swampy Crees; and another settlement of Saulteaux at Baie St Paul on the Assiniboine. The 1849 census (and the colony was systematically enumerated) allows a firm picture to be drawn.[49] The Kildonan Scots maintained their separateness, their Presbyterian religion, and their aloofness from the fur trade. They lived by agriculture, and they did not intermarry with the Indians or with the French. The French community was a self-contained body of French Canadians who had settled round the Roman Catholic mission at St Boniface. At the Upper Settlement Frenchmen were mixed with Métis, mostly discharged servants of the North West Company with their Indian or Métis wives and children, drawn into Red River from all over the Northwest. These were indifferent agriculturists, and they supplemented their farming by the buffalo hunt. In the White Horse Plain, with its centre at Grantown, the Métis were almost undiluted, and although there was some agriculture at that settlement, their chief occupation was the buffalo hunt, eked out by fishing in Lake Manitoba. The Middle Settlement of Scottish and Orkney servants and their wives and half-breed children had been steadily built up since 1821. They had retired from the Company to the colony. With some means at their disposal, they put their savings into farming and formed a stable, and often prosperous, element in the colony, with pride in their wealth and in their derivation. The Lower Settlement completed the building of the stone church of St Andrew's in 1849, and the general standard of living and housing there was superior to that of the rest of the colony. An English-speaking half-breed settlement was by 1849 beginning a couple of miles above the Forks of Red River. Separate from all these groups were the active Hudson's Bay Company's officers and servants, congregated round Upper and Lower Fort Garry. To some extent they remained aloof from the settlers, and they were always liable to find that their interests and their loyalties cut them off from their neighbours.

Despite the recognizable cleavages within the colony, it had its own character, and it presented a pleasing contrast to the wilderness in which it lay. The settlement was a riverside community, and by 1850 not a single farmstead lay back from the river's banks. For the river was the highway, and the Red River cart, despite its capacity for travel over rough country, could not compare with the river as a means of haulage. Another outstanding feature was the number of windmills. A visitor in 1851 noted that there were almost twenty of them, and the 1849 Census listed eighteen windmills and two water mills. Although prosperous and well fed, the colony practised an unsophisticated agriculture, largely for subsistence and for sale to the fur trade. For winter food for cattle the settlers organized the allocation of "hay privileges" lying back from the river behind the plough lands along the river-front. Considerable effort, the Company providing the capital, had gone into improving grains by the introduction of Black Sea wheat, and into improving stock by driving up herds from the Mississippi, by bringing in Galloway cattle on the long route from York Factory, by securing an Ayreshire bull and Ayreshire cows. It was not until Simpson had the famous stallion Fireaway brought out from England, in 1831, and got some mares sent up from the United States, that any fresh blood was brought to improve the horses in the colony—or indeed in the whole of the Northwest. But horses were an important status symbol; races were as much a social pleasure for the white settlers as pride in their horses was a motive for the Indians and the Métis, and once the possibility of improvement in stock was there, the danger was rather that enthusiasm would outrun discretion than that the opportunity would be missed.

As the disputes with the United States came to a head over the Oregon boundary in 1846, the Company managed to secure an imperial garrison for Red River, ostensibly for defence against the possibility of American raids. In fact, however, the garrison was valued for two reasons; it brought to the colony a military officer who might be made Governor and who would not involve the trade in the government of the colony; and it allowed the fur trade to use the military force as a means of coercing the Métis and the petty traders. The fur-traders were equally anxious to keep the Americans at bay and to bring the free-traders to heel. The two went together, for the free-traders went to the Americans with their trade.

By 1844 the colony had thrown up its own leaders, some of them men of fair substance. Andrew McDermot was reputedly the wealthiest man in the colony, and he acted with the half-breed James Sinclair to undertake freighting for the Company to York and back, to trade furs on the American side of the frontier, and to supply fellow-settlers with their day-to-day requirements. They proposed to set up a distillery as a means of absorbing surplus grain, and though this proposal was rejected, though their freighting contract was not renewed, and though their business of shipping tallow to England was discriminated against, nevertheless these two men remained prosperous and stood out among the settlers. They challenged the Company both because they denied its right to regulate the life of the colony and because they denied its control of the trade in furs. In particular they insisted on their right to trade across the frontier to Americans, and to trade even in furs, despite the Company and its prohibitions. Chief Factor Alexander Christie, taking office as Governor of Assiniboia in 1844, turned to the Recorder of the colony, Adam Thom, for a legal opinion on the Company's veto. McDermot and Sinclair refused to declare that they had not traded in furs, and the Council of Assiniboia then levied a prohibitive duty on goods brought up from the States for private traders in the hope that the consequent rise in prices would prevent private traders from getting furs from Indians. The power of the Company was such that both traders offered to engage not to trade in furs on condition that the Company would buy their lands, houses, and merchandise at a fair valuation. They nevertheless declared their right to trade in furs if they wished, and the Recorder began to stage-manage the situation by inserting in the settlers' leases clauses which made their tenure dependent on admission of the Company's control of the trade in furs.

Simpson appeared in the colony in June 1845, in the middle of the trouble; but, although he supported the Recorder and the Governor, the traders at that time had adequate supplies of goods, and without invoking the full weight of the law there was no means of enforcing the rule. The claim to freedom of trade, in fact, appeared so reasonable that the settlers even appealed to the Committee in London and got from them some support against local authority. It was at this juncture, when two army officers, Lieutenant H. J. Warre and Lieutenant M. Vavasour, had been sent out to make a report on the military defences of the frontier against the United States, that Simpson managed to secure troops and officers for Red River. He was greatly helped by the fact that a petition from the colonists, asking for an American post to be set up at Pembina, had secured over a thousand signatures, and by an incident in which a party of American cavalry had met the Métis on their buffalo hunt, on American territory, and had warned them they would no longer be able to hunt there unless they became American citizens. There seemed some likelihood that the colony might secede to the States. But though Simpson was able to put up a plausible case for a garrison to be sent to Red River during the heat of the dispute over the Oregon frontier, he knew well "that nothing but a military force can . . . permanently reconcile the enforcing of our rights with the preserving of the public tranquility."[50] He knew that there might well be riots if the Company's veto on a trade in furs were enforced.

The British government was not only anxious to stabilize the American frontier; it was also still convinced that (whatever the defects of monopoly might be) competition in the fur trade would result in debauching the Indians. This had made it comparatively easy for the Company to secure a renewal of its Licence for Exclusive Trade as recently as 1839, and in 1844-45 a Commission on Indian Affairs had approved of the Company's rules for the conduct of trade.[51] Accordingly, the Company could count on government support when the petty traders brought forward together the issues raised by the Licence for Exclusive Trade, by the American frontier, by the loyalty and good behaviour of the Métis, and by the internal government of the colony.

Simpson had a unique knowledge of the territory under dispute with the United States, in Oregon and elsewhere, and he exploited his position purposefully. "If we succeed in getting a garrison at Red River we shall be able to put down the illicit trade and keep the settlers in order," he wrote.[52] In 1846 he eventually achieved his purpose despite opposition from Gladstone on political grounds and from the Duke of Wellington on military grounds (for Wellington was convinced that so lengthy a frontier was not defensible). The Company agreed to bear part of the costs of a garrison, and some three hundred officers and men of the Sixth Regiment of Foot, with sappers, gunners, and miners attached, were sent out in August 1846, to come up from York Factory in Hudson's Bay to Red River by the same route as Selkirk's settlers had used. Simpson intended that the commanding officer of these troops should be Governor of the colony. In that capacity he would, perforce, support the Company and its claims, for they were legally valid. But the first commanding officer, quickly retiring from the colony, left a successor who seemed unsuitable; so the chief result of the presence of the Sixth Regiment of Foot was that the men, as their wages were paid, brought money and an active market to the colony, taking agricultural produce and stimulating the petty traders.

By 1848 the Oregon crisis was well over, and the utmost which the Company could get in replacement for the regular troops was a contingent of Chelsea Pensioners. The Pensioners, however, came in much smaller numbers than were desired—only fifty-six men, forty-two women, and fifty-seven children instead of two hundred able men with pensions to spend

—and the possibility of a soldier settlement seemed remote in such circumstances. Their commander, Major William Caldwell, moreover, was inefficient, elderly, and dull. He had been nominated by Earl Grey and had been accepted as Governor by the Committee, but he soon aroused alarm both in Simpson and in the settlers.

At this juncture, therefore, the Hudson's Bay Company had almost achieved its object of stabilizing a colony which would not be a drain on the fur trade but which could supply both employees and food for the trade. The colony had been separated off from the trade and had its own independent Governor, its councillors and administrative machinery. Yet the Company had kept its claim to an exclusive trade in furs and had maintained its own trade post, driving a profitable trade in supplying the settlers. The right of the settlers to trade in furs was still under dispute. Of the two champions of the settlers' claims, McDermot made a substantial profit from supplying the troops and then the pensioners; he was reputed to have taken over £1,400 in gold in a few months and had withdrawn his opposition. But Sinclair, the half-breed, although not so good a business man as McDermot, was involved in deeper issues than mere profit. He tried to show that the half-breeds, as natives of the soil, had rights which could not be affected by the Licence for Exclusive Trade. On this score he challenged not only the Company itself, but all settlers who held their lands on tenures derived from the Company's grant, and ultimately from its Charter.

With such issues under discussion, the colony was divided and distracted, and the fact that the Company had managed to hand over responsibility to Caldwell was no advantage in view of the lack of experience of Caldwell and the folly of his subordinate, Captain V. Foss, who got involved in a scandal which produced the first divorce case of the colony. In 1847 Sinclair took a petition from the settlers to London, and another half-breed, Alexander Isbister, son of a clerk of the Company, who had been educated at Red River and had served the Company for a brief period, there lent him support.[53]

Isbister had inherited his father's farm at Red River but had left the country to graduate in law at Edinburgh University; he challenged the general opinion that competition in the fur trade would be disastrous for the Indians, and he held that the Company's lands should not be kept for the fur trade but should be opened for settlement. He set out to show that throughout the North West Territory and Rupert's Land there was almost unlimited land suitable for settlement once the long transport system had been overcome and once legal titles were obtainable; and he held that both these things were possible and that the colonies which might then be created should be annexed to Canada. To these convictions, supported by his knowledge of the territory, Isbister added the conviction, derived from his legal studies, that the Charter itself was invalid. He addressed his "Few Words on the Hudson's Bay Company with a statement of the grievances of the natives and half-caste Indians" to the British government in London, and he took over from Sinclair the petition of the half-breeds and presented it to the Colonial Office in 1847.

The case was strong enough for Earl Grey to institute an enquiry and, although a full Parliamentary Commission was not set up, information was collected from the Governor of the Company, Lord Elgin as Governor General of Canada, Caldwell as Governor of Assiniboia, and the army officers who had returned to England from their tour of duty at Red River. Great weight was attached to the opinion of Lord Elgin, who was achieving success as Governor General; and Elgin supported the Licence for Exclusive Trade. In this one business, competition must result in debauchery. The Governor of the Hudson's Bay Company was able to show that not enough spirits were taken into all the territories allocated to the fur trade to allow the proper employees of the Company more than two tablespoons of spirits a day; and Caldwell testified to the Company's care for the colony, to its efforts to maintain a stable and prosperous society there, and to suppress evil living. The soldiers bore out these views, the Colonial Secretary was satisfied that there was no need for a government enquiry, and the Company was in effect confirmed in its position.[54]

But Isbister challenged the Charter itself. He achieved an address to the House of Common asking for an enquiry, and as a result the papers were printed and made public in the *Parliamentary Blue Book No. 35, 1849*. At the same time John McLaughlin, an ardent opponent of the Company, an Irish nephew of McDermot, who had come to the colony from the United States, appeared in London. McLaughlin had been an advocate of secession by the colony to the United States, and in 1845 he had framed a petition asking that the Métis should be admitted to American citizenship. He was not the only leader of the Métis; they followed closely the teaching of the Roman Catholic priest Georges Antoine Belcourt, a man of active habits who had the great advantage of being able to talk with the Métis and the Indians without using an interpreter. Belcourt was something of an exception; for the priesthood on the whole supported the Company's régime. He denied its claims, partly from genuine sympathy with the Métis, partly because in his career as a mission priest he had found the Company reluctant to support outlying missions and even at times hostile. Nevertheless, Belcourt insisted that the Métis must use only legal means to challenge the Company, and he was instrumental in drawing up two petitions, one in French and one in English, addressed to the Colonial Secretary and asking for free trade and representative government. It was not until Congress had rejected McLaughlin's petition that the Métis should be granted United

States citizenship that Belcourt's petitions were dispatched to the Colonial Office. McLaughlin, on his arrival in England in 1849, therefore appeared with something of a blemish of disloyalty upon him, and his efforts to push Belcourt's petitions before the Colonial Office were not propitious; nor were his methods. He was anxious to secure publicity for an account of the Company's maladministration of the colony. But the Company silenced him by the threat of a libel action.[55]

Nevertheless, the presence of McLaughlin in England, the pressure of Isbister, and the publication of the 1849 *Blue Book* kept the pot boiling. Though Isbister's request for a formal verdict as to the legal validity of the Charter, to be delivered by the Law Officers of the Crown, was met as on former occasions by a declaration that the solution could be found only when a contestant should come forward and fight a test case, the Company could not ignore the challenges.

In the colony Caldwell encountered considerable opposition, especially as the tone of his replies to the Parliamentary questions became known. A kindly man, if lacking in subtlety, he had much sympathy with the settlers; but he gave the impression that he would not accept any criticism of the Company. At the same time his second-in-command brought Caldwell's authority into disrepute by his association with the wife of the Company's Chief Factor at Red River while the Company, at last free of the costs of government, caused uneasiness as it set to work to extirpate the petty traders.

South of the border, American activity was intense. The American Fur Company had gone out of business in 1847, and Simpson's arrangements with them counted for nothing. The enterprising Kittson had taken over most of their business in the Pembina area, and he was successful there. The general attitude of American politicians was expansive, and the extension of American rule right up to Pembina was anticipated by an American military mission in the summer of 1849. There were rumours that the United States government would purchase the land from the Indians, and such rumours brought an influx of Indians and Métis to the site in the hope that they might participate in the sale. The American frontier came into play in another sense when Father Belcourt moved to Pembina. Simpson had refused to sanction a Roman Catholic mission at Moose until Bishop Provencher had withdrawn the priest from the colony. Belcourt's move to Pembina left him outside Simpson's power; he made an easy alliance with Kittson and with H. H. Sibley, who represented Minnesota in Congress and who strongly advocated a forward-moving frontier for the United States. The Métis followed the priest, and within a year over a thousand had migrated to American territory. The Company's effort to counter the drift of furs to the south, by setting up a store near Pembina and offering better prices than the Americans, came to nothing, and Chief Factor Ballenden turned to the civil power to seek support in his efforts to enforce the Company's claim to an Exclusive Trade in furs.

In May 1849, four Métis were therefore accused of an illicit traffic in furs with Indians. The trial of Pierre Guillaume Sayer, the first of these Métis to be brought before the court of the colony, sitting at Fort Garry, not only proved to be a *cause célèbre* but was to be the end of one epoch and the start of another in the North West Territories.[56] The accused had been advised by Belcourt and had been put in touch with Louis Riel, a recent arrival at the colony and a powerful leader of Métis opinion. Belcourt believed that resistance to the Licence for Exclusive Trade would be legal, and he urged the Métis to turn out armed and ready to defend their rights. Himself, he could not be present; but his message was read at the door of the Roman Catholic cathedral, and the trial was attended by a formidable body of Métis, who assembled at the court house. With something like four hundred armed men milling round, whooping and yelling, the Chelsea Pensioners could not have given any support to the court, and Caldwell wisely decided to take his seat as Governor without even his usual guard of honour. With the utmost difficulty proceedings were kept from degenerating into a riot. As mass ended Riel addressed the Métis at the cathedral, urging them to free Sayer and to vindicate their freedom of trade. It was impossible to start the trial until James Sinclair agreed to act as counsel for Sayer. It was admitted that Sayer had not himself trapped all of his furs, but had traded most of them from Indians in exchange for liquor. But it was alleged that the Company's agents had told the Métis that they would accept any furs which were got by such methods and had not forbidden the Métis to trade furs from other Métis, although they denied the right to trade furs with Indians. The jury of five Frenchmen and seven Englishmen found Sayer guilty of trading furs.

The verdict was accompanied by a recommendation to mercy on the ground that the Métis had laboured under a genuinely mistaken opinion that they were permitted a free trade. The Company's Chief Factor accepted both the verdict and the recommendation and dropped his cases against the other three accused Métis. Therefore, when Sayer came out from the court house and appeared before the Métis mob, with no stigma on him and no punishment inflicted, the situation seemed to warrant the conclusion that freedom of trade had been accorded. A *feu de joie* was fired off, and the Métis proclaimed that "*le Commerce est libre.*"

There was an overwhelming realism about this interpretation of the verdict and the recommendation to mercy, and it would have been useless for the Company thereafter to try to enforce restrictions on trade within the colony, or between the colony and free-traders outside. The result of the

Sayer trial was that the Company was forced to admit freedom of trade, even in furs. Henceforth (as often in the past) it made no attempt to support its claims by appeals to its legal status; instead it relied on exploitation of its economic power. In normal circumstances, notwithstanding the existence of American traders, the free-traders within the colony were forced to rely on the Company for the goods with which to trade furs from the Indians or the Métis; they could be charged prices adjusted to the situation, and they could be given prices in excess of anything which the Americans could afford for their furs. For the Hudson's Bay goods were still got to Red River at much less cost by way of Hudson Bay than by any other route. The old geographical advantage was still in the hands of the Company.

Though Caldwell had conducted himself with great courage and dignity during the trial, he was clearly incompetent to deal with problems which would arise from the "concession to the imperative demands from the disaffected halfbreeds." The Company concluded that effective leadership was necessary, and since Simpson was increasingly reluctant to spend his winters at Red River, the Committee decided to appoint Eden Colvile as Associate Governor for Rupert's Land and as a Councillor of Assiniboia. Arriving in the colony in the summer of 1850, Colvile found the settlers prosperous but uneasy. As a member of the London Land Company, with the task of developing the Seigneury of Beauharnois in Lower Canada on behalf of Edward Ellice, Jr., he had already shown an interest in Canadian problems, and he had begun to take an active part in Canadian politics before he came to Red River. He had also travelled across the North West Territories to the Pacific and had some knowledge, and some opinions, on the problems of the Northwest. Reluctant as the Company certainly was, Colvile's assignment indicated that authority and leadership in the colony must still derive from the Company.

But though the Company was thus still in effective control of the colony in 1849, the census reports and the ecclesiastical situation show the stability and the variety which had been achieved. This was a real colony which had been established. It had its freedom of trade, even of the fur trade. It had its churches, its ecclesiastical institutions, its Governor independent of the Company, and its Council. True, although freedom of trade had been achieved and although for a brief period the Americans were able to carry away substantial loads of furs which had been traded by residents in the colony, nevertheless, by 1853-54 the Company was again in command of the situation simply because it commanded the cheapest route of access. This meant that to a large extent the colony was still self-centred economically. The settlers bought from and sold to Americans; but external trade was for luxuries, not necessities.

It was, nevertheless, freedom to trade which the Métis demanded most persistently. They asked for the end of the existing law, imposed by Simpson and the Council of Assiniboia in 1845, exacting customs duties on imports to the colony from the United States; and they asked for a free trade in furs. The two went together, for the customs dues had been aimed at preventing settlers from getting American goods for use in the fur trade rather than at stifling the American trade completely. Duties on American goods were quickly standardized at 4 per cent, which was the same rate as was paid on goods from York Factory. Freedom of trade was not conceded—at least not formally. Indeed, despite the reception of the verdict at Sayer's trial, he had been convicted. Simpson declared that the Licence for Exclusive Trade had been granted by Crown in Parliament and could only be revoked in the same way, and in 1850 the Governor and Committee refused to abandon their right. But they failed to get military support from the British government, they refused to create (and pay) a force of their own, and the Pensioners were manifestly incompetent to enforce their claim. They therefore adopted a policy of licensing private traders and of buying their furs. On these terms a free trade soon became normal and general.[57]

The one aspect of this arrangement which the Company found unpalatable was the trade from the colony to Pembina, where Norman Kittson had set up his post. This took off furs. But an American customs post proved a deterrent, and by 1851 the Company was not dissatisfied. Prices were driven up in competition, Kittson lost trade, and the Métis settlement which had gathered near Father Belcourt's mission at Pembina, providing many of Kittson's customers, suffered from floods and from the acquisition of the Ojibways' lands by Minnesota Territory.

The Company had in effect given up the legal defences of its economic privileges in the colony and was dependent henceforth on its financial strength and its trading ability. On that basis it remained preponderant; and the colony throve. The Company controlled most of the transportation, although the annual cart trade to St Paul was steadily increasing. Most of the goods used for trading with Indians, the seed-corn and the implements of husbandry, had to be got at the Company's store; and constitutional authority and administrative power still rested with the Company.

The Company therefore emerged intact, and in many matters it stood fast upon its rights. The Métis' desire that Thom should be removed from his office of Recorder was refused on the grounds of his competence to conduct judicial business in both French and English and on the grounds of the independence of the judiciary; and although it proved impracticable to use his vast legal knowledge, he remained in the colony until 1854. Similarly, when Simpson was ready to meet another demand and to appoint six Métis to the Council of Assiniboia, the Governor and Committee asserted their authority and added only the French priest Louis Laflèche.

But although the Company was vindicated in its rights and was prepared to exercise them, it was still insistent that the colony must be separated off from the Company. A good harvest and good hunts for the moment took the edge off the problems in 1850, and the free-trade arrangements were giving satisfaction. A recognizable community had emerged, with corporate problems and corporate reactions. But it was by no means a unified community. There were sharp dissensions between Roman Catholics and Protestants and between Anglicans and Presbyterians. The Protestants, Presbyterian and Anglican alike, had hitherto attended services conducted by Anglican priests in the stone church which had been consecrated in 1834. But the church was on land which the Presbyterians claimed, and they also claimed that Selkirk had promised them a Gaelic-speaking minister. In 1849 Rupert's Land was made an Anglican bishopric, and the first bishop, David Anderson, decided to tear down the Church of St John's and build better—a proper cathedral. When at last the Presbyterians got their minister, John Black, they left the English church. But disputes dragged on over rights in the fabric and in the burial-ground. One of the chief results of these dissensions was that neither Protestant nor Catholic clergy were available to give leadership to the colony. They refused nomination as magistrates,[58] and the other rifts in the colony were all the more apt to split and frustrate the settlers.

As Colvile stepped ashore at Lower Fort Garry he was handed a petition signed by the Council and by five hundred English settlers, asking that Governor Caldwell be removed from office.[59] The Sheriff had already resigned, and the Council had told Caldwell that they would never meet again under him and had also threatened resignation. Colvile had been appointed a Councillor of Assiniboia, and with a noticeable corporate spirit (the Anglican and the Roman Catholic bishops and Rev. William Cockran[60] were the only abstainers) the Council asked him to assume the Presidency of Court and Council. Colvile had been told by the Governor and Committee that they were averse from resuming authority over the settlement. Accordingly, he demurred and referred the suggestion to London, adding that "nothing could induce me so to act, but the feeling that it is the only way, by which the tranquility of the Colony can be preserved." Caldwell, however, revealed his own impotence and the need for effective authority in a couple of simple court cases. In one of them, *Matheson v. Thom*, Thom openly showed his contempt for Caldwell's ignorance of the law, and in the other, *Foss v. Pelly*, all the magistrates refused to sit with Caldwell, the colony split on its first major scandal, and the incompetence of the Governor was beyond dispute.

Despite his misgivings, Colvile agreed to act as President of the Council of Assiniboia and of the Quarterly Court. Given confident and competent

leadership—and Simpson thought that Colvile possessed "general information, business habits and conciliatory disposition"—the colony got on with
its business.[61] Solutions were found to local problems, of church sites and
personalities, appointments and land allocations. It was, however, a community which was settling down, not one which was expanding; attention
was focussed on the Upper and the Lower Fort, the churches and schools,
the Council Chamber and the Court Room, not upon the rolling prairies to
north and west. The chief development of the period came when Assiniboia
was organized into three judicial districts, each competent to deal summarily
with petty cases; and it was noteworthy that Canadians and Métis were
among the magistrates appointed, for one of the points for reform was still
the need for judges who spoke both French and English. But this also was
an act of consolidation, not of expansion.

Only the churches were looking outwards as the ageing Bishop Provencher chose as his Coadjutor Bishop of St Boniface the Oblate missionary
priest, Alexandre Taché, in 1851. Taché had served at Ile-à-la-Crosse; he did
not regard his main task as being confined to the settlement but maintained
a strong missionary outlook; and in 1852 he was organizing the departure
of priests for "Fort des Prairies, Athabasca, Peace River, and the vicinity"—
by way of the United States since the Company would not grant facilities.[62]
Normally, Simpson and the Company considered Roman Catholic missions
more appropriate to the Northwest than Protestant ventures. Their discouragement of Taché is an indication of the extent to which they still
regarded the western territories within which they enjoyed the Licence for
Exclusive Trade as a fur-trade preserve in which the Indians should be
encouraged in their nomadic hunting, not turned into agriculturists settled
round a mission. The Protestants also had their frustrations and made even
less impression outside the limits of the colony. Attempts at Portage la
Prairie, at Beaver Creek, and at Brandon House had failed, and plans for
mission stations in Athabasca and on the Winnipeg River had come to
nothing. There was, however, an Anglican mission at Lac la Ronge, another on Lake Manitoba, and a third at The Pas on the Saskatchewan.[63]

Colvile's assumption of the Presidency of the Council of Assiniboia had
seemed to portend a reassertion of the Company's authority—and for their
separate reasons the leaders of the different creeds resented this. They were
therefore relieved when in the spring of 1851 the Winter Express brought
instructions that he should no longer sit on the Council in any official capacity. Caldwell became Governor again. The Company had maintained its
claim that the colony must be independent. But the situation was equivocal.
Though they abstained from authority, Sheriff Ross maintained that the
clergy, Anglican and Roman Catholic, controlled the Council.[64] And though
the Company insisted that it would not control and direct the colony, a

petition signed by five hundred and forty colonists in 1851 asked for British liberty, a Governor appointed by the Crown, a judge able to speak French and English, a council appointed by the Governor, dismissal of councillors for subservience to the Company or loss of public confidence—and the removal of Recorder Thom.[65]

This was a demand for the reality of power, which still lay in the Company's hands, and the Company did not yield. Care had to be taken to divert attention from the fact that all the Bench of Magistrates were "in one way or other in the pay of the Company," and to ensure "with the aid of a little discretion and management" that the Company did not appear in court as either plaintiff or defendant.[66] But Colvile was equal to this. Caldwell remained in office until 1855, and both his retention and his departure were symptomatic of the way in which the Company kept its position and then relaxed as the colony began to steady itself. In 1852 Dr. John Rae had written that "At Red River everything goes on quietly. Provisions seem plentiful and the halfbreeds satisfied. . . . The clergy are the only people that seem at war with each other."[67] Colvile himself left the colony soon after Rae's visit, but the policy of conciliation continued. A new and bilingual Recorder, F. G. Johnson, succeeded Thom in 1854, and Métis members began to find places on the Council from 1853 onwards. The colony, born into the strife of fur companies, inextricably involved in their rivalries, and then placed under the control and protection of the coalition of the companies, had reached an equilibrium.

CHAPTER 14

The Fur-Traders
and the Pacific Slope

When the North West Company followed up David Thompson's journey and developed their own trade to the Columbia they met a lively opposition from the Astorians, working inland to Okanagan, Kamloops, Spokane, and the Snake River. But the War of 1812 isolated the Astorians, and in June 1813 they sold their post to the Nor'westers, thus anticipating capture by a ship which had been sent from England. The Nor'westers created their Departments of New Caledonia and Columbia and maintained them by a transport system which brought goods from Montreal to the Saskatchewan and so over the height of land. They made profits, and continued to do so when in 1818 the British government, anxious to placate the Americans, acquiesced in the return to the United States of the North West post. But the convention of October 20, 1818, gave free access to citizens of the United States and of Great Britain for a period of ten years, and under this system of Joint Occupation the Nor'westers were still able to trade freely.

But they had little experience of shipping, marine insurance, or eastern trade, and they made little of the China trade. The Canton market was upset, and the East India Company unhelpful. Their trade on the Pacific coast, too, was developed during the period of rivalry with the Hudson's Bay Company and with Selkirk, and after the coalition of the fur companies, when Simpson was first able to assess the trade of the Columbia,[1] he declared that it was ruined by extravagance. The most which he could hope was to reduce losses and to use the Columbia Department as a frontier against American opposition, in which modest losses might be accepted while the Department of New Caledonia was recuperated, developed, and brought to a profit.

This view of the Columbia Department was never abandoned. But hopes of profits died hard, and when in 1822 Alexander Kennedy, in command of Spokane House, reported that the Snake Country produced most of the furs of the Columbia Department and that the Snake Country trade could easily be increased, Simpson turned to organize the Snake Country expeditions.[2] The first, in 1823, under a hardened Nor'wester, Finan Macdonald, brought a fair trade; but Macdonald swore he would never go back to the Snake Country again. He had followed the previous practice of outfitting trappers who accompanied him, freemen and Indians (some of them Iroquois who had come over to the West Coast), and control was difficult. Troubles with Indians were inevitable, for the Indians of the Rockies were far more unruly than those of the plains, and by the time Macdonald got back to Spokane he had killed about seventy Indians and lost six of his own men.

At this juncture, in 1824, Peter Skene Ogden took command at Spokane. Educated, the son of an Admiralty Judge of Quebec, a man of indefatigable strength, of indomitable courage, and of acute intellect, Ogden had been barred from the coalition for his outrageous conduct during the conflict of the fur companies. But he had been accepted by the Company in 1822, was appointed to Spokane, and was on hand when an expedition led by Alexander Ross got back from its hunt. Ross had made a fair hunt, but he had met opposition from Americans led by Jedediah Smith and outfitted by the Rocky Mountain Fur Company. The Americans were confident and effective, and Ross was not the man to face them. Simpson, who was also at Spokane in 1824, thought Ross a self-sufficient, empty-headed man and sent him to be a schoolmaster at Red River. He appointed Ogden to lead the Snake Country expeditions.[3] It was an admirable appointment.

Ogden made five expeditions in all, the last in 1828-29. They took him well into American territory, over the height of land and out of the area of joint occupation, to Montana and the headwaters of the Missouri, to Utah, the Humboldt River, and probably to Great Salt Lake itself, to Idaho, to the Klamath country of north California, and into Mexico.[4] His character and his knowledge gave him an increasing hold on his men, and though he wrote that "a convict at Botany Bay is a gentleman at ease compared to my trappers,"[5] he held them together in the face of American opposition. He also made profits. Behind his expeditions lay the assumption that "we cannot expect to have a more southern boundary than the Columbia in any treaty with the Americans." Therefore, "the more we impoverish the country the less likelihood is there of being assailed by opposition," and Ogden should "get all we can from the south side of the Columbia while it is in our power."[6]

Other expeditions followed the same policy of "trapping clean." They went far afield—Ogden's successor, John Work, in 1832 led a party to the Sacramento and down past San Francisco Bay—and they built up their own knowledge of the Pacific Slope, down to San Francisco and inland to Idaho, as they carried their determined opposition into the Americans' own territory. Under the leadership of General William Ashley, with Jedediah

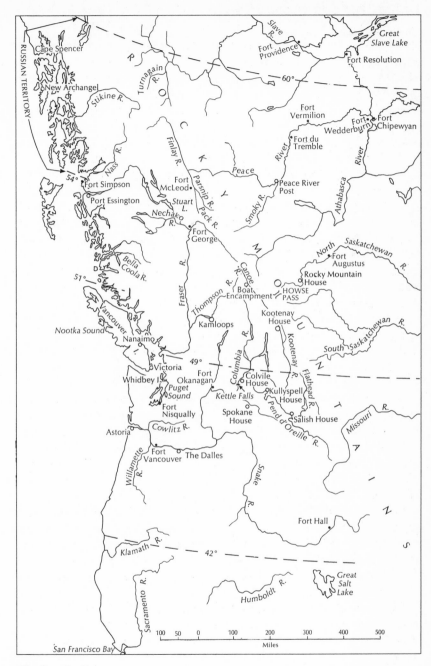

The Pacific Coast

Smith, David Jackson, and William Sublette to command expeditions, the Rocky Mountain Fur Company was a formidable opposition. But Ashley retired in 1826, and Smith, Jackson, and Sublette were forced to sell out in 1830.[7] So far were the Hudson's Bay men in command of the situation that in 1828, when a party led by Smith was massacred by the Umpqua Indians, it was to Fort Vancouver that Smith fled, and it was a Hudson's Bay party which carried out a punitive raid.[8]

From 1824 on, the Snake Country expeditions, and all else in the Columbia Department, were under the direction of Chief Factor John McLoughlin. A former North West wintering partner who had led the revolt against the agents, he also was slow to receive recognition at the coalition. But with his Herculean proportions and his dynamic and dogmatic character, he was, again, admirably suited to his task. Their careers drove McLoughlin and Simpson steadily apart, but as they came overland to the Columbia together in 1824 they were in substantial agreement.[9] Assuming that most of the Columbia Department would eventually go to the United States, they wanted a new depot to be built on Fraser River, to serve New Caledonia; and Simpson optimistically described the Fraser as "formed by Nature as the grand communication from the coast." The Colonial Office was informed of this policy in 1826. But already by 1826 greater knowledge had raised doubts about the Fraser, the Colonial Office seemed ready to support a case for retaining the Columbia area, and Simpson was ready to insist that the Columbia was the only possible route to the interior; if it could not be secured, the trade west of the Rockies must be abandoned.[10]

The main depot inherited from the Nor'westers, Fort George, was, however, south of the Columbia, and there could be little hope of retaining it. Accordingly, in 1825 Simpson and McLoughlin moved their depot seventy-five miles back from the river mouth, to the nearest suitable site on the north bank of the river. Jolie Prairie, where Fort Vancouver was then built, offered chances of farming as well as of trade, and the move was in tune with the mood of the diplomatic discussions of 1826, which gave the impression that Huskisson would let Oregon "gradually and silently slide into the hands of the United States.'[11] But no firm conclusion could be reached, and when in August 1827 the Convention for Joint Occupation west of the Rockies was extended for an indefinite period, the Hudson's Bay men took a new look at the situation.

Attention was still directed to the long-term development of New Caledonia, with the Columbia Department assumed as eventually an American possession; and access to New Caledonia was still assumed to be by way of the Fraser. It was expected that opposition would come in New Caledonia from the Russians rather than from the Americans, and to discover how far Russian influence had penetrated inland, as well as to see if a better route than the Fraser lay to the north, Samuel Black had been sent, in 1824, on his "Rocky Mountain Expedition." Black was another Nor'wester who had been proscribed for his exuberance during the opposition but who had later been accepted in the coalition, and he also brought great courage and ability to his task. His exploration took him from the Peace River up the lower Finlay, past the Big Bend of the Finlay to the River Turnagain in the region of 58° 40′ North. It was a magnificent achievement, and it revealed both the poverty of the country and the extent to which Russian influence had penetrated among the trading Nahanni Indians of the Stikine River.[12]

The Russian American Company controlled the Alaskan coast of the Pacific, opened up by Behring and Chirikoff, since its foundation in 1799. The company had been reorganized in 1819, and Simpson found his plans for New Caledonia threatened by an Imperial Ukase of September 1821 which forbade all access by non-Russians to the coast north of 51°. But joint pressure with the Americans had secured rights of access for fishing and trading for the Americans in 1824 and for the British in 1825. The southern limit of the Russian claims was then agreed at 54° 40′ North, and the Russians were granted rights of access to British and American territories.

Simpson set out to exploit this arrangement by developing a coastal trade; and he had the example of American ships to show that this was a sound project. Ships and ships' captains were difficult to manage, and the *Vancouver* and the *Broughton*, built by McLoughlin on the coast, were no better than ships sent from England. But the "naval department" was greatly strengthened when Aemilius Simpson, a relative of the Governor and a former naval officer, arrived on the coast in 1826.[13] He quickly mastered the coastal trade from Monterey north to the Stikine, he wrote logical and accurate reports, and he directed the Company's attention to the Nass River. In 1828 the Nass River had particular attractions because, when he went to the Columbia for the second time, in that year, George Simpson had himself run Thompson's River from Kamloops to the Forks of the Fraser, and the Fraser down to the ocean. After two hair-raising days in the Canyon of the Fraser he was convinced that in nine cases out of ten it would be fatal to travel that route and that the Fraser "could no longer be thought of as a practicable communication with the interior."[14]

In 1830, therefore, Simpson decided to pursue the development of a coastal trade and to set up a post at Nass. McLoughlin agreed, but the coastal trade revealed fundamental divergencies between the two men. The problem was to oust the American shippers and to create a monopoly of trade with the Russians. For this Simpson was willing to rely on ships; McLoughlin, oppressed by the defects of his shipping, wanted to use shore bases as much as possible. Simpson, too, wanted to drive the Americans to the wall; McLoughlin wanted to supply them, to take their furs from them in payment, and to make a profit from them. This was a divergency which had also arisen in the Snake Country expeditions, with McLoughlin ready to equip Francis Ermatinger, his own stepson Thomas McKay, and others, and Simpson ordering that all rivals must be driven out of business and that no trade goods were to be supplied except to Company expeditions under Company command.[15]

The difference in policy came to a head when in 1829 Captain Dominis of Boston in the brig *Owhyee* was shadowed and undersold on the coast and reduced in a year to offer to sell out. McLoughlin would have bought, but he was forbidden. Apart from economic reasons, he was desperately anxious to end competition because it involved trading spirits to the Indians. But though he could not buy the *Owhyee* and knew the official policy clearly, in 1832, when he was crippled by lack of shipping, McLoughlin not only bought the *Lama* of Boston but took her crew and her captain, William Henry McNeil, into the Company's service. It was a good bargain, and he paid largely in salmon and timber of local origin. McNeil was an experienced and competent trader who won Simpson's approval, and the deal was eventually approved.[16] But when in 1836 McLoughlin decided to sell the *Lama*, he sold her to John Bancroft, an Englishman who hunted sea otter for Americans; and he sold her on credit, to be paid for from the produce of Bancroft's hunts, for which he also supplied an outfit of goods. Again this was a sound move, and Bancroft quickly repaid. But McLoughlin was not driving the opposition out of business with the simple directness which Simpson advocated.[17]

Simpson's notions should have been revised when he received a report from Aemilius Simpson in 1829. Aemilius had been sent to New Archangel to offer to supply the Russians with food and goods, taking payment in furs. His valuable report described the Russian posts and system in detail and concluded that the Americans could not be supplanted in the coastal trade unless the Hudson's Bay Company traded arms and spirits to the Indians. This the Russians would strongly resent. The dilemma was clear and was clearly put.[18] But negotiations were continued at St Petersburg, and in 1831 Ogden was sent to build a post at Nass. Malaria, which was proving a serious handicap at Fort Vancouver, delayed Ogden until 1832, but Fort Simpson, Nass River, then became the centre of coastal opposition, with Ogden trading arms and spirits to counter the Americans.

The death of Aemilius Simpson in 1831 was a severe setback, and the Nass River and Fort Simpson both had defects; but the Russians were impressed and began to negotiate for English supplies. Ogden was to pursue the coastal trade policy, seeking for a site for a post further north, at the Stikine or Port Essington. The Company was commissioning the famous paddle steamer, the *Beaver*, for use on the coast, arguing that she would have great advantages over sail. She arrived out in 1836. But McLoughlin still pinned his faith to land bases, and in 1834 he had sent Ogden to found a post on the Stikine.[19] Under the Convention of 1825 Ogden should have had a right of access to Russian waters and territories. But he was held off by the Russians and retired discomfited. McLoughlin claimed £22,000 damages for this Stikine affair, and Lord Palmerston as Foreign Secretary was called into the fray as Duncan Finlayson took the *Beaver* for her first trip north.

Despite the hostility shown to Ogden, the Russians wanted English supplies; they disliked the Americans' methods, and an arrangement seemed possible. The complexities of European diplomacy had isolated Russia and made a *rapprochement* with England highly desirable. It was therefore opportune that in 1838 and 1839 the Hudson's Bay Company enjoyed the approval of the British government. The signs of such approval came when in 1838 the Licence for Exclusive Trade was gratuitously renewed (it had not yet expired) for a further period of twenty-one years, and when George Simpson and John Henry Pelly, Governor of the Company, were designated for a knighthood and a baronetcy respectively. These honours were directly related to the work which Chief Factor Peter Warren Dease and Chief Trader Thomas Simpson had achieved in 1837 and 1838 in clarifying the coastline of the Arctic Ocean by journeys north from Fort Chipewyan and from Fort Confidence;[20] but they were also a sign of general approval and support of the Company. The Company brought to arctic exploration a great capacity to travel light, and to live off the country by hunting and fishing. It could not sponsor such expensive and heavily-equipped expeditions as those of Franklin and Back, with the British Admiralty behind them. But its men could cover the ground and could live in the Arctic in a way which commanded admiration—and which earned rewards.

Even with such support, Simpson and Pelly were not able to agree on terms with the Russian Company when they visited St Petersburg in 1838. But Simpson met Baron Wrangell in Hamburg in January 1839 and there agreed that the Russians should cede the trade of the coast from Cape Spencer down to 54° 40′ for ten years from June 1, 1840. The Hudson's Bay Company even took over the Russian posts; they were to supply provisions to the Russians at fixed prices and were to pay an annual rent of two thousand land-otter skins.[21] By 1840 Simpson had achieved the monopoly of the coastal trade which he had planned, and he could develop the trade of New Caledonia behind the barriers of his agreement with the Russians and of the Columbia Department.

But agricultural produce was needed to fulfil his agreement with the Russians and, though the farm at Fort Vancouver was promising well, the

Willamette Valley was undoubtedly the most attractive agricultural land on the West Coast. The Willamette lay south of the Columbia, and its fertility had already attracted attention in the United States as early as 1828. The agreement with the Russians therefore merely diverted opposition to American ambitions from a commercial to an agricultural basis, and tension rose in direct proportion to American knowledge and interest.

In 1830 Hall Jackson Kelly, a Boston schoolmaster, arriving by ship from California, had been greatly taken with the prospects of agricultural development in the Columbia. He had publicized his views widely and had also damaged the Company's reputation by recounting rumours of its habitual ill-treatment of Indians and opposition to settlers, alleging among other things that the Company provoked the Indians to attack American traders and American settlers.[22] Then, in 1831-32, Nathaniel Wyeth, founder of the Oregon Colonization Society, started out with a party of thirty-one would-be settlers and brought eleven of them through to Fort Vancouver. They had to be helped on their way by the Hudson's Bay Company's posts, and they suffered severely. But Wyeth came again in 1834, this time representing the Columbia River Fishing and Trading Company. He now brought twenty-four men overland, and he got a cargo of goods round by sea. Following his own notions, McLoughlin made an agreement with Wyeth by which the American would be able to salt salmon and to trade horses but would not interfere with the Company's trade. But McLoughlin rejected a suggestion that Wyeth should hunt deep into American territory on behalf of the Company; so in due course did Simpson. Yet McLoughlin, realizing that Wyeth had brought out goods to supply American trappers and had set up a post for that purpose at Fort Hall on the Snake River, agreed to supply him, to hunt on American territory only, and to take payment in furs. This was a contentious decision, contrary to expressed policy. But it resulted in Wyeth being driven out of business. In 1836-37 Simpson himself bought out the American while McLoughlin, not knowing of this result, also bought Fort Hall and all its equipment.[23]

The Wyeth episode revealed American interest in the Columbia, and the Company's ability to deal with opposition in the fur trade. But in December 1836 McLoughlin was visited by William Slacum, whom he described as "an agent of the American Government, come to see what we are doing."[24] Slacum did indeed make a report to the United States Senate, praising the Willamette as the finest grazing land in the world, claiming American ownership up to the Russian frontier at 54° 40', and urging protection for American settlers. He again propagated stories of the Hudson's Bay men ill-treating Indians and opposing settlers,[25] and his report played its part in spreading "Oregon Fever" in the States.

As "Oregon Fever" began to become a recognizable element in American political life, American settlement in the Willamette also got started. The Methodist missionaries Jason and Daniel Lee had come west with Wyeth in 1834 and had been welcomed by McLoughlin, given a room at Fort Vancouver, and supplied from the Company's store. While Simpson thought that the missions and settlement should not be in any way encouraged, McLoughlin and most of the traders under him regarded settlement as inevitable and missions (whether Roman Catholic or Methodist) as desirable. But McLoughlin forbade the Methodists to trade furs, and in 1838 that seemed a much more realistic issue than the distant problems of agricultural settlement; for at that date the "settlement" contained only ten mission servants and eighteen other Americans, against twenty retired servants of the Company. The total population was about three hundred, and when the Company had yielded to pressure and accepted a Roman Catholic mission to the Cowlitz, McLoughlin had gone further and granted a site for a church in the Willamette also.

The missions showed that McLoughlin was more reconciled to the prospects of settlement than Simpson and the Company were. His views had emerged as early as 1832, when he had proposed to develop grazing by an independent hide and tallow company. This plan was rejected; but by 1837 McLoughlin had farms at Fort Vancouver, on the Cowlitz River, on Whidbey Island, and at Nisqually on Puget Sound. Such projects were so far acceptable that when it was negotiating for the renewal of its Licence for Exclusive Trade in 1837-38, the Company stressed its intention to develop an agricultural colony on the West Coast, and in 1839 the Puget's Sound Agricultural Company was set up as a subsidiary to the main company, and to it the farms at Cowlitz and Nisqually were transferred.[26] But settlement in the Willamette, where American influence was felt to be strong, was still discouraged. Instead, attention was concentrated on Victoria Harbour, at the southeast tip of Vancouver Island. The harbour had been surveyed in 1837, and it seemed to offer every advantage, good grazing and good land for tillage, as well as the safest harbour on the coast.[27]

American interest in the Columbia quickened as these moves went forward and as Slacum presented his report to the Senate. In 1838 Senator Lewis F. Linn of Missouri brought in his Oregon Bill, proposing American military occupation from the agreed frontier with Spain (at 42° North, according to the Spanish-American Treaty of October 1818) right up to the agreed frontier with Russia, at 54° 40′ North. He advocated the ending of the Convention for Joint Occupation west of the Rockies and the encouragement of American settlers by the grant of a square mile of land to each. With Palmerston as Foreign Secretary, the Company could be assured that such views would not be accepted. But its own efforts at farming were going slowly, and English settlers to balance Americans were discouraged by the Company's system of farming "on halves" (by which the Puget's Sound Company provided stock and seed and took half the increase) and by the policy of turning them away from the best lands, in the Willamette. An attempt to recruit families from Red River Colony did indeed produce an additional hundred or so settlers in 1841;[28] but although a party of them settled happily at the Cowlitz Farm under their priest, Father Demers, most of those who were directed to Nisqually soon dispersed to the Willamette.

The party from Red River brought the Canadians on the Willamette up to a total of 350 out of 500 settlers there, but the Americans received a substantial increase in the next year when Dr. Elijah P. White came through with a party of about a hundred and with a commission from the Secretary of War of the United States, to take charge of Indian affairs west of the Rockies. He was followed in 1843 by a much larger party, of 875 people, and the Americans then far outnumbered both the Canadians and the English. In 1842 White had announced that the American government meant to take the settlers under its protection. The Canadians held off from any move to set up a government in the settlement, as they had held off in 1841 when Jason Lee had invited them to do so. The Americans also had hitherto followed the advice of Commodore Wilkes of the American Navy, who had told them not to do anything to challenge the agreement for Joint Occupation until a boundary had been agreed between the two governments. But after White's declaration they held a meeting at Champoeg in May and decided to form their own provisional government. They adopted the Organic Laws and Articles of Oregon, based on the laws of Iowa, by a narrow majority, the Canadians refusing to participate.

McLoughlin and the Company's officers were for the moment able to ignore the Organic Laws, which would have borne hard upon them, for although they made an exception for the missions, the Organic Laws forbade anyone else to hold more than a square mile of land or to claim water privileges or other key positions. The great migration seemed to bring a more tolerant spirit, and the Canadians put their case, that they would not accept any petition to be incorporated into the United States until the boundary had been settled, that they claimed the same rights as the Americans, and that the country should be open to all settlers. These views being accepted, McLoughlin in 1845 gave his support to the formation of a Temporary and Provisional Government. The need was to enforce law and order; the Provisional Government had no reference to the claims of the British and American governments, and it was agreed that it made no claim to any land north of the Columbia.

But "Oregon Fever" could not be allayed so. Fresh accusations of the Company's abuse of its position began after a report from Captain Spalding of the mission ship *Lausanne*, and in 1843 Senator Linn got the Senate to adopt an Oregon Bill which declared Oregon a United States Territory, while a Convention of Citizens from States in the Mississippi Valley met at Cincinnati and asserted the right of the United States to Oregon. The issue was gathering momentum as the Presidential election approached, and candidates asserted their care for American interests. At the end of 1843 President Tyler in his Message to Congress claimed Oregon for the States, with a boundary at 54° 40' and with a chain of military posts to protect Americans from Indians and English alike. It seemed that the Americans would claim New Caledonia as well as the Columbia and that the issue could only be settled by war.

In the Willamette, in the meantime, the Methodist mission had begun to break up. Jason Lee was recalled in 1843, and Rev. George Gary decided to sell the mission's property. McLoughlin took the chance to buy the strategic site of the Falls of the Willamette. Ocean-going shipping could not go past this point, and it had been noted from early days as the place for a salmon fishery and for a sawmill; McLoughlin had a race blasted for a sawmill in 1832, and he built a store-shed there in 1838. When the Methodists moved to the Falls in 1840, he raised no more than formal objections, however, saying that when the boundary had been settled he would make his claim. But in 1842 the missionary Alvin Waller denied McLoughlin's claim, and difficulties arose as it became necessary to state whether McLoughlin was acting on his own account or on behalf of the Company. It was in an effort to establish a clear title that in 1844 he bought out the mission's claim. He thought the whole transaction shady, the price high, and the possibility that in the end the Provisional Government might simply deny his right under its Organic Laws unthinkable. Simpson, who at an early stage had instructed him to make the claim on behalf of the Company, by 1844 had concluded that the Company would not be allowed to hold such claims south of the Columbia, insisted that McLoughlin was acting on his own account, and charged the costs to the "John McLoughlin suspense Account." The dispute over the Falls of the Willamette[29] became part of the growing animosity between the two men, an animosity which prevented their communicating with each other after the death of McLoughlin's son, who had been murdered at Fort Stikine and whose death McLoughlin attributed directly to Simpson's intervention in the affairs of that post. But the Falls of the Willamette had more than a personal significance. The dispute showed American predominance—over 3,000 Americans came to Oregon in 1845—and American determination not to tolerate English claims. Angry as he was at his treatment, McLoughlin himself removed to Oregon City in January 1846. He retired from the Hudson's Bay Company in June 1849.

There was never any great likelihood that the Falls of the Willamette would prove to lie in British territory when the boundary was settled. As the American Presidential campaign continued and the claim to all land north to 54° 40′ gained currency,[30] British statesmen began to work for a boundary at 49°, and the Hudson's Bay Company began to concentrate on the preservation of New Caledonia. The two policies amounted to the same thing, and both statesmen and fur-traders were anxious to keep the whole of Vancouver Island in the British sphere; for Victoria Harbour held promise both as a naval base and as a fur depot. As Foreign Secretary from 1841 onwards, Aberdeen had seemed likely to achieve an agreed solution, and in March 1845 Simpson gave his views to the Foreign Office, supporting the frontier at 49° but with the retention of the whole of Vancouver Island and with the right to navigate the Columbia River and to use the Straits of Juan de Fuca as the approach to the Fraser River.[31] The Company's farms and other "Possessory Rights" south of the frontier (including the Falls of the Willamette) should also be safeguarded, though the Company would surrender them gladly in return for compensation.

But a frontier at 49° could not be accepted by American politicians in the heat of an election; nor when the election was over and it fell to President Polk to vindicate his election pledge to "re-occupy" Oregon up to 54° 40′. In his inaugural address as President, in March 1845, Polk claimed the whole of Oregon; anxious to "look the British lion in the eye" and to secure the support of the western Democrats who rallied to the cry of "Fifty-Four Forty or Fight," he maintained the right of Oregon to join the American Union without any "foreign intervention."[32] Polk mellowed perceptibly in office, and under the influence of his Secretary of State, James Buchanan. But in April 1846 the necessary year's notice to end the Treaty of Joint Occupation was handed to the British, and it seemed that war over the Oregon boundary was inevitable. This was the situation which Simpson exploited to get troops sent to Red River.[33] He was instructed by the government to take any measures necessary to ensure British claims in Oregon, and he was in direct contact with the British Minister in Washington and with the Governor General of Canada, Lord Metcalfe. Two army officers, Lieutenants H. J. Warre and M. Vavasour, were sent on a journey along the frontier to report on the military problems, and two men-of-war were sent to the Columbia. The result was a valuable factual report, taken posthaste to England by Lieutenant Peel, Royal Navy, son of the Prime Minister, in which the size and composition of the settlement was set out, the petition of the American settlers, in August 1845, asking Congress for a "Distinct Territorial Government under American auspices" was summarized, and the point was stressed that the economy of the settlements would collapse if the Company withdrew.[34]

American pressure lessened largely because Oregon was not the only boundary problem with which the régime under Polk was involved. He was as much committed to the "re-annexation" of Texas as to the "re-occupation" of Oregon; there also American settlers were claiming an independent republic and were seeking admission to the United States regardless of the claims of Mexico. The overland approach to California lay through Texas, and in 1845 Polk was declaring that for California also "if the people should desire to unite their destiny with ours they would be received as brethren." Faced with the choice of maintaining the independence of Texas and California or securing a peaceful settlement of the Oregon boundary, the British government chose the latter; and, given the choice, so did the American government. In 1846, therefore, Texas and California were absorbed by the United States, and on June 15, 1846, the Oregon Boundary Treaty was signed. Peel's government had been thrown out over the Repeal of the Corn Laws before the negotiations could be concluded, and Palmerston, taking over the Foreign Office, noted that the treaty "gave the Americans everything that they had ever really wanted." There could be little doubt that "England gave up a just claim to territory" or that the Americans yielded their claims to include the lands up to 54° 40' because of "the desire of Polk to be free to thrash Mexico."[35]

There were certainly defects and uncertainties in the Oregon Boundary Treaty. The right of navigation on the Columbia had been conceded; but the Americans held that this was only so as to give the Company access to its posts and that the right would cease at the end of the Licence for Exclusive Trade, in 1858. The "possessory rights" of the Company south of the new frontier were also safeguarded, but in such loose phrases as to cause endless contention, especially when the implied purpose was implemented and the Company tried to dispose of these rights. In all, the fur trade south of the Columbia, and the property rights of the Company also, were sacrificed to the British government's desire to secure peace and a reasonable understanding with the United States.

But the agreement, when at last it was reached, conformed in its essentials to the purpose which the fur-traders had followed from the beginning. They had meant to sacrifice the Columbia Department and to retain and develop New Caledonia. In 1846 the names were changed, but little else. The United States secured Oregon Territory; the British retained British Columbia.

CHAPTER 15

Epilogue: The Fur Trade
and Confederation

Apart from the Hudson's Bay Company, British financiers and politicians had shown little interest in the Pacific coast up to 1846; and when Vancouver Island and the mainland north from 49° to the Russian boundary at 54° 40' had been acclaimed as British, the Colonial Office was at a loss what to do with it. These lands seemed valueless except for the fur trade; even on Vancouver Island the problems of settlement and government seemed insuperable. For the island Earl Grey, as Colonial Secretary, concluded that "settlement could only advantageously be effected under the auspices of the Hudson's Bay Company," and in September 1848 the Company accepted a grant of Vancouver Island for the purpose of colonization.[1] Land was to be sold on reasonable terms, a representative assembly was to be set up in due course, a Governor was to be appointed by the Crown and not by the Company, and although the grant purported to be in perpetuity it was agreed that it might be revoked in 1859, when the Licence for Exclusive Trade would expire.

Within that limited period little was accomplished on Vancouver Island even when the forceful and wise Chief Factor of the Hudson's Bay Company, James Douglas, became the island's second Governor in 1851.[2] The attraction and the price of land in Oregon were too alluring, the journey from England was incomparably more costly and difficult than that to the United States or Canada, and the heavy hand of the Company lay over all the island. Apart from the so-called "Fur Trade Reserve" of twenty square miles at Victoria Harbour, the Company was suspected of keeping for itself and for its satellite, the Puget's Sound Company, all the best lands. Accordingly, by 1852, even allowing for the indentured labourers and the bailiffs whom the Company brought out, only 435 colonists had come to the island, and by 1855 there were only forty-three established independent settlers.[3] Though a party of miners was sent to work a coal seam at Nanaimo, the coal would not serve for ships' boilers, and the miners added more to the difficulties of government than they contributed to the economic stability of the "colony."

In such circumstances the nomination of an independent Council was necessarily unrealistic, and when the Assembly met for the first time, in 1856, three of the seven elections were still under dispute.[4] The Company claimed that it had been "tolerably successful" in establishing a colony; but as the end of the first five years of its grant of the island approached it was well prepared to hand over. The Colonial Secretary and a strong body of Parliamentary critics were equally anxious to seize the opportunity. It was, however, not easy to arrange terms for recompensing the Company for its expenditure. Figures varied between £225,699 claimed by the Company and £46,524 offered by the Colonial Office. Agreement was eventually reached at £57,500,[5] and the "resumption" of Vancouver Island was officially carried through in January 1862. But technicalities prolonged the completion of the Indenture of Surrender until April 1867.[6]

The terms were agreed as the result of the recommendation of the Select Committee of the House of Commons which the Colonial Secretary, Henry Labouchere, had called to deal with the problems of "British Oregon" in February 1857. The Committee included Edward Ellice, Member of Parliament for Coventry, and other friends of the Company. It also included Gladstone, Roebuck, Charles Fitzwilliam, and other severe critics of the Company. In the event, Vancouver Island got scant attention from the Committee, which turned to a general review of the Company as a factor in the agricultural settlement of British North America. But the Committee's Report was, for this very reason, an outstanding landmark in the history of Canada, of the North West Territories, and of the Hudson's Bay Company.

The revocation of the grant of Vancouver Island was recommended, and the Company's record there was held to invalidate its claims to approve of agricultural settlement anywhere at all. But its failure in Vancouver Island was not entirely its own fault; the price of land (a pound an acre, which government insisted on), the difficulty of the passage, and the need for capital for cattle, all played their parts. But the contrast with development on the mainland of British Columbia was challenging.

The great difference between Vancouver Island and the mainland arose from the discovery of gold in Thompson's River in 1857.[7] Within a year something like 25,000 men had joined the rush, at least 18,000 coming by sea from California with experience of the Diggers' Republics and the Constitutional Convention of 1849 behind them. The miners' convention had secured the admission of California to full statehood in the United States. The experience might well have been repeated. But as the diggers passed through Victoria on their way to the Fraser and the Thompson,

James Douglas took them in hand. He subjected them to rigid controls, and as they posed problems of government and administration he moved over in person and brought order to the territory largely by virtue of his sterling character and his great experience. He insisted on an oath of allegiance to the British Crown and never faltered from the principle that the Fraser and Thompson rivers were in British territory.

In this Douglas was acting on his own authority; but with the weight of the Hudson's Bay Company and with his own knowledge as a fur-trader behind him. He was taken to task by the Colonial Office for exceeding his powers as Governor of Vancouver Island. But as the mainland territory settled down in 1858 with a population of about eleven thousand, it was taken out from the Hudson's Bay Company's Licence for Exclusive Trade and was made the Colony of British Columbia, with Douglas as its first Governor.[8] The fur-traders had preserved the British claim to New Caledonia from American settlers in 1846 and then had preserved it from American diggers in 1858.

It was entirely acceptable, under the terms of the renewal of the Licence for Exclusive Trade in 1838, that British Columbia should be withdrawn from the Company's control, just as it was acceptable that Vancouver Island should be "resumed" under the terms of the grant of 1848. Both moves were made in the context of the Select Committee of 1857, and both brought under review the general position of the fur trade as the controller of land which might be used for settlement, and the position and rights of the Hudson's Bay Company as the owner of such lands. When the colony of British Columbia was established, the Colonial Secretary, Bulwer Lytton, declared that the colony had two distinguishing features. It would maintain the British connection in the face of American expansion; and it would be one of a chain of British colonies which would stretch from the Atlantic to the Pacific.[9] For either purpose British Columbia was isolated. If British Columbia was to survive the prairies also must be settled.

At the approach to the prairies there could be no doubt that Red River Colony, by the middle of the century, showed an encouraging example of what might be achieved. With its two bishops, its cathedrals, its council and its courts it was, with all its imperfections, a firmly established colony. As George Simpson reached and passed the zenith of his powers and matured his plans for exploiting the opportunities which the union of the fur companies and the Licence for Exclusive Trade had put in his hands, the rich black soil of Red River was being capably developed, and the changes which had taken place at Red River by 1857 had turned what was already a coherent community into a stable society.

As population steadily increased and as cash purchases became common, the general trade of the Company's store became more lucrative than its fur trade, and the Company fell into the role of one (important) element in the settlement. The "informal and slovenly balance of forces" which developed left the settlers, as Simpson had foretold, with the capacity to become the happiest and most comfortable population in the British Empire.[10] It was a balance of forces which left the Company dependent on its competence, not upon chartered rights, and the Company viewed the issues of access to Red River and of trade there from a cost-analysis point of view. The advantages of an approach to Red River from the Bay steadily diminished as railway development took hold of North America, and the Company itself began to bring up goods to the colony from the United States through St Paul, Minnesota. This route offered a chance to save a year's interest on the capital involved, and Simpson and his officers increasingly worked to a method in which heavy goods and immigrants came up from the Bay, lighter commodities came from Boston, New York, and St Paul, and swift expresses from Quebec and Montreal.[11]

Despite its efforts to place the responsibility upon government, at Red River the Hudson's Bay Company remained the source of authority; it supplied the machinery of government—and continued to do so until 1870. Elsewhere in British North America there seemed to be equally fertile soil, and no greater difficulties of access. But even on Vancouver Island by the middle of the century there were no bodies of settlers to form the bases of colonies. The one area of promise, Oregon, had been yielded to the United States; and except on Vancouver Island the Hudson's Bay Company was opposed to settlement and unwilling to provide the machinery for government. The Colonial Office also had shown that it was reluctant to undertake this task even for Vancouver Island, and the prospect that Canada might provide the financial, constitutional, and administrative backing for settlement was, if anything, more remote still.

Reluctance to accept the costs of settlement was not confined to Vancouver Island. The prairies posed the same problems in an expanded form, especially where defence against the United States was concerned. As the Governor General put the issue against the background of the Montreal Annexation Manifesto of 1849, there was "Only one absurdity . . . greater than the absurdity of supposing that the British Parliament will pay £200,000 for Canadian Fortifications— . . . the absurdity of supposing that the Canadians will pay for it themselves."[12] Nevertheless, if Canada was not to be drawn inexorably into the expanding American economy, the Canadian Middle West must not only be secured but must be settled and developed. Canada must create her own balanced economy, with its own internal market and with its export staples. Above all, she must develop an export trade in wheat to the great consuming area, industrialized Free-

Trade England; and she must herself handle the transportation of that wheat to the Atlantic coast.

In 1849, the creation of "a federal union of all the British North American Provinces" was under discussion as one means of developing such a balanced Canadian economy. But at that time the "Upper Country" was not in view, only "the vast extent of territory . . . from the Gulf of the St Lawrence to Lake Superior."[13] Yet as the Reciprocity Treaty with the United States drew to its close in 1866, and the problems of creating an independent Canadian economy again demanded attention, the Middle West assumed an importance which was all the greater because the previous decade had seen the transportation of wheat to the Atlantic coast lead to the development, first of rival canal systems, and then of a considerable railway system. In 1850, however, there were only sixty-six miles of railroad in all the provinces of British North America as against over nine thousand miles in the United States. If Canada was not to yield control of access to the Middle West, and therewith much of her economic independence, Montreal must secure railway contact with the Atlantic and railway contact with the prairies.

In 1853 the Canadian legislature passed the charter of the Grand Trunk Railway. The original proposal had been that Canada should play its part in building a line from Halifax to Quebec and should undertake construction of a line from Quebec through the St Lawrence valley, along the north shore of Lake Ontario to Hamilton. There the line would join the Great Western, which ran on to Windsor and Detroit; two hundred and fifty miles of the system were already open to traffic, and though the Quebec-Halifax part of the project was dropped, the Grand Trunk was able to lease traffic rights on the St Lawrence and Atlantic line to the Atlantic at Portland. The bonds were guaranteed by the Canadian government, an impressive list of Canadian and English directors was available, and powerful English bankers and engineering firms supported the Trunk. The line was completed by 1860—indeed, more than completed since an independent line west from Toronto to Sarnia and Detroit was built instead of the Great Western's track being taken over. But by 1860 the Trunk was almost bankrupt. It had already proved "too expansive and too expensive for the Canada of today."[14] The remedy for this great Canadian venture was found, not in any contraction of its interests, but in expansion—"through the extension of the railway communication to the Pacific." The prairies must be traversed, and they must yield their harvests, if the Grand Trunk was to be saved.

Ten years of uneasy progress at Red River were drawing to a close, and the grants to the Hudson's Bay Company of a Licence for Exclusive Trade and of Vancouver Island were both due to expire in 1859, as federation and railway policy, and the very existence of Canada as a separate North American state and economy, brought to a head the issues of the development of the prairies and of settlement and government on the Pacific coast. To the Colonial Office, Vancouver Island seemed to hold pride of place, and discussions of the terms on which the Company might surrender its grant of the island were in hand from 1855 onwards.[15] There was considerable feeling in the British Parliament that the Company's record, both in Vancouver Island and at Red River, showed a hostility to colonization and a perpetuation of fur-trading privileges; and although there were no insuperable difficulties in the way of an arrangement for Vancouver Island, the Colonial Secretary seized upon the occasion to call a Select Committee of the House of Commons, to report on "British Oregon."

But although "British Oregon" was the reason why the Committee had been called, it turned most of its attention to the wider aspects of the Company's lands and privileges, declaring that its interest in the territory administered by the Company was solely to see that it was developed and used for the best interest of the North American British subjects "and especially in the mode which is best calculated to add to the strength of the great colony of Canada."[16]

The Select Committee, like the Government of Canada, had available the evidence of the first Annual Report of the Commissioner of Crown Lands, of 1856; and the conclusion was that in Canada proper little good land remained available. From the Saguenay up to Lake Huron, settlement had taken up the land until the farms were on the fringes of the Shield. This was described as "the rough country" or "the lumbering counties," and the impossibility of developing agricultural communities in such territory, when Iowa and Minnesota beckoned, was recognized. Government survey parties had been sent out, and some good land was discovered, especially between Georgian Bay and the upper Ottawa River. Roads were driven into such areas, and the immigrants of the 1850's were directed there. But conditions were hard, many "pulled out" for the States, and those who remained were often at odds with the lumbermen. The story was basically the same in Upper and in Lower Canada, though in Upper Canada the settlers were often immigrant Germans or Irish, whereas in Lower Canada they were most often native-born French, more acclimatized, moving under their priests in groups, and more successful. In either case, shortage of good land was beginning to drive settlers up to contact with the Shield and up to conflict with the lumbermen.

The fur-traders also had their troubles with lumbermen, who were apt to turn traders and to dispense spirits. Simpson had taken twelve years to drive the American firm of McConnell Brothers out of the fur trade of Timiskaming and had then been forced to pay them £500 a year for their acquiescence.[17] In the attack on the Shield the lumbermen stood between the settlers, who could make nothing of the rough country, and fur-traders, whose natural preserve it was.

For the moment, however, in 1857 it was not the Shield but the prairies which were under discussion. In his *Journey Round the World* Simpson (or more probably his ghost writer) had written enthusiastically of the charm and fertility of the area between Lake of the Woods and Rainy Lake and of the suitability of the Red River territory for settlement, the richness of its deep black mould and the value of its crops. He was mercilessly harried by the Committee when he tried to make it appear that he had been writing only of limited areas, for there was a growing belief that a vast "Fertile Belt" spread westwards from Lake Winnipeg up the valley of the Saskatchewan, across the prairies to the foot of the Rockies—as is, indeed, substantially true. Accordingly, when Simpson maintained that the Company was not opposed to colonization so long as the exclusive right to trade with Indians was maintained (and with two exceptions the Committee agreed that competition in the fur trade would be unacceptable), it was essential to know whether he had in mind small pockets of settlement or something on a scale which would open up the prairies.

Simpson undoubtedly made a poor impression on the Committee, and some members were convinced that "a fur company has interests in direct opposition to the colonisation of the country." Edward Ellice was in a way more convincing. He declared that settlement was steadily driving the frontier of the fur trade further north, that supplies had dwindled since the beginning of the century, that furs were almost extinct in the United States, and that "all the countries easily reached have been entirely destroyed." The fur trade, he said, ceased to matter south of about 60° North, and the Hudson's Bay Company made no profit on its southern trade and lost on its trade near the American frontier. This, in effect, meant that all the territory under discussion could be taken for settlement without damage to the fur trade or to the Company; and Ellice gave his view that "the Hudson's Bay Company would be too glad to make a cession of any part of that territory for the purpose of settlement, upon the one condition that Canada shall be at the expense of governing it and maintaining a good police, and preventing the introduction, so far as they can, of competition with the fur trade."

The Select Committee took the fur-traders at their word, and recommended that Canada should be allowed to acquire any lands on her borders suitable for settlement, that the Company should yield up Red River (which should if possible be attached to Canada), and that Vancouver Island should be "resumed" from the Company as soon as possible.[18] The Company and the fur-traders had had their day: they had, indeed, surrendered their claims in principle. But they had maintained the British-Canadian titles to the Shield, to the Northwest, and to a Pacific shoreline.

But though the Company had conceded the principle of settlement, it was not ready to abandon its chartered rights without compensation. The legal validity of the chartered rights was a question on which the members of the Select Committee were not qualified to speak. They suggested that the British government should deal with this question. The extent of the land to be made available, and consequently the boundary with Canada, were also left for subsequent arrangement. But on three points the Select Committee was conclusive: the Company's Licence for Exclusive Trade should be renewed in the interests of the Indian population, its ownership of land in the Fertile Belt should be ended in the interests of the white population, and Vancouver Island should be "resumed."

Negotiations for Vancouver Island were immediately started and success-fully concluded, although agreement on finance could not be reached, and the Indenture of Surrender signed, until 1862. The Licence for Exclusive Trade, as renewed in 1838, had made explicit provision for the fur trade to yield to settlement, so that it was not an issue and there was no compelling reason why the Licence for Exclusive Trade should be involved. The Select Committee recommended renewal; the chartered rights of the Company were something separate from the Licence for Exclusive Trade. But Bulwer Lytton, then Colonial Secretary, was convinced that a decision on the chartered rights should be reached, and that if necessary the Company should be compelled to seek a verdict.[19] Therefore, although in 1858 the Company was informed that the Licence would be renewed, this decision was cancelled in January 1859 on the ground that renewal of the Licence was impossible until the validity of the chartered rights had been ascer-tained. A renewal for a single year was offered, to avoid the consequences of a sudden break, but this the Company declined—and declined again when the offer was increased to two years.[20] This should not have affected the chartered territory of Rupert's Land, but to the end of the story some confusion persisted between the legal status of Rupert's Land, which the Company owned and where it enjoyed exclusive trade under its Charter, and the North West Territories, for which a Licence for Exclusive Trade had first been granted in 1821, on condition that the Company accept respon-sibility for law and order and for proper treatment of the Indians.[21]

In 1859 the Licence for Exclusive Trade was not renewed; Lytton's suc-cessor at the Colonial Office, Newcastle, was still thinking on much the same lines as Lytton. Negotiations foundered, not because the Colonial Office had changed its view that competition in the fur trade was undesir-able nor because it had any alternative available for such administration as was needed in the North West Territories, but because Newcastle wanted to make the prairie portion of Rupert's Land available for settlement and for railway development.[22]

The North West Territories affected by these events were (except for British Columbia) what Sir Edmund Head called the "wild portion of the country not set apart for colonisation." Little was involved in 1859 except the Company's control over its own men; and the possibility of serious competition in the fur trade was remote. Had this not been so, the Company might well have taken a softer line in the negotiations. But the Company's approach to renewal of the Licence was uncompromising.[23] Renewal of the Licence for anything less than twenty-one years (with an option on withdrawal) would be taken to show lack of confidence and would be rejected.

In sharp contrast with this firm attitude was the approach towards the cession of land for settlement. Simpson, Ellice, and other members of the Company had, in varying phrases and with varying degrees of conviction, stated the view which the Governor, Sir John Pelly, communicated to the Colonial Office in 1857: "Assuming, however, that the object of the proposed inquiry is to obtain for Canada land fit for cultivation and the establishment of agricultural settlers, I would observe that the Directors are already prepared to recommend to the shareholders of the Company to cede any lands which may be required for that purpose. The terms of such cessions would be a matter of no difficulty between Her Majesty's Government and the Company."[24]

The principle of cession was early accepted and unequivocally phrased —Ellice gave his view that "if the place is fit for settlement, and you can obtain the means for settling it, it ought to be settled, and it ought not to be occupied by a set of fur-hunters," and "that there is not an acre of land fit for settlement which should be kept under any other dominion than that of the settlers." But before the easy solution foreshadowed by Sir John Pelly could be reached, twelve years were taken up in strenuous and tortuous negotiation. It was not merely a question of price. But price was an obstacle; Canada had no resources, and Ellice was not overstating the issue when he declared that "it is a question of a million of money."[25]

Before any realistic discussions could take place (even assuming that the money could be raised), the chartered rights and the Company's territorial claims would have to be authenticated; and the successor to the Company would have to be named. Would it be Canada? Or a series of new provinces? Or the home government?

Labouchere proposed that Canada should be represented before the Select Committee of 1857, and the Canadian government seized the chance to put the view that "the western boundary of Canada extended up to the Pacific Ocean" and the hope that "there is an inherent right on the part of Canada to some of the spoils of the Hudson's Bay Company."[26] But moderate views prevailed as William Henry Draper, Chief Justice of Canada West, was named to put the Canadian case. He was a witness only, without power to accept commitments; and he was instructed to put the case for Canadian settlement at Red River and across the prairies to the Pacific and to oppose any licences or rights which would prevent occupation of land adapted for settlement.[27] Draper was convinced that a monopoly of trade must be illegal, but he was not much concerned with that; he wanted to challenge the territorial rights granted in the Charter, and he suggested that the Judicial Committee of the Privy Council should conduct an enquiry and deliver a verdict. The Company, confident of the law, accepted this suggestion when it appeared in the first draft of the Committee's Report, and the Law Officers of the Crown (who had been consulted as Draper's suggestion was under discussion) would have agreed that the territorial clauses of the Charter were valid and would stand up to challenge. But, probably because the known opinions of the Law Officers made abrogation of the territorial rights by judicial action unlikely, the Select Committee ruled out the Judicial Committee of the Privy Council and merely left the home government to make an arrangement with the Company.[28]

By the end of 1857 the Canadian government also was reluctant to provoke an appeal to the Judicial Committee of the Privy Council—at least upon the territorial rights only. Instead, the general validity of the Charter should be discussed. This the Colonial Office refused to sponsor, and the Company declined to provoke a legal action so as to secure a decision on the Charter in general. It was not unreasonable to insist that, if Canada wished to dispute the Charter, it was for Canada to bring on a case. For the immediate problem, the Company declared that it would cede the territories required for settlement—and it had been indicated that the lands of Red River and the Saskatchewan would be required first—but it would expect the Canadian government to preserve order there.[29]

Canada had herself set up a Select Committee to examine the Company's claims and its administration, and this Committee had sifted the views of a number of men who were confident that easy communication could be established from Lake Superior to Red River, and it had received several petitions asking for annexation of the Company's lands, and especially for incorporation of Red River Colony into Canada.[30]

The need to counter the Americans was strongly felt, and the visit of the Prince of Wales to Canada in 1860 (a visit during which Sir George Simpson died, shortly after entertaining the Prince) increased the feeling of hostility, especially in the mind of the Colonial Secretary, Newcastle, who accompanied the Prince and who was confirmed in his determination to build a strong British confederation in North America. The middle provinces would have to come from Rupert's Land, the ancient area of the fur trade; the "obstacle interposed by a proprietary jurisdiction" would have to be removed.

As it became clear that the Company would not oppose settlement as long as acceptable terms could be secured, the status which any new settlements would enjoy came under serious discussion. If they were merely incorporated into Canada, the balance of politics would obviously be affected by any influx of Protestant English-speaking immigrants. But, as Reciprocity drew to an end, Confederation again became attractive for economic reasons, and a federal constitution seemed to offer the chance of creating separate prairie provinces which could be made responsible for their own costs (including the costs of buying out the Company) and which might later be admitted to a federation with less direct effect on the position of the French-speaking population of Canada East.

Knowledge of the "Fertile Belt" was growing, and three official reports —from George Gladman on the route between Lake Superior and Lake Winnipeg, from Captain John Palliser on the extent and nature of the fertile land in the prairies, and from Professor H. Y. Hinds on the potential wealth, mineral and agricultural, of the prairies—all added weight to the movement. Realization of the value of the land emphasized the need for railway access; and for British Columbia even a telegraph communication across the prairies would be invaluable. But railways, and even telegraphs, would need land, and delegations from Canada in 1857 and 1858, to underline the need for an Intercolonial Railway and for a "military road," found that the Company's Territorial Rights were still "an obstruction" which would have to be removed before any progress could be made.

In 1860, therefore, the Colonial Office prepared to follow up the Company's declared willingness to cede land whenever required for settlement. A draft bill was sent to the Company, which would enable the British Government to take land at Red River, on the Saskatchewan, or anywhere else, in five years' time.[31] Colonies would then be created by Letters Patent. Compensation would be settled by arbitration; it would be for loss of the right of exclusive trade, for roads and bridges taken over, and it would be the first charge on revenue from land sales. The Company raised many detailed points for discussion. But principally it required that its freehold title to the land, under the Charter, should be recognized in the bill.[32] Otherwise that right would seem to be denied.

This was no longer the problem of "British Oregon" which had led (ostensibly) to the calling of the Select Committee of the House of Commons in 1857—the problem of a territory which had been granted to the Hudson's Bay Company under specific terms for a specific period. The lands particularly under review in 1860 were the prairie lands of Red River, the

Assiniboine and the Saskatchewan, and the chartered territorial rights of the Company could neither be ignored nor overriden in those territories. Until its rights were disproved at law—and neither the Canadian nor the British government would undertake this—the Company professed its willingness to sell the lands but would not begin to negotiate until its rights were acknowledged. Newcastle was not so much anxious to challenge the chartered rights as to negotiate their surrender and to set up Crown Colonies. Patience and diplomacy might well have achieved a solution; but at Red River there was an immediate need to devise an effective form of government.

The urgency was largely derived from American pressure. Pro-American and pro-Canadian parties had emerged in the colony by 1860, and with Métis and Indians to confuse the issue, to deny the Company's and the settlers' right to the soil, a breakdown in government was probable. It was clear that the Company's rule would be difficult to sustain but that Company rule must be maintained until an alternative was available.[33] An effective form of government, to replace the Company if the Company withdrew, had therefore to be devised in the face of the unsettled conditions at Red River; and it had to be ready before the Company withdrew.[34]

Canada's intentions at this juncture were obscure. Her government refused to provoke a legal challenge to the Hudson's Bay Charter, and the Colonial Secretary could not even discover whether the purpose was to create independent prairie colonies, to annex the prairie lands to the existing province, or perhaps simply to bring the prairies under the rule of Canada West. Unable to allow time to soften the problem, Newcastle turned to the Company and insisted that it was responsible for preserving order at Red River until some other system had been established.[35]

Newcastle's attempt to establish Crown Colonies in 1860 failed. The Company had to be called in. But the evidence given before the Select Committee of 1857 had revealed all the factors in the situation—the fertility of much of the prairies, the desire of Canada to participate in the "spoils of the Hudson's Bay Company," the complexities of Canadian politics as the debate of Confederation went forward, the drag of the United States, the stimulus of railway development, and the willingness of the Hudson's Bay Company to make its lands available. As the Report was received and approved it became clear that notwithstanding changes in the British government and in the office of Colonial Secretary, the lasting purpose was "to add to the strength of the great colony of Canada." With so much of common purpose it is perhaps surprising that the achievement of Confederation, and the transfer of the prairie provinces to the Kingdom of Canada, took ten years and that the last act involved the sending of British troops to end a rebellion at Red River.

These were ten years of fascinating interchanges, and there would be a logic in including the story here—if only for the reason that the final act at Red River was achieved by the personal intervention, the character, and the knowledge of Donald Smith, Chief Factor of the Hudson's Bay Company. But the critical years between 1857 and 1873 have been dealt with in all their complexity in another volume in this series; and once the policy declarations of 1857 had been made, the fur-trader as such became relatively unimportant. From then on, the Hudson's Bay Company was indeed still a major participant in all negotiations. But even before control of the Company passed in May 1863 to the International Financial Society, the Company had changed its character. The traditionalists were gone; above all, George Simpson was gone. The fur-traders had learned at Red River how to live with settlement. In 1857 the Company had yielded its case; in 1859 it had forfeited its Licence for Exclusive Trade. The fur trade, as such, was prepared to retire north of 60°, and the protracted negotiations which led to the Deed of Surrender of the Company's lands were over territorial rights, not over trading capacity.

But although the fur-traders were little concerned with the last acts which brought the Northwest into Confederation, they had played a vital role in making the very concept possible. They had not only pioneered the routes, mastered the techniques for the break-out through the Shield, and learned how to approach the prairies from the Bay as well as from the St Lawrence; they had also made it seem normal and acceptable to live and to travel in the Northwest, and they had dreamed their dreams of a route from coast to coast and had made them come true. It was not only in their explorations and discoveries that the fur-traders opened up the Northwest for settlement, and so for inclusion in the Dominion of Canada, and it was not only by fostering the pioneer prairie colony at Red River that they showed that Canada was far more than the valley of the St Lawrence. They lived in the "Upper Country," year after year; and although it needed governmental enquiries, Blue Books, and Reports of Select Committees to penetrate the secrecy in which they veiled their knowledge and their familiarity, when the record had been compiled it was evident that the fur-traders had mastered the Northwest. Rupert's Land and the North-Western Territory, it must be remembered, in 1870 included Manitoba, Saskatchewan, Alberta, the District of Ungava, and the northern part of the Province of Ontario. If the fur-traders had not opened up these territories someone else, with other incentives, would have done so. As things stood, these great areas were the territorial contribution of the fur-traders to Canada.

ABBREVIATIONS

A.H.R. : *American Historical Review.*
A.N. : Archives Nationales.
B.M. : British Museum.
B.N. : Bibliothèque Nationale.
C.H.R. : *Canadian Historical Review.*
C.O. : Colonial Office, Public Record.
C.S.P., *C.: Calendar State Papers, Colonial.*
C.S.P., *D. : Calendar State Papers, Domestic.*
C. *Treasury B.: Calendar Treasury Books.*
Ec.H.R. : *Economic History Review.*
E.H.R. : *English Historical Review.*

H.B.C.A. : Hudson's Bay Company Archives. (All citations of documents in the Archives of the Hudson's Bay Company are made with the kind permission of the Governor and Committee.)
H.B.R.S. : Hudson's Bay Record Society.
N.A. : Nouvelles Acquisitions, Bibliothèque Nationale.
P.A.C. : Public Archives of Canada.
P.R.O. : Public Record Office.
R.C.A. : *Report on Canadian Archives.*
T.R.S.C.: *Transactions of the Royal Society of Canada.*

NOTES TO CHAPTER ONE

1. *Revised Statutes of Canada*, 1906, c. 50. The District of Keewatin, adjoining Hudson Bay, was created in 1876 but was restored to the North West Territories in 1905.

2. For a detailed analysis of the rock formations of the Shield, and a summary of the literature, see G. A. Young, "The Geological Investigation of the Canadian Shield, 1882 to 1932," T.R.S.C., 1933, Vol. 26, Sec. IV, pp. 341–71; Vol. 27, Sec. IV, pp. 67–108.

3. *Canada Year Book*, 1946, p. 4.

4. Cf. *Loc. cit.*, pp. 18–21.

5. Ch.-A. Julien, R. Herval, et Th. Beauchesne (eds.), *Les Français en Amérique pendant la première moitié du XVIe siècle* (Paris, 1946), "Deuxième voyage de Jacques Cartier au Canada," p. 125; cf. J. B. Brebner, *The Explorers of North America, 1492–1806* (London, 1933), pp. 120–21.

6. E. E. Rich, "Russia and the Colonial Fur Trade," *Ec.H.R.*, 2nd Series, Vol. VIII, No. 3, pp. 307–28.

7. For Champlain see H. P. Biggar (ed.), *The Works of Samuel de Champlain* (6 vols.; Toronto: Champlain Society, 1922–36); Morris Bishop, *Champlain, the Life of Fortitude* (New York, 1948).

8. C. W. Cole, *Colbert and a Century of French Mercantilism* (New York, 1939), I, 174, 177–80.

9. For Groseilliers and Radisson see Grace Lee Nute, *Caesars of the Wilderness* (New York, London, 1943), *passim*.

NOTES TO CHAPTER TWO

1. Nute, *Caesars of the Wilderness*, p. 109, n. 10.

2. P.R.O., C.O. 1/66/272; H.B.R.S., XI, 70, 91.

3. Nute, *Caesars of the Wilderness*, pp. 115–16; Grace Lee Nute, "Radisson and Groseilliers' Contribution to Geography," *Minnesota History*, XVI (Dec. 1935); P.R.O., State Papers Domestic, 251/180; C.S.P., D., 1668–69, p. 139.

4. Cf. B. de Voto, *Westward the Course of Empire* (London, 1954), p. 88.

5. *Minnesota History*, XVI (Dec. 1935), 423–24.

6. C.S.P., D., 1668–69, p. 543.

7. C. *Treasury B.*, 1669–72, Vol. III, Part 1, p. 401; Historical Manuscripts Commission, 15th Report, 1897, App. 2, p. 11; *Charters, Statutes, Orders in Council, etc., relating to the Hudson's Bay Company*, pp. 3–25.

8. A. M. Johnson, "First Governor on the Bay," *The Beaver*, June, 1945.

9. Nute, *Caesars of the Wilderness*, App. 2, pp. 286–92.

10. Cf. W. J. Eccles, *Canada under Louis XIV* (Toronto, 1964) pp. 39–44.

11. Nute, *Caesars of the Wilderness*, p. 125.

12. B.N., MSS Fonds Français, N.A., 9284, fos. 18 ff.; 9285, fo. 257.

13. C.S.P., C., *America and West Indies, 1669–74*, p. 85.

14. Eccles, *Canada under Louis XIV*, pp. 63 ff.; C. de Bonnault, *Histoire du Canada Français* (Paris, 1950), pp. 67–76; A.N., Col. C/11/A/4/33; B/1/112.

15. C.S.P., C., *1661–68*, p. 440.

16. Pierre Margry, *Découvertes et établissements* (Paris, 1879–88), I, 84–85.

17. Albanel's Instructions are in A.N., Col. F/3/2/22. His report is in B.N., MSS Fonds Français, N.A., 9284, fos. 8 ff.; cf. also Jacques Rousseau, "Les voyages du Père Albanel," *Revue d'Histoire de l'Amérique Française*, March, 1950; Jacques Rousseau and Antoine Roy, "Lettre de Talon au Père Albanel" and "La Mission politique du Père Albanel à la Baie d'Hudson," *Bulletin des Recherches Historiques*, June, 1950; cf. also H.B.R.S., VIII, xviii, xlii.

18. A.N., Col. C/11/A/4/5.

19. H.B.R.S., XI, 71–72.

20. For this period cf. John Oldmixon, "British Empire in America," in J. B. Tyrrell (ed.), *Documents Relating to the Early History of Hudson Bay* (Toronto: Champlain Society XVIII, 1931), pp. 383 ff.; and H.B.R.S., V, *passim*.

21. B.N., MSS Fonds Français, N.A., 9284, fos. 44 d. ff.; 9285, fos. 206–7; for the

Wood Assiniboines cf. A. S. Morton, *History of the Canadian West* (London, New York, 1939), p. 16.
22. A.N., Col. C/11/A/4/12/68d.
23. Cf. Eccles, *Canada under Louis XIV*, pp. 103–4.
24. A.N., Col. C/11/A/4/5.
25. *Loc. cit.*, C/11/A/4/81d.–82.
26. B.N., MSS Fonds Français. N.A., 9284, fos. 44 ff.; H.B.R.S., XI, 311–12; J. A. Bur-

gesse, "Jolliet on James Bay," *Beaver*, Dec., 1947.
27. B.N., MSS Fonds Français, N.A., 9284, fos. 50 ff.
28. H.B.R.S., XI, 2–13.
29. A.N., Col. C/11/A/5/359 ff.
30. H. A. Innis, *The Fur Trade in Canada* (revised ed.; Toronto, 1956), p. 50 and n. 31.

NOTES TO CHAPTER THREE

1. A.N., Col. C/11/A/5/86d.
2. *Loc. cit.*, C/11/A/7/131; F/3/2/28.
3. *Loc. cit.*, F/3/2/32.
4. *Loc. cit.*, C/11/A/5/316.
5. B.N., MSS Fonds Français, N.A., 9284, fos. 44 ff.
6. H.B.R.S., XI, 35–36.
7. *Loc. cit.*, VIII, 228–30 *et passim*; XI, 46, 53, 83.
8. *Loc. cit.*, VIII, 258–59.
9. R.C.A., 1895, *Relation of Pierre Esprit Radisson*, p. 62.
10. P.R.O., C.O. 1/66/66; H.B.R.S., XI, 68–69.
11. *Loc. cit.*, 70–71.
12. *Loc. cit.*, 92.
13. For Radisson's exploits see H.B.R.S., XX, 167 ff.
14. *Loc. cit.*, 292.
15. B.N., MSS Fonds Français, N.A., 9284, fo. 4d.
16. *Loc. cit.*, fos. 2–10; P.R.O., C.O. 135/1/67–68, 94; C.O. 135/2/25/49; H.B.R.S., XI, 285–90.
17. P.R.O., C.O. 135/2/40, 59.
18. A.N., Col. C/11/A/6/176, 223; Col. B/11/27; Col. F/3/6/105; Archives de la Marine, B/2/49/329.
19. H.B.R.S., XI, 73.
20. P.R.O., C.O. 134/3/8, 13, 39; A.N., Col. C/11/A/33; Col. E/9/11–18; B.N., MSS Fonds Français, N.A., 9284, fos. 108, 116d.
21. Nute, *Caesars of the Wilderness*, p. 211, n. 28.
22. A.N., Col. C/11/A/6/382d.
23 *Loc. cit.*, fos. 151, 263d.
24. H.B.R.S., XI, 150.
25. Eccles, *Canada under Louis XIV*, pp. 122–24; A.N., Col. C/11/A/5/359; C/11/A/6/382d.

26. B.N., MSS Fonds Français, N.A., 9258; H.B.R.S., XI, 307–10.
27. A.N., Col. C/11/A/7/198d.; Col. C/11/A/8/194d.
28. Tyrrell (ed.), *Documents*, pp. 35–101; A.N., Col. C/11/A/6/406 ff.
29. H.B.R.S., XX, 167 ff.
30. A.N., Col. C/11/A/6/248d.; B.N., MSS Fonds Français. N.A. 9297, fo. 7.
31. F. A. Middlebush, "Charles II and Louis XIV in 1683," E.H.R. 1925, p. 258.
32. B.N., MSS Fonds Français, N.A., 9284, fo. 61.
33. P.R.O., C.O. 134/1/225; A.N., Col. C/11/A/7/102d.; H.B.R.S., XI, 154, 214.
34. See E. E. Rich, *History of the Hudson's Bay Company* (London, 1958), I, 202–4.
35. A.N., Col. C/11/A/7/124–25, 178, 212, 250–53.
36. B.N., MSS Clairambault, 284, fos. 613 ff.; P.R.O., C.O. 135/2/32–33; H.B.R.S., XI, 306.
37. B.N., MSS Fonds Français, N.A., 9284, fos. 108d., 111d.
38. A.N., Col. C/11/A/8/247d.
39 Hubert Jaillot, *Atlas Français* (Paris, 1695). Partie de la Nouvelle France, 1685.
40. I. Caron, *Journal de l'expédition du Chevalier de Troyes à la Baie d'Hudson* (Beauceville, 1918), *passim*; B.N., MSS Clairambault, 1026/284, fos. 409 ff.; MSS Fonds Français, N.A., 9297, fos. 32 ff. Iberville's account is in N.A., 9284, fos. 117 ff.; H.B.R.S., XI, 313 ff.; P.R.O., C.O. 134/1/191 ff.
41. Caron, *Journal*, p. 7; A.N., Col. C/11/A/8/100, 107, 112, 164.
42. H.B.R.S., XI, 77.
43. *Loc. cit.*, 328–30.
44. Eccles, *Canada under Louis XIV*, 159.
45. P.R.O., C.O. 135/1/50.

46. P.R.O., C.O. 135/2, passim; B.M., Stowe MSS, 480; H.B.R.S., XI, 222 ff., 284–85.

47. P.R.O., C.O. 135/1/113; C.O. 135/2/71; A.N., Col. C/11/A/8/45d., 112d.; H.B.R.S., XI, 234, 300.

48. D. MacKay, The Honourable Company (revised ed.; Toronto, 1948), p. 339.

49. P.R.O., C.O. 135/1/122, 150; Acts of Privy Council, Colonial, 1680–1720, p. 132; H.B.R.S., XX, 6.

50. A.N., Col. C/11/A/9/148; Col. C/11/A/10/94; B.N., MSS Fonds Français, N.A., 9297, fo. 53.

51. P.R.O., C.O. 134/1/255; A.N., Col. C/11/A/10/4, 119, 127d.; H.B.R.S., XX, 81–84.

52. The river called Dering's River cannot be precisely identified. Cf. H.B.R.S., XX, xvi, 14, 66, 78.

53. Tyrrell (ed.), Documents, p. 380; H.B.R.S., V, 126; XI, 120–21, 180, 195, 197–98; XX, xlii–xlv.

54. H.B.R.S., XI, 121.

55. Loc. cit., XX, 66.

56. Loc. cit., XX, 12.

57. Journals, House of Commons, X, 369, 392, 401, 410, 412; Journals, House of Lords, XIV, 495–98; H.B.R.S., XX, xxxi–xxxiii, 100, 105. Charters, Statutes, Orders in Council, etc., relating to the Hudson's Bay Company, 75–78; P.R.O., C.O. 134/3/14; H.B.C.A., A/9/6/17d.–23.

58. Cf. H.B.R.S., XX, 118; G. S. Graham, Empire of the North Atlantic (Toronto, 1958), pp. 68–75.

59. A.N., Col. C/11/A/10/299; B.N., MSS Fonds Français, N.A. 9287, fo. 21.

60. B.N., MSS Clairambault, 879, fos. 278, 280, 291, 294.

61. B.N., MSS Fonds Français, N.A., 9287, fo. 21.

62. Tyrrell (ed.), Documents, p. 255.

63. Loc. cit., p. 257; Iberville's own Mém-

oire is in B.N., MSS Fonds Français, N.A., 9297.

64. B.N., MSS Clairambault, 879, fo. 379.

65. Tyrrell (ed.), Documents, pp. 107–9, 256.

66. B.N., MSS Clairambault, 881, fos. 162 ff., MSS Fonds Français, N.A., 9284, fo. 119; 9297, fos. 99 ff.

67. Loc. cit., 9297, fos. 108 ff.; P.R.O., C.O. 134/2/25; Tyrrell (ed.), Documents, pp. 105 ff.

68. Loc. cit., pp. 25 ff.; N. Jérémie, Twenty Years of York Factory (Ottawa, 1926), p. 27; A.N. Col. C/11/A/14/28, 157d., 244, 321d.; B.N., MSS Fonds Français, N.A., 9284, fo. 117; P.R.O., C.O. 134/2/2.

69. Cf. Rich, Hudson's Bay Company, I, 340–41; A.N. Marine, B/2/125/370.

70. W. Coxe, Private and Original Correspondence of Charles Talbot, Duke of Shrewsbury (London, 1821), p. 319; L. G. Wickham Legg, Matthew Prior (Cambridge University Press, 1921), p. 55; British Diplomatic Instructions, France, 1689–1721 (Camden Society, 1925), p. xii.

71. B.N., MSS Clairambault, 879, fos. 350–55.

72. Eccles, Canada under Louis XIV, pp. 202–4.

73. Coxe, Correspondence of Charles Talbot, p. 362.

74. Legg, Prior, p. 56; H.B.C.A., A/1/19/34d., 37d., 38; A/1/20/2; A/6/3/36; A/9/3/2d.; A/9/4/24–26d., 39d.–41; P.R.O., C.O. 134/3, passim.

75. Loc. cit., 25, 54d.

76. Morton, Canadian West, pp. 118–19; J. B. Tyrrell (ed.), Letters of La Potherie (Toronto: Champlain Society XVIII, 1931), passim; Jérémie, York Factory, p. 28; cf. G. Frégault. Iberville le Conquérant (Montreal, 1944), pp. 212–31. The most authoritative French account is in B.N., MSS Fonds Français, N.A., 9297.

NOTES TO CHAPTER FOUR

1. H.B.R.S., XI, 197–98; XX, 14–15, 114; P.R.O., C.O. 134/1/1; C.O. 135/1/26.

2. H.B.R.S., XX, 100, 115, and n. 2.

3. Loc. cit., XIV, xix–xx; XV, xiv.

4. Eccles, Canada under Louis XIV, pp. 108–9, 124.

5. M. Giraud, Le Métis Canadien (Paris, 1945), p. 147.

6. H.B.R.S., IX, 232, n. 3.

7. Loc. cit., XX, 18.

8. Cf. p. 59, n. 52 supra.

9. H.B.R.S., XX, 97.

10. Loc. cit., 18.

11. A. G. Doughty and Chester Martin (eds.), The Kelsey Papers (Ottawa, 1929), p. 28.

12. *Loc. cit.*, p. 27. Kelsey's "Buffilo" must have been musk-oxen. He described them as having a "Body bigger than an ox, leg and foot like the same but not half as long, a long neck and head a hog, their Horns not growing like other Beast but Joyn together upon their forehead and so come down the side of their head and turn up till the tips be Even with the Buts, their Hair is near a foot long."

13. *Loc. cit.*, p. xx; Morton, *Canadian West*, pp. 16, 111.

14. Doughty and Martin, *Kelsey Papers*, p. 111; H.B.R.S., XI, 198, records a similar journey inland by Chouart in 1685.

15. Doughty and Martin, *Kelsey Papers*, p. 5.

16. *Loc. cit.*, p. 7,—i.e., "Buck Muse."

17. *Loc. cit.*, pp. 3, 12–13.

18. H.B.R.S., XX, 187.

19. *Report from the Committee Appointed to enquire into the State and Condition of the Countries adjoining to Hudson's Bay*, 1749, pp. 276–81; Doughty and Martin, *Kelsey Papers*, "Introduction."

20. H.B.R.S., XX, 115, 138, 187; there is, however, support for the notion that Kelsey had somehow misbehaved in the instruction to Governor Geyer (Doughty and Martin, *Kelsey Papers*, p. 194) that "As for the Service Henery Kelsey has done us in travelling up into the Counterey You being imediate Judges of his demerits we leave it to your discretion to gratifie him for the same."

21. Giraud, *Le Métis*, p. 148.

22. H.B.R.S., XX, 17, 101.

23. Giraud, *Le Métis*, p. 149, n. 4.

24. H.B.C.A., B/239/a/2/59.

25. A.N., Col. C/11/A/16/207 ff.

26. B.N., MSS Fonds Français, N.A., 9284, fos. 62d.–64; A.N., Col. C/11/A/7/5, 212, 264d.–65; C/11/A/8/247d.; C/11/A/16/207.

27. *Loc. cit.*, C/11/A/17/361–65.

28. *Loc. cit.*, C/11/A/16/207 ff.

29. *Loc. cit.*, C/11/A/15/184; C/11/A/18/366; Archives de la Marine, B/2/149/249.

30. A.N., Col. C/11/A/18/356–57d.

31. *Loc. cit.*, C/11/A/19/308.

32. *Loc. cit.*, C/11/A/19/299.

33. B. Sulte, "Le Commerce de France avec le Canada avant 1760," T.R.S.C., 1906, p. 45.

34. A.N., Col. C/11/A/34/10–13d.; *Cal. Journals of Commissioners for Trade and Plantations, 1722–28*, pp. 170, 176, 177.

35. H.B.C.A., A/1/109/22d.; A/6/3/100–100d.; A/6/7/34–35d.

36. Cf. E. E. Rich, "The Hudson's Bay Company and the Treaty of Utrecht," *Cambridge Historical Journal*, 1954.

37. P.R.O., C.O. 134/3/20; C.O. 135/3/130 ff.

38. *Cal. Trade and Plantations, 1722–28*, p. 164.

39. H.B.C.A., A/9/6/52; A/9/11/27, 36.

40. P.R.O., C.O. 134/2/270, 307; H.B.C.A., A/1/117/27–32; A/9/3/76–77; B.N., MSS Fonds Français, N.A., 9284, fo. 270; N.A. 9287, fo. 4.

41. B.N., MSS Clairambault, 1016, fo. 375.

42. H.B.C.A., A/6/4/15, 28d., 116; A/6/5/19, 40, 42; A/11/114/48, 53; B/42/a/5/24d.

43. *Loc. cit.*, B/3/a/2, *passim*.

NOTES TO CHAPTER FIVE

1. Giraud, *Le Métis*, pp. 152–57, esp. p. 156, n. 4.

2. *Loc. cit.*, pp. 151–52. La Noue was to build his post at the mouth of Kaministikwia River, not at the mouth of Nantokonagane River (Pigeon River, the site of the later Grand Portage, which was already receiving attention).

3. H.B.C.A., A/11/114/48d.

4. *Loc. cit.*, A/1/143/64d.; A/1/121/173; A/11/2/59d.

5. *Loc. cit.*, A/11/72/46, 64.

6. Cf. M. Giraud, *Histoire de la Louisiane Française* (Paris, 1953) I, 14 ff.

7. F. X. de Charlevoix, *Histoire et description générale de la Nouvelle France avec le journal historique d'un voyage fait par ordre du Roi dans l'Amérique Septentrionale* (Paris, 1744).

8. Cf. Morton, *Canadian West*, pp. 166 ff.

9. *Loc. cit.*, p. 171.

10. Giraud, *Le Métis*, pp. 159–60.
11. L. J. Burpee (ed.), *Journals and Letters of Pierre Gaultier de Varennes de la Vérendrye and his Sons* (Toronto: Champlain Society, XVI, 1927) pp. 91, 436–37, makes it clear that the meeting was at Grand Portage and that the party then wintered at Kaministikwia, fifteen leagues distant.
12. Morton, *Canadian West*, p. 174.
13. Burpee (ed.). *Journals*, pp. 95–97, 438.
14. *Loc. cit.*, pp. 98, 183.
15. H.B.C.A., A/11/114/48d., 64d.
16. Burpee (ed.), *Journals*, pp. 128 ff., 173 ff. La Vérendrye had considerable misgivings about giving his son to go to

war with the Indians. But Maurepas (*Loc. cit.*, p. 196) was particularly pleased by this action.
17. *Loc. cit.*, p. 191. Pigeon River and the Grand Portage were not yet in use.
18. *Loc. cit.*, p. 214 and n. 2, pp. 442–43. Cf. Morton, *Canadian West*, p. 185.
19. *Loc. cit.*, pp. 208–31, 262–66.
20. Giraud, *Le Métis*, pp. 165–66.
21. Burpee (ed.), *Journals*, pp. 271–356, esp. p. 345; 445–47.
22. *Loc. cit.*, pp. 450, 453–54, 456, 496.
23. *Loc. cit.*, pp. 378–79.
24. *Loc. cit.*, pp. 406 ff.; Morton, *Canadian West*, pp. 196–98.
25. Burpee (ed.), *Journals*, pp. 485–92.

NOTES TO CHAPTER SIX

1. J. F. Kenney (ed.), *The Founding of Churchill* (Toronto, 1932); Morton, *Canadian West*, pp. 134–35.
2. H.B.C.A., A/6/4/12, 16–16d.
3. J. Barrow (ed.), *The Geography of Hudson's Bay* (London: Hakluyt Society, 1852), p. 32; A. Dobbs, *Remarks upon Captain Middleton's Defence* (London, 1744), p. 25; H.B.C.A., A/1/117/21d.; B/42/a/1/22d., 29.
4. Cf. p. 76 *supra*.
5. H.B.C.A., A/11/114/17.
6. *Loc. cit.*, A/1/33/159d., A/6/3/137–38; A/6/4/4, 20d., 22.
7. *Loc. cit.*, A/6/4/24–27.
8. *Loc. cit.*, B/42/a/2/47, 51.
9. Kenney (ed.), *Churchill*, pp. 81–82; H.B.C.A., B/42/a/1/84, 127; B/42/a/2/45.
10. *Loc. cit.*, B/42/a/1/127, 131d., 136–42.
11. *Loc. cit.*, A/6/4/48d., 54d.
12. *Loc. cit.*, A/6/4/95d.–98d.; B/42/a/4/29–30.
13. *Loc. cit.*, B/42/a/1/52, 132d.
14. Cf. Rich, *Hudson's Bay Company*, I, p. 529.
15. H.B.C.A., A/6/4/30; A/6/5/7d., 42d., 48d.–51d., 60, 69.
16. *Loc. cit.*, A/11/2/81; A/11/43/ *passim*.
17. *Loc. cit.*, A/11/2/141; B/3/a/35/30d.; cf. Sulte, "Le Commerce."
18. Cf. the evidence of Anthony Henday, *infra* p. 125.

19. H.B.C.A., A/11/2/145; A/11/43/18, 50d.
20. *Loc. cit.*, A/11/2/84, 137, 141, 145; A/6/5/85, 118; A/6/6/31d.–32.
21. *Loc. cit.*, A/11/43/1d., 4.
22. *Loc. cit.*, A/11/2/114d.; A/11/13/30d.
23. *Loc. cit.*, A/11/114/124.
24. *Loc. cit.*, A/6/5/87; A/11/13/*passim*; A/11/114/64; B/43/d/21.
25. *Loc. cit.*, A/6/4/75, 86; A/11/2/52d., 56, 64; B/3/a/4/31.
26. *Loc. cit.*, A/11/2/117; A/11/114/137; B/3/a/4/34.
27. *Loc. cit.*, A/6/7/34; A/11/2/117; A/11/114/137; B/3/a/4/34.
28. *Loc. cit.*, A/11/2/116d., 128d., 129d., 149d.
29. *Loc. cit.*, A/1/36/141, 145; A/6/7/34, 34d., 42d., 90d., 104d., 106d.; A/11/114/137.
30. *Loc. cit.*, A/11/3/12 ff.
31. *Loc. cit.*, A/11/3/17.
32. *Loc. cit.*, A/11/2/165, 173, 175; A/11/43/77, 85; B/182/a/7/31.
33. *Loc. cit.*, A/11/2/129d.; A/11/3/17, 21; B/3/a/34/5–6d.; B/3/a/35/6.
34. *Loc. cit.*, A/11/3/51.
35. For the Dobbs episode see H.B.R.S., XII, xlvii ff.
36. B.N., MSS Fonds Français, N.A., 9287, fo. 228d.
37. C. Middleton, *A Vindication of the Conduct of Captain Christopher Middleton* (London, 1743), p. 125.
38. Middleton, *Vindication*; Dobbs, *Mid-*

dleton's *Defence*; C. Middleton, *Reply to the Remarks of Arthur Dobbs, Esq.* (London, 1744); A. Dobbs, *Account of the Countries adjoining to Hudson's Bay* (London, 1744). The issue was also taken up in two anonymous articles in the *Gentleman's Magazine* in 1742.
39. H.B.R.S., XII, 207.

NOTES TO CHAPTER SEVEN

1. H.B.R.S., IX, 73, n. 2; XI, 5–6.
2. H.B.C.A., A/1/23/30; A/6/3/35, 48d., 89d., 92–93, 120d.; A/6/4/33d.; A/6/14/22, 33d.–34, 41d.; B/3/a/2/6, 9.
3. *Loc. cit.*, A/6/6/11, 15d., 32, 36, 57, 69, 96; A/11/2/93.
4. *Loc. cit.*, A/6/7/14d.–15, 29–30, 126; B/3/a/35/5d., 33 ff.
5. *Loc. cit.*, A/6/7/166, 171d.; A/11/2/145d., 180; A/11/57/15.
6. *Loc. cit.*, A/6/7/178; A/9/4/80.
7. *Loc. cit.*, A/11/2/152; A/11/43/63; A/11/57/22–24; B/182/a/6/34, 59; B/182/b/1/passim.
8. *Loc. cit.*, A/6/9/35d.; A/11/13/126.
9. *Loc. cit.*, A/6/8/116; A/6/9/9d., 10–10d., 33–33d.; H.B.R.S., XII, lxx, 114, 180, 207.
10. H.B.C.A., A/6/8/118d.–119.
11. *Loc. cit.*, A/6/8/47; A/6/9/33d.; A/11/114/164, 166. For the Henday episode see L. J. Burpee (ed.), "York Fort to the Blackfeet Country. The Journal of Anthony Hendry, 1754–55," *T.R.S.C.*, 1907.
12. H.B.C.A., B/2/6; B/239/a/40; E/2/11.
13. For the Earchthinues see H.B.R.S., XII, 312–13 and n.
14. Morton, *Canadian West*, pp. 245 ff.
15. Burpee (ed.), "Journal of Anthony Hendry," p. 342, n. 1.
16. *Loc. cit.*, pp. 350–51.
17. H.B.C.A., A/6/9/34.
18. *Loc. cit.*, fo. 4d.
19. *Loc. cit.*, A/11/114/190d.; B/239/a/39.
20. *Loc. cit.*, B/239/a/44/43; B/239/a/46/37.
21. *Loc. cit.*, B/239/a/43.
22. *Loc. cit.*, B/239/a/44; B/239/a/45, *passim*.
23. *Loc. cit.*, B/239/a/47/30.
24. *Loc. cit.*, A/11/13/passim.
25. *Loc. cit.*, B/239/a/48/34, 35.

NOTES TO CHAPTER EIGHT

1. F. Parkman, *The Conspiracy of Pontiac* (London, 1893), I, 174, n. 1.
2. H.B.C.A., A/11/3/51d.
3. Parkman, *Pontiac*, I, 329; J. Bain (ed.), *Alexander Henry, Travels and Adventures in Canada and the Indian Territories* (Toronto, 1901).
4. V. T. Harlow, *The Founding of the Second British Empire* (London, New York, 1952), Vol. I, Chap. 5.
5. P. C. Phillips, *The Fur Trade* (U. of Oklahoma Press, 1961), I, 561 ff.
6. Cal., *Journal of the Commissioners for Trade and Plantations, Jan. 1759–Dec. 1763*, pp. 374, 380; W. P. M. Kennedy, *Documents of the Canadian Constitution, 1759–1915* (Toronto, New York, 1918), pp. 18–21.
7. Phillips, *Fur Trade*, I, 574–76; Kennedy, *Documents*, pp. 40–42.
8. A. S. Morton, "Forrest Oakes, Charles Boyer, Joseph Fulton and Peter Pangman," *T.R.S.C.*, 1937, pp. 87 ff.
9. Innis, *Fur Trade in Canada*, pp. 192–93; W. Stewart Wallace, "The Pedlars from Quebec," *C.H.R.*, 1932, pp. 387 ff.
10. M. G. Reid, "The Quebec Fur-traders and Western Policy, 1763–1774," *C.H.R.*, 1925.
11. Phillips, *Fur Trade*, I, 578–79, 583.
12. *Loc. cit.*, 618, n. 39.
13. *Loc. cit.*, 579–80; Reid, "Fur-traders," pp. 27–30; G. C. Davidson, *The North West Company* (Berkeley, 1918), pp. 5–6.
14. Morton, *Canadian West*, pp. 270–71.
15. H.B.C.A., A/11/115/41, 66d.
16. *Loc. cit.*, A/11/115/96d., 101.
17. *Loc. cit.*, B/239/a/58. Cf. Wallace, "Pedlars."
18. H.B.C.A., A/11/57/59d.; A/11/115/114d.
19. *Loc. cit.*, A/11/115/116d.

20. *Loc. cit.*, A/6/10/87d., 111d.
21. *Loc. cit.*, A/6/11/50d., 79d.
22. *Loc. cit.*, 55d.
23. *Loc. cit.*, 124; B/239/a/61/21.
24. L. R. Masson, *Les bourgeois de la Compagnie du Nord-Ouest* (New York, 1960), p. 14.
25. H.B.C.A., A/11/115/132, 148.

26. *Loc. cit.*, fos. 142d. ff.; W. Stewart Wallace (ed.), *Documents Relating to the North West Company* (Toronto: Champlain Society XXII, 1934), pp. 40–41.
27. H.B.C.A., A/9/4/99; A/1/43/151, 172; A/1/44/17; A/6/11/143, 145.
28. *Loc. cit.*, A/6/11/55d.
29. *Loc. cit.*, B/239/a/63/3d., 24d.–25d.

NOTES TO CHAPTER NINE

1. MacKay, *Honourable Company*, p. 340.
2. H.B.C.A., A/6/11/55d. ff.
3. *Loc. cit.*, A/11/115/124.
4. *Loc. cit.*, A/11/57/63d.
5. *Loc. cit.*, A/11/115/144, 161 ff.; Wallace (ed.), *Documents*, p. 39.
6. L. J. Burpee (ed.), "An Adventurer from Hudson Bay: Journal of Matthew Cocking, from York Factory to the Blackfeet Country, 1772–73," T.R.S.C., 1908, Sec. II, pp. 91–121. Wallace, *Documents*, pp. 44–45, purports to add to Burpee's summary of Cocking's journal. But his additions relate to Cocking's journey of 1775–76, not to that of 1772–73. There are indeed many important omissions in Burpee, whose account is that contained in H.B.C.A., E/2/11 (prepared by Graham). Cocking's original is in H.B.C.A., B/239/a/69.
7. H.B.C.A., A/6/11/173 ff.
8. For Hearne cf. J. B. Tyrrell (ed.), *Journey from Prince of Wales Fort, in Hudson Bay, to the Northern Ocean, 1769–72* (Toronto: Champlain Society, VI, 1911) and *The Journals of Samuel Hearne and Philip Turnor between the years 1774 and 1792* (Toronto: Champlain Society, XXI, 1934).
9. H.B.C.A., A/11/14/3d.
10. *Loc. cit.*, B/239/a/59/6.
11. *Loc. cit.*, A/11/115/142d.; cf. Wallace, *Documents*, p. 42.
12. H.B.C.A., A/11/115/156.
13. *Loc. cit.*, fo. 161 ff.; B/239/a/65/32, 36d.
14. For Hearne's journal see J. B. Tyrrell (ed.), *Journal of a Journey Inland from York Fort towards Basquiau Commencing 23d June 1774 and Ending 23d June 1775, by Samuel Hearne* (Toronto: Champlain Society XXI, 1934), pp. 97 ff.
15. L. J. Burpee, *The Search for the Western Sea* (Toronto, 1935), pp. 162–63.

16. H.B.R.S., XIV, xxiii ff.; Tyrrell (ed.), *Journey . . . by Samuel Hearne*, p. 114.
17. *Loc. cit.*, pp. 156–61.
18. Wallace, *Documents*, pp. 4–5.
19. Cf. H. A. Innis, *Peter Pond: Fur Trader and Adventurer* (Toronto, 1930), *passim*.
20. *Loc. cit.*, pp. 76–77.
21. Wallace, *Documents*, p. 53.
22. H.B.C.A., A/11/15/11–11d.; Morton, *Canadian West*, p. 289; Alexander Mackenzie, *Voyages from Montreal through the Continent of North America to the Frozen and Pacific Oceans in 1789 and 1793 with an Account of the Rise and State of the Fur Trade* (London, 1800), I, xi.
23. H.B.R.S., XIV, 215–16, *et passim*.
24. *Loc. cit.*, 235.
25. *Loc. cit.*, 111–15, 120, 129.
26. *Loc. cit.*, 165–68.
27. *Loc. cit.*, 175–245.
28. *Loc. cit.*, 243–45.
29. *Loc. cit.*, 309, n. 1, 317–18, 324–25.
30. *Loc. cit.*, XV, 94–97, 134–35, 261–64, 270.
31. *Loc. cit.*, 263 ff.
32. *Loc. cit.*, XIV, lxxxiv ff. From B.N., MSS Fonds Français, N.A., 9418, fos. 274, 305, it is clear that Lapérouse's expedition had been planned as early as 1780.
33. B.N., MSS Fonds Français, N.A., 9427, fos. 316, 318 ff.
34. *Loc. cit.*, N.A., 9421, fos. 85 ff.; H.B.R.S., XIV, lxxxvi.
35. H.B.C.A., E/2/12/627.
36. R. Glover, "La Pérouse on Hudson Bay," *The Beaver*, March 1951, discusses the published accounts of this episode and gives a transcript of an account by the French officer du Tremblier. The Hudson's Bay Company's account, preserved by Andrew Graham, is in

H.B.C.A., E/2/12/623 ff. The account of the Marquis de la Jaille, who commanded one of the French ships, is in B.N., MSS Fonds Français, N.A., 9421, fos. 85 ff.

37. H.B.C.A., E/2/12/631; B.N. MSS Fonds Français, N.A., 9421, fo. 88.
38. H.B.C.A., E/2/12/635.

NOTES TO CHAPTER TEN

1. H.B.C.A., B/239/a/59/246, 263, 269.
2. Loc. cit., 182–83.
3. Loc. cit., 59, 69, 250, 266.
4. H.B.R.S., XVII, 350–53.
5. Loc. cit., 367.
6. Loc. cit., 331–34.
7. For Turnor see J. B. Tyrrell (ed.), *The Journals of Samuel Hearne and Philip Turnor between the years 1774 and 1792* (Toronto: Champlain Society, XXI, 1934), pp. 67 ff.; H.B.R.S., XIV, *passim*.
8. H.B.C.A., A/5/2/161d.
9. A. B. Keith, *Selected Speeches and Documents on British Colonial Policy, 1763–1917* (London, 1961), pp. 53 ff.
10. Phillips, *Fur Trade*, II, Chap. 32; Harlow, *Second British Empire*, pp. 433 ff.
11. W. E. Stevens, *The Northwest Fur Trade* (Urbana, Illinois, 1928), pp. 95, 110–16, 167–75.
12. E. Umfreville, *The Present State of Hudson's Bay* (Toronto, 1954), pp. 143 ff.; Wallace, *Documents*, pp. 72–73; Davidson, *North West Company*, p. 48.
13. H.B.C.A., A/11/5/35.
14. Loc. cit., fos. 59, 74, 77.
15. H.B.R.S., XVII, 327.
16. Loc. cit., XIV, 6, 327; XV, 5n.; Innis, *Fur Trade in Canada*, p. 156; Innis, *Peter Pond*, pp. 85–86.
17. Wallace, *Documents*, pp. 5–8; R.C.A., 1888, p. 59; Davidson, *North West Company*, pp. 9–10.
18. Innis, *Peter Pond*, pp. 89–93.
19. Wallace, *Documents*, pp. 8–9, 68–75;

Davidson, *North West Company*, pp. 11–13.
20. Loc. cit., pp. 42–44.
21. H.B.C.A., A/1/46/41–41d.
22. Wallace, *Documents*, pp. 11–12; Innis, *Peter Pond*, pp. 106–7; Mackenzie, *Voyages from Montreal*, pp. xix–xx.
23. Wallace, *Documents*, pp. 13–14, 75–84.
24. Morton, *Canadian West*, p. 441.
25. H.B.C.A., A/5/2/161; A/11/5/74, 77; A/6/13/156.
26. Loc. cit., A/6/13/156d.
27. Loc. cit., A/6/14/33, 75; A/11/45/127d.
28. Loc. cit., A/11/5/105, 169, 173–175d.; A/6/15/14d., 17, 49, 97.
29. Mackenzie, *Voyages from Montreal*, *passim*; Davidson, *North West Company*, p. 61.
30. H.B.C.A., B/239/b/53/68d.–69d.; Tyrrell (ed.), *Hearne and Turnor*, p. 398 n.
31. Loc. cit., pp. 317 ff.
32. Loc. cit., p. 588; H.B.C.A., B/239/b/58/32d., 57, 72.
33. Tyrrell, *Hearne and Turnor*, p. 588.
34. J. B. Tyrrell (ed.), *The Journals of David Thompson* (Toronto: Champlain Society, XII, 1916), p. 55; Morton, *Canadian West*, pp. 440–41.
35. H.B.C.A., C/7/175/4–7, 10, 13; A/6/14/105d., 139d.–140; A/11/15/184–85. Duncan had already explored parts of the northwest coast, seeking a passage from west to east. His task was approved by the British Admiralty.
36. For Malchom Ross see Tyrrell, *Hearne and Turnor*.

NOTES TO CHAPTER ELEVEN

1. H.B.C.A., A/1/49/78; A/1/147/40; A/6/17/153.
2. Loc. cit., A/1/49/78, 85.
3. Loc. cit., A/1/48/passim.

4. Loc. cit., A/6/16/156.
5. Loc. cit., A/11/117/163–65; Morton, *Canadian West*, pp. 338, 444, 456.
6. Innis, *Fur Trade*, pp. 260–61.

7. Mackenzie, *Voyages from Montreal*, pp. xliv–xlv; Davidson, *North West Company*, pp. 229–38; Wallace, *Documents*, p. 73.
8. Wallace, *Documents*, pp. 84 ff.; Masson (ed.), *Les Bourgeois*, I, 38.
9. H.B.C.A., F/3/1/65d., 66d.
10. Wallace, *Documents*, pp. 432, 437, 449, 453; Stevens, *Northwest Fur Trade*, pp. 125 ff.
11. Wallace, *Documents*, p. 15; H.B.C.A., F/3/1/151 ff.
12. R. Harvey Fleming, "The Origins of Sir Alexander Mackenzie and Company," *C.H.R.*, June, 1928; Innis, *Fur Trade*, pp. 255–59; H.B.C.A., A/6/16/70, 73; F/3/2/3; Masson, *Les Bourgeois*, I, 74; Wallace, *Documents*, pp. 95–96.
13. Mackenzie, *Voyages*, p. xxiii; R.C.A., 1892, pp. 147–52.
14. Wallace, *Documents*, pp. 108–25.
15. H.B.C.A., A/6/16/160; A/6/17–17d., 22 ff.; A/10/1/45, 47, 49.
16. *Loc. cit.*, A/6/16/102.
17. *Loc. cit.*, B/39/a/1/6d.; A/5/4/103d.
18. *Report of the Select Committee on the Hudson's Bay Company, 1857*, p. 344.
19. H.B.C.A., A/1/48/106d.; A/5/4/132d., 134.
20. *Loc. cit.*, B/121/a/1/150; Innis, *Fur Trade*, p. 271; Davidson, *North West Company*, p. 91.
21. Cf. Morton, *Canadian West*, pp. 514–15.
22. Masson, *Les Bourgeois*, II, 482 ff.; Wallace, *Documents*, pp. 143–70.
23. Davidson, *North West Company*, p. 88.
24. Tyrrell (ed.), *Journals of David Thompson*, pp. lxxi–lxxvi, 237 ff.
25. J. B. Tyrrell, "David Thompson and the Columbia River," *C.H.R.*, March, 1937, and A. S. Morton, "Did Duncan McGillivray and David Thompson cross the Rockies in 1801?" *C.H.R.*, June, 1937; Morton, *Canadian West*, pp. 458–68; R. Glover (ed.), *David Thompson's Narrative, 1784–1812* (Toronto: Champlain Society, XL, 1962), xliv–xlvii.
26. Wallace, *Documents*, p. 203.
27. For Frazer's journal see Masson, *Les Bourgeois*, II, 155 ff.
28. Tyrrell (ed.), *David Thompson*, p. 328.
29. For Thompson's crossing of the Rockies see *Loc. cit.*, pp. 375 ff.; R. Glover (ed.), *David Thompson*, pp. xlvii–lxiv, 273 ff.; Morton, *Canadian West*, pp. 465 ff.
30. H.B.C.A., A/1/220/5.
31. *Loc. cit.*, A/1/219/38, 45; A/1/220/38; A/10/1/85, *et passim*.
32. *Loc. cit.*, A/1/220/54.
33. *Loc. cit.*, A/1/49/91d.–94d.
34. *Loc. cit.*, fos. 86 ff.
35. *Loc. cit.*, A/6/17 and A/6/18, *passim*; J. H. Clapham, *An Economic History of Modern Britain* (3 vols.; Cambridge, Eng., 1926), I, 237–38; R. G. Albion, *Forests and Sea Power* (Cambridge, Mass., 1926), pp. 316–45.
36. H.B.C.A., A/1/147/29d.; A/5/4/158–62d.; A/6/17/81, 87.
37. For Colin Robertson see H.B.R.S., II, *passim*.
38. For Selkirk see Chester Martin, *Lord Selkirk's Work in Canada* (Oxford, 1916); Davidson, *North West Company*, pp. 118 ff.; J. P. Pritchett, *Red River Valley* (New Haven, 1942); J. M. Gray, *Lord Selkirk of Red River* (Toronto, 1963).
39. H.B.C.A., A/1/49/114; A/6/17/68d., 93d., 125d.; H.B.R.S., II, xxxi–xxxii.
40. H.B.C.A., A/1/50/19, 33–35.
41. H.B.R.S., II, xlvi. Selkirk Correspondence, St. Mary's Isle (since destroyed by fire, but which the writer enjoyed the privilege of perusing in 1937–38), Memorandum.

NOTES TO CHAPTER TWELVE

1. Martin, *Selkirk's Work*, pp. 201 ff., and map p. 226.
2. *Loc. cit.*, p. 36, n. 4.
3. H.B.R.S., II, xxxix.
4. H.B.C.A., A/6/18/25.
5. H.B.R.S., II, xxxix.; H.B.C.A., A/6/18/32.
6. H.B.R.S., I, 423–24; II, lii.
7. *Loc. cit.*, III, lvii, 242, 280.
8. Martin, *Selkirk's Work*, pp. 50–51; Gray, *Selkirk*, pp. 77–84.
9. Martin, *Selkirk's Work*, pp. 53 ff.
10. Selkirk Correspondence, Auld to Macdonell, Mar. 13, 1814.

11. Cf. Morton, *Canadian West*, p. 525; H.B.C.A., F/3/2/108, 113; A/6/18/63–68.
12. H.B.C.A., A/11/76/10d.
13. H.B.R.S., XVIII, xxx.
14. H.B.C.A., A/6/17/106d., 139, 170.
15. H.B.R.S., II, 221–23.
16. H.B.C.A., B/42/b/50/19–20; B/60/a/9/16d.–17; Morton, *Canadian West*, pp. 496–97.
17. H.B.C.A., A/6/8/93.
18 H.B.R.S., II, Introduction, *passim*.
19. Martin, *Selkirk's Works*, pp. 92–94.
20. *Loc. cit.*, pp. 57 ff.
21. Gray, *Selkirk*, p. 89.
22. Martin, *Selkirk's Work*, Chap. V, "The Pemican War."
23. *Loc. cit.*, p. 79 and n. 2; Gray, *Selkirk*, Chap. IV, *passim*.
24. H.B.R.S., II, lxiii–lxvi.
25. *Loc. cit.*, 241; H.B.C.A., A/6/18/278 ff.
26. For accounts of the "Massacre" see Martin, *Selkirk's Work*, Gray, *Selkirk*, and Morton, *Canadian West*, pp. 572 ff. For a treatment of the incident as a "battle" see M. W. Campbell, *The North West Company* (Toronto, 1957), pp. 215–18.
27. H.B.R.S., II, lix–lx; Gray, *Selkirk*, p. 120.
28. W. Stewart Wallace, "The Literature Relating to the Selkirk Controversy," C.H.R., XIII (1932), pp. 45–50.
29. *Papers Relating to the Red River Settlement* (Blue Book, 1819), pp. 57 ff.; Selkirk Correspondence, Lady Selkirk to Selkirk, Hogmanay, 1816; Selkirk to Lady Selkirk, April 29, 1817.

30. *Blue Book, 1819*, pp. 72–73, 96; Gray, *Selkirk*, p. 186; Martin, *Selkirk's Work*, pp. 128 ff.
31. H.B.CA., A/8/1/31; *Blue Book, 1819*, pp. 72–73; Martin, *Selkirk's Work*, Appendix C, pp. 215–18.
32. H.B.C.A., A/8/1/42d., 129; Morton, *Canadian West*, pp. 594–95; *Blue Book, 1819*, *passim*.
33. Gray, *Selkirk*, pp. 230 ff.
34. A. Amos, *Report of Trials in the Courts of Canada* (London, 1820); Martin, *Selkirk's Work*, Chap. X, "The Mud of the Law."
35. *Loc. cit.*, p. 150.
36. H.B.R.S., II, 151–52.
37. H.B.C.A., B/39/a/6/63 ff.; Selkirk Correspondence, Clarke to Selkirk, Aug. 1816.
38. H.B.C.A., B/39/a/6; B/39/a/7; B/39/a/8; *passim*.
39. H.B.R.S., II, 41 ff., and 292 ff., for Robertson's own accounts of his winter in Athabasca.
40. William's account of the affair is in H.B.R.S., II, 284 ff.
41. H.B.R.S., I, 273–74, 420–21.
42. For Simpson cf. H.B.R.S., I, Introduction by Chester Martin, *passim*; pp. 466–67; A. S. Morton, *Sir George Simpson, Overseas Governor of the Hudson's Bay Company* (Toronto, 1944).
43. Cf. H.B.R.S., III, 411, 423–24.
44. *Loc. cit.*, II, cxix–cxx; H.B.C.A., B/39/a/19.
45. H.B.R.S., I, *Simpson's Athabasca Journal*.

NOTES TO CHAPTER THIRTEEN

1. H.B.C.A., A/8/1/1, 6, 15, 19, 22.
2. *Loc. cit.*, fos. 27d.–29d.
3. *Blue Book, 1819*, pp. 5–7, 15, 39–42.
4. Martin, *Selkirk's Work*, pp. 92 ff.
5. *Loc. cit.*, pp. 102–3.
6. Cf. pp. 226–27 *supra*.
7. H.B.C.A., A/10/2/3; Martin, *Selkirk's Work*, pp. 162–63; Gray, *Selkirk*, pp. 307–9 and note p. 366. Cf. also J. Halkett, *Statement Respecting the Earl of Selkirk's Settlement of Kildonan, upon the Red River, in North America, its Destruction in the years 1815 and 1816, and*

the Massacre of Governor Semple and his Party (London, 1817).
8. H.B.C.A., A/8/1/54d.
9. P.C.A., *Pamphlet 1070*; Selkirk Correspondence, Selkirk to Colvile, Dec. 11, 1819; Montgomery to Colvile, Dec. 2, 1819.
10. *Report from the Select Committee on the Hudson's Bay Company, 1857*, p. 415.
11. Statutes 1 and 2, George IV, 1821.
12. Martin, *Selkirk's Work*, p. 92.
13. *Report from the Select Committee*,

1857, Nos. 5785–86, 5889; H.B.C.A., A/10/2/36d.

14. Martin, *Selkirk's Work*, Appendix D, pp. 218–22.

15. *Report from Select Committee*, 1857, pp. 328, 338.

16. H.B.R.S., II, 302 ff. for the coalition.

17. *Loc. cit.*, 327 ff.

18. "Diary of Nicholas Garry," *T.R.S.C.*, 1900, pp. 3–204.

19. H.B.R.S., II, 169.

20. Wallace, *Documents*, p. 328.

21. H.B.R.S., II, 175; H.B.C.A., D/4/85/10d.

22. H.B.R.S., III, 293–98.

23. Wallace, *Documents*, p. 328; *Report from Select Committee*, 1857, No. 5784.

24. H.B.R.S., II, 308; H.B.C.A., A/6/21/37.

25. Wallace, *Documents*, pp. 332, 373–74, 387–422.

26. H.B.R.S., I, 401–2; cf. *Loc. cit.*, III, *passim*.

27. *Loc. cit.*, I, p. 26, n. 4, p. 401.

28. For the Bow River Expedition see *Loc. cit.*, III, xviii and n. 3, xxvii, 12, 312, 355–56.

29. *Loc. cit.*, 418.

30. *Loc. cit.*, 28 ff.

31. H.B.C.A., Simpson's Private Journal, unclassified, Mar. 14, May 18, 25, 1822.

32. H.B.R.S., III, 360–62.

33. *Loc. cit.*, 392–98.

34. *Loc. cit.*, 33 *et passim*.

35. A. Ross, *Red River Settlement* (London, 1856), pp. 64, 76; Pritchett, *Red River Valley*, pp. 244–54; H.B.C.A., A/12/1/188, 350; H.B.R.S., III, 80, 109–11d.

36. Pritchett, *Red River Valley*, pp. 226–27; F. Merk (ed.) *Fur Trade and Empire* (Cambridge, Mass., 1931), p. 179.

37. Ross, *Red River Settlement*, and Pritchett, *Red River Valley*, *passim*; G. P. de T. Glazebrook (ed.), *The Hargrave Correspondence*, 1821–43 (Toronto: Champlain Society, XXIV, 1938), pp. 47, 51, 119–21.

38. H.B.C.A., A/12/2/180d., 386d.

39. F. B. Head, *A Narrative* (3rd Edition: London, 1839), Appendix A, p. 4.

40. For the buffalo hunt see Ross, *Red River Settlement*, pp. 255 ff.; Giraud, *Le Métis Canadien*, pp. 801–17; H.B.R.S., XIX, xxxvi ff.

41. H.B.C.A., A/12/1/91, 162d.

42. *Loc. cit.*, 152d., 163d.

43. *Loc. cit.*, 429, 590.

44. Head, *Narrative*, Appendix A.

45. H.B.C.A., A/6/19/57d.–58; A/10/2/307a; A/12/2/243, 390d.

46. *Loc. cit.*, A/12/2/524–29.

47. Martin, *Selkirk's Work*, p. 223. The arrangement was made in 1834; payment was completed in 1836.

48. Pritchett, *Red River Valley*, p. 253; Ross, *Red River Settlement*, pp. 174–76.

49. Cf. H.B.R.S., XIX, *Eden Colvile's Letters*, Introduction by W. L. Morton, *passim*.

50. H.B.C.A., A/12/2/569.

51. P.R.O., C.O. 42/515; B.M., Harleian MSS 6394; H.B.C.A., A/8/2/49.

52. H.B.R.S., XIX, lxvii ff.

53. For Alexander Isbister see *Report from Select Committee*, 1857, pp. 120–21; *Parliamentary Papers*, 1849, XXXV, No. 227, Copies of any Memorials presented to the Colonial Office by Inhabitants of the Red River Settlement, p. 597.

54. *Report from Select Committee*, 1857, pp. 370–71; H.B.C.A., A/11/95, Caldwell to Governor and Committee, Mar. 28, 1849.

55. *Report from Select Committee*, 1857, Nos. 3412–14; H.B.C.A., A/8/3 and A/8/4, *passim*, A/11/95, Caldwell to Grey, Mar. 22, 1849; A/13/4, McLaughlin to Grey, Jan. 16, 1850.

56. For the Sayer Trial see H.B.R.S., XIX, lxxxii ff.

57. *Ibid.*, lxii–lxiii, xcii; H.B.C.A., A/6/28; Mar. 25, 1850; D/5/26; Oct. 26, 1850; D/5/28; Apr. 12, 1850.

58. H.B.R.S., XIX, 207.

59. *Loc. cit.*, 22–24.

60. So spelt in H.B.R.S. XIX, *Eden Colvile's Letters*, *passim*. Also rendered as Cochrane.

61. H.B.C.A., D/5/24, Pelly to Simpson, Jan. 12, 1849, enclosing Simpson's note of Sept. 7, 1848.

62. H.B.R.S., XIX, 162.

63. *Loc. cit.*, l and notes.

64. *Loc. cit.*, 207; H.B.C.A., D/5/31, Aug. 1, 1851.

65. H.B.R.S., XIX, cviii; H.B.C.A., A/13/5.

66. H.B.R.S., XIX, 207–8.

67. *Loc. cit.*, XVI, 219.

NOTES TO CHAPTER FOURTEEN

1. H.B.R.S., III, xxx–xxxv; IV, xi–xx.
2. Loc. cit., III, xxxiii; IV, xxi–xxii.
3. Cf. Loc. cit., XIII, xiii–xxv for Ogden's early career and character; III, 53n. for Finan Macdonald and Ross.
4. Loc. cit., XIII and XXIII; T. C. Elliott, "Peter Skene Ogden, Fur Trader," Oregon Historical Quarterly, XI: T. C. Elliott (ed.), "Journal of Alexander Ross, Snake Country Expedition, 1824," Oregon Historical Quarterly, XIV; F. Merk, "Snake Country Expedition, 1824–25," Oregon Historical Quarterly, XXXV.
5. Oregon Historical Quarterly, XI, 214–17.
6. H.B.C.A., A/6/21/78–79; B/23/b/1/21; D/4/6/2d.
7. H. M. Chittenden, The American Fur Trade of the Far West (New York, 1936), I, Chap. 16; H. C. Dale, The Ashley-Smith Explorations and the Discovery of a Central Route to the Pacific, 1822–29 (Glendale, 1941), pp. 92 ff.; Phillips, Fur Trade, II, 395 ff.
8. H.B.R.S., IV, 68 ff.
9. John McLoughlin was a highly controversial figure, the "White-headed Eagle" of Oregon. For his relations with Simpson and the Hudson's Bay Company see H.B.R.S., IV, VI, and VII, McLoughlin's Fort Vancouver Letters, with introductions by W. Kaye Lamb, and Burt Brown Barker (ed.), Letters of Dr. John McLoughlin written at Fort Vancouver, 1829–1832 (Portland, 1948).
10. Merk, Fur Trade and Empire, p. 266.
11. Loc. cit., p. 87; H.B.R.S., X, 68; H.B.C.A., A/8/1/131d.; A/12/1/123, 133d.–134, 139, 149.
12. J. S. Galbraith, The Hudson's Bay Company as an Imperial Factor, 1821–69 (Toronto, 1957), p. 187. Cf. H.B.R.S., XVIII, Black's Rocky Mountain Journal, 1824.
13. H.B.R.S., III, 454–55; IV, 42–44.
14. Loc. cit., XX, xxix ff., 173 ff.
15. Loc. cit., XIV, 166 et passim.
16. Merk, Fur Trade and Empire, pp. 321–26.
17. H.B.R.S., IV, 195, 211; V, 206, 212.
18. Loc. cit., X, 73 ff. Aemilius's own report has not survived, but George Simpson summarizes it.

19. Loc. cit., IV, 317–22; H.B.C.A., B/223/b/10/7, 39–44d.; Alaskan Boundary Tribunal, Appendix to the British Case, I, 158–59.
20. For the Dease and Simpson explorations see H.B.R.S., XVI, Introduction; D. MacKay and W. Kaye Lamb, "More Light on Thomas Simpson," The Beaver, 1938; A. Simpson, The Life and Travels of Thomas Simpson (London, 1845); T. Simpson, Narrative of the Discoveries of the North Coast of America (London, 1843).
21. S. B. Okun, The Russian-American Company (Cambridge, Mass., 1951), Chap. IX; Galbraith, Hudson's Bay Company as an Imperial Factor, pp. 151–54; Alaskan Boundary Tribunal, Appendix to the British Case, I, 150–60; II, 307–8.
22. H.B.R.S., IV, 126–27; VII, 269 n.
23. H.B.C.A., B/223/b/10/26d., 34–35; B/223/b/15/14d.–15; D/4/126; H.B.R.S., IV, xcvi–xcvii, cix, 125–28, 177–82, 195–202, 208.
24. H.B.C.A., B/223/b/15/76d.
25. Oregon Historical Quarterly, XIII, 176–224; H.B.R.S., V, 30–33.
26. Report from Select Committee, 1857, p. 417; Galbraith, Hudson's Bay Company as an Imperial Factor, Chap. 10; H.B.C.A., A/1/61/50; A/6/25/28.
27. H.B.R.S., IV, 286–87.
28. Sir George Simpson, Narrative of a Journey Round the World (London, 1847), I, 90–93, 150; H.B.C.A., D/4/25/57–58, 103d.–104; D/5/6/137; H.B.R.S., VI, 77–79.
29. Cf. H.B.R.S., VI and VII, passim, especially VII, xxxvi–xxxvii, for a discussion of the Champoeg meeting.
30. F. Merk, The Oregon Question in the Webster-Ashburton Negotiations (Mississippi Valley Historical Society, 1956); Galbraith, Hudson's Bay Company as an Imperial Factor, pp. 229–30.
31. H.B.C.A., D/4/66/107d.
32. Cf. H. C. Allen and P. C. Hill (eds.), British Essays in American History (London, 1957), pp. 136–39.
33. H.B.C.A., D/4/66/107d. ff.
34. Galbraith, Hudson's Bay Company as an Imperial Factor, Chap. 11, F. Merk,

"The American Pioneers and the Boundary," A.H.R., 1924; H.B.C.A., A/8/3/ 62d. ff.
35. Galbraith, *Hudson's Bay Company as*

an Imperial Factor, p. 250; S. E. Morison and H. S. Commager, *The Growth of the American Republic* (London, 1942), I, 594.

NOTES TO CHAPTER FIFTEEN

1. W. P. Morrell, *British Colonial Policy in the Age of Peel and Russell* (London, 1930), pp. 444–45; *Parliamentary Papers*, 1849, XXXV, 15–16; *Hansard Debates*, Third Series, Vol. ci, 263–303; H.B.C.A., F/11/1/93 ff.
2. Douglas had been appointed Governor in September 1848. But the dangers of having an employee of the Hudson's Bay Company hold that office were accepted, and this was merely a temporary appointment. The first proper governor, Richard Blanshard, was a nominee of the Company though he was never an employee, and he was so critical of the Company and its control of the Island that he resigned in November 1851, after only eighteen months in office. Cf. Morrell, *Colonial Policy*, p. 445.
3. *Parliamentary Papers*, 1852–53, lxv (H.C. 83), p. 2; H.B.C.A., A/8/7/74d.; Galbraith, *Hudson's Bay Company as an Imperial Factor*, p. 298.
4. *Report from Select Committee, 1857*, pp. 451–58 and Appendix 19.
5. H.B.C.A., A/8/8/–, A/8/9/–, A/8/10/–, *passim*. For the final agreement at £32,500 in addition to £25,000 which had already been paid, see A/1/75/31d., 43, 59d.; A/8/10/194, 204, 207.
6. *Loc. cit.*, A/8/10/121 ff., 131–34, 152; *Charters, Statutes, Orders in Council, etc., relating to the Hudson's Bay Company*, pp. 223–25.
7. W. P. Morrell, *The Gold Rushes* (London, 1940), pp. 74–135.
8. H.B.C.A, A/8/8/99d., 102, 111, 121; *Charters, etc., relating to Hudson's Bay Company*, pp. 127–28; cf. W. L. Morton, *The Critical Years* (Toronto, 1964), pp. 27–28.
9. H.B.C.A., A/8/9/73.
10. Galbraith, *Hudson's Bay Company as an Imperial Factor*, pp. 71 ff.; H.B.R.S., XIX, lxxxvii.

11. H.B.C.A., A/11/118/375d., 384d., 422d.
12. A. G. Doughty (ed), *The Elgin-Grey Papers, 1846–1852* (Ottawa, 1937), II, 559.
13. *Loc. cit.*, 654–60; IV, 1600–2.
14. E. W. Watkin, *Canada and the States: Recollections, 1851 to 1886* (London, 1887), pp. 11–14.
15. H.B.C.A., A/8/8/9-10, 35.
16. *Report from Select Committee, 1857*, p. xi.
17. H.B.C.A., A/12/2/223d., 232d.
18. *Report from Select Committee, 1857*, *passim* and p. xii.
19. H.B.C.A., A/8/9/2.
20. *Loc. cit.*, A/8/8/44; A/8/9/36, 38, 40, 41.
21. *Loc. cit.*, A/10/2/36d.; *Report from Select Committee, 1857*, pp. 415, 425–26.
22. H.B.C.A., A/7/2/48; P.R.O., C.O. 42/615/32d.
23. *Report from Select Committee, 1857*, pp. 405–6; H.B.C.A., A/8/8/44.
24. *Report from Select Committee, 1857*, p. 405; pars. 5841, 5847, 5856–60.
25. H.B.C.A., A/7/2/48; D. G. Creighton, *John A. Macdonald: the Young Politician* (Toronto, 1952), p. 244.
26. *Report from Select Committee, 1857*, par. 4103.
27. *Loc. cit.*, p. 436.
28. *Loc. cit.*, pp. 403–4.
29. H.B.C.A., A/8/8/59; cf. Creighton, *Macdonald*.
30. *Report from Select Committee, 1857*, pp. 435, 437–39; P.R.O., C.O. 6/23/196 ff.
31. H.B.C.A., A/8/9/230–35.
32. *Loc. cit.*, A/8/10/3.
33. *Loc. cit.*, A/7/2/47.
34. *Loc. cit.*, A/8/10/183.
35. *Ibid.*; P.R.O., C.O. 42/614/278. Minute by Merivale.

SELECT BIBLIOGRAPHY

MANUSCRIPT SOURCES

An invaluable guide to the archive and manuscript sources for the history of the Northwest is H. P. Beers' *The French and British in the Old Northwest*, Detroit, 1965. This statement is made on the authority of a signed review by the Dominion Archivist; the author himself has not yet been able to consult this work.

1. The Archives of the Hudson's Bay Company are indispensable for an approach to this subject. For over twenty years the author had free and privileged access, for which he is grateful to the Governor and Committee of the Company. For a summary of the system of classification, and of the contents of the different classes, see E. E. Rich, "The Hudson's Bay Company's Activities," *Pacific Historical Review*, September, 1938. Microfilm copies of most of the Company's Archives—those down to 1870—are now in the Public Archives of Canada.

2. The Archives Nationales in Paris probably contain the next most important collection of manuscript material. Most (but not all) of the relevant documents are to be found in the Archives des Colonies.

Col. Séries B contains instructions outwards from Paris. No printed list or inventory is available, and although there is a card index up to 1718, it is not completely reliable.

Séries C contains reports inwards from governors, intendants and other officials. There is no index of any kind; the catalogue is merely a list of the years covered. Col. C/11/A contains endless and valuable information on the internal social and economic problems of Canada under the French regime. Col. C/11/E deals with boundary problems and the rivalry between English and French traders, and Col. C/11/G records decisions taken in France for the regulation of the fur trade of Canada.

Séries F/2 deals with the over-all problems of colonial trade; Col. F/2/A/13 gives the documentation on the *Compagnie du Nord et de la Baie d'Hudson*, F/2/B/1 gives a wide range of documents on trade with the colonies from 1663 to 1747, and F/2/B/8 the memorials from merchants and Chambers of Commerce on colonial trade.

The Archives du Ministère des Affaires Etrangères contain the diplomatic documents on the disputes between France and England, the series H/1/89/F in particular being devoted to the struggle for the Bay.

In addition, the Collection de Moreau de Saint-Méry in the Archives Nationales contains some hundreds of important documents on the history of Canada, Séries F/3. An *Inventaire* is available.

The Archives de la Marine are housed and administered separately from the Archives Nationales. They contain much which would not normally be expected in naval administration. In the Séries Marine B/2 are the orders outwards from Paris for expeditions to Canada, including those of Heemskerk and Iberville, together with much on the fur trade. Marine B/2/235 is on *Le commerce du nord et du Moscovie*.

Séries Marine B/3 contains mainly diplomatic documents, including several on the Hudson's Bay posts. Séries Marine B/4 consists of ships' logs, including those of the ships placed under command of Iberville.

3. The Bibliothèque Nationale affords almost equally valuable documentation, but whereas the series in the Archives Nationales are remarkable for their completeness the collections in the Bibliothèque are random, but immensely valuable, survivals. In the Manuscrits du Fonds Français, in the Nouvelles Additions (Papers

of Margry and of Renaudot), in the Mélanges de Colbert, the Colbert Collection des Cinq Cents, and in the Collection de Clairambault, is to be found a vast wealth of material.

4. The Public Record Office, London, contains material which, though essential, is less in volume than might be expected. Prior to 1763, the papers on Hudson Bay have been put together in CO/134 and CO/135; they deal almost exclusively with Anglo-French disputes from 1672 to 1687. Series CO/1/66 and 67 deal with general colonial policy, Series E/190, the Port Books of London, gives information on imports into the United Kingdom, and Series 30/24 (the Papers of the First Earl of Shaftesbury) gives much on the English attitude to colonial trade at the Restoration. The Colonial Entries, Series CO/389, give much on colonial policy; the Journals of the Board of Trade from 1675 to 1688 are in CO/389/101-109, while the Board of Trade papers from 1688 onwards are in CO/323/1-30. From 1763 onwards Series CO/42 contains reports and correspondence of governors and other officials in Canada. A summary of this series, and of much of the other documentation available in the Public Record Office, appeared in the *Preliminary Inventory of the Manuscript Division of the Public Archives of Canada*, published in 1952. To the *Inventory* should be added CO/42/303, The King's Posts; CO/42/571, Isbister and the Hudson's Bay Company's Charter, 1849; CO/42/614, Petition against the Charter, 1858.

Series CO/325 contains miscellaneous memoranda and tracts on the colonies, including CO/325/1, Report from the Board of Trade of June 8, 1763 on the creation of an Indian Reserve, and the frontiers of Canada.

5. The British Museum documents are not easy to discover by use of the lists and catalogues, especially where the Additional MSS are concerned. The maps in the Additional MSS were used by Professor Taylor in her introduction to the *Letters Outwards, 1679-94*, of the Hudson's Bay Record Society, and Davidson's *North West Company* also makes full use of British Museum material. Among other documents relevant to this study are Stowe MS 480, Lord Preston's Papers (including evidence from Radisson); Sloane MS 2716, the *Compagnie du Nord*; Sloane MS 2902, on trade and the Coinage Current; Additional MS 17677, Dutch Negotiations, 1660-1669; Additional MSS 21661-21982, Haldimand's Papers.

6. By courtesy of Major Sir Charles Hope-Dunbar, in 1938 the author was allowed to use the Selkirk Correspondence then preserved at St Mary's Isle, Kirkcudbright, Scotland. These documents have since been destroyed by fire. Copies of parts of the collection are available in the Selkirk Papers in the Public Archives of Canada.

7. The Public Archives of Canada contain much copied and microfilmed material from both public and private archives in the United Kingdom and in France. Among other collections, they now contain a microfilm copy of the Archives of the Hudson's Bay Company. Inventories and reports are periodically and systematically published.

In addition, the Public Archives of Canada contain a number of valuable collections of private papers of Canadian provenance—among them the Askin Papers, the Bulger Papers, the Coltman Papers, the Council of Assiniboia Minutes, 1832-61, the John McGillivray Papers, 1783-1857, the Journals of William McGillivray, the Memoirs of Roderick Mackenzie, the Macdonell Papers, the John McLeod Papers, the Richardson Letters, and the Trials Between the Hudson's Bay Company and the North West Company. The Letters of Joseph Frobisher and Simon McTavish are in Series Q.

8. The Library of McGill University, Montreal, contains the Masson MSS, collected for the preparation of Masson's *Les Bourgeois de la Compagnie du Nord-Ouest* and including many journals and narratives of fur-traders. There are also Frobisher's Letter Book of the North West Company, 1787-88; An account of the Athabasca Indians, and Alexander Henry's Travels in the Red River Department of the North

West Company, 1806. The McCord Museum of McGill University contains a number of papers on the North West Company.

9. The Baby MSS in the Library of the Université de Montréal contain many relevant documents, including the Minutes of the Northwest Company, 1801-8.

10. The documents available in the archives of the religious establishments of Canada are described and analysed by M. Giraud in the Preface to his *Le Métis Canadien*.

11. The Toronto Public Libraries periodically publish guides to the manuscript collection in their possession; in 1931 they published a *Bibliography of the Sources of Information in the Public Reference Library of the City of Toronto, Canada, in Regard to the Hudson's Bay Company, the Fur Trade and the Early History of the Canadian North West.*

PUBLISHED DOCUMENTS

ALASKAN BOUNDARY TRIBUNAL: *Proceedings of the Alaskan Boundary Tribunal, convened at London... under the Treaty concluded at Washington, January 24, 1903. 7 vols.* Washington, 1904.

BLANCHET, J. (ed.) *Collection des manuscrits relatifs à l'histoire de la Nouvelle France. 4 vols.* Quebec, 1883-85.

CANADA, Legislative Assembly: *Report of the Select Committee appointed to receive and collect evidence and information as to the rights of the Hudson's Bay Company.* Toronto, 1857

CANADA, Public Archives: see under Publications of Societies, and Journals, Bulletins, Reports and Publications; *Preliminary Inventory of the Manuscript Division,* 1952.

H. M. STATIONERY OFFICE: *Acts of the Privy Council, Colonial, 1613-1783; Calendar of State Papers, Colonial, America and the West Indies, 1574-1737; Journals of the Commissioners for Trade and Plantations, 1704-1782.*

HISTORICAL MANUSCRIPTS COMMISSION, REPORTS: *V, The Shelburne Papers in the possession of the Marquis of Lansdowne; VII, The Manuscripts and Letters of Lord Preston; LXXII, The Laing Manuscripts preserved in the University of Edinburgh; LXXV, i and ii, The Papers of Sir William Trumbull; LXXVI, The Manuscripts of the Earl of Bathurst.*

HUDSON'S BAY COMPANY: *Charters, Statutes, Orders in Council, etc. relating to the Hudson's Bay Company* (London, 1949); *Proceedings of the General Court of Proprietors, 1860-69* (London); *Reports of the Governor and Committee to the Shareholders, 1863-69* (London).

INNIS, H. A. *Select Documents in Canadian Economic History, 1497-1783.* Toronto, 1929.

INNIS, H. A. and LOWER, A. R. M. *Select Documents in Canadian Economic History, 1783-1885.* Toronto, 1933.

KENNEDY, W. P. M. *Documents of the Canadian Constitution, 1759-1915.* Toronto, 1918.

LINDSAY, W. B. (ed.) *Edits, ordonnances royaux, déclarations d'état du Roy concernant le Canada. 3 vols.* Quebec, 1854.

MARGRY, P. (ed.) *Mémoires et documents pour servir à l'histoire des origines françaises des pays d'outre mer. 6 vols.* Paris, 1879-88.

—— *Rélations et mémoires inédits pour servir à l'histoire de la France dans les pays d'outre mer.* Paris, 1867.

O'CALLAGHAN, E. B. *Documentary History of the State of New York. 4 vols.* Albany, 1850.

—— (ed.) *Documents Relative to the Colonial History of the State of New York, procured in Holland, England and France by John Romeyn Brodhead, Esq. 15 vols.* Albany, 1856-83.

PARLIAMENT, HOUSE OF COMMONS, JOURNALS: *Papers Relating to the Red River Settlement, 1819; Reports from Committees, 1715-1801; Report from the Committee appointed to inquire into the State and Condition of the Countries Adjoining to Hudson's Bay, 1749; Report from the Select Committee on Aborigines, 1837; Return of an Address of the Hon. the House of Commons... for copy of the existing charter of Grant by the Committee to the Hudson's Bay Company, 1842; Return to an Address of the House of Commons (Red River Settlement), 1849; Papers relating to the Legality of the Powers of the Hudson's*

Bay Company in respect to Territory, Trade, Taxation and Government, 1850; Parliamentary Papers, Vol. LXV, The Discovery of Gold, and the Returns of the Hudson's Bay Company on Vancouver Island, 1852; Report from the Select Committee on the Hudson's Bay Company, 1857.

────── HOUSE OF LORDS, JOURNALS:

REID, J. H. STEWART, MCNAUGHT, K., and CROWE, H. S. (eds.) A Source-book of Canadian History. Toronto, 1959.

ROY, P. G. (ed.) Ordonnances, Commissions, etc. des Gouverneurs et Intendants de la Nouvelle France, 1639-1760. 2 vols. Beauceville, 1924.

SHORTT, A. (ed.) Documents Relating to Canadian Currency, Exchange and Finance during the French Period. Ottawa, 1925.

SHORTT, A. and DOUGHTY, A. G. (eds.) Documents Relating to the Constitutional History of Canada, 1759-1791. 2 vols., Revised ed. Ottawa, 1918.

STATUTES AT LARGE, UNITED KINGDOM.

THWAITES, R. G. (ed.) Early Western Travels, 1748-1846. 32 vols. Cleveland, 1904-07.

WRAXALL, PETER. An Abridgement of the Indian Affairs . . . Transacted in the Colony of New York from the Year 1678 to the Year 1751. C. H. McIlwain (ed.). Cambridge, Mass., 1915.

PUBLICATIONS OF SOCIETIES, ANNUALS AND SERIES

American Historical Association, Annual Reports

MANNING, W. R. "The Nootka Sound Controversy," American Historical Association Annual Report for 1904.

TEGGERT. F. J. "Notes supplementary to any edition of Lewis and Clark," American Historical Association Annual Report for 1908.

────── "Calendar of the American Fur Company's Papers," American Historical Association Annual Report for 1844.

Champlain Society, Publications

BIGGAR, H. P. (ed.) The Works of Samuel de Champlain. 6 vols. 1922-36.

BURPEE, L. J. (ed.) Journals and Letters of Pierre Gaultier de Varennes de La Vérendrye and his Sons." 1926.

GANONG, W. F. (ed.) The Description and Natural History of the Coast of America by N. Denys. 1908.

GLAZEBROOK, G. P. DE T. (ed.) The Hargrave Correspondence, 1821-43. 1938.

GLOVER, R. (ed.) David Thompson's Narrative, 1784-1812. A new edition, 1962.

GRANT, W. L. and BIGGAR, H. P. (eds.) The History of New France by M. Lescarbot. 3 vols. 1907-14.

MACLEOD, MARGARET. (ed.) The Letters of Letitia Hargrave. 1947.

MORTON, W. L. (ed.) Alexander Begg's Rea River Journal and other Documents Relating to the Red River Resistance of 1869-70. 1956.

TYRRELL, J. B. (ed.) A Journey from Prince of Wales's Fort in Hudson's Bay, to the Northern Ocean, in the years 1769, 1770, 1771 and 1772. 1911.

────── David Thompson's Narrative of his Explorations in Western America, 1784-1812. 1916.

────── Documents Relating to the Early History of Hudson Bay (i.e. "Journal of Father A. Silvy from Belle Isle to Port Nelson," "Letter from Father Gabriel Marest," "Letters of Claude Charles le Roy de la Potherie," "Oldmixon's History of Hudson's Bay"). 1931.

WALLACE, W. STEWART (ed.) Notes of a Twenty-five Years' Service in the Hudson's Bay Territories by John McLean. 1932.

────── Documents Relating to the North West Company. 1934.

WHITE, P. C. T. (ed.) Lord Selkirk's Diary, 1803-04. 1958.

WRONG, G. M. (ed.) Sagard's Long Journey to the Country of the Hurons. 1939.

Hudson's Bay Record Society Publications

DAVIES, G. F. K. (ed.) Letters from Hudson Bay, 1703-40. Introduction by R. Glover. 1965.

────── Peter Skene Ogden's Snake Country Journal, 1826-27. Introduction by Dorothy O. Johansen. 1961.

RICH, E. E. (ed.) Peter Skene Ogden's Snake Country Journals, 1824-25 and 1825-26. Introduction by Burt Brown Barker. 1950.

────── Moose Fort Journals, 1783-85. Introduction by G. P. de T. Glazebrook. 1954.

—— Cumberland and Hudson House Journals, 1775-82. 2 vols. Introductions by R. Glover. 1951-52.
—— Minutes of Council Northern Department of Rupert Land, 1821-31. Introduction by H. A. Innis. 1940.
—— McLoughlin's Fort Vancouver Letters, 1825-46. 3 vols. Introduction by W. Kaye Lamb. 1941-44.
—— Simpson's Athabasca Journal. Introduction by Chester Martin. 1938.
—— Eden Colvile's Letters, 1849-52. Introduction by W. L. Morton. 1956.
——Black's Rocky Mountain Journal, 1824. Introduction by R. M. Patterson. 1955.
—— Colin Robertson's Correspondence Book, September 1817 to September 1822. Introduction by E. E. Rich. 1939.
—— James Isham's Observations on Hudson's Bay, 1743. Introduction by E. E. Rich. 1949.
—— Simpson's 1828 Journey to the Columbia. Introduction by W. Stewart Wallace. 1947.
—— John Rae's Correspondence with the Hudson's Bay Company on Arctic Exploration, 1844-1855. Introduction by J. M. Wordie and R. J. Cyriax. 1953.

Public Archives, Publications

BIGGAR, H. P. (ed.) The Voyages of Jacques Cartier. 1924.
BURPEE, L. J. (ed.) A. H. Murray's Journal of the Yukon, 1847-48. 1910.
—— Journal of F. J. Laroque from the Assiniboine to the Yellowstone, 1805. 1911.
DOUGHTY, A. G. (ed.) The First Journal of Simon Fraser, 1806. 1929.
—— and MARTIN, CHESTER (eds.) The Kelsey Papers. 1929.
OLIVER, E. H. The Canadian North-West, Its Early Development and Legislative Records. 2 vols. 1914.

Public Archives, Reports

Alexander Mackenzie's Proposed General Fur and Fishery Company. 1892.
Duncan McGillivray, Some Account of the Trade carried on by the North West Company, 1808. 1928.
Journal of Legardeur de Saint-Pierre. 1886.
Letter-book of Miles Macdonell. 1886.
Northwest Disputes. 1897.

The Northwest Trade. 1888.
The Origins of the Northwest Company. 1886.
Radisson's Rélation des Voyages dans les années 1682, 1683 et 1684. 1895.
Transactions between England and France relating to Hudson's Bay. 1883.

Wisconsin Historical Collections

CRUICKSHANK, E. A. Robert Dickson, the Indian Trader. 1892.
—— Papers from the Canadian Archives, 1767-1814. 1892.
——American Fur Company Employees, 1818-19. 1892.
THWAITES, R. G. Letter Book of Thomas Forsyth, 1814-1818. 1888.
——The American Fur Company, 1821-22. 1888.
—— Papers from the Canadian Archives, 1778-1783. 1888
—— The Story of Mackinac. 1898.
—— The Journal of Peter Pond, 1740-75. 1908.
UPHAM, W. Groseillers and Radisson, the first White Men in Minnesota, 1655-66 and 1659-60. 1890.

PERIODICAL ARTICLES

ADAIR, E. R."France and the Beginnings of New France," C.H.R., 1944.
ALCOCK, J. F. "Past and Present Trade Routes to the Canadian Northwest," Geographical Review, 1920.
ATKIN, W. T. "Snake River Fur Trade, 1816-24," Oregon Historical Quarterly, 1934.
BARRY, J. N. "Astorians," Washington Historical Quarterly, 1933.
BIGGAR, H. P. "The French Hakluyt; Marc Lescarbot of Vervins," A.H.R., 1901.
BROSHER, HELEN. "The First Push Westward of the Albany Traders," Mississippi Valley Historical Review, 1920.
BRYCE, G. "The Further History of Pierre Esprit Radisson," T.R.S.C., 1898.
—— "Extracts from Lord Selkirk's Diaries in Upper and Lower Canada in the years 1803 and 1804," ibid., 1912.
—— "The Pre-Selkirk Settlers of Old Assiniboia," ibid., 1918.
BUFFINTON, A. D. "The Policy of Albany and English Westward Expansion," Mississippi Valley Historical Review, 1922.
BUFFINTON, A. H. "New England and the Western Fur Trade, 1629-75," Publica-

tions of the Colonial Society of Massachusetts, 1917.

BURPEE, L. J. (ed.) "Some Letters of David Thompson," *C.H.R.*, 1923.

—— "La Vérendrye's 1738-1739 Journal," *ibid.*, 1942.

—— "Highways of the Fur Trade," *T.R.S.C.*, 1914.

—— "York Factory to the Blackfeet Country, the Journal of Anthony Hendry, 1754-55, *ibid.*, 1907.

—— "Fur-trader's Journal, June 1772-June 1773," *ibid.*, 1908.

—— "An Adventurer from Hudson Bay. Journal of Matthew Cocking from York Fort to the Blackfeet Country, 1772-73," *ibid.*, 1909.

CAMPBELL, H. C. "Radisson and Groseillers, Problems in Western History," *A.H.R.*, 1896.

CAREY, C. E. "Lee, Walker and McLoughlin," *Oregon Historical Quarterly*, 1932.

CARRIERE, G. "L'Honorable Compagnie de la Baie d'Hudson et les missions des Oblats, 1844-61," *Revue de l'Université de Ottawa*, XXV.

CHAPIN, J. L. "Letters of John McLoughlin, 1805-49," *Oregon Historical Quarterly*, 1936.

CLARK, R. C. "Aberdeen and Peel on Oregon, 1844," *Oregon Historical Quarterly*, 1933.

COMMAGER, H. S. "England and the Oregon Treaty, 1846," *Oregon Historical Quarterly*, 1927.

COWAN, I. MCT. "The Fur Trade and the Fur Cycle, 1825-57," *British Columbia Historical Quarterly*, 1938.

CRUIKSHANK, E. A. "Early Traders and Trade-routes in Ontario and the West, 1760-1783," *Royal Canadian Institute, Transactions*, 1893.

—— "The Fur Trade, 1783-1787," *ibid.*, 1898.

DEAN, C. "Early Fur-trading in the Red River Valley, from the Journals of Alexander Henry, Junior," *North Dakota Historical Collections*, 1910.

—— "Summary of Evidence in the Controversy between the Hudson's Bay Company and the Northwest Company, Reprinted from Papers Relating to the Red River Settlement, 1815-19," *ibid.*, 1913.

DE LAND, C. E. "The Vérendrye Explorations and Discoveries: Leading to the Planting of the Fort Pierre Tablet," *South Dakota Historical Society, Collections*, 1914.

ECCLES, W. J. "Frontenac and the Iroquois, 1672-1682," *C.H.R.*, 1955.

—— "Frontenac's Military Policies, 1689-1698. A Reassessment," *ibid.*, 1956.

ELLIOTT, T. C. (ed.) "Journal of John Work, April 30 to May 31, 1830," *Oregon Historical Quarterly*, 1909.

—— "Journals of Peter Skene Ogden," *ibid.*

—— "Journals of Peter Skene Ogden, ctd.," *ibid.*, 1910.

—— "Peter Skene Ogden, Fur Trader," *ibid.*

—— "Journal of John Work, Covering the Snake Country Expedition of 1830-31," *ibid.*, 1912.

—— "The Snake Country Journal of Alexander Ross, 1824," *ibid.*, 1913.

—— "Journal of David Thompson," *ibid.*, 1914.

—— "Narrative of the Expedition to the Kootenay and Flat Bow Indian Countries . . . by David Thompson," *ibid.*, 1925.

—— "The Fur Trade in the Columbia Basin Prior to 1811," *Washington Historical Quarterly*, 1915.

—— "The Journals of John Work, 1824-26," *ibid.*, 1912-15.

—— "David Thompson's Journeys in the Spokane Country," *ibid.*, 1917-19.

FLEMING, R. H. "Phyn, Ellice and Co. of Schenectady," Contributions to *Canadian Economics*, 1932.

—— "The Origin of Sir Alexander Mackenzie and Company," *C.H.R.*, 1928.

—— "McTavish, Frobisher and Company of Montreal," *ibid.*, 1929.

FURNISS, O. C. "Some Notes on Newly-Discovered Fur Posts on the Saskatchewan River," *C.H.R.*, 1943.

GALBRAITH, J. S. "A Note on the British Fur Trade in California, 1821-46," *Pacific Historical Review*, 1955.

—— "Fitzgerald versus the Hudson's Bay Company: the Founding of Vancouver Island," *British Columbia Historical Quarterly*, 1952.

—— "The Hudson's Bay Company under Fire, 1847-62," *C.H.R.*, 1949.

GARRY, N. "The Diary of Nicholas Garry, Deputy-Governor of the Hudson's Bay Company, from 1822-35," *T.R.S.C.*, 1900.

GIBSON, J. A. "The Colonial Office View of Canadian Federation, 1856-68," C.H.R., 1954.

—— "The Duke of Newcastle and British North American Affairs, 1859-64," ibid., 1963.

GLAZEBROOK, G. P. de T. "A Document Concerning the Union of the Hudson's Bay Company and the Northwest Company," C.H.R., 1932.

GLOVER, R. "The Difficulties of the Hudson's Bay Company's Penetration of the West," C.H.R., 1948.

—— "The Witness of David Thompson," ibid., 1950.

—— "A Note on John Richardson's 'Digression Concerning Hearne's Route,'" ibid., 1951.

GLUCK, A. C., JR. "Imperial Protection for the Trading Interests of the Hudson's Bay Company, 1857-1861," C.H.R., 1956.

GRAHAM, G. S. "The Indian Menace and the Retention of the Western Posts," C.H.R., 1934.

GUNN, H. G. "The Fight for Free Trade in Rupert's Land," Mississippi Valley Historical Association, Proceedings, 1912.

HARPER, I. M. "The First Complete Exploration of Hudson's Bay," Cambridge Historical Journal, 1929.

HILL, J. J. "Ewing Young in the Fur Trade of the Far Southwest, 1822-34," Oregon Historical Quarterly, 1923.

HITSMAN, J. MACKAY. "David Thompson and Defence Research," C.H.R., 1959.

HOROWITZ, M. and PRITCHETT, J. P. "Five 'Selkirk' Letters," C.H.R., 1941.

HOWAY, F. W. "An Outline Sketch of the Maritime Fur Trade," Canadian Historical Association, Reports, 1932.

—— "Early Days of the Maritime Fur Trade on the Northwest coast," C.H.R., 1932.

—— "Indian Attacks upon Maritime Traders of the Northwest coast, 1785-1805," ibid., 1925.

—— "The raison d'être of Forts Hope and Yale," ibid., 1922.

—— "Early Navigation of the Straits of Fuca," Oregon Historical Quarterly, 1911.

—— "Voyages of Kendrick and Gray in 1787-80," ibid., 1929.

—— "David Thompson's Account of His First Attempt to Cross the Rockies," Queen's Quarterly, 1933.

—— "A Yankee Trader on the North-

west Coast, 1791-95," Washington Historical Quarterly, 1930.

HUMPHREYS, R. A. "Governor Murray's Views on the Plan of 1764 for the Management of Indian Affairs," C.H.R., 1935.

—— "Lord Shelburne and the Proclamation of 1763," E.H.R., 1934.

—— "Lord Shelburne and British Colonial Policy, 1766-68," ibid., 1935.

INNIS, H. A. "The Northwest Company," C.H.R., 1927.

—— "Some Further Material on Peter Pond," ibid., 1935.

—— "Peter Pond and the Influence of Captain James Cook on Exploration in the Interior of North America," T.R.S.C., 1928.

JACKSON, MARJORY C. "The Beginnings of British Trade at Michilimackinac," Minnesota History, 1930.

JAMES, J. A. "Some Phases of the History of the Northwest, 1783-86," Mississippi Valley Historical Association, Proceedings, 1913.

JENNESS, D. "The Indians of Canada," National Museum, Bulletin, 1934.

—— "The Indians' Interpretation of Men and Nature," T.R.S.C., 1930.

JUDSON, K. B. "Dr. McLoughlin to Sir George Simpson, March 20, 1944., Oregon Historical Quarterly, 1916.

KENNEY, J. R. "The Career of Henry Kelsey," T.R.S.C., 1929.

KING, J. E. "The Glorious Kingdom of the Saguenay," C.H.R., 1950.

KITTSON, W. "Journal Covering Peter Skene Ogden's 1824-25 Snake Country Expedition," Utah Historical Quarterly, 1954.

KNAPLUND, P. "James Stephen on Granting Vancouver Island to the Hudson's Bay Company, 1846-1848," British Columbia Historical Quarterly, 1945.

—— "Letters from James Edward Fitzgerald to W. E. Gladstone Concerning Vancouver Island and the Hudson's Bay Company, 1848-1850," ibid., 1949.

—— "Gladstone on the Red River Rebellion," Mississippi Valley Historical Review, 1934.

LAMB, W. KAYE. "The Governorship of Richard Blanshard," British Columbia Historical Quarterly, 1950.

LART, C. E. (ed.) "Fur Trade Returns, 1767," C.H.R., 1922.

LEAVITT, O. A. "British Policy on the Canadian Frontier, 1782-92," *Wisconsin Historical Society, Proceedings*, 1915.

LEFROY, H. "Sir Henry Lefroy's Journey to the Northwest," *T.R.S.C.*, 1938.

LONG, D. E. "English Interest in the Fur Trade of Hudson Bay before 1670," *C.H.R.*, 1933.

LONG, DOROTHY E. T. "The Elusive Mr. Ellice," *C.H.R.*, 1942.

LOWER, A. M. "The Assault on the Laurentian Barrier, 1850-1870," *C.H.R.*, 1929.

MACLEOD, M. A. "Cuthbert Grant of Grantown," *C.H.R.*, 1940.

―― "Memoranda Regarding the Affairs of York Factory, Winter Season, 1839-40," *ibid.*, 1948.

―― "A Note on the Red River Hunt by John Norquay," *ibid.*, 1957.

MARBOIS, F. DE. "The Fur Trade, 1784," *A.H.R.*, 1923.

MARTIN, CHESTER "British Policy in Canadian Federation," *C.H.R.*, 1932.

―― "The Hudson's Bay Company's Monopoly of the Fur Trade at the Red River Settlement, 1821-1850," *Mississippi Valley Historical Association, Proceedings*, 1914.

MARTIN, CHESTER and DOUGHTY, A. G. (eds.) "The Kelsey Papers," *C.H.R.*, 1929.

MASSICOTE, E. Z. "La Compagnie du Nord," *Bulletin des Recherches Historiques*, XXIV.

MCCABE, J. O. "Arbitration and the Oregon Question," *C.H.R.*, 1960.

MERK, F. (ed.) "The Snake Country Expedition Correspondence, 1824-25," *Mississippi Valley Historical Review*, 1934.

―― "The Oregon Question in the Webster-Ashburton Negotiations," *ibid.*, 1956.

―― "The Snake Country Expedition, 1824-25," *Oregon Historical Quarterly*, 1934.

MEYERS, J. A. "Finnan McDonald—Explorer, Fur Trader and Legislator," *Washington Historical Quarterly*, 1932.

MITCHELL, E. A. "Edward Watkin and the Buying-Out of the Hudson's Bay Company," *C.H.R.*, 1953.

―― "The North West Company Agreement of 1795," *ibid.*, 1955.

―― "New Evidence on the Mackenzie-McTavish Break," *ibid.*, 1960.

MORISON, S. E. "Letters on the Northwest Fur Trade of Elijah Grimes," *Washington Historical Quarterly*, 1920.

MORTON, A. S. "The Place of Red River Settlement in the Plans of the Hudson's Bay Company, 1812-25," *Canadian Historical Association, Reports*, 1929.

―― "La Vérendrye: Commandant, Fur-trader and Explorer," *C.H.R.*, 1929.

―― "The Early History of Hudson Bay," *ibid.*, 1931.

―― "The North West Company's Columbian Enterprise and David Thompson," *ibid.*, 1936.

―― "Forrest Oakes, Charles Boyer, Joseph Fulton and Peter Pangman," *ibid.*, 1937.

―― "The Canada Jurisdiction Act (1803) and the North-West," *ibid.*, 1938.

MORTON, W. L. "Agriculture in the Red River Colony," *C.H.R.*, 1949.

MUNRO, W. B. "The Brandy Parliament of 1678," *C.H.R.*, 1921.

―― "The *Coureurs de Bois*," *Publications of the Colonial Society of Massachusetts*, 1923-34.

MURRAY, J. E. "The Early Fur Trade in New France and New Netherland," *C.H.R.*, 1938.

NUTE, GRACE LEE. "A British Legal Case and Old Grand Portage," *Minnesota History*, 1940.

―― "Radisson and Groseillers' Contribution to Geography," *ibid.*, 1935.

O'NEIL, MARION. "The Maritime Activity of the North West Company, 1813-21," *Washington Historical Quarterly*, 1930.

PAULLIN, C. O. "The Early Choice of the Forty-Ninth Parallel as a Boundary Line," *C.H.R.*, 1923.

PORTER, K. W. "John Jacob Astor and Lord Selkirk," *North Dakota Historical Quarterly*, 1930.

PRATT, J. W. "Fur Trade Strategy and the American Left Flank in the War of 1812," *A.H.R.*, 1935.

PRITCHETT, J. P. "A Letter by Lord Selkirk on Trade between Red River and the United States," *C.H.R.*, 1936.

―― "The Appeal of the North West Company to the British Government, to Forestall John Jacob Astor's Columbian Enterprise," *ibid.*, 1936.

―― "Some Red River Fur-trade Activities," *Minnesota Historical Bulletin*, 1923-24.

PRITCHETT, J. P. and WILSON, F. J. "A Winter at Hudson Bay, 1811-12," *C.H.R.*, 1943.

PRUDHOMME, L. A. "Pierre Gaultier de Varennes, Sieur de la Vérendrye . . . 1685-1749," *T.R.S.C.*, 1905.

—— "Les successeurs de la Vérendrye sous la domination française," *ibid.*, 1906.

—— "La Baie d'Hudson," *ibid.*, 1909-11.

—— "La regne de la Compagnie de la Baie d'Hudson, 1821-69," *ibid.*, 1914.

REID, A. G. "Representative Assemblies in New France," *C.H.R.*, 1946.

—— "Intercolonial Trade during the French Regime," *ibid.*, 1951.

—— "General Trade between Quebec and France during the French Regime," *ibid.*, 1953.

REID, MARJORIE G. "The Quebec Furtraders and Western policy, 1763-1774," *C.H.R.*, 1925.

RICH, E. E. "The Hudson's Bay Company and the Treaty of Utrecht," *Cambridge Historical Journal*, 1954.

—— "Trade Habits and Economic Motivation among the Indians of North America," *Canadian Journal of Economics and Political Science*, 1960.

—— "Russia and the Colonial Fur Trade," *Ec.H.R.*, 1955.

RIFE, C. W. "Norman W. Kittson, a Furtrader at Pembina," *Minnesota History*, 1925.

ROBINSON, P. J. "Yonge Street and the North West Company," *C.H.R.*, 1943.

ROE, F. G. "The Extermination of the Buffalo in Western Canada," *C.H.R.*, 1934.

—— "Buffalo and Snow," *ibid.*, 1936.

—— "Buffalo as a Possible Influence in the Development of Prairie Lands," *ibid.*, 1939.

—— "Early Opinions on the 'Fertile Belt' of Western Canada," *ibid.*, 1946.

—— "The Numbers of Buffalo," *T.R.S.C.*, 1937.

ROSS, F. E. "The Retreat of the Hudson's Bay Company in the Pacific Northwest," *C.H.R.*, 1937.

ROUSSEAU, J. "Les Voyages du Père Albanel au lac Mistassini et à la Baie de James," *Revue d'Histoire de l'Amérique Française*, 1950.

ROUSSEAU, J. and ROY, A. "Lettre de Talon au Père Albanel," *Bulletin des Recherches Historiques*, 1950.

—— "La mission politique du Père Albanel à la Baie d'Hudson," *ibid.*, 1950.

SAGE, W. N. "Two North West Company Documents," *C.H.R.*, 1930.

—— "The Oregon Treaty of 1846," *ibid.*, 1946.

—— "The Annexationist Movement in British Columbia," *T.R.S.C.*, 1927.

—— "Sir Alexander Mackenzie and His Influence on the History of the Northwest," *Queen's University, Bulletin of the Departments of History and Political and Economic Science*, 1922.

SAUNDERS, R. M. "Coureur de Bois: A Definition," *C.H.R.*, 1940.

SAVELLE, M. "The Forty-Ninth Degree of North Latitude as an International Boundary, 1719. The Origin of an Idea," *C.H.R.*, 1957.

SCHAFER, J. (ed.) "Letters of Sir George Simpson, 1841-43," *A.H.R.*, 1908.

—— "Dr. John McLoughlin's Last Letter to the Hudson's Bay Company," *ibid.*, 1915.

SCULL, G. D. "The voyages of Pierre Esprit Radisson," *Minnesota History*, 1927.

SOSIN, J. M. "The French Settlements in British Policy for the North American Interior, 1760-1774," *C.H.R.*, 1958.

STACEY, C. P. "The Hudson's Bay Company and Anglo-American Military Rivalries during the Oregon Dispute," *C.H.R.*, 1937.

STANLEY, G. F. G. "Documents Relating to the Swiss Immigration to Red River in 1821," *C.H.R.*, 1941.

STEVENS, WAYNE E. "The Organisation of the British Fur Trade, 1760-1800," *Mississippi Valley Historical Review*, 1916.

STEWART, W. M. "David Thompson's Surveys in the North-West," *C.H.R.*, 1936.

SULTE, B. "Le Fort de Frontenac, 1668-78," *T.R.S.C.*, 1901.

—— "Le Haut-Canada avant 1615," *ibid.*, 1904.

—— "Le commerce de France avec le Canada avant 1760," *ibid.*, 1906.

—— "Les Français dans l'Ouest en 1671," *ibid.*, 1918.

TOMPKINS, S. R. "Drawing the Alaskan Boundary," *C.H.R.*, 1945.

TURNER, F. J. "The character and Influence of the Fur Trade in Wisconsin," *Wisconsin Historical Society, Proceedings*, 1889.

TWAY, D. C. "The Wintering Partners and the Hudson's Bay Company, 1863 to 1871," *C.H.R.*, 1952.

TYRRELL, J. B. (ed.) "David Thompson and the Rocky Mountains," *C.H.R.*, 1934.

—— "Did Duncan McGillivray and David Thompson Cross the Rock.es in 1801?," *ibid.*, 1937.

—— "David Thompson and the Columbia River," *ibid.*, 1937.

—— "Duncan McGillivray's Movements in 1801," *ibid.*, 1939.

—— "Peter Fidler, Trader and Surveyor, 1769-1822," *T.R.S.C.*, 1913.

VAN ALSTYNE, R. W. "International Rivalries in the Pacific Northwest," *Oregon Historical Quarterly*, 1945.

WAITE, P. B. "A Chapter in the History of the Intercolonial Railway, 1864," *C.H.R.*, 1951.

WALLACE, W. STEWART "The Pedlars from Quebec," *C.H.R.*, 1932.

—— "The Literature Relating to the Selkirk Controversy," *ibid.*, 1932.

WILLIAMS, GLYNDWR "Arthur Dobbs and Joseph Robson; New Light on the Relationship between Two Early Critics of the Hudson's Bay Company," *C.H.R.*, 1959.

WILSON, CLIFFORD P. "La Vérendrye Reaches the Saskatchewan," *C.H.R.*, 1952.

WISLEZENUS, F. A. "Journey to the Rocky Mountains," *Missouri Historical Society*, 1912.

WRINCH, L. A. "The Formation of the Puget's Sound Agricultural Company," *Washington Historical Quarterly*, 1933.

ZOLTVANY, J. A. "New France and the West, 1701-1713," *C.H.R.*, 1965.

PUBLISHED WORKS

AITKEN, H. G. J. See under Easterbrook, W. T.

AMOS, C. *Report of the Trials in the Courts of Canada Relative to the Destruction of the Earl of Selkirk's Settlement.* London, 1820.

ATCHESON, N. *American Encroachments on British Rights; or Observations on the Importance of the British North American Colonies and on the Late Treaties with the United States.* London, 1808.

—— *On the Origin and Progress of the North-West Company of Canada, with a History of the Fur Trade, as Connected with that Concern.* London, 1811.

BACK, SIR G. *Narrative of the Arctic Land Expedition to the Mouth of the Great Fish River and along the Shores of the Arctic Ocean.* London, 1836.

BAIN, J. (ed.) *Travels and Adventures in Canada and the Indian Territories between the Years 1760 and 1766 . . . by Alexander Henry, Fur Trader.* Toronto, 1901.

BALLANTYNE, R. M. *Hudson's Bay; or Everyday Life in the Wilds of North America, during Six Years' Residence in the Territories of the Honourable Hudson's Bay Company.* Edinburgh, 1848.

BANCROFT, H. H. *History of the Northwest Coast, 1543-1846.* 2 vols. San Francisco, 1884.

—— *History of British Columbia, 1792-1887.* San Francisco, 1884.

BARROW, J. See under Coats, W.

BEGG, ALEXANDER. *History of the North-West.* 3 vols. Toronto, 1894-95.

—— *The Creation of Manitoba, or a History of the Red River Troubles.* Toronto, 1871.

BIGGAR, H. P. *The Early Trading Companies of New France.* Toronto, 1901.

BREBNER, J. B. *The Explorers of North America, 1492-1806.* London, 1933.

BRYCE, G. *The Remarkable History of the Hudson's Bay Company, including that of the French Traders of North-western Canada and of the North-West, XY and Astor Fur Companies.* London, 1900.

BURPEE, L. J. *The Search for the Western Sea: the Story of the Exploration of North-western America.* Toronto, 1908.

BURT, A. L. *The Old Province of Quebec.* Minneapolis, 1933.

—— *The United States, Great Britain and British North America from the Revolution to the Establishment of Peace after the War of 1812.* New Haven, 1940.

CALLAHAN, J. M. *American Foreign Policy in Canadian Relations.* New York, 1937.

CARON, I. *Journal de l'expédition du Chevalier de Troyes à la Baie d'Hudson en 1686.* Beauceville, 1918.

CARVER, JONATHAN. *Travels through the Interior Parts of North-America in the Years 1766, 1767 and 1768.* London, 1781.

—— *Three Years Travels throughout the Interior Parts of North America for more than Five Thousand Miles.* London, 1797.

CHARLEVOIX, F. X. DE. *Histoire et description générale de la Nouvelle France avec le journal historique d'un voyage fait par ordre du Roi dans l'Amérique Septentrionale.* 3 vols. Paris, 1774.

CHITTENDEN, H. M. *The American Fur Trade of the Far West.* 3 vols. vol. 1, New York, 1902; vols. 2 and 3, New York, 1935.

COATS, W. *The Geography of Hudson's Bay: Being the Remarks of Captain W. Coats, in many Voyages to that Locality, between the years 1727 and 1751,* ed. J. Barrow. London: Hakluyt Society, 1852.

COLE, C. WOLSEY. *Colbert and a Century of French Mercantilism.* 2 vols. New York, 1939.

COUES, E. (ed.) *New Light on the Early History of the Greater Northwest. The Manuscript Journals of Alexander Henry, Fur Trader of the Northwest Company, and of David Thompson, Official Geographer and Explorer of the Same Company.* 3 vols. New York, 1897. See also under Pike, Z. M.

COWIE, I. *The Company of Adventurers; a Narrative of Seven Years in the Service of the Hudson's Bay Company during 1867-74 on the Great Buffalo Plains.* Toronto, 1913.

COX, ROSS. *Adventures on the Columbia River.* London, 1831. See also under Stewart, E. I.

CREIGHTON, D. G. *The Commercial Empire of the St. Lawrence, 1760-1850.* Toronto, 1937.

—— *Dominion of the North.* London, 1947.

—— *John A. Macdonald: the Young Politician.* Toronto, 1952.

—— *John A. Macdonald: the Old Chieftain.* Toronto, 1955.

CROUSE, N. M. *Le Moyne d'Iberville: Soldier of New France.* Ithaca, New York, 1954.

DALE, H. C. *The Ashley-Smith Explorations and the Discovery of a Central Route to the Pacific, 1822-29.* Cleveland, 1918.

DAVIDSON, G. C. *The North West Company.* Berkeley, California, 1918.

DENYS, N. *Description géographique et historique des costes de l'Amérique Septentrionale.* 2 vols. Paris, 1672. See also under Champlain Society.

DE VOTO, B. *Westward the Course of Empire.* London, 1954.

—— (ed.) *The Journals of Lewis and Clark.* London, 1954.

DOBBS, A. *An Account of the Countries adjoining to Hudson's Bay in the Northwest Part of America.* London, 1744.

—— *Remarks upon Captain Middleton's Defence.* London, 1744.

DRAGE, T. F. (The Clerk of the "California"). *An Account of a Voyage for the Discovery of a North-West Passage by Hudson's Streights to the Western and Southern Ocean of America, Performed in the Year 1746 and 1747.* 2 vols. London, 1748.

DUGAS, G. *The Canadian West: its Discovery by the Sieur de la Vérendrye. Its Development by the Fur-trading Companies, down to the Year 1822.* Montreal, 1905.

EASTERBROOK, W. T. and AITKEN, H. G. J. *Canadian Economic History.* Toronto, 1956.

ECCLES, W. J. *Canada under Louis XIV, 1663-1701.* Toronto, 1964.

ELLIS, H. *A Voyage to Hudson's Bay by the Dobbs Galley and California in the Years 1746 and 1747 for Discovering a North West Passage.* London, 1748.

ELTON, C. *Voles, Mice and Lemmings.* Oxford, 1942.

FISHER, R. H. *The Russian Fur Trade, 1550-1700.* Berkeley, 1943.

FITZGERALD, J. E. *An Examination of the Charter and Proceedings of the Hudson's Bay Company with Reference to the Grant of Vancouver's Island.* London, 1849.

FRANCHERE, G. *Narrative of a Voyage to the Northwest Coast of America in the Years 1811, 1812, 1813 and 1814.* New York, 1854. See also under Huntington, J. V.

FRANKLIN, SIR J. *Narrative of a Journey to the Shores of the Polar Sea, in the Years 1819, 1820, 1821 and 1822.* 2 vols. London, 1824.

FREGAULT, GUY. *Iberville le Conquérant.* Montreal, 1940.

FUCHS, V. R. *The Economics of the Fur Industry.* New York, 1957.

GAGNON, F. E. A. *Louis Jolliet.* Montreal, 1913.

GALBRAITH, J. *The Hudson's Bay Company as an Imperial Factor, 1821-69.* Toronto, 1957.

GATES, C. M. (ed.) *Five Fur Traders of the Northwest*. Minnesota, 1933.

GIRAUD, M. *Le Métis Canadien: son rôle dans l'histoire des provinces de l'Ouest.* Paris, 1945.

GLAZEBROOK, G. P. DE T. *A History of Transportation in Canada.* Toronto, 1938.

GLOVER, R. *A Journey from Prince of Wales's Fort in Hudson's Bay to the Northern Ocean . . . by Samuel Hearne.* Toronto, 1958. See also under Champlain Society.

GOLDER, F. A. *Russian Expansion on the Pacific, 1641-1850.* Cleveland, 1914.

GOURLAY, R. *Statistical Account of Upper Canada.* 2 vols. London, 1822.

GRAHAM, G. S. *British Policy and Canada, 1774-91.* London, 1930.

—— *Empire of the North Atlantic.* Toronto, 1950.

GREENHOW, R. *The History of Oregon and California.* Revised ed. New York, 1845.

GUNN, G. and TUTTLE, C. R. *History of Manitoba.* Ottawa, 1880.

HALKETT, J. *Statement Respecting the Earl of Selkirk's Settlement of Kildonan upon the Red River in North America.* London, 1817.

HARGRAVE, J. J. *Red River.* Montreal, 1871.

HARMON, D. W. *Journal of Voyages and Travels in the Interior of North America.* Andover, New Hampshire, 1820. New York, 1903.

HAZLITT, R. (ed. and trans.) *The Journal of François Antoine Laroque from the Assiniboine to the Yellowstone, 1805.* Missoula, 1934.

HENNEPIN, L. *Nouvelle Découverte d'un très grand pays situé dans l'Amérique, entre le Nouveau Mexique et la mer Glaciale.* Utrecht, 1697.

—— *A New Discovery of a Vast Country in America*, ed. Thwaites, R. G. Chicago, 1903.

HENRY, ALEXANDER. See Bain, J. (Alexander Henry the Elder) and Coues, E. (Alexander Henry the Younger).

HIND, H. Y. *Narrative of the Canadian Red River Exploring Expedition of 1857, and of the Assiniboine and Saskatchewan Exploring Expeditions of 1858.* 2 vols. London, 1860.

HOWAY, F. W. *British Columbia, the Making of a Province.* Toronto, 1928.

HUDSON'S BAY COMPANY. *A Brief History.* London, 1934.

—— *Reports of the Governor and Committee to the Shareholders, 1863-69.* London.

—— *Proceedings of the General Court of Proprietors, 1860-69.* London See also under Collections of Documents.

HUNTINGTON, J. V. (ed. and trans.) *Narrative of a Voyage to the Northwest Coast of America in the Years 1811, 1812, 1813 and 1814.* New York, 1854.

INNIS, H. A. *The Fur Trade in Canada.* Revised ed. Toronto, 1956.

—— *Peter Pond: Fur Trader and Adventurer.* Toronto, 1930.

IRVING, WASHINGTON. *The Adventures of Captain Bonneville, U.S.A., in the Rocky Mountains and the Far West.* New York, 1837.

—— *Astoria.* Philadelphia, 1836.

—— *The Fur Traders of the Columbia River and the Rocky Mountains.* London, 1903.

ISBISTER, A. K. *A Few Words on the Hudson's Bay Company, with a Statement of the Grievances of the Native and Half-Caste Indians.* London, 1847.

JENNESS, D. *The Indians of Canada.* Ottawa, 1934.

JEREMIE, N. *Twenty Years of York Factory,* trans. and ed. R. Douglas and J. N. Wallace. Ottawa, 1926.

JESUIT RELATIONS AND ALLIED DOCUMENTS. *Travels and Explorations of the Jesuit Missionaries in New France, 1610-1791.* See under Thwaites, R. G.

KELLOG, L. P. *Early Narratives of the Northwest, 1634-99.* New York, 1917.

—— *The French Régime in Wisconsin and the Northwest.* Madison, 1925.

KELSEY, H. *The Kelsey Papers,* eds. A. G. Doughty and Chester Martin. Ottawa, 1929.

KENNEY, J. F. (ed.) *The Founding of Churchill, being the Journal of Captain James Knight, Governor-in-chief in Hudson Bay, from the 14th of July to the 13th of September, 1717.* Toronto, 1932.

KIRKE, H. *The First English Conquest of Canada.* London, 1871.

LAHONTAN, L. A. *New Voyages to North-America.* London, 1703. See also under Thwaites, R. G.

LAMB, W. KAYE (ed.) *Sixteen Years in the Indian Country. The Journal of Daniel Williams Harmon, 1800-1816.* Toronto, 1957.

LA POTHERIE, B. DE. *Histoire de l'Amérique Septentrionale.* Paris, 1772.

LAROQUE, F. A. See under Hazlitt, R.

LAUT, A. *The Adventurers of England on Hudson Bay.* Toronto, 1914.

—— *The Conquest of the Great Northwest.* 2 vols. in 1. New York, 1918.

—— *Pathfinders of the West.* Toronto, 1904.

LESCARBOT, M. *Histoire de la Nouvelle France.* Paris, 1609. See also under Champlain Society.

LEWIS, M. *Original Journals of the Lewis and Clark Expedition, 1804-1806,* ed. Thwaites, R. G. 8 vols., New York, 1904-5. See also under De Voto, B.

LONG, J. *Voyages and Travels of an Indian Interpreter and Trader.* London, 1791.

M'DONELL, A. *A Narrative of Transactions in the Red River Country.* London, 1819.

MCGILLIVRAY, D. *The Journal of Duncan M'Gillivray of the North West Company at Fort George on the Saskatchewan, 1794-95,* ed. A. S. Morton. Toronto, 1929.

MCGILLIVRAY, S. (Simon McGillivray, reputed author.) *A Narrative of Occurrences in the Indian Countries of North America.* London, 1817; Montreal, 1818.

MACKENZIE, A. *Voyages from Montreal through the Continent of North America to the Frozen and Pacific Oceans in the Years 1789 and 1793, with an account of the Rise and State of the Fur Trade,* ed. Grant, W. L. 2 vols. Toronto, 1911. See also under Quaife, M. M.

MCILWAIN, C. H. *An Abridgement of the Indian Affairs . . . Transacted in the Colony of New York, from the Year 1678 to the Year 1751, by Peter Wraxall.* Cambridge, Mass., 1915.

MCLEAN, J. *Notes of a Twenty-five Years' Service in the Hudson's Bay Territory.* 2 vols. London, 1849. See also under Champlain Society.

MCLEOD, J. *Journals and Correspondence of John McLeod, Senior, Chief Trader, Hudson's Bay Company, Who Was One of the Earliest Pioneers in the Oregon Territory,* ed. R. E. Gosnell. Victoria, 1903.

MCLOUGHLIN, J. *Letters from Fort Vancouver.* See under Hudson's Bay Record Society.

—— *Letters, 1829-32,* ed. Burt Brown Barker. Portland, 1848.

MARTIN, CHESTER. *Lord Selkirk's Work in Canada.* Oxford, 1916.

MARTIN, R. M. *The Hudson's Bay Territories and Vancouver's Island.* London, 1849.

MASSON, L. R. *Les bourgeois de la Compagnie du Nord-Ouest; Récits de voyages, lettres, et rapports inédits relatifs au Nord-Ouest canadien.* 2 vols. Quebec, 1889-90.

MEARES, J. *Voyages made in the Years 1788 and 1789, from China to the Northwest Coast of America.* 2 vols. London, 1791.

MERK, F. (ed.) *Fur Trade and Empire. George Simpson's Journal. Remarks Connected with the Fur Trade in the Course of a Voyage from York Factory to Fort George and back to York Factory, 1824-25; together with Accompanying Documents.* Cambridge, Mass., 1931.

MORGAN, DALE L. *Jedediah Smith and the Opening of the West.* New York, 1953.

MORICE, A. G. *The History of the Northern Interior of British Columbia, formerly New Caledonia, 1660-1880.* Toronto, 1904; London, 1906.

MORRELL, W. P. *The Gold Rushes.* London, 1940.

MORTON, A. S. *A History of the Canadian West to 1870-71.* London, 1939.

—— *Sir George Simpson, Overseas Governor of the Hudson's Bay Company.* Toronto, 1944.

MORTON, W. L. *The Kingdom of Canada.* Toronto, 1963.

—— *The Critical Years: The Union of British North America, 1857-1873.* Toronto, 1964.

MYERS, J. *The Life, Voyages and Travels of Captain John Myers, Detailing his Adventures during Four Voyages round the World . . . and Exhibiting a Most Instructive Description of the Northwest Trade.* London, 1817.

NASATIR, A. P. (ed.) *Before Lewis and Clark.* 2 vols. St. Louis, 1952.

NUTE, GRACE LEE. *Caesars of the Wilderness: Médard Chouart, Sieur des Groseilliers and Pierre Esprit Radisson, 1618-1710.* New York, 1943.

OGDEN, P. S. *Traits of American-Indian Life and Character. By a Fur Trader.* London, 1853. See also under Hudson's Bay Record Society.

OKUN, S. B. *The Russian-American Company.* Cambridge, Mass., 1951.

OLDMIXON, JOHN. *The British Empire in America.* 2 vols. London, 1708.

OLIVER, E. H. (ed.) *The Canadian Northwest, its Early Development and Legislative Records.* 2 vols. Ottawa, 1914-15.

ORMSBY, M. *British Columbia: A History.* Toronto, 1958.

PARKMAN, F. *La Salle and the Discovery of the Great West.* Boston, 1918.

────── *Conspiracy of Pontiac.* 2 vols. London, 1908.

────── *France and England in North America.*

────── *The Jesuits in North America in the Seventeenth Century.* Boston, 1886.

────── *The Pioneers of France in the New World.* Boston, 1907. All Parkman's works are available in several editions.

PHILLIPS, C. P. *The Fur Trade.* 2 vols. Norman, Oklahoma, 1961.

PIKE, Z. M. *The Expeditions of Zebulon Montgomery Pike to the Headwaters of the Mississippi River, through Louisiana Territory and in New Spain, during the years 1805, 1806 and 1807,* ed. E. Coues. 3 vols. New York, 1895.

PORTER, K. W. *John Jacob Astor, Business Man.* 2 vols. Cambridge, Mass., 1931.

PRITCHARD, J. *Narratives of John Pritchard, Pierre Chrysalogue Pambrun and Frederick Damien Heurter, respecting the Aggressions of the North-west Company, against the Earl of Selkirk's Settlement upon Red River.* London, 1819.

PRITCHETT, J. P. *The Red River Valley, 1811-1849.* New Haven, 1942.

QUAIFE, M. M. (ed.) *Alexander Mackenzie's Voyage to the Pacific Ocean in 1793.* Chicago, 1931.

RADISSON, P. E. *Voyages of Pierre Esprit Radisson, Being an Account of his Travels and Experiences among the North American Indians, from 1652 to 1684,* ed. G. D. Scull. Boston, 1885.

REED, C. B. *The First Great Canadian: The Story of Pierre Le Moyne, Sieur d'Iberville.* Chicago, 1910.

RICH, E. E. *The Hudson's Bay Company, 1660-1870.* 3 vols. Toronto, 1960. See also under Hudson's Bay Record Society.

RIOUX, J. DE LA CROIX (ed.) *Le Grand Voyage du Pays des Hurons situé en l'Amérique vers la Mer douce, by Gabriel*

Sagard-Théodat. Montreal, 1964. See also under Sagard-Théodat, G.

ROBSON, J. *An Account of Six Years' Residence in Hudson's-Bay, from 1733 to 1736 and 1744 to 1747.* London, 1752.

ROE, F. G. *The North American Buffalo.* Toronto, 1951.

ROLLINS, P. A. *The Discovery of the Oregon Trail.* New York, 1935.

ROSS, A. *Adventures of the First Settlers on the Oregon or Columbia River, 1810-13.* London, 1849. See also under Thwaites, R. G.

────── *The Fur Hunters of the Far West: A Narrative of Adventures in the Oregon and Rocky Mountains.* 2 vols. London, 1855.

RYERSON, J. *Hudson's Bay; or a Missionary Tour in the Territory of the Honorable Hudson's Bay Company.* Toronto, 1855.

SACHS, J. C. *Furs and the Fur Trade.* London, 1923.

SAGARD-THEODAT, G. *Histoire du Canada et voyages que les Frères mineurs Recollets y ont faicts pour la conversion des infidèles depuis l'an 1615.* Paris, 1636. 4 vols. Paris, 1866.

────── *Le Grand Voyage du Pays des Hurons situé en Amérique vers la Mer douce.* Paris, 1632. 2 vols. Paris, 1865.

SAGE, W. N. *Sir James Douglas and British Columbia.* Toronto, 1930.

SCHOOLING, SIR W. *The Governor and Company of Adventurers of England Trading into Hudson's Bay during Two Hundred and Fifty Years, 1670-1920.* London, 1920.

SCULL, G. D. (ed.) See under Radisson, P. E.

SELKIRK, THOMAS DOUGLAS, EARL OF. *A Sketch of the British Fur Trade in North America; with Observations Relative to the North-West Company of Montreal.* London, 1816.

SIMPSON, ALEXANDER. *The Life and Travels of Thomas Simpson, the Arctic Discoverer.* London, 1845.

SIMPSON, SIR GEORGE. *Narrative of a Journey round the World during the Years 1841 and 1842.* 2 vols. London, 1847. See also under Merk, F.

SIMPSON, THOMAS. *Narrative of the Discoveries of the North Coast of America; Effected by the Officers of the Hudson's Bay Company.* London, 1843.

STECK, F. B. *The Jolliet-Marquette Expedition of 1673.* Washington, 1927.

SELECT BIBLIOGRAPHY

STEFANSSON, V. Hunters of the Great North. London, 1923.

STEVENS, WAYNE E. The Northwest Fur Trade, 1763-1800. Urbana, 1928.

STEWART, E. I. and STEWART, J. R. (eds.) The Columbia River, by Ross Cox. Oklahoma, 1957.

STUART, R. The Discovery of the Oregon Trail, ed. P. A. Rollins. New York, 1936.

SULLIVAN, M. S. The Travels of Jedediah Smith. Santa Anna. 1934.

TERRELL, J. U. Furs by Astor. New York, 1963.

THOMPSON, DAVID. Narrative of Explorations in Western America, 1784-1812, ed. E. Coues. New York, 1897. See also under Champlain Society.

THWAITES, R. G. Early Western Travels. 32 vols. Cleveland, 1904-7.

—— Jesuit Relations and Allied Documents, 1610-1791. 73 vols. Cleveland, 1896-1901.

—— Original Journals of the Lewis and Clark Expedition, 1804-6. 8 vols. New York, 1904-5.

—— Lahontan's New Voyages to North-America. 2 vols. Chicago, 1905.

TURNER, F. J. The Character and Influence of the Indian Trade in Wisconsin, a Study of the Trading Posts as an Institution. Baltimore, 1891.

—— The Frontier in American History. New York, 1921.

TUTTLE, C. R. See under Gunn, G.

UMFREVILLE, E. Nipigon to Winnipeg: a Canoe Voyage through Western Ontario by Edward Umfreville in 1784. Ottawa, 1929.

—— The Present State of Hudson's Bay, Containing a Full Description of That Settlement, and the Adjacent Country, and Likewise of the Fur Trade, with Hints for Its Improvement . . . and a Journal of a Journey from Montreal to New York. London, 1790.

VANDIVER, C. A. The Fur Trade and Early Western Exploration. Cleveland, 1929.

WALLACE, J. N. The Wintering Partners on Peace River from the Earliest Records to the Union of 1821; with a Summary of the Dunvegan Journal, 1806. Ottawa, 1929.

WALLACE, W. STEWART (ed.) The Maseres Letters, 1776-98. Toronto, 1919.

WARRE, H. J. Sketches in North America and the Oregon Territory. London, 1848.

WATKIN, SIR E. W. Canada and the States; Recollections 1851 to 1886. London, 1887.

WEST, J. The Substance of a Journal during a Residence in the Red River Colony. London, 1824.

WHITE, C. The Journals of David Thompson. Missoula, 1950.

WILLSON, BECKLES. The Great Company, 1667-1871. 2 vols. London, 1900.

WINTHER, O. O. The Great Northwest. New York, 1947.

WISLIZENUS, F. A. A Journey to the Rocky Mountains in the Year 1839. St. Louis, 1912.

WOOD, E. O. Historic Mackinac. 2 vols. New York, 1918.

WORK, J. The Journal of John Work, a Chief-trader of the Hudson's Bay Company, during his Expedition from Vancouver to the Flatheads and Blackfeet of the Pacific Northwest, eds. W. S. Lewis and P. C. Phillips. Cleveland, 1923.

WRAXALL, P. An Abridgement of the Indian Affairs Contained in Four Folio Volumes, Transacted in the Colony of New York, from the Year 1678 to the Year 1751, ed. C. H. McIlwain. Cambridge, Mass., 1915.

YOUNG, F. G. (ed.) The Correspondence and Journals of Captain Nathaniel J. Wyeth, 1831-36. Eugene, 1899.

ACKNOWLEDGEMENTS

We wish to thank the following sources for permission to use their material in the illustration sections.

BRITISH MUSEUM, *London*: for "The Buffalo Hunt by George Catlin."

GLENBOW FOUNDATION, *Calgary, Alberta*: for "York Boat on Lake Winnipeg, 1848, by George E. Finlay."

MANITOBA ARCHIVES, *Winnipeg, Manitoba*: for "York Factory, 1853."

OREGON HISTORICAL SOCIETY, *Portland, Oregon*: for the portrait of Doctor John McLoughlin.

PUBLIC ARCHIVES OF CANADA: for "Fort William, 1866 by W. Armstrong," "A North-west View of Prince of Wales's Fort in Hudson's Bay, North America, by Samuel Hearne," and "Edmonton, From Point Below Wesleyan Mission, December, 1871"; and for the portraits of Lord Selkirk, Alexander Mackenzie, William McGillivray and Sir George Simpson.

QUEBEC—ARCHIVES DE LA PROVINCE, *Quebec, P.Q.*: for the portrait of Pierre Lemoine d'Iberville.

THE
CANADIAN
CENTENARY
SERIES

A HISTORY OF CANADA IN SEVENTEEN VOLUMES

The Canadian Centenary Series is a comprehensive history of the peoples and lands which form the Dominion of Canada.

Although the series is designed as a unified whole so that no part of the story is left untold, each volume is complete in itself. Written for the general reader as well as for the scholar, each of the seventeen volumes of *The Canadian Centenary Series* is the work of a leading Canadian historian who is an authority on the period covered in his volume. Their combined efforts have made a new and significant contribution to the understanding of the history of Canada and of Canada today.

W. L. Morton, Master of Champlain College, Trent University, is the Executive Editor of *The Canadian Centenary Series*. A graduate of the Universities of Manitoba and Oxford, he is the author of *The Kingdom of Canada; Manitoba: A History; The Progressive Party in Canada; One University: A History of the University of Manitoba;* and other writings. He has also edited *The Journal of Alexander Begg and Other Documents Relevant to the Red River Resistance.* He holds the honorary degree of Doctor of Laws from the University of Toronto and honorary Doctorates of Letters from the Universities of New Brunswick, McGill and Manitoba, and has been awarded the Tyrrell Medal of the Royal Society of Canada and the Governor General's Award for Non-Fiction.

D. G. Creighton, Professor of History, University of Toronto, is the Advisory Editor of *The Canadian Centenary Series*. A graduate of the Universities of Toronto and Oxford, he is the author of *John A. Macdonald: The Young Politician; John A. Macdonald: The Old Chieftain; Dominion of the North; The Empire of the St Lawrence,* and many other works. He has received honorary Doctorates from the Universities of Manitoba, McGill, Queen's, New Brunswick, Saskatchewan, and British Columbia. Twice winner of the Governor General's Award for Non-Fiction, he has also been awarded the Tyrrell Medal of the Royal Society of Canada, the University of Alberta National Award in Letters, and the University of British Columbia Medal for Popular Biography.